Questions & Answers

Secured Transactions

Carolina Academic Press
Questions & Answers Series

Questions & Answers: Sales & Leases
Aviva Abramovsky

Questions & Answers: Administrative Law,
Third Edition
Linda D. Jellum, Karen A. Jordan

Questions & Answers: Antitrust
Shubha Ghosh

Questions & Answers: Bankruptcy
Bruce A. Markell, Mary Jo Wiggins

Questions & Answers: Business Associations,
Second Edition
Douglas M. Branson

Questions & Answers: Civil Procedure,
Fourth Edition
William V. Dorsaneo, III, Elizabeth Thornburg

Questions & Answers: Constitutional Law,
Third Edition
Paul E. McGreal, Linda S. Eads, Charles W. Rhodes

Questions & Answers: Contracts, Second Edition
Scott J. Burnham

Questions & Answers: Copyright Law
Dave Fagundes, Robert C. Lind

Questions & Answers: Criminal Law, Third Edition
Emily Levine, Paul Marcus

Questions & Answers: Criminal Procedure —
Police Investigation, Third Edition
Neil P. Cohen, Michael J. Benza, Wayne A. Logan

Questions & Answers: Criminal Procedure —
Prosecution and Adjudication, Third Edition
Neil P. Cohen, Michael J. Benza, Wayne A. Logan

Questions & Answers: Environmental Law
Dru Stevenson

Questions & Answers: Evidence, Third Edition
David P. Leonard, Paul Giannelli

Questions & Answers: Family Law, Second Edition
Mark Strasser

Questions & Answers: Federal Estate & Gift
Taxation, Second Edition
Elaine Gagliardi

Questions & Answers: Federal Income Tax
David L. Cameron

Questions & Answers: Intellectual Property,
Second Edition
Gary Myers, Lee Ann W. Lockridge

Questions & Answers: International Law
Rebecca Bratspies

Questions & Answers: Patent Law
Cynthia Ho

Questions & Answers: Payment Systems,
Second Edition
Timothy R. Zinnecker

Questions & Answers: Professional Responsibility,
Fourth Edition
Patrick Emery Longan

Questions & Answers: Property, Second Edition
John Nagle

Questions & Answers: Remedies
Rachel Janutis, Tracy Thomas

Questions & Answers: Secured Transactions,
Third Edition
Bruce A. Markell, Timothy R. Zinnecker

Questions & Answers: Taxation of Business Entities
Kristofer Neslund, Nancy Neslund

Questions & Answers: The First Amendment,
Third Edition
Russell L. Weaver, William D. Araiza

Questions & Answers: Torts, Third Edition
Anita Bernstein, David P. Leonard

Questions & Answers: Trademark and
Unfair Competition
Vince Chiappetta

Questions & Answers: Wills, Trusts, and Estates,
Third Edition
Thomas Featherston

Questions & Answers
Secured Transactions

THIRD EDITION

Multiple-Choice and Short-Answer
Questions and Answers

Bruce A. Markell
PROFESSOR OF BANKRUPTCY LAW AND PRACTICE
NORTHWESTERN PRITZKER SCHOOL OF LAW

Timothy R. Zinnecker
PROFESSOR OF LAW
CAMPBELL UNIVERSITY SCHOOL OF LAW

CAROLINA ACADEMIC PRESS
Durham, North Carolina

ISBN 978-1-53100-689-1
e-ISBN 978-1-53100-690-7

Carolina Academic Press, LLC
700 Kent Street
Durham, North Carolina 27701
Telephone (919) 489-7486
Fax (919) 493-5668
www.cap-press.com

Printed in the United States of America

To Douglass G. Boshkoff,
a better mentor and friend there never was.

B.A.M.

To my beloved wife, Lisa, truly a "Proverbs 31" woman.

T.R.Z.

Contents

About the Authors   ix

Preface   xi

Questions   1

   Topic 1: Scope   3

   Topic 2: Definitions   7

   Topic 3: Attachment   11

   Topic 4: Perfection   17

   Topic 5: Proceeds   29

   Topic 6: Fixtures   37

   Topic 7: Priority (Secured Party v. Secured Party; No PMSI)   43

   Topic 8: Priority (Secured Party v. Secured Party; PMSI)   53

   Topic 9: Priority (Secured Party v. Buyer of Collateral)   65

   Topic 10: Priority (Secured Party v. Lien Creditor)   71

   Topic 11: Priority (Secured Party v. IRS)   77

   Topic 12: Default   79

   Topic 13: Bankruptcy (Excluding Voidable Preferences)   85

   Topic 14: Bankruptcy (Voidable Preferences)   93

Practice Final Exam   99

Answers   117

   Topic 1: Scope   119

   Topic 2: Definitions   123

   Topic 3: Attachment   133

   Topic 4: Perfection   141

   Topic 5: Proceeds   163

   Topic 6: Fixtures   179

Topic 7: Priority (Secured Party v. Secured Party; No PMSI)   187

Topic 8: Priority (Secured Party v. Secured Party; PMSI)   199

Topic 9: Priority (Secured Party v. Buyer of Collateral)   211

Topic 10: Priority (Secured Party v. Lien Creditor)   221

Topic 11: Priority (Secured Party v. IRS)   229

Topic 12: Default   231

Topic 13: Bankruptcy (Excluding Voidable Preferences)   239

Topic 14: Bankruptcy (Voidable Preferences)   249

Practice Final Exam Answers   257

Index   279

About the Authors

Bruce A. Markell is the Professor of Bankruptcy Law and Practice at Northwestern Pritzker School of Law. From 2004 to 2013, he was a United States bankruptcy judge for the District of Nevada; from 2007 to 2013 he was also a member of the Bankruptcy Appellate Panel for the Ninth Circuit.

Before taking the bench, Professor Markell practiced bankruptcy and business law in Los Angeles for 10 years (where he was a partner at Sidley & Austin), and was a law professor for 14. After law school, he clerked for then-judge Anthony M. Kennedy on the United States Court of Appeals for the Ninth Circuit.

He is the author of numerous articles on bankruptcy and commercial law, and a co-author of four law school casebooks. He contributes to COLLIER ON BANKRUPTCY and is a member of COLLIER's editorial advisory board.

He is a conferee of the National Bankruptcy Conference, a fellow of the American College of Bankruptcy, a member of the International Insolvency Institute, and a member of the American Law Institute. He is a founding member of the NITA-trained faculty of the Advanced Consumer Bankruptcy Practice Institute.

He has served as an advisor on bankruptcy and secured transaction reform to the Republic of Indonesia, and was the International Bar Association's representative to the sessions of United Nations Commission on International Trade Law (UNCITRAL) that led to the creation of UNCITRAL's model law on the assignment of international receivables. He was also asked by the United Nations to be an expert consultant to its project to create a legislative guide for secured transactions. He recently completed a project redrafting Kosovo's bankruptcy law. He consults regularly with the International Monetary Fund on insolvency-related issues (having been part of the IMF's missions to Ireland, Bosnia, Montenegro, Serbia, and Greece).

Timothy R. Zinnecker is a law professor at Campbell University, where he teaches Secured Transactions. He joined the Campbell faculty in 2011 after teaching commercial law courses for several years at South Texas College of Law. Professor Zinnecker received his J.D. degree from Brigham Young University. After serving as a judicial clerk for the Hon. Frank X. Gordon (Arizona Supreme Court), and the Hon. Edith H. Jones (United States Court of Appeals for the Fifth Circuit), he practiced commercial law in Dallas and Houston for five years.

Preface

The primary source of law for Secured Transactions is Article 9 of the Uniform Commercial Code. This study guide uses multiple-choice and short-answer questions to test your knowledge of Article 9 and its occasional intersection with other sources of law (e.g., the Federal Tax Lien Act [part of the Internal Revenue Code], and the Bankruptcy Code). These materials are based on the uniform version of Article 9 (sometimes referred to as "Revised Article 9"), which became effective in every (or almost every) state on July 1, 2001. Our occasional citations to other UCC articles (such as Articles 1, 2, and 8) are to the versions most recently approved by the American Law Institute and the National Conference of Commissioners on Uniform State Laws. Our materials do not reflect non-uniform amendments enacted by any particular state. You will find a copy of the UCC in any of the several softback statutes books adopted for use by most commercial law professors.

The short-answer questions should be answered in no more than 10 sentences and less than 20 minutes. We believe that you will better understand the materials if you prepare your own answer before peeking at the model answer.

We love teaching Secured Transactions and are delighted that you are using our study guide to supplement your understanding of this challenging subject. We invite you to contact us with your questions and comments.

This study guide quotes selected passages of the Uniform Commercial Code (UCC) copyright © Articles 1 (2001), 2 (2011), 8 (1994), 9 (2010), by The American Law Institute and the National Conference of Commissioners on Uniform State Laws. Reproduced with the permission of the Permanent Editorial Board for the UCC. All rights reserved.

Professor Bruce A. Markell
bmarkell@law.northwestern.edu
Chicago, Illinois
September 2017

Professor Timothy R. Zinnecker
zinneckert@campbell.edu
Raleigh, North Carolina
September 2017

Questions

Scope

1. ZinnCorp sells and leases office equipment. It desires to raise some needed capital by selling selected assets to Purchaser. As a general rule, Article 9 will *not* apply to ZinnCorp's sales of its

    (A)   accounts.

    (B)   equipment lease contracts.

    (C)   negotiable promissory notes, each individually evidencing debt of $5,000 (or less) and executed by consumer customers.

    (D)   customer lists.

2. Meredith wants to borrow $5,000 from her sister, Grace, to remodel her kitchen. Grace insists on collateral. Meredith offers three lottery tickets that she recently purchased (the drawing will be held next week), six bottles of vintage wine, and an assignment of her claim for next week's wages from her employer.

    Article 9 will apply to

    (A)   all three items of collateral.

    (B)   only the lottery tickets and the bottles of wine.

    (C)   only the lottery tickets and the assignment of Meredith's claim for wages.

    (D)   only the bottles of wine and the assignment of Meredith's claim for wages.

3. BizCorp wants to borrow $10 million from Lender for general corporate purposes. The parties agree that the loan will be secured by all of BizCorp's assets. BizCorp's assets include (i) a claim against a competitor for trademark infringement that will go to trial later in the year, (ii) rights as a beneficiary on a life insurance policy covering BizCorp's visionary founder, and (iii) a condominium located in Florida.

    Article 9 will cover BizCorp's property interest in

    (A)   only the trademark infringement claim.

    (B)   only the rights under the life insurance policy.

    (C)   only the trademark infringement claim and the condominium.

    (D)   none of these three assets.

4.   Three months ago, Ingrid borrowed $2,500 from Matt. To secure repayment, Ingrid agreed in writing that repayment of the debt was secured by Ingrid's bank account maintained with SmallBank.

      Yesterday, Ingrid defaulted on the loan, still owing $1,300 to Matt. Ingrid's bank account has a balance of approximately $835.

      Is Matt's claim to Ingrid's bank account balance covered by Article 9?

      ANSWER:

5.   Lisa's three daughters recently started college and rarely, if ever, ride their bicycles anymore for recreational pleasure. The bikes are in good shape and each has a fair market value in the range of $200-$300.

      Two months ago, with permission of her daughters, Lisa took the three bikes to Joe's Bike Shop. She asked Joe, the owner, if he would buy the bikes. Joe declined, but he offered to take them on consignment, agreeing to sell each of them for $225, retaining a $50 commission for each bike he could sell. Lisa agreed.

      Does Article 9 cover this transaction between Lisa and Joe's Bike Shop?

      (A)   Yes, because Article 9 covers consignments, and this transaction is a consignment.

      (B)   No, because Article 9 does not cover consignments.

      (C)   No, because Article 9 does not cover consignments if the merchant is retaining a per-item commission less than $100.

      (D)   No, because Article 9 does not cover consignments in goods with an aggregate value under $1,000.

6.   Several months ago, Erin lost her job. She remains unemployed. As a result, she has suffered significant financial hardships. Her creditors have turned aggressive. The county assessor has placed a statutory lien on her boat for unpaid property taxes. A neighbor who won a defamation lawsuit against Erin has received a judgment lien on some of Erin's non-exempt jewelry. Six nights ago, Erin's car was seized from the street in front of her home by an agent of the dealer exercising its rights as a creditor under the only contract signed by Erin (a "Promissory Note" under which the dealer retained title to the car until Erin satisfied all purchase obligations). And just this morning, the bank posted a foreclosure notice on her residence under a mortgage document executed by Erin on the purchase date.

      Article 9 governs the property interest claimed by

      (A)   the neighbor and the mortgage bank.

      (B)   the county assessor, the mortgage bank, and the car dealer.

      (C)   the county assessor, the neighbor, and the car dealer.

      (D)   the car dealer.

7. A few months ago, ZinnCo borrowed $800,000 from Bank. Bank insisted on collateral. ZinnCo offered all of its current and future equipment, and a negotiable promissory note executed by ZinnCo's president, payable to the order of ZinnCo, and itself secured by a recorded mortgage on the president's residence.

Can the president's negotiable promissory note held by ZinnCo serve as Article 9 collateral? Or is the note excluded from the scope of Article 9 because it is itself secured by real estate?

ANSWER:

Definitions

8. Sarah is an architect who lives in Dallas. She wants to borrow $4,000 from her sister, who insists on collateral.

    Which of the following assets offered by Sarah is a "consumer good"?

    (A)   Her two cats.

    (B)   Her checking account, which she uses exclusively for personal reasons.

    (C)   Her laptop computer that she uses half the time for personal matters and half the time for business matters.

    (D)   Her claim against a consumer client for unpaid services rendered.

9. Rebecca is a lawyer who lives in Baltimore. She wants to borrow $10,000 from her brother, who insists on collateral.

    Which of the following assets offered by Rebecca is "investment property"?

    (A)   A $2,500 certificate of deposit issued to her by Fidelity Bank, bearing an annual interest rate of 4% and a one-year maturity date.

    (B)   Two hundred shares of Myspace capital stock, which is now worth considerably less than what Rebecca paid for it.

    (C)   A rare baseball (autographed by legendary pitcher Sandy Koufax) that Rebecca inherited from her grandfather, and that Rebecca is holding for market appreciation.

    (D)   Her cabin located in Lake Placid, New York (the cabin has doubled in market value since she bought it six years ago).

10. Ellen is a veterinarian who lives in Phoenix. She wants to borrow $15,000 from her parents, who insist on collateral.

    Which of the following assets offered by Ellen is *not* a "general intangible"?

    (A)   Her unpaid claim against the IRS for a federal tax refund.

    (B)   Her three patents.

    (C)   Her claim against the State of Arizona for winnings to be paid on a lottery ticket she purchased.

    (D)   Her claim against her brother, Jeff, who borrowed $2,500 from Ellen last year and has yet to honor his oral promise of repayment.

11.   Give an example of a secured transaction involving an "obligor" who is not a "debtor."

     ANSWER:

12.   All of the following are examples of a "registered organization" except

     (A)   a limited partnership.

     (B)   a sole proprietorship that has filed a "d/b/a" ("doing business as") certificate with the appropriate state official.

     (C)   a limited liability company (created under the laws of Florida) that is delinquent in paying its property taxes.

     (D)   a corporation (chartered under the laws of Texas) that recently filed a bankruptcy petition.

13.   Lender has an enforceable security interest in BizCorp's current and future inventory. This morning, BizCorp sold a unit of its inventory to Jessalyn. The sale did *not* create "cash proceeds" if Jessalyn

     (A)   paid with her personal check.

     (B)   tendered Canadian dollars.

     (C)   paid with a cashier's check payable to her, which she indorsed to BizCorp.

     (D)   orally promised to make full payment within three business days.

14.   Give an example of a "consumer transaction" that is not a "consumer-goods transaction."

     ANSWER:

15.   Yesterday, ZinnCorp purchased a large shipment of copier paper on credit. ZinnCorp will *not* be an "account debtor" if its authorized agent paid for the shipment by

     (A)   executing a negotiable, but unsecured, promissory note.

     (B)   authenticating the seller's standard contract, which evidenced the debt and reserved in the seller's favor a security interest in the shipment of the copier paper.

     (C)   orally agreeing to repay the purchase price within 30 business days.

     (D)   signing a non-negotiable, non-transferable, writing, and the debt is unsecured.

16.   What action must Secured Party take in order to achieve "control" of a deposit account maintained by Debtor with Bank (who is not the same person as Secured Party)?

     ANSWER:

17. Each of the following is a "good" as defined by Article 9 except

    (A) a microwave oven that has become a fixture in a residence.

    (B) $123.17 (in coin and paper bills) in a company's "petty cash" drawer.

    (C) a rare baseball card held for investment purposes.

    (D) a litter of unborn puppies.

18. Lender has an enforceable security interest in the debtor's current and after-acquired "inventory." Lender's security interest will *not* include

    (A) a fleet of vehicles that the debtor leases at an airport site to customers for short periods.

    (B) thousands of tomatoes, which the debtor will soon harvest and then use to make its prize-winning pasta sauce that it sells throughout the world.

    (C) office supplies (e.g., paper clips, pens, and photocopier paper) at an elementary school.

    (D) sugar, chocolate, and other ingredients used by a cookie company to make its products.

19. What action must Secured Party take in order to achieve "control" of a certificated stock certificate that has been issued to, and registered in the name of, Debtor?

    ANSWER:

20. Meredith owes $500 to Grace. Which explanation for this monetary claim has created a "payment intangible"?

    (A) Meredith orally promised to pay $500 to purchase Grace's sofa.

    (B) Meredith signed a negotiable promissory note, evidencing her obligation to pay $500 to purchase a puppy from Grace.

    (C) Meredith borrowed $500 from Grace and signed only a one-sentence writing that stated: "Meredith promises to pay $500 to Grace upon demand."

    (C) Meredith executed a written lease, obligating her to pay $100 per month, for five months, to use Grace's riding lawnmower.

21. Describe a transaction in which Bank's security interest attaches to a "supporting obligation."

    ANSWER:

22. What is the "lowest intermediate balance" rule?

    ANSWER:

23. Lender is making a $500,000 secured loan to MegaCorp. Part of the collateral offered by MegaCorp will include (i) a stock certificate, issued in MegaCorp's name, evidencing 1,000 shares of SubCorp capital stock (SubCorp is a wholly owned corporate subsidiary of Mega-Corp) and (ii) its investment portfolio of stocks, bonds, and mutual funds in an account managed by its broker, ZinnMark Investments Group.

    Which party (or parties) is (are) an "entitlement holder"?

    (A)   SubCorp and MegaCorp.

    (B)   MegaCorp and ZinnMark.

    (C)   MegaCorp only.

    (D)   SubCorp and ZinnMark.

24. Continuing with the previous set of facts, which party (or parties) is (are) a "securities intermediary"?

    (A)   ZinnMark and SubCorp.

    (B)   MegaCorp.

    (C)   ZinnMark.

    (D)   MegaCorp and ZinnMark.

25. What is a "strict foreclosure"?

    ANSWER:

26. In what Article 9 context might the term "recognized market" arise?

    ANSWER:

27. Article 9 includes within its scope an "agricultural lien." As defined, an "agricultural lien" refers to a property interest in

    (A)   farm products.

    (B)   goods.

    (C)   crops.

    (D)   livestock.

Attachment

28. A security interest becomes enforceable when it

    (A) is perfected.

    (B) has attached.

    (C) enjoys priority over a lien creditor.

    (D) is memorialized in writing.

29. To create an enforceable security interest, the

    (A) secured party must give value to the debtor.

    (B) debtor must own the collateral.

    (C) collateral must be personal property or fixtures.

    (D) debtor must authenticate a security agreement that provides an adequate description of the collateral.

    NOTE: These facts apply to Questions 30 through 35.

30. BigBank is lending $10 million to ZinnCorp for general corporate purposes. The loan will be secured by all of ZinnCorp's current and after-acquired personal property.

    To create an enforceable security interest in ZinnCorp's assets, the written security agreement

    (A) may describe the collateral as "all of Debtor's rights in its personal property, whether now or hereafter existing."

    (B) must state the location(s) of the inventory, equipment, motor vehicles, and other tangible collateral.

    (C) must state the original principal amount of the loan if it equals or exceeds $1 million.

    (D) need not state the scheduled final payment date, even if that date is more than five years after the date of the security agreement.

31. BigBank is insisting that ZinnCorp's primary shareholder, Jane Smith, unconditionally guaranty repayment of the secured debt.

To create an enforceable security interest in ZinnCorp's property, the written security agreement must be executed by

(A)   BigBank, ZinnCorp, and Smith.

(B)   ZinnCorp and Smith.

(C)   BigBank and ZinnCorp.

(D)   ZinnCorp.

32.   To create an enforceable security interest in ZinnCorp's assets, the written security agreement must describe the collateral in a manner that

(A)   is "commercially reasonable."

(B)   is specific.

(C)   "reasonably identifies" the collateral.

(D)   utilizes Article 9's defined terms, such as "accounts," "equipment," "inventory," and "general intangibles."

33.   To create an enforceable security interest in ZinnCorp's assets that fall within the following defined terms, the parties cannot rely *solely* on the term

(A)   "commercial tort claims."

(B)   "security entitlements."

(C)   "negotiable instruments."

(D)   "general intangibles."

34.   The purpose of including an after-acquired property clause in the written security agreement is to include within the collateral any assets in which ZinnCorp acquires rights after the date on which

(A)   BigBank's financing statement is recorded in the public records.

(B)   ZinnCorp first borrows any money under the $10 million loan.

(C)   ZinnCorp authenticates the security agreement.

(D)   BigBank agrees to make the $10 million loan.

35.   For some unknown reason, BigBank and ZinnCorp never produce a written security agreement. Both parties are willing to testify that they had an oral understanding that the $10 million loan would be secured by all of ZinnCorp's assets.

The oral understanding will create an enforceable security interest in

(A)   any tangible collateral in BigBank's possession.

(B)   all collateral, whether tangible or intangible.

(C)   all tangible and intangible collateral in which ZinnCorp has rights as of the date of the understanding, but not tangible and intangible collateral in which ZinnCorp acquires rights thereafter (rephrased, an oral security agreement is ineffective to cover after-acquired property).

(D)   no collateral (rephrased, an oral security agreement is ineffective).

36.   Meredith recently moved to Denver to begin a new job. To furnish her apartment, Meredith borrowed $3,000 from her sister, Grace. Grace insisted on collateral, so Meredith executed a security agreement on July 1, in which Meredith granted to Grace a security interest in all of Meredith's "household furnishings, whether now owned or hereafter acquired." Grace delivered the $3,000 check to Meredith on July 4.

In July, Meredith purchased the following household furnishings, in each instance using her own funds:

refrigerator	July 3
bedroom furniture	July 6
television	July 9
kitchen table	July 12
sofa	July 15

In which of these household furnishings will Grace have an enforceable security interest?

ANSWER:

37.   ZeeCo builds roads and clears land for governmental, commercial, and private parties. In February, Hoover Finance loaned $2 million to ZeeCo. To secure repayment of the loan, ZeeCo granted to Hoover Finance a security interest in its excavation equipment. During the year, Hoover Finance funded additional advances to ZeeCo. Also during the year, ZeeCo bought additional excavation equipment. A summary of the activity follows:

February 1	Parties execute security agreement and other loan papers
	Hoover Finance advances $2 million
	Value of existing excavation equipment is $1.7 million
April 10	Hoover Finance advances $350,000
May 20	ZeeCo buys road grader for $250,000
June 25	ZeeCo buys bulldozer for $300,000
August 15	Hoover Finance advances $250,000

In November, ZeeCo defaulted on its obligations to Hoover Finance, having repaid none of the loans.

Ignore any market changes or depreciation in the value of the equipment. Assume that the security agreement included an after-acquired property clause, but not a future advance clause.

Calculate the amount of Hoover Finance's *secured* claim.

ANSWER:

38. Ignore any market changes or depreciation in the value of the equipment. Assume that the security agreement included a future advance clause, but not an after-acquired property clause.

    Calculate the amount of Hoover Finance's *unsecured* claim.

    ANSWER:

39. Helen borrowed $5,000 from her mother, Sarah, last week. Helen and Sarah orally agreed that six specific pieces of Helen's jewelry will serve as collateral for the loan. To Helen, the pieces of jewelry are "consumer goods."

    Which of the following statements is true?

    (A)   Sarah does not have an enforceable security interest in the jewelry because Article 9 does not permit oral security agreements when the original loan exceeds $1,000.

    (B)   Sarah does not have an enforceable security interest in the jewelry because Article 9 does not permit oral security agreements when the collateral is a consumer good.

    (C)   Sarah has an enforceable security interest in the jewelry if she takes possession of it.

    (D)   Article 9 does not cover this transaction because the amount of the original loan does not exceed $5,000.

40. Assume, instead, that Helen borrowed the $5,000 from Puritan Bank. To secure repayment of the loan, Puritan Bank insisted on taking a security interest in Helen's personal checking account maintained with Puritan Bank. Helen orally agreed to this arrangement, which was never memorialized in writing or otherwise authenticated.

    Which of the following statements is true?

    (A)   Puritan Bank does not have an enforceable security interest in Helen's checking account because Article 9 requires a written security agreement for this type of collateral.

    (B)   Article 9 does not apply to this transaction because Article 9 excludes from its scope of coverage a transaction in which a checking account serves as collateral.

    (C)   Puritan Bank does not have an enforceable security interest in Helen's checking account because Article 9 does not permit oral security agreements if the debtor is a consumer.

(D) Puritan Bank has an enforceable security interest in Helen's checking account if she uses the loan proceeds for a business purpose — even if Helen uses the checking account primarily to pay for personal, family, or household expenses.

41. BAMCO, a corporation, sells various musical instruments through its retail stores. BAMCO's customers include symphonies, houses of worship, schools and colleges, professional musicians, and many consumer households. Friendly Finance has agreed to make a $5 million loan to BAMCO that will be secured by its musical instruments.

If the parties desire to use Article 9 terminology when describing the musical instruments, the security agreement should describe the collateral as

(A) instruments.

(B) inventory.

(C) inventory, equipment, and consumer goods.

(D) goods.

42. Lender has agreed to make a $25 million secured loan to ZinnMark, a corporation that makes power tools for carpenters, homeowners, and others. Lender's lawyer has drafted the security agreement, which describes the collateral as:

Debtor's rights, whether now owned or hereafter acquired or created, in each of the following: accounts, chattel paper, commercial tort claims, deposit accounts, documents, equipment, farm products, general intangibles, instruments, inventory, investment property, letter-of-credit rights, and money.

The after-acquired property clause will be ineffective against

(A) letter-of-credit rights.

(B) money.

(C) commercial tort claims.

(D) deposit accounts.

43. Two years ago, Rebecca borrowed $10,000 from Bank to assist her in starting a catering business. To secure repayment of the loan, Bank obtained an enforceable security interest in 10 specific pieces of Rebecca's jewelry. Bank timely perfected its security interest by filing.

Three weeks ago, Thief broke into Rebecca's home and stole several items, including several of the pieces of jewelry serving as collateral for Bank's loan.

Rebecca sought recovery of the value of the stolen items by filing a claim against Superior Insurance under her homeowner's insurance policy (which included a jewelry rider). Three days ago, Rebecca received a $17,000 check from Superior Insurance (the amount includes payment for more than just the stolen jewelry; the amount attributable to stolen jewelry collateral is $8,000). This morning, Rebecca deposited the check into her personal checking account, raising the total balance in the account to $21,500.

Which of the following statements is true?

(A)   Bank has no enforceable security interest in any part of the checking account because the insurance check has been commingled with other funds to which Bank has no claim.

(B)   Bank has no enforceable security interest in any part of the checking account because the check was issued under an insurance policy, and Article 9 excludes from its scope any interest in an insurance policy and amounts paid thereunder.

(C)   Bank has an enforceable security interest in the entire balance of the checking account.

(D)   Bank may have an enforceable interest in the checking account, capped at no more than $8,000.

Perfection

44. BigBanc will loan $5 million to Friendly Furniture Corp. Friendly Furniture Corp. is a corporation organized under California law. It operates furniture stores in San Francisco, California; Las Vegas, Nevada; and Phoenix, Arizona. Repayment of the loan will be secured by all of Friendly's accounts, inventory, equipment, chattel paper, instruments, documents, general intangibles, investment property, letter-of-credit rights, commercial tort claims, and deposit accounts.

    The BigBanc loan officer asks its lawyer to determine whether any other parties have non-fixture security interests in the collateral. In response, the lawyer should order a UCC search report against Friendly from the appropriate filing officer in

    (A)   California only.

    (B)   California, Nevada, and Arizona.

    (C)   California and, if different, the state in which Friendly maintains its chief executive office.

    (D)   California and, if different, the state in which Friendly's stores generate the greatest percentage of Friendly's gross sales revenues.

45. After filing its financing statements, BigBanc's lawyer submits a written request for a search report on Monday, July 20, and each filing officer receives the request on Wednesday, July 22.

    Each filing officer must communicate the results of its search to BigBanc's lawyer no later than

    (A)   Friday, July 24.

    (B)   Wednesday, July 29.

    (C)   Monday, July 27.

    (D)   Friday, July 31.

46. The information on any search report received under BigBanc's request made in Question 45 must be current through at least

    (A)   Monday, July 20.

    (B)   Friday, July 10.

(C)   Friday, July 17.

(D)   Wednesday, July 1.

47.   BigBanc's lawyer receives the search report and sends a copy to its client. BigBanc's loan officer forwards a copy to Friendly's general counsel. The general counsel reviews the information and concludes that two filings on the report pertain to the assets of "Friendly's Furniture, Inc.," a different legal entity.

Article 9 permits either BigBanc or Friendly's general counsel to

(A)   file a termination statement against the two filings.

(B)   take no unilateral filing action.

(C)   unilaterally file an information statement.

(D)   file an information statement that explains the problem, provided that the information statement is authenticated by an authorized officer of "Friendly's Furniture, Inc."

48.   BigBanc's lawyer is preparing the financing statement for the loan to Friendly Furniture Corp. The financing statement

(A)   will not perfect a security interest in any of Friendly's "fixtures" unless the filing is recorded in the real estate records of the county where the fixture is (or will be) located.

(B)   need not include an after-acquired property clause to perfect a security interest in Friendly's future personal property.

(C)   must be authenticated by Friendly.

(D)   cannot be filed before Friendly authenticates the security agreement.

49.   To be effective, the financing statement must

(A)   state the maximum amount of debt that will be secured by the designated collateral.

(B)   provide the name of the secured party (BigBanc).

(C)   avoid using a supergeneric collateral description (such as "all assets" or "all personal property").

(D)   be filed in each state where Friendly maintains the type of collateral described (so if inventory is in Indiana and Kentucky, for example, the financing statement must be filed in both states).

50.   Before Friendly signs any loan agreement or any security agreement, BigBanc files a financing statement with the central filing office in California naming Friendly as debtor and indicating that the collateral is "all assets." Friendly does not consent to this filing when it is made, and sends a letter to BigBanc to that effect. BigBanc's loan terms, however, are the best it can obtain, and so one month after the financing statement is filed, Friendly

signs a loan and security agreement with BigBanc under which BigBanc agrees to lend Friendly $1 million, and Friendly grants to BigBanc a security interest in "all inventory, now owned or hereafter acquired." The loan and security agreement is silent about the earlier financing statement, and BigBanc does not file a new financing statement. BigBanc then loans Friendly $1 million.

BigBanc's loan

(A) is unsecured, because Friendly never consented to the filing of a necessary financing statement.

(B) is attached, but not perfected, in Friendly's inventory only because BigBanc's financing statement was not authorized.

(C) is perfected by Friendly's inventory, and nothing else.

(D) is perfected by all of Friendly's personal property.

51. Assume BigBanc only files one financing statement with respect to the loan to Friendly. BigBanc's lawyer prepares the financing statement and submits it, along with the necessary fees, to the appropriate filing officer(s) on Monday, August 10. Each filing officer receives the filing on Wednesday, August 12. Give three of the reasons why a filing officer may *rightfully* reject the filing.

ANSWER:

52. In addition to the information statement, BigBanc ultimately files amendments to the financing statement against Friendly: restating the indication of collateral by adding examples of inventory (but not changing the basic indication of inventory as collateral); changing BigBanc's address after a move; and releasing some large lots of furniture from the indication of collateral. When reading Article 9, references to the "financing statement" related to Friendly include

(A) only the first, full, financing statement filed by BigBanc.

(B) only the first, full, financing statement filed by BigBanc, and the amendment changing BigBanc's address.

(C) only the first, full, financing statement filed by BigBanc, and all amendments, but not the information statement.

(D) the first, full, financing statement filed by BigBanc, all amendments, and the information statement.

53. Immediately after BigBanc files its financing statement, in which of the following items of collateral will BigBank *not* have a perfected security interest (or, put another way, the filing of the financing statement will *not* perfect BigBanc's interest in which of the following items)?

(A) Domain name (https://www.FriendlyFurniture.com)

(B) Fleet of delivery trucks

(C)   Bank accounts, unless the bank accounts are insured by the Federal Deposit Insurance Corporation

(D)   Stocks, bonds, and other investment property managed by a person or entity subject to regulatory oversight by the Securities and Exchange Commission

54.   A filed financing statement is the *only* method by which BigBanc will perfect its security interest in Friendly's

(A)   cash that is received from customers and prior to its deposit into a bank account.

(B)   rights under a life insurance policy owned by Friendly that will pay Friendly more than $1 million upon the death of its founder and chief executive officer, Felix Friendly.

(C)   lease contracts executed by local entities that lease furniture from Friendly to furnish apartment units.

(D)   payment claims against Friendly's customers who sign simple form agreements obligating themselves to pay for their purchases over time. These agreements do not take or retain a security interest in the goods sold, and contain standard warranty clauses regarding the quality of the goods sold.

55.   BigBanc's financing statement is filed on November 1, 2018. The parties contemplate that Friendly will be making periodic loan payments through November 2023. BigBanc's lawyer anticipates filing a continuation statement sometime prior to Friendly's last loan payment. Which of the following dates will be the best date on which to file the continuation statement?

(A)   November 2, 2018.

(B)   December 1, 2023.

(C)   June 1, 2023.

(D)   Any date after Friendly has paid more than 50% of the original principal amount of the loan.

56.   Five years have passed since BigBanc filed its initial financing statement on November 1, 2018. It is now November 10, 2023, and BigBanc's lawyer realizes that the bank never filed a continuation statement. The lawyer checks the central filing office and the records of the local court. It finds that there is one other financing statement on file (filed after Big-Banc's initial financing statement). It covers Friendly's obligation to pay for a copier Friendly bought. There is also a judicial lien on Friendly's collateral, which was effective on October 15, 2023.

Friendly still owes BigBanc a lot of money. Assuming the other creditors will not cooperate, what should BigBanc do to achieve maximum protection of its present and future position?

(A)   File a continuation statement, its mistake falls within Article 9's statutory grace period applicable to untimely filed continuation statements.

(B)   File an amendment to the initial financing statement.

(C)   File a new initial financing statement.

(D)   Do nothing, because each of the other creditors obtained their interests when Big-Banc's financing statement was effective.

57.   Friendly makes its last monthly loan payment to BigBanc in December 2023. What filing action (if any) must BigBanc take, and what penalties (if any) might BigBanc incur for failing to do so?

ANSWER:

58.   Chump Bank has made four secured loans to Gasoline Motors, Inc. Three loans are secured by the inventory at three of Gasoline Motors' plants; the final loan is secured by all of Gasoline Motors' equipment, regardless of location. All loans were properly perfected by four separate filings at the central filing office in Delaware, where Gasoline Motors is incorporated. Gasoline Motors wishes to repay the inventory loan in full (while not touching the equipment loan), and informs Chump Bank of that fact. Chump Bank, to save costs, agrees that Gasoline Motors' attorneys may draft all documents, including the termination statement for the financing statement related to the inventory loans.

Due to Gasoline Motors' attorneys' unintentional mistake, the termination statement provided to Chump for its review (and which it and its attorneys did review) contained the file numbers for all four loans, including the equipment loan. Neither Chump nor its attorneys caught the mistake. The erroneous termination statement was thus filed.

Several years later, Gasoline Motors files for bankruptcy, and its trustee searches the Delaware filing office for UCC-1 filings. It finds none.

Which of the following best describes the most likely outcome?

(A)   Chump will be held to be perfected because it did not authorize the filing of the termination statement as to the equipment loan.

(B)   Chump will be held to be perfected because no one subjectively intended to terminate the financing statement related to the equipment loan.

(C)   Chump will be held to be perfected so long as it files a new financing statement within the first 30 days of Gasoline Motors' bankruptcy.

(D)   Chump will be held to be unperfected, and the trustee will have priority as to the equipment.

59.   Miguel Garza borrowed $15,000 from Friendly Financing to open a restaurant. The loan will be secured by an enforceable interest in Miguel's personal and business assets. In

addition to a filing at a central filing office, Friendly Financing should consider a local filing with the county recorder if

(A)   Miguel is a debtor.

(B)   Miguel is married, and he and his wife maintain their primary residence in a community property state.

(C)   the collateral includes the restaurant equipment.

(D)   the collateral includes his personal automobile, on which Miguel pays county personal property taxes each calendar year.

60.   Jim's current and valid passport lists his name as "James Fallon Lump." His birth certificate reads "James Fallow Lump." His current and valid driver's license reads "Jim F. Lump." Which of the following is his correct name according to Article 9, if Jim's state of residence has adopted Alternative A to Section 9-503?

(A)   Jim F. Lump

(B)   James F. Lump

(C)   James Fallon Lump

(D)   James Fallow Lump

61.   Jillian does not have a driver's license. All her friends call her Jill Smith, and that is the name her employer uses on her paychecks. Her mother calls her Jillian Francis Smith, and that is the name on her birth certificate. She occasionally signs her name "Jill Smyth," just to be fancy. Which of the following is most likely her correct name according to Article 9?

(A)   Jillian Francis Smith

(B)   Jill Smith

(C)   Jill Smyth

(D)   Jillian Smith

62.   The full name of the singer Shakira is Shakira Isabel Mebarak Ripoll. Her name adopts the Hispanic convention of two surnames (*apellidos*). Mebarak is taken from her father's surname (her *apellido paterno*); Ripoll is taken from her mother's surname (*apellido materno*).

Were you to loan money to Shakira secured by her jewelry, which of the following best describes how you would fill in and complete a financing statement for such a transaction (assume that there is no extra charge for each additional debtor name added to a financing statement)?

(A)   You would fill in three debtors, each with three different surnames; one with Mebarak, one with Ripoll; and one with Mebarak Ripoll.

(B) You would fill out two debtor names; one with the surname Mebarak, and one with the surname Ripoll.

(C) You would insert the surname Mebarak only.

(D) You would insert the surname Ripoll only.

63. Jim runs a bar and restaurant. On its menus, stationery, and checks, its name is listed as "Jim's Bar and Grill." That is also the name that appears in neon over its front door. In his business records, however, are the original articles of incorporation, which have never been amended. They state that Jim incorporated a company called "James's Food and Drink, Inc."

You have been retained by a bank that wishes to lend money to Jim's corporation on a secured basis. Which of the following should be used as the debtor's name on the financing statement?

(A) Jim's Bar and Grill

(B) James's Food and Drink, Inc., dba Jim's Bar and Grill

(C) James's Bar and Grill

(D) James's Food and Drink, Inc.

64. Acme Paints!, LLC, is a Delaware limited liability company. Swoop Bank agrees to lend it $5 million secured by all of Acme's inventory, accounts, equipment and general intangibles. Swoop Bank, however, fills out the financing statement incorrectly; it states the debtor's name as "Acme Paints, *Inc.*" instead of "Acme Paints*!, LLC.*" It files the financing statement with this error at Delaware's central filing office. Discuss why the use of this incorrect name likely *will not invalidate* Swoop Bank's financing statement.

ANSWER:

65. Assume the same facts as Question 64 except Swoop Bank inserts "Acme Painters, LLC" as the debtor's name on the filed financing statement. Discuss why the use of this incorrect name is likely to *invalidate* Swoop Bank's financing statement.

ANSWER:

66. BigBank, MidBank, and SmallBank are the sole members of a syndicate that is making a $250 million loan to ZinnCorp. The loan is secured by an enforceable security interest in ZinnCorp's "accounts, inventory, and equipment, now owned or hereafter acquired." The three banks have appointed BigBank as the collateral agent for the syndicate.

The loan papers were executed earlier today, and the financing statement has been mailed to the appropriate filing office. BigBank's loan officer (your client), just called to express concern that the secured party identified on the filing is "Bigbanc, As Agent"—but the names of the three syndicate banks do not appear anywhere on the filing.

Should you and your client be concerned that the filing fails to perfect BigBank's security interest? Why or why not?

ANSWER:

67. Robert W. Zimmer lives in Kansas City, Missouri (Jackson County). His driver's license states his name as "Robert W. Zimmer." Zimmer operates a consulting service ("RWZ Consulting") that he has incorporated under the laws of Delaware. The sole business office is located in Kansas City, Kansas (Johnson County). Yesterday, Zimmer—acting on behalf of his consulting service—bought a new computer system on credit from Bradford Computer Co. ("BCC"). To secure repayment of the loan, BCC retained an enforceable security interest in the computer system.

    To perfect its security interest, BCC should file its financing statement against

    (A)   "Robert W. Zimmer" in Jackson County, Missouri.

    (B)   "Robert W. Zimmer" in Missouri's central filing office.

    (C)   "RWZ Consulting" in Delaware's central filing office.

    (D)   "RWZ Consulting" in Kansas's central filing office.

68. Why is BCC's purchase-money security interest in the computer system *not* automatically perfected?

    ANSWER:

69. BizCorp sells office equipment to businesses and consumers, often on credit. These credit purchases are evidenced by a single-page contract (captioned "PROMISSORY NOTE AND SECURITY AGREEMENT") that memorializes the buyer's monetary obligation and BizCorp's retention of title in the item(s) until the buyer has fulfilled all monetary obligations.

    BizCorp wants to use these contracts to obtain necessary financing from Lender. The parties are contemplating two possible transaction structures. In the first, Lender will extend credit that will be secured by the contracts. Alternatively, in the second structure, Lender will purchase the contracts for a discounted price.

    Discuss whether Article 9 applies to both forms of proposed transactions and what action Lender must take to perfect any Article 9 interest in the contracts.

    ANSWER:

70. Would any of your analysis change if the single-page contracts were negotiable, but unsecured, promissory notes?

    ANSWER:

71. On July 1, The Book Nook ("TBN"), a retail bookseller, executed a written security agreement granting to Bank a security interest in TBN's existing and future equipment to secure repayment of a loan in an amount not yet agreed upon by the parties. On July 4, Bank filed a proper financing statement against "equipment" with the proper official. Loan negotiations concluded on July 7, when Bank executed a binding commitment to lend up to $500,000 to TBN in one or more advances. On July 10, TBN requested the initial advance of $100,000. Bank funded the $100,000 advance on July 12.

    Bank's interest in a new computer system, purchased by TBN on July 3 (and identified to the contract on that date) and delivered and installed on July 11, became perfected on

    (A) July 4.

    (B) July 7.

    (C) July 11.

    (D) July 12.

72. When did Bank obtain a perfected security interest in a shipment of children's books that TBN ordered on July 2 and received on July 8?

    ANSWER:

73. Maria Garza, a resident of Dallas, Texas, intends to borrow $25,000 from SmallBank. The loan will be secured by the following collateral:

    • 100 shares of 3X, Inc. stock, represented by a stock certificate in Maria's possession;

    • 200 shares of the Franklin Large Cap Fund (the Fund is organized under Delaware law; the account agreement is governed by New York law); and

    • all of the investments in her brokerage account managed by the Houston office of Providence Securities, an entity organized under Delaware law (the account agreement is governed by New York law).

    SmallBank wants to perfect its security interest in all of these investments by filing. To do so, it must file its financing statement

    (A) in the county records in Dallas County, Texas.

    (B) in the county records of Dallas County, Texas, and in the central filing offices of Texas, Delaware, and New York.

    (C) in the central filing offices of Texas, Delaware, and New York.

    (D) in the central filing office of Texas.

74. Three years after funding the loan mentioned in Question 73, SmallBank discovers that Maria had recently sold all shares of her 3X, Inc., stock to her father, Arturo, who lives full time in Rochester, New York.

What filing action, if any, should SmallBank take to continue to perfect its interest in the shares of 3X stock, following Maria's unauthorized transaction?

ANSWER:

75. A few weeks after Maria sold all of her shares of 3X, Inc., stock to her father, Maria moved from Dallas, Texas, to Santa Fe, New Mexico, and now resides in Santa Fe full time.

What filing action, if any, should SmallBank take to continue to perfect its security interest in Maria's investment property, following Maria's relocation to a different state?

ANSWER:

76. Chi-Town Bank wants to perfect an enforceable security interest in BAMCO's inventory, accounts, equipment, investment property, and deposit accounts. BAMCO does business in Nevada, Colorado, and Utah. Its chief executive office is located in Las Vegas.

Explain why this statement is true or false: *If BAMCO is a corporation organized under Delaware law, then Chi-Town Bank must file in both Delaware and Nevada; Delaware to perfect its security interest in inventory and equipment, and Nevada to perfect its security interest in accounts and investment property.*

ANSWER:

77. Explain why this statement is true or false: *If BAMCO is a general partnership, then Chi-Town Bank should file in each state where inventory and equipment are located to perfect its security interest in that collateral and in Nevada to perfect its security interest in accounts and investment property.*

ANSWER:

78. Explain why this statement is true or false: *BAMCO's relocation of its chief executive office to Denver has no impact on the continued effectiveness of Chi-Town Bank's financing statement if BAMCO is a corporation.*

ANSWER:

79. How would your answer to the previous question change, if at all, if BAMCO was a corporation organized under the laws of the United Kingdom, a country that you may assume has a personal property security filing and registration system substantially equivalent to that found in the United States?

ANSWER:

80. In which transaction does Bank have a perfected security interest?

(A) Bank has an enforceable security interest in 100 shares of BAMCO stock owned by Meredith. The shares are evidenced by a certificate issued in Meredith's name.

Meredith delivers the certificate to Bank without indorsing it. Bank never files a financing statement.

(B) Bank has an enforceable purchase-money security interest in Tom's boat (which is not subject to any certificate-of-title laws). Bank never files a financing statement. Ever since he acquired it, Tom has used the boat equally for personal and business purposes.

(C) Bank has an enforceable security interest in all of the motor vehicles owned by Zippy Rental Agency that it leases to travelers, on a short-term basis, from its facility at Reagan National Airport in Washington, D.C. Bank files a financing statement against Zippy's vehicle inventory, rather than complying with certificate-of-title laws.

(D) Bank has an enforceable security interest in BizCorp's deposit accounts maintained with other financial institutions. Bank files a financing statement.

81. The ownership of intellectual property such as copyrights, trademarks, and patents is often registered with national registries in Washington, D.C. Under current caselaw, which of the following types of property can be perfected by filing a financing statement (rather than registering its property interest in the relevant national registry)?

(A) Trademarks, but not patents or copyrights.

(B) Trademarks and copyrights, but not patents.

(C) Patents and trademarks, but not registered copyrights.

(D) Patents, copyrights, or trademarks.

82. Give an example of collateral in which a security interest can be perfected three different ways.

ANSWER:

83. GetSmart! is a Nevada corporation that operates several tutorial clinics in Las Vegas. Most of its customers are individuals who want to maximize their score on any of a number of standardized tests (such as the ACT, the SAT, the GMAT, the LSAT, etc.). GetSmart! owns or leases office furniture, photocopiers, and computers, and its customers pay—with cash, checks, or credit cards—prior to each tutorial. GetSmart! also maintains an up-to-date, and rather lengthy, customer list.

GetSmart! wants to open several tutorial clinics in Reno, Nevada. It approaches Omega Bank for a $1 million loan. Omega Bank agrees to fund the loan, and GetSmart! executes a promissory note and a security agreement that describes the collateral as "all accounts, equipment, and general intangibles." The security agreement includes an after-acquired property clause. Omega Bank files its financing statement (describing the collateral as "all of Debtor's personal property") with the appropriate office.

Upon filing the financing statement, Omega Bank has (or, upon attachment, will have) a perfected security interest in

(A)   none of GetSmart!'s assets because its financing statement fails to provide a proper collateral description.

(B)   everything, other than the customer list and the cash.

(C)   everything, other than the cash and the checks and the customer list.

(D)   everything, other than the cash and the checks.

Proceeds

84. BAM, LLC, borrowed $1 million from ZinnBank. BAM granted to ZinnBank an enforceable security interest in all of BAM's inventory, equipment, and accounts, now owned or hereafter acquired. ZinnBank filed a sufficient financing statement with the appropriate central filing office. One month after the loan was made, without ZinnBank's permission, BAM traded one of its forklifts (not subject to a certificate of title) to a nearby company, Sadie, Inc., in return for 100 wooden pallets and a check for $500. After the sale, ZinnBank has an attached security interest in

    (A)   neither the forklift, the check, or the pallets.

    (B)   the forklift, but not the check or the pallets.

    (C)   the forklift and the pallets, but not the check.

    (D)   the forklift, the pallets, and the check.

85. Same facts as Question 84. It is now one month after the trade mentioned in the question. Assume BAM has not yet cashed the check. ZinnBank now has a perfected security interest in

    (A)   neither the forklift, the check, or the pallets.

    (B)   the forklift, but not the check or the pallets.

    (C)   the forklift and the pallets, but not the check.

    (D)   the forklift, the pallets, and the check.

86. Larabie, Inc., borrows $5 million from Sturm Bank. Larabie gives a security interest to Sturm in all its inventory, now owned or hereafter acquired, to secure the loan. Sturm files an adequate and complete financing statement with the appropriate central filing office, indicating the collateral as "all assets."

    Larabie sells air conditioning units. After Sturm makes its loan, Hank shows up in Larabie's store and buys two units, at $1,000 each. He pays cash for one (with 10 Benjamins), and signs a contract promising to pay $1,000 to Larabie in a month for the other. Larabie takes the $1,000 in cash, goes next door, and buys a new set of display racks for $2,000, paying with the cash Hank gave him and a check drawn on Larabie's account at Sturm. One month passes, and Hank honors his contract by giving his check for $1,000 to Larabie.

Sturm has a perfected security interest in

(A)   the display racks only.

(B)   Hank's check only.

(C)   both Hank's check and the display racks.

(D)   neither Hank's check nor the display racks.

87.   BizCorp is in the business of selling and leasing photocopiers to individuals and businesses. Omega Bank extended credit to BizCorp in return for an enforceable security interest in BizCorp's inventory. Omega Bank perfected its security interest in BizCorp's inventory by filing a financing statement with the appropriate state official. The security agreement and the financing statement described the collateral as "inventory"; neither description mentioned an after-acquired property clause.

BizCorp sold one of its photocopiers in the ordinary course of its business to a law firm, which paid for the purchase by tendering a cashier's check for the full price.

Omega Bank

(A)   cannot claim an enforceable security interest in the cashier's check because the loan papers failed to mention an after-acquired property clause, and BizCorp did not acquire rights in the cashier's check until after it had authenticated the security agreement.

(B)   cannot claim an enforceable security interest in the cashier's check because the loan papers describe the collateral merely as "inventory" and fail to use language (such as "checks" or "proceeds") that would cover the check.

(C)   can claim an enforceable security interest in the cashier's check, but the security interest will not be perfected if the sale of the photocopier to the law firm effectively terminated Omega Bank's security interest in the photocopier.

(D)   can claim an enforceable and perfected security interest in the cashier's check, assuming it is identifiable as proceeds of the photocopier.

88.   Frank borrows $2,000 from Wolf Bank to buy a computer for his work. To secure this loan, Wolf has Frank sign an otherwise valid security agreement that describes the collateral as "that certain Dell X400 computer acquired or to be acquired by Frank, and all accessions, accessories and substitutions related thereto." On June 1, Wolf lends the money (via a check jointly payable to Frank and Dell), and Frank buys the computer. It also on that date files an adequate and complete financing statement with the appropriate central filing office indicating the collateral as "equipment."

On August 1, Frank determines that there is not enough random access memory (RAM) in the computer, and goes to Mark's Memory, Inc., and buys $500 worth of memory chips that will fit the Dell, and that will double its memory capacity. The terms of the sale are that Frank will pay $100 down, and $100 a month until the $500 purchase price is paid in full. Mark's Memory will retain title in the chips until it is paid in full.

Frank returns home, pulls the original chips from the computer, and inserts the new chips. The computer boots up fine, and shows full use of the new chips.

If Frank defaults by not paying either Wolf or Mark's Memory, which of the following is the best description of the relative rights as between Wolf and Mark's Memory?

(A)   Wolf has a perfected security interest in the computer and the old memory chips, but not the new memory chips.

(B)   Wolf has a perfected security interest in the computer, the old memory chips, and the new memory chips.

(C)   Mark's Memory has a perfected security interest in the computer and the new memory chips, but not the old ones.

(D)   Mark's Memory has a perfected security interest in the new memory chips only.

89.   Sandy is a baker, and has three secured creditors, B1, B2, and B3. B1 has a perfected security interest in Sandy's eggs. B2 has a perfected security interest in Sandy's flour and sugar. B3 has a perfected security interest in Sandy's dairy products and vanilla extract. The financing statements for each bank only state the ingredient in which they have an attached security interest.

Sandy bakes 60 mini-cakes for sale in her store, for a price of $2 each. In making the mini-cakes, she uses $20 worth of eggs, $30 worth of flour, and $10 worth of milk, butter, and vanilla extract. Each secured creditor is owed more than $100.

The relative rights of B1, B2, and B3 in the cakes are

(A)   Neither B1, B2, or B3 has any interest in the cakes because the cakes are no longer eggs, flour, dairy products, or vanilla extract.

(B)   B2 has a perfected security interest in all the cakes because flour was the main ingredient.

(C)   B1, B2, and B3 each have a coequal perfected security interest in the cakes in proportion to the value of the ingredients used to bake them, less 20% to account for Sandy's labor and overhead.

(D)   B1, B2, and B3 each have a coequal perfected security interest in the cakes in proportion to the value of the ingredients used to bake them.

90.   Trinity Finance holds a perfected security interest in the inventory of The Avid Reader bookstore. Both the security agreement and the financing statement describe the collateral as "debtor's current and after-acquired inventory."

Last month a hurricane caused significant damage to the bookstore, including $1 million in lost, damaged, or destroyed inventory. The bookstore is insured against this loss.

Trinity Finance has

(A)   an unperfected security interest in the bookstore's insurance claim.

(B)   a perfected security interest in the bookstore's insurance claim, but only for 20 days from the date of the hurricane damage, after which the security interest will become unperfected.

(C)   a perfected security interest in the bookstore's insurance claim.

(D)   no security interest in the bookstore's insurance claim because Article 9 excludes from its coverage a debtor's interest arising under an insurance policy.

91.   A month goes by, and the bookstore receives a $1 million check from its insurance company.

Trinity Finance has

(A)   no security interest in the check because the check is "money" under the UCC and Article 9 excludes from its coverage a debtor's rights in money.

(B)   a perfected security interest in the check, but only for 20 days after the bookstore's receipt of the check, after which the security interest is unperfected unless Trinity Finance takes possession of the check.

(C)   an unperfected security interest in the check, unless and until the bookstore indorses and delivers the check to Trinity Finance.

(D)   a perfected security interest in the check.

92.   Assume, instead, that the insurance company does not pay the claim by delivering a check to the bookstore. Instead, the insurance company sends a $1 million wire transfer (a "funds transfer" under UCC Article 4) directly to the bookstore's general operating bank account that the bookstore maintains with ZinnBank.

Assuming that Trinity Finance can satisfy its tracing burden, Trinity Finance has

(A)   a perfected security interest in the bookstore's bank account for $1 million.

(B)   a perfected security interest in the bookstore's bank account for $1 million, but only for 20 days, after which the security interest is unperfected unless Trinity Finance obtains control over the bank account.

(C)   an unperfected security interest in the bookstore's bank account, unless and until Trinity Finance obtains control over the bank account.

(D)   no security interest in the bookstore's bank account because Article 9 excludes from its coverage the debtor's interest in a bank account arising from a funds transfer covered by UCC Article 4.

93.   On July 20, Omega Bank obtained an enforceable security interest in the current and after-acquired inventory of Gershwin Pianos, a business that sells and leases pianos. Omega Bank filed its financing statement in the appropriate place against Gershwin's inventory on August 1.

On November 1, Lauren bought an upright piano from Gershwin. Lauren operates a sole proprietorship that sells office equipment, and she paid for the piano by trading to Gershwin a photocopier of comparable value (for in-store use).

As of December 1, does Omega Bank have a perfected security interest in the photocopier?

ANSWER:

94. Discuss whether your answer to Question 93 would change if Lauren paid $750 for her piano with a check, Gershwin then immediately deposited that check in its bank account (which had a $100 balance at the time) and, later that day, Gershwin bought the photocopier from Dealer for $500, using a check drawn on the account into which Lauren's check was deposited.

ANSWER:

95. Lender has a perfected security interest in Debtor's inventory and accounts. Contrary to the terms of the security agreement, Debtor deposited cash proceeds in a bank account in April that contained non-proceeds. Evidence reveals the following activity during April:

   •   The opening balance on April 1 was $8,000 ($2,000 of which is proceeds)

   •   Debtor deposited cash proceeds into the account as follows:

       $6,000 on April 5

       $3,000 on April 24

   •   Debtor deposited non-proceeds into the account as follows:

       $4,000 on April 15

       $2,000 on April 28

   •   Debtor made the following withdrawals from the account:

       $7,000 on April 7

       $5,000 on April 20

As of April 30, under the lowest intermediate balance rule, Lender can claim a security interest in

(A) $11,000.

(B) $10,000.

(C) $9,000.

(D) $8,000.

96. Assume that Debtor also deposited cash proceeds of $4,000 on April 12 and non-proceeds of $2,000 on April 22, and withdrew $8,000 on April 17. Calculate the amount of Lender's security interest as of April 30 under the lowest intermediate balance rule.

ANSWER:

97. Tim, an avid and part-time professional chess player, borrowed $15,000 from his parents in August 2018 to purchase a Civil War chess set later that month on an Internet auction site; he planned to bring this set to his professional matches. At his parents' insistence, Tim authenticated a security agreement that granted to his parents a security interest in all chess sets Tim owned or would own in the future (which is an adequate description). Tim also executed a promissory note payable to his parents, with a maturity date of December 31, 2020. His parents filed a financing statement against Tim in Ohio, where Tim lived and had a day job, indicating that the collateral was "chess sets." Tim never told his parents that someone else won the auction, or that he then used his parents' money to take a vacation to New Zealand and pay off some credit card debt.

In October 2018, Tim purchased an identical Civil War chess set at the same Internet auction site.

In July 2019, Tim was promoted by his employer; that month he moved to Rochester, New York, to assume his new responsibilities. He continues to play chess professionally.

In February 2020, Tim sold the Civil War chess set to another collector in exchange for three baseballs, each in mint condition and autographed by a different member of baseball's Hall of Fame.

Tim failed to repay the $15,000 to his parents when the promissory note came due on December 31, 2020.

On that date, his parents have

(A) no security interest in the baseballs.

(B) an unperfected security interest in the baseballs.

(C) a perfected security interest in the baseballs, but only if the chess set was a consumer good as used by Tim.

(D) a perfected security interest in the baseballs, regardless of whether the chess set was a consumer good as used by Tim.

98. BankOne has a security interest in Frank's inventory and accounts to secure a $1 million line of credit. The security agreement has an after-acquired property clause. BankOne has perfected this interest with a financing statement filed with the appropriate state central authority that indicates the collateral as "inventory and accounts." Frank also has a banking relationship with BankTwo, whose depositor agreement states that "Depositor [Frank] grants a security interest in all deposit accounts maintained with Bank to secure all debts

now owed or hereafter incurred to Bank." Frank set up his account with BankTwo after BankOne lent its money and filed its financing statement. BankTwo makes no UCC-1 filings, and has lent Frank $5,000.

Frank sells high-end luggage. He sells a set of luggage to Harold for $1,000, taking a check for that amount in payment. He deposits the check in BankTwo. After Harold's check clears,

(A)   BankOne has no security interest in the deposit account at BankTwo.

(B)   BankOne has an unperfected security interest in the deposit account at BankTwo only if it can trace Frank's check into the existing balance at BankTwo.

(C)   BankOne has a perfected security interest in the deposit account at BankTwo only if it can trace Harold's check into the existing balance at BankTwo.

(D)   BankOne has a security interest in the account at BankTwo only if BankTwo consents.

99.   Same facts as Question 98, except that after depositing Harold's check, Frank buys new luggage for resale with a check drawn on BankTwo in the amount of $1,000. After depositing Harold's check, the balance in the account at BankTwo increased to $1,500. There were no deposits or withdrawals between the time of the deposit of Harold's check and the purchase of the new luggage for resale.

After Frank takes delivery of the new luggage purchased,

(A)   neither BankOne nor BankTwo has a security interest in the new luggage.

(B)   only BankOne has a security interest in the new luggage.

(C)   only Bank Two has a security interest in the luggage.

(D)   both BankOne and BankTwo have a security interest in the luggage.

100. In Question 99, does either BankOne or BankTwo have a perfected security interest in the new luggage after 20 days have passed? Why?

ANSWER:

101. BankOne has lent $5 million to Lucent Corp. Lucent Corp. sells computer systems. BankOne and Lucent have signed a security agreement under which Lucent secured its obligation to repay the $5 million with "all its accounts, chattel paper, and instruments, now owned or hereafter acquired." BankOne has filed a financing statement with this description in the proper central filing office.

Lucent sells a computer system to Balrog, Inc., for $500,000. Under the contract of sale, which is on a form Lucent has developed, Balrog is to pay $50,000 down, and $10,000 a month for 45 months. Lucent retains title until Balrog pays the entire amount owed.

Lucent is strapped for cash. Contrary to its agreement with BankOne, Lucent sells the Balrog contract to High End Factors, Inc. (HEFI), a factor who enters into these types of transactions as its business. It takes possession of the written contract, but does not search the central filing records. HEFI immediately sends an adequate and sufficient notice to Balrog that it should pay HEFI all amounts owed to Lucent. In compliance with this notice, Balrog makes two payments to HEFI, which HEFI puts in a bank account in its name. The payments are still in the account, and are the only amounts in the account.

HEFI, Lucent, and Balrog are all located in the same state. With respect to the Balrog contract, BankOne has a perfected security interest in

(A)   the Balrog contract and the deposit account in HEFI's name.

(B)   the Balrog contract only.

(C)   the HEFI deposit account only.

(D)   neither the Balrog contract nor the HEFI account.

102.   In Question 101, who has priority as to the Balrog contract and the HEFI deposit account, and why?

ANSWER:

103.   Would the answer change in Question 102 if HEFI did not take possession of the Lucent/ Balrog contract? Why?

ANSWER:

Fixtures

104. Bank is making a large commercial loan to TZ Farms, Inc., a North Carolina corporation that owns 100 acres in Wake County on which it grows strawberries. Bank should conduct a search for fixture filings against TZ Farms's

   (A)   equipment.

   (B)   inventory.

   (C)   farm products.

   (D)   goods.

105. Bank intends to file a fixture filing against TZ Farms. Must the filing mention "fixtures" in the collateral description?

   ANSWER:

106. Bank has agreed to make a $25,000 loan to Tim for a business purpose. Collateral will include all of Tim's consumer goods located, at the time of the loan, at his primary residence. Tim never has been, nor does he ever intend to be, engaged in any farming operation.

   Bank believes that because the collateral will include consumer goods, rather than equipment, it need not conduct a fixture filing search as part of its due diligence.

   Discuss the merits of Bank's belief.

   ANSWER:

107. Brenda Banker asserts that the only way to perfect a security interest in a fixture is by filing a fixture filing. Lauren Lender begs to differ, asserting that a secured party can perfect a security interest in a fixture (i) by filing a financing statement with the central filing office, (ii) by filing a fixture filing in the county where the relevant real property is located, and (iii) (in appropriate instances) automatically on attachment if the secured party can claim a purchase-money security interest in a consumer good.

   Discuss whether Brenda or Lauren has the better argument.

   ANSWER:

108.   Which of the following is most likely to merit a fixture filing?

   (A)   A large video monitor that drops down from the ceiling of a university auditorium.

   (B)   A new driver's side exterior mirror affixed to a motor vehicle.

   (C)   Oil reserves not yet extracted from the ground.

   (D)   "Greens fees" collected by a country club from its golfing clientele.

109.   To be effective as a fixture filing, a fixture filing

   (A)   must include a description of real estate to which the fixture is attached.

   (B)   must be recorded no later than the twentieth day after the date on which the collateral became a fixture.

   (C)   must be authenticated by the debtor and, if the debtor does not have an interest of record in the real estate, the record owner of the real estate.

   (D)   can be filed with either the central filing office or the local filing office.

110.   Grappino Corporation ("GC"), chartered under Delaware law, owns and operates three wineries and related vineyards in the Sonoma Valley, north of San Francisco. Bay Area Bank holds a valid mortgage on the real estate and "all fixtures now or hereafter affixed thereto." The mortgage (which is not a construction mortgage) was filed in the local property records in February.

   On July 20, GC purchased four storage tanks on credit from BAMCO (with BAMCO retaining an enforceable security interest in the tanks). BAMCO delivered and installed the tanks (each a "fixture" under applicable law, and not readily removable) on August 15.

   In November, GC defaulted on his obligations to Bay Area Bank and BAMCO. The two creditors are disputing whose property interest in the storage tanks enjoys priority.

   Which of the following statements is true?

   (A)   BAMCO has perfected its security interest in the tanks if it filed a standard financing statement with the central filing office in California.

   (B)   BAMCO will win the priority dispute with Bay Area Bank if BAMCO filed a standard financing statement on August 1.

   (C)   BAMCO will win the priority dispute with Bay Area Bank if BAMCO filed a fixture filing on September 1.

   (D)   BAMCO's security interest in the tanks is automatically perfected because BAMCO is a purchase-money creditor.

111.   Now that GC is in default, BAMCO wants to enforce its rights and remedies. Which of the following statements is true?

(A) BAMCO's rights and remedies as to the tanks/ fixtures are provided by real estate law, rather than Article 9.

(B) BAMCO cannot remove the tanks/fixtures (absent GC's consent).

(C) BAMCO can remove the tanks/fixtures, but only if its security interest in them enjoys priority over the competing claim asserted by Bay Area Bank.

(D) BAMCO cannot remove the tanks/fixtures if GC has paid off more than 60% of the purchase-money debt associated with them.

112. Assume that BAMCO exercises due care in removing the tanks under applicable law, but still causes physical damage of $5,000 to the property. In addition, the absence of the tanks has caused GC's property to decrease in value by $15,000.

Bay Area Bank and GC each contend that BAMCO owes $20,000 to it.

Which of the following statements is true?

(A) BAMCO owes $20,000 to Bay Area Bank, and nothing to GC.

(B) BAMCO owes $5,000 to Bay Area Bank, and nothing to GC.

(C) BAMCO owes $15,000 to Bay Area Bank, and $5,000 to GC.

(D) BAMCO owes nothing to Bay Area Bank, and $5,000 to GC.

113. Five months ago, Tasty Treats, Inc., obtained a $2 million loan from Fidelity Finance to purchase land on which it intended to build a restaurant. The loan is secured by a valid construction mortgage on the property (and all buildings, improvements, and fixtures then or thereafter added to the property), filed in the real property records at the time of the loan. Fidelity Finance made no other filings.

Two months ago, still during the construction phase, Kitchen Appliances, Inc. ("KAI") agreed to sell and install three new appliances at the restaurant for $200,000. Tasty Treats paid $40,000 in cash and agreed to pay the balance, with interest, over the next 12 months. To secure the deferred part of the purchase price, KAI retained an enforceable purchase-money security interest in the three appliances. KAI promptly filed a financing statement with the central filing office of the appropriate state, but it did not file any fixture filings.

Under applicable local law, the three appliances—when installed—will be "fixtures" (and will not be readily removable).

As agreed, KAI delivered the appliances to the restaurant three days ago, with the intent to install them yesterday. Two days ago, however, Tasty Treats defaulted on all of its material contracts and filed a bankruptcy petition. The appliances have not yet been installed. And construction is not yet complete.

In a priority contest between Fidelity Finance and KAI concerning the three appliances,

(A) KAI will win because Fidelity Finance has no interest in the units until they are installed (which has not yet happened).

(B) Fidelity Finance will win because KAI never filed a fixture filing.

(C) Fidelity Finance will win because KAI's PMSI secured repayment of less than the full purchase price of $200,000.

(D) Fidelity Finance will win because its mortgage is a construction mortgage.

114. Assume the same facts, except Tasty Treats filed its bankruptcy petition one day after KAI had installed the three appliances. Who will win the dispute between Fidelity Finance and KAI under these revised facts?

ANSWER:

115. Continue to assume the revised facts. The bankruptcy trustee seeks to convert KAI's secured claim into an unsecured claim by exercising its avoidance powers under Bankruptcy Code § 544(a), the so-called strong-arm clause. Will the trustee be successful?

ANSWER:

116. Grace bought her first home in March of this year. Friendly Finance financed the purchase and holds a valid mortgage on the home, "all fixtures now or hereafter affixed thereto," and the underlying real estate. The mortgage (which is not a construction mortgage) was filed in the appropriate real property records in March.

On August 1, Grace purchased a chandelier for her home on credit from ZinnCo Lighting, which retained an enforceable security interest in the chandelier as of that date. ZinnCo installed the chandelier (a "fixture" under applicable law, and not readily removable) at Grace's home on August 7.

ZinnCo's security interest in the chandelier

(A) is automatically perfected.

(B) is automatically perfected, but only until the chandelier becomes a fixture, at which time automatic perfection ceases.

(C) enjoys priority over the competing claim asserted by Friendly Finance in October, whether or not ZinnCo has filed a proper fixture filing.

(D) enjoys priority over the competing claim asserted by Friendly Finance in October if ZinnCo filed a proper fixture filing in August.

117. Assume, instead, that ZinnCo's priority dispute is not with Friendly Finance, but with Nancy Neighbor. Nancy recently won a dog-bite lawsuit against Grace and obtained a lien on Grace's residence (and fixtures thereto) on September 1. ZinnCo has never filed a standard financing statement or a fixture filing.

Who will win this priority dispute in the chandelier?

ANSWER:

118. In February, the Dallas Sports Bar & Grill (the "Bar") bought five big-screen televisions on credit from Dealer. Dealer installed the televisions later that month and retained an enforceable security interest in them to secure repayment of the aggregate purchase price. Dealer filed a standard financing statement, proper in all respects, with the appropriate central filing official.

In May, the Bar borrowed $10,000 from one of its co-owners, Big Tex. To secure repayment of the loan, the Bar granted to Big Tex an enforceable security interest in various assets, including the five televisions. A week after making the loan, Big Tex filed a proper fixture filing against the five televisions in the appropriate real estate records.

In August, the Bar borrowed $35,000 from Bank. To secure repayment of the loan, the Bar executed a mortgage in favor of Bank (the mortgage is not a "construction mortgage"). The collateral description included not only the land and the restaurant, but all fixtures thereto. Bank properly recorded its mortgage in the appropriate real estate records.

By December, the Bar had fallen on hard financial times and had defaulted on its obligations. Soon thereafter, a priority dispute in the five televisions arose among Dealer, Big Tex, and Bank. The parties have stipulated that the five televisions are "fixtures" under applicable law and not readily removable from the Bar.

The court should conclude that

(A) Big Tex has priority over Dealer and Bank.

(B) Dealer has priority over Big Tex, but not Bank.

(C) Bank has priority over Dealer and Big Tex.

(D) Bank and Big Tex have priority over Dealer.

Priority (Secured Party v. Secured Party; No PMSI)

119. Six months ago, Grace borrowed $5,000 from her sister, Meredith. Meredith was aware that Grace had had financial challenges in the past, so Meredith insisted on some collateral. In response, Grace offered all of her jewelry as collateral. Meredith agreed, but out of convenience the sisters did not memorialize their agreement in writing, nor did Meredith take possession of any jewelry other than a diamond necklace valued at $3,500. Being unfamiliar with UCC Article 9, Meredith never filed a financing statement.

Four months ago, Grace borrowed $3,000 from her brother, Ethan. Ethan, too, insisted on collateral. In response, Grace offered all of her jewelry as collateral. Ethan agreed, and Ethan and Grace memorialized their agreement in writing (signed by both parties and adequately describing the jewelry). Out of convenience, Ethan did not take possession of any jewelry. Being unfamiliar with UCC Article 9, Ethan never filed a financing statement.

Last week, Grace defaulted on both loans, having made no payments.

Meredith and Ethan are having a family squabble over which of them have the greater claim to Grace's jewelry (each piece of which was acquired by Grace at least seven months ago). Meredith still has possession of the diamond necklace.

Which of the following statements is true?

(A) Meredith and Ethan have coequal claims to the jewelry, as neither of them filed a financing statement.

(B) Meredith has no enforceable security interest in any of the jewelry because Grace never authenticated a security agreement in Meredith's favor.

(C) Ethan has no enforceable security interest in any of the jewelry because he does not have possession of any of the jewelry, and he never filed a financing statement.

(D) Meredith has a perfected security interest in the diamond necklace, which enjoys priority over Ethan's claim to it, but Ethan has an enforceable security interest in all remaining jewelry, which enjoys priority over Meredith's unsecured claim in that jewelry.

120. Assume the original facts, except Meredith and Grace timely memorialized their agreement in writing before Ethan made his loan to Grace.

With respect to all jewelry still in Grace's possession,

(A)   Meredith and Ethan have coequal enforceable security interests.

(B)   Meredith has the greater of the two security interests.

(C)   Ethan has the greater of the two security interests.

(D)   Neither Meredith nor Ethan has an enforceable security interest in the jewelry.

121.   Assume the original facts, except that Ethan filed a proper financing statement with the appropriate clerk three days after Grace executed the security agreement in his favor.

With respect to the diamond necklace in Meredith's possession,

(A)   Meredith and Ethan have coequal perfected security interests.

(B)   Meredith and Ethan have perfected security interests, but Meredith's interest enjoys priority.

(C)   Meredith and Ethan have perfected security interests, but Ethan's interest enjoys priority.

(D)   Meredith and Ethan have perfected security interests, which share priority in the ratio of unpaid debt (e.g., Meredith enjoys a 5/8 claim, and Ethan enjoys a 3/8 claim).

122.   ZinnCorp wants to borrow funds to address certain corporate needs.

In February, ZinnCorp began negotiating the terms of a $35,000 secured loan from First Bank. With ZinnCorp's permission, First Bank filed a financing statement against ZinnCorp's "accounts, inventory, and equipment" on February 20. Negotiations continued for several weeks thereafter. On the afternoon of April 10, First Bank funded the $35,000 loan, only hours after ZinnCorp had executed a written security agreement in which it granted to First Bank a security interest in its "accounts, inventory, and equipment." The security agreement included an after-acquired property clause.

Meanwhile, in March, ZinnCorp began negotiating the terms of a $25,000 secured loan from Second Bank. On the morning of March 15, Second Bank funded the $25,000 loan within minutes after ZinnCorp executed a written security agreement in which ZinnCorp granted to Second Bank a security interest in its "accounts, inventory, and equipment." The security agreement included an after-acquired property clause. Second Bank filed its financing statement against the same collateral on March 23.

In October, ZinnCorp defaulted under both agreements. First Bank and Second Bank are fighting over which of them has the greater claim to a piece of equipment acquired by ZinnCorp on March 1.

Which of the following answers is true?

(A)   First Bank wins because it was the first party to both file its financing statement against, and perfect its security interest in, the piece of equipment.

(B) Second Bank wins because it was the first party to both file its financing statement against, and perfect its security interest in, the piece of equipment.

(C) First Bank wins because of its filing date.

(D) Second Bank wins because of its perfection date.

123. How would your analysis change if ZinnCorp had acquired the piece of equipment on July 1?

ANSWER:

124. How would your analysis change if ZinnCorp had acquired the piece of equipment on July 1 and First Bank had failed to include an after-acquired property clause in its security agreement with ZinnCorp?

ANSWER:

125. How would your analysis change if (i) ZinnCorp had acquired the piece of equipment on July 1, (ii) First Bank had failed to include an after-acquired property clause in its original security agreement with ZinnCorp, but (iii) First Bank and ZinnCorp executed an amended security agreement (that covered equipment and that included an after-acquired property clause) on August 1?

ANSWER:

126. MegaCorp is a Delaware corporation. It has one wholly owned corporate subsidiary: Longhorn Corporation, Inc. ("LCI"), incorporated under Texas law.

On March 15, MegaCorp executed a valid security agreement in favor of First Bank, granting a security interest in "all shares of Longhorn Corporation, Inc., capital stock, whether now owned or hereafter acquired" by MegaCorp. First Bank gave value for the first time on March 18.

On April 10, Second Bank advanced $23,000 to MegaCorp. With MegaCorp's permission, Second Bank filed its financing statement against MegaCorp's "investment property" on April 13. MegaCorp did not authenticate its security agreement in favor of Second Bank (covering "investment property, whether now owned or hereafter acquired") until April 20.

MegaCorp encountered financial difficulties later in the year and defaulted on both loans in early November. First Bank and Second Bank are fighting over the priority of their respective security interests in the LCI shares of capital stock, all of which are evidenced by a single stock certificate issued in registered form to MegaCorp.

Which of the following statements is true?

(A) First Bank has priority if it filed a financing statement in Texas on March 25.

(B) First Bank has priority if it filed a financing statement in Delaware on April 15.

(C)   Second Bank has priority if it takes delivery of the LCI certificate on October 1 and continues to hold it, even if First Bank perfected its security interest by an earlier filing.

(D)   Filing a financing statement will not perfect a security interest in the LCI shares.

127.   On July 15, Debtor borrowed $400,000 from Alpha Bank. The loan is secured by an enforceable security interest in Debtor's equipment. The security agreement included an after-acquired property clause. Alpha Bank filed its financing statement against Debtor and its equipment on August 1, 2013.

On September 15, Debtor borrowed $300,000 from Omega Bank. The loan is secured by an enforceable security interest in Debtor's equipment. The security agreement included an after-acquired property clause. Omega Bank filed its financing statement against Debtor and its equipment on October 1, 2013.

Alpha Bank filed its UCC-3 continuation statement against Debtor on July 15, 2018.

Omega Bank filed its UCC-3 continuation statement against Debtor on May 15, 2018.

It is now December 1, 2018. The banks are fighting over priority in two pieces of equipment (neither of which is purchase-money collateral). Debtor acquired rights in Item #1 on February 1, 2017, and Item #2 on November 1, 2018.

Which bank has priority in these two pieces of equipment?

(A)   Alpha Bank has priority in Item #1, and Omega Bank has priority in Item #2.

(B)   Alpha Bank has priority in Item #1 and Item #2.

(C)   Omega Bank has priority in Item #1 and Item #2.

(D)   Omega Bank had priority in Item #2 until Alpha Bank filed its UCC-3 continuation statement (after which Alpha Bank had priority in Item #2).

128.   Would your analysis change if Alpha Bank filed its UCC-3 continuation statement on January 15, 2018, before Omega Bank filed its UCC-3 continuation statement four months later?

ANSWER:

129.   On March 1, First Finance obtained an enforceable security interest in the existing and future accounts of Odyssey Furniture, a business that sells furniture to businesses and consumers. First Finance filed its financing statement against the accounts on March 4.

On June 1, Midway Bank obtained an enforceable (but non-purchase money) security interest in the current and after-acquired inventory of Odyssey Furniture. Midway Bank filed its financing statement against the inventory on June 4.

On September 1, a local hotel bought several pieces of bedroom furniture that had been part of Odyssey's inventory since February. The hotel paid for the furniture with a $40,000 check, delivered at the time of purchase, and then it took delivery of the furniture a week later.

On August 15, a local college bought several pieces of bedroom furniture that had been part of Odyssey's inventory since July. The college took delivery of the furniture on August 23, and then it mailed a $50,000 check (as full payment) to Odyssey Furniture, which received the check on September 1.

Odyssey Furniture still has possession of both checks.

Which of the following statements is true?

(A) First Finance has priority in both checks.

(B) Midway Bank has priority in both checks.

(C) First Finance has priority in the $40,000 check, and Midway Bank has priority in the $50,000 check.

(D) Midway Bank has priority in the $40,000 check, and First Finance has priority in the $50,000 check.

130. Assume that Odyssey Furniture deposits both checks into a "proceeds only" deposit account maintained with Paragon Bank on September 3. Paragon Bank has held an enforceable security interest in the deposit account for over a year, but it has never filed a financing statement. Both First Finance and Midway Bank can satisfy any tracing burden as to the credits. At all relevant times, the balance in the deposit account exceeds $90,000, and Paragon Bank is owed more than $50,000 by Odyssey Furniture.

Which of the three financial institutions has priority in the $40,000 credit and the $50,000 credit?

(A) All three financial institutions can claim a one-third priority claim to each credit (in sum, they each claim priority for $30,000).

(B) Paragon Bank has priority in both credits.

(C) Midway Bank has priority in the $40,000 credit, and First Finance has priority in the $50,000 credit.

(D) Midway Bank and Paragon Bank have a one-half priority claim to the $40,000 credit (each for $20,000), and First Finance and Paragon Bank have a one-half priority claim to the $50,000 credit (each for $25,000).

131. Metro Bank loaned $250,000 to ZeeCorp, an entity that sells office equipment. The loan was secured by an enforceable security interest in ZeeCorp's inventory. Metro Bank filed its financing statement on February 15, three days after it funded the loan and ZeeCorp authenticated the security agreement (which included an after-acquired property clause).

In need of additional funding, ZeeCorp sold numerous accounts and chattel paper contracts to Friendly Finance in June for $35,000 (the accounts and chattel paper contracts resulted from inventory sales). Friendly Finance, in the business of buying accounts and commercial paper, took possession of the chattel paper contracts (but it never filed a financing statement against ZeeCorp). As part of its due diligence, Friendly Finance ordered and received a UCC search report against ZeeCorp that revealed Metro Bank's earlier filing.

When Metro Bank discovered what ZeeCorp had done, it sued Friendly Finance for conversion of the accounts and chattel paper contracts.

The judge should rule that

(A)   Metro Bank has priority in the accounts, and Friendly Finance has priority in the chattel paper.

(B)   Friendly Finance has priority in the accounts, and Metro Bank has priority in the chattel paper.

(C)   Metro Bank has priority in the accounts and the chattel paper.

(D)   Friendly Finance has priority in the accounts and the chattel paper.

132.   Clinic maintained a deposit account with Bluebird Bank. On May 1, Bluebird Bank obtained an enforceable security interest in that deposit account pursuant to a security agreement authenticated by Clinic.

On September 1, Clinic borrowed $250,000 from Fidelity Finance for general corporate purposes. The loan was secured by an enforceable security interest in Clinic's current and after-acquired equipment. Fidelity Finance filed a proper financing statement against Clinic and its "equipment" with the appropriate authority on September 12.

On November 1, Clinic purchased a new piece of medical equipment (the "Item"), paying for the purchase with a $25,000 check drawn on its deposit account at Bluebird Bank.

In a priority dispute over the Item that is resolved as of November 15,

(A)   Fidelity Finance has priority over Bluebird Bank, which has no security interest in the Item.

(B)   Fidelity Finance has priority over Bluebird Bank, which has an unperfected security interest in the Item.

(C)   Fidelity Finance has priority over Bluebird Bank, which has a perfected security interest in the Item.

(D)   Bluebird Bank has priority over Fidelity Finance.

133.   Assume that Bluebird Bank discovers on November 10 that Clinic purchased the Item and, with Clinic's permission, files a financing statement against the Item on November 18.

In a priority dispute over the Item that is resolved as of December 1,

(A)   Bluebird Bank's security interest enjoys priority because Fidelity Finance's security interest in after-acquired equipment is unperfected.

(B)   Fidelity Finance enjoys priority because Bluebird Bank never had control over the deposit account on which Clinic wrote the $25,000 check that Clinic issued as payment for the Item.

(C)   Bluebird Bank has a perfected security interest that enjoys priority over Fidelity Finance's perfected security interest.

(D)   Fidelity Finance has a perfected security interest that enjoys priority over Bluebird Bank's perfected security interest.

134.   On February 1, 2015, Beta Bank obtained an enforceable security interest in the current and after-acquired equipment of BetaTech, a Delaware corporation. Beta Bank filed its financing statement in Delaware on February 4, 2015.

On June 4, 2016, Alpha Bank obtained an enforceable security interest in the current and after-acquired equipment of AlphaTech, Inc., a Delaware corporation. Alpha Bank filed its financing statement in Delaware on June 10, 2016. The security agreement prohibited any dispositions of the equipment.

On August 10, 2017, AlphaTech sold an item of equipment (the "Item") to BetaTech, for use as equipment.

On September 1, 2018, Alpha Bank seeks a declaratory judgment that its security interest in the Item enjoys priority over the competing security interest in the Item claimed by Beta Bank.

The judge should rule that

(A)   Alpha Bank enjoys priority.

(B)   Beta Bank enjoys priority because its filing date is earlier than Alpha Bank's filing date.

(C)   Beta Bank enjoys priority because Alpha Bank's security interest became unperfected on the date of sale.

(D)   Beta Bank enjoys priority because the sale terminated Alpha Bank's security interest.

135.   Assume that Alpha Bank filed its financing statement in Texas, rather than Delaware, because AlphaTech is a Texas corporation. All other facts remain unchanged.

How should the judge rule under the revised facts?

ANSWER:

136.   In July 2017, Tim borrowed $10,000 from his sister, Karen, to pay off some uninsured medical expenses. To secure repayment of the loan, Karen took an enforceable security interest

in Tim's grand piano. Karen perfected her interest by filing a financing statement against Tim and his piano in Texas, where Tim resides.

On March 15, 2018, Tim moved to North Carolina.

In May 2018, Tim borrowed $10,000 from his other sister, Diana, to pay off some credit card debt. To secure repayment of the loan, Diana took an enforceable security interest in Tim's grand piano. Diana perfected her interest by filing a financing statement against Tim and his piano in North Carolina on May 10, 2018.

Which sister has priority in the grand piano on July 1, 2018? Assume that Karen has taken no further filing action.

(A) Diana has priority in the grand piano because she has the only filing in North Carolina.

(B) Diana has priority in the grand piano because Karen's security interest is unperfected.

(C) Diana has priority in the grand piano because Karen lost her security interest when Tim moved to North Carolina.

(D) Both sisters are perfected, and Karen has priority.

137. Assume that Karen filed a financing statement against Tim and his piano in North Carolina on July 20, 2018.

It is now November 2018, and Tim has defaulted on the loans to his two sisters, each of whom asserts a priority claim to the grand piano.

Which of the following statements is true?

(A) Diana has priority in the grand piano because she filed first in North Carolina.

(B) Karen has always had priority in the grand piano.

(C) Karen had priority until July 15, then Diana had priority until July 20, and then Karen regained priority when she filed in North Carolina.

(D) Both sisters are perfected, and Diana has priority.

138. Bank made a $1 million loan to HealthNet Corp. (a Delaware corporation) in January. The loan was secured by a security interest in HealthNet's accounts and equipment, and the security agreement included an after-acquired property clause. Bank promptly filed its financing statement.

HealthNet changed its name to "Houston Healthcare Corp." on March 15. Bank knew of the name change, but it took no action in response.

Lender made a $1 million loan to Houston Healthcare in July. The loan was secured by a security interest in Houston Healthcare's accounts and equipment, and the security agreement included an after-acquired property clause. Lender filed its financing statement on July 8. Lender was aware of Bank's security interest in the collateral, but the UCC search report that Lender ordered against "Houston Healthcare Corp." did not disclose Bank's filing.

Houston Healthcare defaulted on both loans in December. A priority dispute in three pieces of equipment has erupted. Evidence reveals that the debtor used its own funds during the year to acquire Item #1 on May 10, Item #2 on July 20, and Item #3 on September 18.

As of December 15, Bank has priority in

(A)   none of the Items.

(B)   Item #1 only.

(C)   Items #1 and #2 only.

(D)   all three Items.

139.   Would your analysis change if Lender filed a UCC-3 amendment, reflecting the name change, on August 1?

ANSWER:

140.   Bank made a $3 million loan to BizCorp in January. The loan was secured by a security interest in all of BizCorp's current and future "contract rights." All contract rights are evidenced by writings and arise from the following transactions:

contracts executed by BizCorp's customers who buy BizCorp's inventory on credit (the "Customer Contracts");

contracts executed by parties who agree to pay BizCorp for licensing BizCorp's intellectual property (the "IP Contracts"); and

contracts executed by BizCorp's corporate officers who, from time to time, borrow money from BizCorp for a year or less (the "Officer Contracts").

Rather than file a financing statement, Bank has taken possession of all of the writings (and BizCorp has faithfully honored its contractual obligation to timely deliver future writings to Bank).

Lender made a $1 million loan to BizCorp in June. The loan was secured by a security interest in all of BizCorp's current and future "contract rights." Lender filed its financing statement against BizCorp and its "contract rights" on June 10.

In July, BizCorp defaulted on both loans. Bank and Lender are fighting over the contract rights evidenced by writings in Bank's possession (each of which BizCorp had delivered before Lender filed its financing statement).

Which of the following statements is true?

(A)   Bank has priority in all contract rights evidenced by the writings in its possession.

(B)   Bank has priority in all contract rights evidenced by writings in its possession that are, or have created, "instruments" or "chattel paper" or "accounts."

(C)   Lender has priority in all contract rights evidenced by writings that have created "accounts" or "general intangibles."

(D)   Bank has a perfected security interest in all contract rights evidenced by writings in its possession.

Priority (Secured Party v. Secured Party; PMSI)

141. Jennifer J. Jacklin operates a music studio in her home, where she gives piano and voice lessons. She and her spouse also play the piano for personal enjoyment. Jennifer operates her studio under the name of "JJJ Music Studio" (but Jennifer does not operate her business as a separate legal entity).

      About 15 months ago, Jennifer borrowed $6,000 from her parents, which she and her spouse used to pay some uninsured family medical bills. At the time of the loan, Jennifer executed a security agreement that granted to her parents a security interest in "any and all pianos, whether now owned or hereafter acquired" by Jennifer (at this time, Jennifer owned one piano in her home). Jennifer's parents promptly filed a financing statement with the appropriate clerk, naming Jennifer as the debtor and describing the collateral as "all pianos in which debtor now or hereafter has rights."

      About six months ago, Jennifer added a second piano to her studio. She purchased the piano on credit from Dealer. Dealer retained an enforceable purchase money security interest in the piano. Dealer delivered the piano to Jennifer's home six days after the purchase date. Twenty-five days after the purchase date, Dealer filed a financing statement with the appropriate clerk, naming JJJ Music Studio as the debtor and adequately describing this piano as the collateral.

      Jennifer has defaulted on her financial obligations to her parents and Dealer, and both creditors are claiming a superior interest in the second piano. Evidence reveals that the second piano is used by Jennifer's family for personal use 60% of the time, and in Jennifer's business 40% of the time.

      Which of the following statements is true?

      (A) Dealer's PMSI is perfected and enjoys priority over the parents' unperfected security interest.

      (B) Both security interests in the second piano are unperfected and share coequal priority.

      (C) Dealer has priority because it has the only enforceable security interest in the second piano.

      (D) The parents have a perfected security interest that enjoys priority over Dealer's perfected security interest.

142.   Assume that the second piano is used by Jennifer's family for personal use 35% of the time, and in Jennifer's business 65% of the time. All other facts remain the same.

   Which of the following statements is true?

   (A)   Dealer's PMSI is perfected and enjoys priority over the parents' unperfected security interest.

   (B)   Both security interests in the second piano are unperfected and share coequal priority.

   (C)   Dealer has priority because it has the only enforceable security interest in the second piano.

   (D)   The parents have a perfected security interest that enjoys priority over Dealer's unperfected security interest.

143.   Assume that the second piano is used by Jennifer's family for personal use 35% of the time, and in Jennifer's business 65% of the time. Also assume that the parents described the collateral on their financing statement as "pianos" rather than "all pianos in which debtor now or hereafter has rights." All other facts remain the same.

   How, if at all, does this change in collateral description on the parents' filing affect priority (as addressed in Question 142)?

   ANSWER:

144.   Assume that the second piano is used by Jennifer's family for personal use 35% of the time, and in Jennifer's business 65% of the time. Also assume that Dealer used Jennifer's name as shown on her current driver's license, rather than the studio's trade name, as the debtor on its financing statement. All other original facts remain the same.

   Which of the following statements is true?

   (A)   Dealer's filing was not sufficiently timely, so it lost its purchase-money status; it retains an enforceable generic security interest that is unperfected (and the parents have priority).

   (B)   Dealer's filing was not sufficiently timely, but it retains an enforceable PMSI that is unperfected (and the parents have priority).

   (C)   Dealer's filing was not sufficiently timely, but it has a perfected PMSI in the piano; the parents have priority.

   (D)   Dealer's filing was sufficiently timely, giving it a perfected PMSI that enjoys priority over the parents' perfected security interest.

145.   ZinnCo is a Delaware corporation that manufactures spark plugs. Its corporate headquarters and manufacturing plant are located in Birmingham, Alabama.

ZinnCo borrowed $1 million from Alpha Bank last year. The loan is secured by a perfected security interest in ZinnCo's current and after-acquired inventory, equipment, and accounts.

On March 5 of this year, ZinnCo bought five new photocopiers from BizCorp for general corporate use. BizCorp delivered and installed the photocopiers on March 12. BizCorp retained an enforceable PMSI in the photocopiers and perfected its interest by filing a financing statement on March 30.

By November, ZinnCo had defaulted on its obligations to Alpha Bank and BizCorp. The two creditors are fighting over the five photocopiers that BizCorp sold to ZinnCo in March.

The priority dispute should be resolved in favor of

(A)   Alpha Bank, because it filed before BizCorp filed.

(B)   Alpha Bank, because its interest became perfected before BizCorp's interest became perfected.

(C)   Alpha Bank, because BizCorp failed to timely perfect its PMSI.

(D)   BizCorp, because its perfected PMSI qualifies for superpriority over Alpha Bank's perfected security interest.

146.   Assume that BizCorp filed its original financing statement in Alabama on March 30. It discovered its mistake and filed a new financing statement in Delaware on April 17.

Which secured creditor wins the priority dispute in the photocopiers under these revised facts?

ANSWER:

147.   Assume that ZinnCo did not buy five new photocopiers from BizCorp on March 5. Instead, assume that ZinnCo had been leasing the five new photocopiers since January 15 of this year (the lease is a true lease, not a disguised secured financing).

ZinnCo's employees loved the new photocopiers, so ZinnCo and BizCorp agreed on August 1 of this year that ZinnCo would cease leasing the photocopiers and instead purchase them. BizCorp agreed to finance the purchase price, which ZinnCo agreed to pay in monthly installments for three years. ZinnCo executed a security agreement that created an enforceable security interest in the five photocopiers. BizCorp perfected its security interest by filing a financing statement on August 15. BizCorp never sent notice of its security interest in the photocopiers to Alpha Bank.

By November, ZinnCo had defaulted on its obligations to Alpha Bank and BizCorp. The two creditors are fighting over the five photocopiers that BizCorp leased, and then sold, to ZinnCo.

The priority dispute should be resolved in favor of

(A) BizCorp, which has a perfected PMSI that enjoys superpriority.

(B) Alpha Bank, because BizCorp's failure to send notice of its interest in the photocopiers to Alpha Bank precludes superpriority.

(C) Alpha Bank, because BizCorp's filing date of August 15 is more than 20 days after the date in January when ZinnCo took possession of the photocopiers.

(D) Alpha Bank, because Article 9 does not permit a creditor to convert a lease transaction into a secured transaction that disadvantages a then-existing perfected security interest held by another secured party.

148. Three years ago, Clinic borrowed $2 million from Lender. The loan was secured by Clinic's current and after-acquired equipment. Lender timely filed its proper financing statement with the appropriate clerk within days after funding the loan.

Two years ago, Clinic bought a $250,000 machine on credit from Dealer. Dealer retained a security interest in the machine, which attached on the first day of the month when Clinic authenticated the security agreement that contained a definitive description of the machine. Dealer filed its financing statement against that specific machine, proper in all respects, 28 days later, with the appropriate central filing officer. Dealer delivered and installed the machine 10 days after the attachment date.

Last week, without Dealer's consent, Clinic sold the machine to a competitor for $150,000. Clinic is still holding the check.

Assuming that both Lender and Dealer can satisfy any tracing burden, which creditor has the superior claim to the check?

(A) Dealer, because its PMSI in the machine qualified for superpriority that extends to the proceeds.

(B) Lender, because its filing date is earlier than Dealer's filing date and perfection date.

(C) Lender, because Dealer failed to file its financing statement on a date that would have made its PMSI in the machine eligible for superpriority that would have extended to proceeds.

(D) Lender, because Dealer's superpriority in the machine does not extend to the proceeds.

149. Assume that Clinic deposited the check into its deposit account yesterday. Bank maintains that deposit account and has held an enforceable security interest in that account for two years to secure a loan in excess of $150,000. Bank has never filed a financing statement against Clinic and the deposit account, however.

As between Lender, Dealer, and Bank, which creditor has priority in the $150,000 deposit made into the deposit account? Continue to assume that both Lender and Dealer can satisfy any tracing burden.

ANSWER:

150. Assume that Clinic did not deposit the check (which it received last week). Instead, two days after receiving the check, Clinic negotiated the check to Seller (that is, signed it over, or indorsed it over, to Seller), as payment for new equipment.

As between Dealer and Lender, whose security interest in this new equipment enjoys priority as of today, as well as in two months?

(A)   Dealer has priority today, as well as in two months.

(B)   Dealer has priority today; Lender will have priority in two months.

(C)   Dealer has priority today; Dealer and Lender will both be unperfected in two months and share priority.

(D)   Lender has priority today, as well as in two months.

151. Two years ago, Heather borrowed $12,000 from her brother, Luke. She used the money to purchase a car. Luke insisted on collateral (other than the car). Heather then executed a security agreement, granting to Luke a security interest in all of Heather's "investment property in Account 345-6789 managed by Paragon Investments." The security agreement included an after-acquired property clause. Luke timely filed a proper financing statement with the appropriate recording office.

A year ago, Heather borrowed $4,000 from her sister, Lauren. Heather used the $4,000 to purchase 200 shares of MegaCorp capital stock. Heather indorsed Lauren's $4,000 check and mailed it to her financial advisor, Paragon Investments, which used the check proceeds to purchase the shares on Heather's behalf. Paragon Investments added the Mega-Corp shares to Heather's account 345-6789 via a bookkeeping entry (there is no physical certificate). Lauren filed a proper financing statement, with the appropriate filing office, against Heather and the MegaCorp shares within three days after the purchase was made and posted by Paragon Investments to Heather's account.

Three weeks ago, Heather defaulted on her loan obligations to her siblings. Luke and Lauren are fighting over the priority of their respective security interests in the MegaCorp shares.

Which of the following statements is true?

(A)   Lauren has a perfected PMSI in the MegaCorp shares, which enjoys priority.

(B)   Luke has no security interest in the MegaCorp shares because an after-acquired property clause is ineffective when the collateral is investment property.

(C)   Both Lauren and Luke hold an unperfected security interest in the MegaCorp shares because filing a financing statement is ineffective to perfect a security interest in investment property that is not evidenced by a physical certificate; their unperfected security interests enjoy coequal priority.

(D)   Luke has a perfected security interest in the MegaCorp shares, which enjoys priority over Lauren's perfected security interest.

152.   ToyCo is a Delaware corporation that sells games and toys through its retail stores located in several states.

Three years ago, Lender made a $1 million loan to ToyCo. The loan is secured by an enforceable security interest in ToyCo's inventory, equipment, and accounts. The security agreement included an after-acquired property clause. Lender filed its financing statement against ToyCo and the collateral with the appropriate filing office within days of funding the loan.

In recent weeks, a new toy—the "FidgetyWidget"—has taken the market by storm. ToyCo wants to place a large order for it from the distributer, FW Corporation. FW will agree to ToyCo's request to purchase on credit, but FW is insisting on retaining a security interest in the shipment, and (as most creditors do) wants its security interest to enjoy priority over competing claims.

Which statement best states the filing duty imposed on FW if FW expects to win a priority dispute with Lender?

(A)   FW does not need to file a financing statement if it includes a "title retention" clause in the security agreement with ToyCo.

(B)   FW must file a financing statement, in Delaware, against the shipment before delivering it to ToyCo.

(C)   FW must file a financing statement, in Delaware, against the shipment no later than 20 days after delivering it to ToyCo.

(D)   FW must file a financing statement, in Delaware and in the states where ToyCo's stores that will be selling the FidgetyWidgets are located, against the shipment no later than 20 days following the delivery date to ToyCo.

153.   Which of the following statements best states the notice duty imposed on FW if FW expects to win the priority dispute with Lender?

(A)   FW must send notice of its property interest in the FidgetyWidgets to Lender before FW delivers them to ToyCo.

(B)   Lender must receive FW's notice of its property interest in the FidgetyWidgets before FW delivers them to ToyCo.

(C)   Lender must receive FW's notice of its property interest in the FidgetyWidgets no later than 20 days following FW's delivery to ToyCo.

(D)   FW's priority does not turn on satisfying any notice requirement.

154.   FW knows that ToyCo will sell its collateral, the FidgetyWidgets. In fact, FW wants ToyCo to sell the FidgetyWidgets (along with its other inventory products) in order to generate sufficient revenue to honor ToyCo's payment obligations to FW.

ToyCo's customers exercise a variety of purchase options at the checkout counter. Some pay with cash. Some pay with a check. Others swipe a credit card or a debit card. If the purchase exceeds $1,000, ToyCo permits the purchaser to buy "on account" with payment due in 30 days. If the purchase exceeds $5,000, ToyCo permits the purchaser to sign a negotiable promissory note with payment due in one year.

Which of the following statements best states the result of a priority dispute between Lender and ToyCo in these various forms of identifiable proceeds arising from ToyCo's sale of the FidgetyWidgets to its customers? Assume in all transactions that the customer takes possession of the FidgetyWidgets at the checkout counter before leaving the store.

(A)   If FW has superpriority in the FidgetyWidgets, then its superpriority extends to all identifiable proceeds, regardless of form.

(B)   FW will have priority in the cash and the checks, but nothing more.

(C)   FW will have priority in the cash and the checks and the "accounts," but nothing more.

(D)   FW will have priority in the cash, the checks, the "accounts," and the receivables generated by debit card and credit card swipes, but nothing more.

155.   BAM, Inc., is an Illinois corporation that operates an upscale restaurant in Chicago. On July 12, it purchased two new food freezers from Dealer. The aggregate purchase price was $100,000. Dealer financed $70,000 and retained an enforceable security interest in the freezers to secure repayment of the credit. Dealer delivered the freezers on July 20 and filed its financing statement on August 5. BAM financed the remaining $30,000 with funds borrowed from its principal shareholder, Emily Capella. Emily, too, retained an enforceable security interest in the freezers to secure repayment of her $30,000 loan. Emily filed her financing statement on August 1.

Several months later, the restaurant failed and BAM defaulted on its payment obligations to Dealer ($60,000) and Emily ($20,000).

If the equipment liquidator sells the two freezers for $60,000, then it should distribute

(A) $60,000 to Dealer.

(B) $45,000 to Dealer and $15,000 to Emily.

(C) $42,000 to Dealer and $18,000 to Emily.

(D) $40,000 to Dealer and $20,000 to Emily.

156.   Assume the same facts as in Question 155, except Dealer refused to extend any credit. BAM then borrowed the $70,000 from Fidelity Bank (which wired the funds directly to Dealer).

Fidelity Bank retained an enforceable security interest in the freezers to secure repayment of the $70,000 loan. Fidelity Bank filed its financing statement on July 30.

Again, the restaurant failed and BAM defaulted on its payment obligations to Fidelity Bank ($60,000) and Emily ($20,000).

How should the liquidator distribute the $60,000 under these revised facts? Would your analysis change if Fidelity Bank filed its financing statement on August 7?

ANSWER:

157. Blissful Comfort, Inc. ("BCI") is a corporate entity that operates three spas in Asheville, North Carolina. On May 1, BCI and Upscale Furnishings entered into a contract whereby Upscale Furnishings agreed to sell to BCI numerous furnishings on credit. Upscale Furnishings retained an enforceable security interest in all furnishings that it sold to BCI, and the security agreement included an after-acquired property clause and a future advance clause. The agreement also called for BCI's payments to be applied first to amounts outstanding related to the oldest purchase. Upscale Furnishings filed a proper financing statement with the appropriate official on May 10.

BCI purchased the following items from Upscale Furnishings during the year:

June	beds	($100,000)
July	chairs and lamps	($45,000)
August	mirrors and pictures	($35,000)

Near the end of the year, BCI defaulted on its financial obligations not only to Upscale Furnishings (which at that time, after various payments, are $60,000), but also to Big-Bank ($540,000), which had extended credit to BCI two years ago, secured by an enforceable security interest in all of BCI's current and future equipment, and perfected by a financing statement filed at the time of the loan.

The two creditors are fighting over the items sold by Upscale Furnishings to BCI during the year.

If a liquidator sells the beds for $80,000, then Upscale Furnishings should receive

(A) $60,000.

(B)   approximately $42,000.

(C) $8,000.

(D) $0.

158. If a liquidator sells the chairs and lamps for $30,000, then Upscale Furnishings should receive

    (A) $30,000.

    (B) $25,000.

    (C) $3,000.

    (D) $0.

159.   If a liquidator sells the mirrors and pictures for $15,000, then Upscale Furnishings should receive

    (A) $15,000.

    (B) $12,000.

    (C) $8,000.

    (D) $1,500.

160.   What is the transformation rule? When might it apply?

    ANSWER:

161.   On February 1, Tennessee National Bank ("TNB") made a $2 million loan to MusicLand Company, a corporation that sells musical instruments through its two retail stores in Nashville. To secure repayment of the loan, TNB obtained an enforceable security interest in MusicLand's inventory, accounts, and equipment. TNB filed its financing statement against the collateral on February 10. An after-acquired property clause appeared in the collateral description found in the security agreement, but not in the financing statement.

On July 1, Keyboard Corporation sold 15 pianos and 10 electric keyboards to MusicLand. Keyboard Corporation shipped the pianos from its Atlanta warehouse and delivered them to MusicLand on July 10. It shipped the electric keyboards from its Raleigh warehouse and delivered them to MusicLand on July 20. Keyboard Corporation retained an enforceable security interest in the pianos and electric keyboards and filed its financing statement against the collateral on July 15. On July 13, Keyboard Corporation sent a written notice of its security interest in the pianos and electric keyboards to TNB; the contents of the notice satisfied the statutory requirements of UCC Article 9. TNB received the notice on July 17.

MusicLand defaulted on its obligations to both creditors in November. Each creditor asserts priority in the pianos and electric keyboards sold by Keyboard Corporation that MusicLand has not yet sold.

Which of the following statements is true?

    (A)   Keyboard Corporation has a perfected PMSI in the pianos and electric keyboards that enjoys superpriority over TNB's competing security interest.

    (B)   Keyboard Corporation has superpriority in the electric keyboards, but TNB has priority in the pianos.

(C)   Keyboard Corporation has priority because its security interest is perfected, whereas TNB's security interest is unperfected because its financing statement failed to include an after-acquired property clause.

(D)   TNB has a perfected security interest in the pianos and the electric keyboards, which has priority over Keyboard Corporation's perfected security interest in those musical instruments.

162.   Yesterday morning, Meredith bought one of the electric keyboards and paid with a check. Yesterday afternoon, First Church bought two electric keyboards after executing MusicLand's retail installment contract, in which MusicLand retained title to the two keyboards until First Church completed its obligation to pay the purchase price in installments over a two-year period. All of these proceeds remain identifiable and are in MusicLand's possession. Both Meredith and First Church left the store with their respective keyboards.

Keyboard Corporation has priority in

(A)   neither the check nor the contracts.

(B)   the check, but not the contracts.

(C)   the contracts, but not the check.

(D)   the check and the contracts.

163.   On November 1, 2017, BankOne made a loan to Alpha Corporation, a Delaware corporation. The loan was secured by an enforceable security interest in Alpha's equipment. The security agreement included an after-acquired property clause. BankOne filed its financing statement in Delaware on November 10, 2017. The security agreement prohibited any dispositions of the equipment.

On February 1, 2018, Alpha sold three pieces of its equipment (the "Items") to Omega Corporation. The purchase price was $100,000. Omega borrowed that amount from BankTwo, which obtained an enforceable purchase-money security interest in the Items to secure repayment of the loan. Omega took delivery of the Items on February 5, 2018, and BankTwo perfected its security interest by filing a financing statement in Delaware on February 23, 2018.

On September 1, 2018, BankOne seeks a declaratory judgment that its security interest in the Items enjoys priority over the competing purchase-money security interest in the Items claimed by BankTwo.

The judge should rule that

(A)   BankOne enjoys priority.

(B)   BankTwo has a perfected PMSI which enjoys superpriority over BankOne's perfected non-PMSI.

(C)   BankTwo enjoys priority because Alpha's disposition of the Items terminated BankOne's security interest in the Items.

(D)   BankOne's security interest in the Items became unperfected at the time of sale because its financing statement filed against Alpha ceased to accomplish the notice function against Omega.

Priority (Secured Party v. Buyer of Collateral)

164. Dongles, LLC, makes connectors for computers. Dongles has borrowed $5 million from HedgeBanc, and has secured that loan with a properly perfected security interest in all its "inventory, accounts, and equipment."

Dongles' accounting department is upgrading its computers. It offers its existing computers, worth $1,000 each, to its employees for their fair market value, or $1,000. Ten employees buy the 10 available computers. Dongles takes the money from the sales, and tenders it to HedgeBanc, which takes the funds and applies them to Dongles' outstanding loan balance.

It then turns around and sues each of the 10 employees for conversion. Which of the following best describes the most likely outcome of each lawsuit?

(A) The employees will win because they did not know of HedgeBanc's interest.

(B) The employees will win because the proceeds of the sales were immediately paid to HedgeBanc, and HedgeBanc took the money and reduced Dongles' debt.

(C) The employees will win because they did not buy the computers for resale.

(D) HedgeBanc will win because it was perfected.

165. Same facts as Question 164, except that the security agreement between Dongles and HedgeBanc has the following provision: "Dongles may sell up to $15,000 in office equipment free and clear of HedgeBanc's security interests, without the prior consent of HedgeBanc, so long as Dongles gives HedgeBanc notice within 20 days of any such sale."

Which of the following best describes the most likely outcome of HedgeBanc's conversion suit?

(A) HedgeBanc will win, but only if Dongles does not send notice of the sales.

(B) HedgeBanc will win because it did not consent to the sales specifically before they were made.

(C) HedgeBanc will win because Dongles' sale was contrary to the security agreement.

(D) The employees will win only if they did not have any notice of the security interest before paying their consideration.

166.   Trevor raises chickens, both for sale and for the eggs they produce. BankOne has lent Trevor $50,000, which is secured by a perfected security interest in "farm products."

Every Friday, Trevor donates about $100 worth of eggs to a local foodbank as a charitable donation. Giving away eggs is a default under the security agreement between BankOne and Trevor. Despite knowing about the practice, however, BankOne has never in the last year taken any action to stop it.

Last Friday, Trevor defaulted on the loan from BankOne. BankOne then sues the foodbank for conversion seeking $5,200 in damages—the value of all eggs donated by Trevor within the last year. Which of the following best describes the most likely result of this lawsuit?

(A)   The food bank will win because it took the eggs as a buyer in the ordinary course of business, given the year's practice.

(B)   The food bank will win because BankOne's security agreement does not cover eggs.

(C)   The foodbank will win only if BankOne expressly consented to each donation.

(D)   The food bank will win because BankOne took no action for a year with respect to the donations despite its knowledge of the practice.

167.   ZinnMark is a Delaware corporation that operates three retail stores in Seattle, from which it sells and leases computers, photocopiers, and other office equipment to commercial and consumer customers. ZinnMark's current and after-acquired inventory is subject to a security interest held by MegaBank, perfected by an accurate and complete financing statement filed in Delaware. There are no filings anywhere else.

Two months ago, ZinnMark engaged in a routine cash sale of three photocopiers to a Seattle law firm (structured as a limited liability company organized under Washington law) for an aggregate sales price of $30,000.

In a priority dispute between MegaBank and the law firm over the three photocopiers,

(A)   MegaBank will win if the law firm had knowledge, before it took possession of the photocopiers, of MegaBank's filing in Delaware.

(B)   MegaBank will win if the law firm had knowledge, before it purchased the photocopiers, of MegaBank's security interest.

(C)   MegaBank will lose because it never filed a financing statement in Washington, the state in which the law firm is located.

(D)   MegaBank will lose.

168.   Assume that the law firm did not pay cash, but instead executed ZinnMark's standard form of a 90-day, negotiable promissory note (a form that comports with industry-wide standards). MegaBank's security agreement expressly prohibits non-cash dispositions (loosely defined as a disposition to a customer who does not pay with cash, a check, a credit card, or a debit card).

How would your analysis change, under these revised facts?

ANSWER:

169. Assume that the law firm paid for the three photocopiers at the time of purchase with a cashier's check for $30,000. ZinnMark promptly deposited the cashier's check into its general operating account that it maintains with SmallBank.

     If MegaBank can satisfy its tracing burden,

     (A)   it cannot claim a security interest in the $30,000 unless the collateral description in its security agreement mentions "proceeds" or "cash proceeds" or "deposit accounts" (or similar language).

     (B)   it cannot claim a security interest in the $30,000 unless its security interest in the photocopiers survived the sale to the law firm.

     (C)   it can claim a perfected security interest in the $30,000, but only for 20 days following ZinnMark's receipt of the check.

     (D)   it can claim a perfected security interest in the $30,000 for 20 days following ZinnMark's receipt of the check, and thereafter.

170. Erewhon, LLC, is a Delaware limited liability company. It sells trail guides for the Mt. Charleston area north of Las Vegas. It has only one store, and that is in Las Vegas, Nevada. Hank, a private investor, lends $500,000 to Erewhon. Erewhon and Hank sign a security agreement granting to Hank a security interest in all of Erewhon's "inventory, accounts, equipment, chattel paper, instruments, general intangibles, investment property and deposit accounts, now owned or hereafter acquired to secure all amount owing from Erewhon to Hank, whenever arising." Hank files a financing statement indicating the collateral as "all assets" and that is otherwise adequate with the Nevada Secretary of State.

     Explore-O-Rama, Inc., a Nevada corporation (EOR), needs trail guides for a tour it has arranged. It normally prints its own, but its current batch has flaws. EOR approaches Erewhon, and offers to buy 4,000 trail guides at $2 each. Even though this is more than half of Erewhon's inventory, it is a good price, and Erewhon accepts and delivers the guides to Erewhon, receiving a check in return. Erewhon does not tell EOR of Hank's interest, and deposits the check in its main checking account.

     The sale is a default under Hank's security agreement with Erewhon. If Hank sues EOR for conversion, the most likely result is

     (A)   EOR will lose because it did not check the Nevada UCC filing system before purchasing the trail guides.

     (B)   EOR will lose because it was not a buyer in the ordinary course of business.

     (C)   EOR will lose because Hank did not consent, explicitly or implicitly.

     (D)   EOR will win.

171. GoGetter, Inc. is a Washington corporation. It serves as a clearing house for jobs in the Seattle area. It has been very profitable, and sunk lots of money into Microsoft Corporation stock, which is publicly traded on NASDAQ. It, however, has pressing cash needs, but doesn't want to sell its holdings in Microsoft stock. It thus arranges with BankOne to lend it $1 million dollars. GoGetter signs a security agreement that describes the collateral as "investment property;" at the time, its Microsoft stock is worth $5 million. BankOne, due to a mistake in its loan department, never files a UCC-1 financing statement, and never contacts GoGetter's brokerage firm.

GoGetter needs more money, and BankOne refuses to lend more or release its security interest. GoGetter discovers that BankOne has filed no financing statement and has not contacted its broker. Without telling its broker of BankOne's interest, GoGetter instructs its broker to sell all its Microsoft stock, and it does. BankOne promptly sues the broker for conversion (which you may assume would be an appropriate action if GoGetter had no ability to sell the stock free of BankOne's interest).

Which of the following best describes the most likely outcome of the lawsuit?

(A) The broker will win because it had no knowledge of BankOne's interest.

(B) The broker will win because it had no knowledge of BankOne's interest and it gave value in the form of brokerage services.

(C) The broker will win because it had no knowledge of BankOne's interest, it gave value in the form of brokerage services, and BankOne was not perfected.

(D) The broker will lose.

172. Manufacturer, who is in the business of manufacturing appliances, owns manufacturing equipment subject to a perfected security interest in favor of Lender. Having no further need for some equipment, Manufacturer sells the equipment to Dealer, who is in the business of buying and selling used equipment. Lender learns of the sale to Dealer but does nothing to assert its security interest, even though there was time and opportunity to do so.

Buyer buys the equipment for cash for its fair market value from Dealer (cash being the primary manner in which Dealer is paid). Buyer bought it for use in its business, and knew nothing of Lender's interest. Manufacturer defaults, and Lender then seeks to foreclose on the equipment Buyer bought.

Which of the following best describes the most likely outcome of this attempted foreclosure?

(A) Buyer will lose because Lender did not consent to the sale from Manufacturer to Dealer.

(B) Buyer will lose because Lender did not consent to the sale from Dealer to Buyer.

(C) Buyer will lose because Lender was initially properly perfected in the equipment.

(D) Buyer will win.

173. Eight months ago, Sandra bought a dining room suite on credit from Friendly Furniture for everyday use in her home. To secure repayment of the purchase price, Friendly Furniture retained a security interest in the furniture. Friendly Furniture never filed a financing statement, but its security agreement expressly prohibited Sandra from disposing of the furniture or using it as collateral to secure any other debt.

Two months ago, and without the permission of Friendly Furniture, Sandra sold the dining room suite to Fred. Friendly Furniture discovered the sale and has sued Fred for conversion of its collateral.

Friendly Furniture will

(A) lose the lawsuit because its security interest in the furniture was never perfected.

(B) lose the lawsuit if the sale generated cash proceeds that remain identifiable.

(C) lose the lawsuit if Fred was a good-faith purchaser, with no knowledge of Friendly Furniture's interest, who is using the dining room suite as a consumer good.

(D) win the lawsuit.

174. Assume that Fred bought the furniture for his secondhand furniture store. Would your analysis change under these revised facts?

ANSWER:

175. Same facts as Question 173, but assume that Friendly Furniture had timely filed a financing statement against Sandra and the dining room suite at the time of her purchase.

How would your analysis change, under these revised facts?

ANSWER:

176. Two years ago, Omega Bank loaned $1 million to Allegro Music Company ("AMC"), a Texas corporation that operates two retail stores in Dallas, from which it sells musical instruments, songbooks, and related items. The loan was secured by an enforceable security interest in AMC's inventory, equipment, and accounts. The security agreement included an after-acquired property clause and prohibited AMC from selling any unit of collateral, except for inventory sales to customers who paid with cash, a check, or a debit card. Omega Bank perfected its security interest by filing a financing statement within days after funding the loan.

Six months ago, AMC sold a $35,000 harp to Ima Virtuoso (a Dallas resident). Ima executed a promissory note (an industry practice for such an expensive purchase), agreeing to make equal monthly payments for five years. Ima is a professional musician and will use the harp in a studio where she earns her livelihood by giving private lessons. Ima has no knowledge of the business relationship between Omega Bank and AMC.

Two months ago, AMC sold some in-house computer equipment to Hewey Dell, an employee (and Dallas resident), for his personal use. Hewey was not aware of the business relationship between Omega Bank and AMC.

In a priority dispute between Omega Bank and Ima over the harp,

(A)   Omega Bank wins, because its security interest in the harp survived AMC's disposition of it.

(B)   Ima wins, because she can invoke the protections afforded to a buyer in the ordinary course of business.

(C)   Omega Bank wins, because Ima is not using the harp as a consumer good.

(D)   Ima wins, because Omega Bank never filed a new financing statement against her.

177.   In a priority dispute between Omega Bank and Hewey over the computer equipment,

(A)   Hewey wins, because he is using the computer equipment as a consumer good.

(B)   Omega Bank wins, because AMC's sale of the computer equipment violated the terms of its security agreement.

(C)   Hewey wins, because he is a buyer in the ordinary course of business.

(D)   Omega Bank wins, because Hewey is AMC's employee.

178.   Redbird Bank has a perfected security interest in the current and after-acquired inventory of Dealer, a merchant that sells baseball cards, autographed sporting goods, and other sports memorabilia. The security agreement permits Dealer to sell its goods to customers who pay with cash, a debit card, a credit card, or a check. Credit sales (excluding credit card transactions) are prohibited.

Last week, Mickey bought two autographed baseballs from Dealer (which he intends to add to his collection that he displays at his law office). At Mickey's request, Dealer allowed him to pay by executing a negotiable, unsecured promissory note for the purchase price, payable in 90 days.

After Redbird Bank discovered the transaction and its terms, it sued Mickey for conversion. Mickey responded by invoking the protection afforded by section 9-320(a) to buyers in the ordinary course of business.

Mickey cannot be a buyer in the ordinary course of business

(A)   because the sale violated Redbird Bank's security agreement.

(B)   because the baseballs are not inventory in Mickey's hands.

(C)   if Mickey had actual knowledge of Redbird Bank's filing.

(D)   if negotiable, unsecured promissory notes are not typical forms of payment for Dealer or the sports memorabilia industry.

Priority (Secured Party v. Lien Creditor)

179. For two years, MegaBank has had an enforceable security interest in ZinnCorp's inventory, equipment, and accounts. The security agreement included an after-acquired property clause. MegaBank perfected its security interest by filing a financing statement in the appropriate filing office soon after making the initial advance.

Six months ago, BAMCO won a lawsuit against ZinnCorp for property damage negligently caused by one of ZinnCorp's employee-drivers. Notwithstanding the adverse judgment, ZinnCorp has never paid it. As a result, on BAMCO's instructions under local law, a court official visited ZinnCorp's warehouse three days ago and constructively seized its entire contents, including inventory and equipment that serve as MegaBank's collateral. Under Article 9, BAMCO became a "lien creditor" at the moment of the constructive seizure. Evidence reveals that ZinnCorp acquired rights in some of the assets in the warehouse before BAMCO won its lawsuit (the "pre-lawsuit assets"); the rights in the remainder were acquired by ZinnCorp after BAMCO won its lawsuit (the "post-lawsuit assets").

In a priority dispute between MegaBank and BAMCO over the inventory and equipment that were constructively seized by the court official,

(A)   MegaBank enjoys priority in the pre-lawsuit assets, but not the post-lawsuit assets.

(B)   MegaBank enjoys priority in the pre-lawsuit assets, and any post-lawsuit assets in which ZinnCorp acquired rights within 45 days after the court entered judgment in favor of BAMCO.

(C)   BAMCO enjoys priority in the pre-lawsuit assets and the post-lawsuit assets because BAMCO is an involuntary creditor (as contrasted with a consensual or contractual creditor).

(D)   MegaBank enjoys priority in both the pre-lawsuit assets and the post-lawsuit assets.

180. On September 1, Allegro Music Company ("AMC") sold a violin on credit to Timmy Zee, who wants to learn how to play violin (he'd read that Sherlock Holmes played the violin to relax, and wants to see if that will work for him). To secure payment of the purchase price, AMC retained an enforceable security interest in the violin pursuant to agreement executed by both parties on that date. AMC delivered the violin to Timmy Zee on September 5.

On September 10, Timmy Zee's neighbor, Ima Victum, acquired the status of "lien creditor" against Timmy Zee (a status that arose from Ima's successful lawsuit against Timmy Zee following an unfortunate canine encounter). Ima's lien encumbers the violin.

On October 1, AMC seeks a declaratory judgment that its security interest in the violin enjoys priority over Ima's lien.

The court should rule in favor of

(A)   AMC, but only if AMC files a financing statement before September 26.

(B)   AMC, but only if AMC files a financing statement before September 26, and if the financing statement describes the violin specifically and does not use general terms such as consumer goods.

(C)   Ima, so long as she acquired lien creditor status before AMC filed any financing statement.

(D)   AMC, regardless of whether it ever files a financing statement.

181.   Would your answer change if Zee was a professional musician? Why or why not?

ANSWER:

182.   Ralph, Inc., (RI) sells pottery, including flower vases. Clueless, LLC, makes flower vases, and trades with RI on the following basis: Clueless ships its vases to RI, and RI sells them to the public. RI takes the money received in each sale, deducts a 7% commission, and returns the rest to Clueless. The agreement between RI and Clueless states: "Clueless shall retain title to all vases delivered to RI, and authorizes RI to sell the vases to others as its agent." Clueless delivers more than $1 million worth of vases to RI each year. RI does not have any signage indicating that it is acting as Clueless's agent, or that RI is doing anything other than selling goods it owns. Clueless does not file a financing statement or take any other action to protect its interest other than inserting the above clause in the RI-Clueless contract.

RI was sued last year by TIG, a competitor, for anticompetitive behavior. Last week, TIG obtained a judgment against RI for $50 million. Using local process, it sends the sheriff to RI's place of business with a valid writ of execution for all of RI's inventory. The sheriff arrives and takes steps to levy upon the inventory by marshaling and segregating the inventory; under local law, TIG obtains a lien on all of RI's inventory at that point.

Clueless finds out about the seizure the next day, and sues TIG for conversion of its vases that were in RI's possession. Which of the following best describes the most likely outcome?

(A)   Clueless will win because it contractually held title to the vases.

(B)   Clueless will win because consignments are outside the scope of Article 9.

(C)   TIG will win because it became a lien creditor before Clueless took any action under Article 9.

(D)   TIG will win because it obtained its judgment before Clueless took any action under Article 9.

183.   Sander Ochre, Inc. (SOI) glazes pottery and other ceramic items for others. This work requires heavy capital investment in kilns and other large equipment. Its customers, however, demand and get 30-day terms for their purchases; that is, they deliver their wares to SOI, SOI glazes them, SOI returns the glazed product to the customer, and the customer then has 30 days to pay the bill.

On July 1, SOI's total receivables from its customers are $2 million; that is, it has rendered services billed at $2 million, and sometime in the next 30 days, its customers should pay it $2 million. Yesterday, however, its major kiln failed, and SOI will need $1 million to fix it, and now. Factors, Inc. approaches SOI and tells it that it will buy $1.5 million of SOI's receivables for a purchase price of $1.3 million (the discount is to account for any non-payment and for Factors' profit). SOI agrees. It signs an agreement assigning specific receivables aggregating $1.5 million to Factors, and then delivers to Factors copies of all of the invoices related to such receivables. Among these receivables is a $500,000 debt owed to SOI by Ralphs, Inc. (RI), a pottery store. Upon receipt of the invoices, Factors pays SOI the $1.3 million as promised.

For the last several years, SOI has been involved in a discrimination lawsuit with Fred, a former employee. Last week, Fred obtained a $4 million judgment against SOI. Fred now works for RI, and knows they owe a lot of money to SOI. Based upon his judgment, Fred obtains a writ of garnishment against all of SOI's receivables. The writ specifically identifies RI. Fred has this writ served on RI (at which time Fred acquires a lien on all debts RI owes SOI), and RI pays Fred $500,000.

Factors immediately sues Fred for conversion. Which of the following best describes the most likely outcome?

(A)   Factors will win because SOI made an absolute assignment of its receivables to Factors.

(B)   Factors will win because sales of receivables are not covered by Article 9.

(C)   Fred will win because his judgment was obtained before the sale of the receivables from SOI to Factors.

(D)   Fred will win because he became a lien creditor of SOI upon service of the writ of garnishment on RI.

184.   Software, LLC, is a Delaware limited liability company that holds all the registered software copyrights for its owner, Microhard, Inc. Although the corporate structure was suggested by tax accountants, Software borrows money using the copyrights as collateral, and then upstreams the proceeds to its parent. At present, there are two lenders, SC1 and SC2. SC1 has lent $5 million; SC2 has lent $10 million. Both have security agreements that adequately grant security interests in all of Software's copyrights; both have filed accurate and complete UCC financing statements with the appropriate Delaware central filing office (SC1's filing predates SC2's filing by six months). Neither, however, has made any filings in the United States Copyright Office.

GeeHard, LLC, obtains a judgment against Software after SC1 makes its Delaware filing, but before SC2 makes its filing. GeeHard then obtains a writ setting in motion a seizure and sale of the intangible copyrights. Upon service of the writ upon Software, GeeHard obtains a lien and property interest in all of Software's copyrights. SC1 and SC2 intervene in the collection proceeding and contend that each of their security interests have priority.

Which of the following best describes the most likely outcome?

(A)   SC1 will prevail over GeeHard, but SC2 will not.

(B)   SC2 will prevail over GeeHard, but SC1 will not.

(C)   Both SC1 and SC2 will prevail over GeeHard.

(D)   GeeHard will prevail over both SC1 and SC2.

185.   Same facts Question 184, except that Software, as part of a restructuring involving Microhard, files an assignment for the benefit of creditors. Alice is the named assignee, and she files a declaratory judgment action seeking a declaration that her interest as assignee is superior to both SC1's and SC2's interest in the copyrights.

Which of the following best describes the most likely outcome?

(A)   There is not enough information to answer because assignments for the benefit of creditors are not covered in Article 9.

(B)   Both SC1 and SC2 will prevail over Alice because their interests arose before the commencement of the assignment for the benefit of creditors.

(C)   Both SC1 and SC2 will prevail over Alice because they filed accurate and complete financing statements.

(D)   Alice will prevail over both SC1 and SC2.

186.   Same facts as Question 185, except that instead of an assignment for the benefit of creditors, SC2 filed a request for a state court receiver, and one was appointed. It is now the receiver who seeks a declaration that the receiver's interest in the copyrights is superior to the rights of SC1. What result, and what additional facts would you need to know to answer completely?

ANSWER:

187.   ZeeTech is a corporation chartered under Delaware law. It operates three retail outlets in Detroit.

In June 2018, Omega Bank loaned money to ZeeTech. To secure repayment of the loan, Omega Bank took an enforceable security interest in all of ZeeTech's current and after-acquired equipment, and properly perfected its security interest by filing immediately thereafter.

In February 2019, ZeeTech changed its legal name to "Quantum Technologies." ZeeTech timely informed Omega Bank of the change, but Omega Bank never took any action in response.

In August 2019, a constable constructively seized two pieces of Quantum's equipment pursuit to a writ of execution obtained by Meredith, a tort creditor of Quantum. At the moment of seizure Meredith became a "lien creditor" under UCC Article 9.

Evidence reveals that Quantum had acquired one of the pieces of equipment ("Item #1") on April 15, 2019, and the other piece of equipment ("Item #2") on July 15, 2019.

A priority dispute now exists between Omega Bank and Meredith in the two pieces of seized equipment.

If the dispute is resolved as of September 1, 2019, then

(A)   Omega Bank has priority in both Item #1 and Item #2.

(B)   Meredith has priority in both Item #1 and Item #2.

(C)   Omega Bank has priority in Item #1, but priority in Item #2 cannot be resolved without additional information.

(D)   Omega Bank has priority in Item #1, and Meredith has priority in Item #2.

188.   On September 1, Debtor granted to Bank a security interest in equipment worth $150,000 (the "Equipment") to secure a $50,000 loan. The security agreement had a future advance clause, but Bank was not obligated to make any future advances. Bank filed an adequate and complete financing statement in the proper place on September 5.

On September 10, Hannah obtained a $75,000 judgment against Debtor. Hannah became a "lien creditor" under UCC Article 9 on September 20 when the sheriff levied upon and seized the Equipment to satisfy Hannah's judgment.

Bank learns of the levy when it occurred, but advanced another $35,000 on October 1, another $25,000 on November 1, and another $20,000 on November 15.

With the consent of both Bank and Hannah, the sheriff sold the Equipment for $120,000 on December 1.

How should the sheriff distribute the proceeds?

ANSWER:

189.   Same facts as Question 188, but now assume that the security agreement between Bank and Debtor included the following statement:

> "Secured Party agrees to loan $150,000 to Debtor in one or more advances; provided that Secured Party may refuse to fund an advance if an Event of Default exists."

Assume that *"Event of Default"* is defined to include judgments against Debtor in excess of $25,000.

Would these assumptions affect the sheriff's distribution of the $120,000?

ANSWER:

190. In January 2014, Redbird Bank made a $1 million loan to Friendly Furniture Company, a corporate entity that sells furniture through several retail outlets in the St. Louis area. Repayment of the loan was secured by an enforceable security interest in Friendly's inventory, equipment, and accounts. The security agreement included an after-acquired property clause. Redbird Bank perfected its security interest by filing a financing statement on January 18, 2014.

In December 2018, a law enforcement official constructively seized all of the furniture inventory located at one of Friendly's stores, pursuant to court order arising from a successful lawsuit initiated earlier that year by Bradford Industries against Friendly. At the moment of the constructive seizure, Bradford Industries became a "lien creditor" under UCC Article 9.

With the permission of all interested parties, a professional liquidator sold all of the furniture for $700,000 on February 15, 2019, an amount considerably less than what Friendly owes to Redbird Bank.

Redbird Bank has priority in the $700,000

(A)   if it filed a continuation statement on July 10, 2018.

(B)   if it filed a continuation statement on January 24, 2019.

(C)   only if it timely filed a continuation statement before the constructive seizure.

(D)   even if it never filed a continuation statement.

Priority (Secured Party v. IRS)

191.   As a general rule, a creditor's security interest in collateral acquired by the taxpayer-debtor after the IRS files its tax lien notice is subordinate to the tax lien. An exception exists for "commercial financing security" that is timely acquired by the taxpayer-debtor.

Each of the following types of Article 9 collateral is "commercial financing security" except

(A)   accounts.

(B)   chattel paper.

(C)   equipment.

(D)   inventory.

192.   ZinnMark Fashions operates several retail clothing stores.

On May 1, Bank entered into a binding commitment to make advances to ZinnMark Fashions in an aggregate amount not to exceed $2 million. On that date, ZinnMark Fashions executed a security agreement in which it granted to Bank a security interest in all of its inventory, accounts receivable, and equipment. The security agreement included an after-acquired property clause and a future advance clause. Bank filed a proper financing statement with the appropriate official on May 8. Pursuant to its binding commitment, Bank made the following advances to ZinnMark Fashions (none of which have been repaid):

DATE	AMOUNT
5/8	$300,000
7/12	$200,000
8/3	$400,000
8/22	$100,000
9/9	$300,000

On July 1, the IRS assessed a $700,000 tax lien against ZinnMark Fashions. The IRS filed a tax lien notice with the appropriate officials on August 1. Bank discovered the tax lien notice on August 21.

Assuming that the type and value of collateral are adequate, the IRS lien will be subject to Bank's security interest that secures debt of

(A) $1,300,000.

(B) $1,000,000.

(C) $900,000.

(D) $500,000.

193.   In a priority dispute concerning a shipment of dresses and shoes acquired by ZinnMark Fashions on September 7,

(A)   Bank's security interest enjoys priority.

(B)   the tax lien enjoys priority because the items are not "commercial financing security."

(C)   the tax lien enjoys priority because ZinnMark Fashions acquired the items after Bank discovered the tax lien notice.

(D)   the tax lien enjoys priority because ZinnMark Fashions acquired the items more than 45 days after the IRS assessed the tax lien.

194.   In a priority dispute concerning new computers purchased by ZinnMark Fashions on July 25,

(A)   the tax lien enjoys priority because the computers are not "commercial financing security."

(B)   the tax lien enjoys priority because ZinnMark Fashions acquired the computers after the IRS assessed the tax lien.

(C)   the tax lien enjoys priority because ZinnMark Fashions acquired the computers before Bank acquired knowledge of the tax lien notice.

(D)   Bank's security interest enjoys priority.

Default

195. Part Six of Article 9 provides the secured party with specific rights and remedies following "default." Which of the following statements regarding that term is true?

    (A)   Article 9 does not define the term, leaving it to the parties to address its meaning in the loan documents.

    (B)   For consumer transactions, Article 9 defines the term in a manner limited to nonpayment of an amount exceeding $2,000.

    (C)   For transactions other than consumer transactions, Article 9 defines the term in a manner limited to nonpayment of an amount exceeding $5,000.

    (D)   Article 9 defines the term in a manner with no minimum dollar thresholds, but it also permits the parties to vary the statutory definition through contract language that is not manifestly unreasonable.

196. Following a default, Article 9 permits the secured party to take possession of collateral

    (A)   if the collateral is not a consumer good.

    (B)   if the security interest in the collateral has attached.

    (C)   only if the security interest in the collateral is perfected.

    (D)   only if the security interest in the collateral is perfected and has priority over all other security interests.

197. BigBank is aware that Article 9 permits self-help repossession as long as the repossession does not trigger a breach of the peace. BigBank wishes to take reasonable steps to avoid being liable for breaching the peace when it exercises this remedy.

    Which of the following statements is true?

    (A)   BigBank should include in its loan papers a well-drafted "waiver of liability for breaching the peace" provision.

    (B)   BigBank should include in its loan papers a very narrow (but not manifestly unreasonable) standard of behavior that will trigger liability for breaching the peace.

    (C)   BigBank should delegate all repossessions to independent contractors, therefore avoiding liability for any breach of the peace.

    (D)   Article 9 does not permit BigBank to take any of the foregoing actions.

198. AutoCorp sold a car on credit to Tim. AutoCorp holds a perfected purchase-money security interest in the car. With Tim's knowledge and consent, AutoCorp has installed a "starter interruption device" on the vehicle, which allows AutoCorp to send a signal that effectively blocks Tim's car from starting. AutoCorp sends the signal when Tim misses a car payment.

Which of the following statements is true?

(A)   Section 9-609 permits AutoCorp to take possession of Tim's car, but it does not address whether AutoCorp can render Tim's car unusable.

(B)   Section 9-609 permits AutoCorp to render Tim's car unusable, but only if Tim is using the car as equipment.

(C)   Section 9-609 permits AutoCorp to render Tim's car unusable, even if Tim is using the car as a consumer good, but only if Tim is at least 30 days late in making a payment.

(D)   Section 9-609 permits AutoCorp to render Tim's car unusable, but only if AutoCorp takes such action when Tim's vehicle is parked at his home address or place of employment.

199. A year ago, Elliott borrowed $3,000 from his sister, Ruth, for a business purpose. Ruth insisted on some collateral, but Elliott had none to offer. Two other siblings then stepped in to move the transaction forward. Brother Kevin guaranteed payment of the debt. And sister Carmen granted a security interest in specific items of jewelry. All parties executed necessary paperwork.

A month ago, Elliott defaulted on the loan, still owing $1,400. Ruth intends to sell the jewelry, which Carmen peaceably surrendered.

Article 9 requires Ruth to send notice of the sale to

(A)   Elliott, Kevin, and Carmen.

(B)   Kevin and Carmen.

(C)   Elliott and Carmen.

(D)   Carmen.

200. Assume Ruth intends to sell the jewelry at a public disposition. Her disposition notice must

(A)   be received by the intended recipient to be effective under Article 9.

(B)   mention a sale date that is at least 20 calendar days later than the date on which she sends the notice.

(C)   offer an accounting of the total unpaid debt.

(D)   provide a telephone number that the recipient can call in order to obtain the redemption price.

201. Assume that Ruth does not wish to sell the jewelry. Instead, Ruth is interested in keeping the jewelry (which has a market value of approximately $3,500) and forgiving all of the unpaid debt.

Which of the following statements is true?

(A) Ruth cannot accept the jewelry and forgive the remaining unpaid debt of $1,400 because Elliott has paid more than 50% of the original $3,000 loan.

(B) Ruth cannot accept the jewelry and forgive the remaining unpaid debt if the pieces of jewelry are Carmen's consumer goods.

(C) Ruth cannot accept the jewelry and forgive the remaining unpaid debt of $1,400 because the market value of the jewelry is more than twice the amount of remaining unpaid debt.

(D) Ruth can accept the jewelry and forgive the remaining unpaid debt, but Carmen must consent to the transaction.

202. Assume that Ruth wishes to move forward with her intent to keep the jewelry and forgive the unpaid debt.

Ruth must send her Article 9 "proposal" to

(A) Elliott, Kevin, and Carmen.

(B) Kevin and Carmen only.

(C) Carmen only.

(D) none of the three parties.

203. Debtor is a corporate entity that operates a group of dental clinics.

Two years ago, BankOne obtained a perfected security interest in Debtor's dental equipment. The security agreement included an after-acquired property clause.

One year ago, BankTwo obtained a perfected security interest in Debtor's dental equipment. The security agreement included an after-acquired property clause.

Eight months ago, BankThree obtained a perfected security interest in Debtor's dental equipment. The security agreement included an after-acquired property clause.

A few weeks ago, Debtor defaulted on its payment obligations to each of the three banks, triggering a default under each of the security agreements.

BankTwo peaceably seized several pieces of dental equipment with Debtor's consent. Two days ago, BankTwo sold the equipment for $310,000 at an Article 9 foreclosure sale, all aspects of which were commercially reasonable. BankTwo complied with all notice requirements. It received no replies from any party. Throughout the disposition process, BankTwo acted in good faith with no knowledge that its conduct violates the rights of any other party.

Immediately prior to the sale, Debtor owed $250,000 to BankOne, $150,000 to BankTwo, and $50,000 to BankThree. No party is claiming a PMSI in any of the equipment.

After subtracting $10,000 to cover the costs of the sale, BankTwo should distribute the remaining $300,000 as follows:

(A) $250,000 to BankOne, and then $50,000 to itself.

(B) $150,000 to itself, and then $150,000 to Debtor.

(C) $150,000 to itself, and then $150,000 to BankOne.

(D) $150,000 to itself, and then $50,000 to BankThree, and then $100,000 to Debtor.

204. After BankTwo appropriately distributes the sale proceeds, Debtor will remain liable to

(A) BankOne for $50,000; BankTwo for $100,000; and BankThree for $50,000.

(B) BankOne for $250,000; BankTwo for zero dollars; and BankThree for zero dollars.

(C) BankOne for $250,000; BankTwo for zero dollars; and BankThree for $50,000.

(D) BankOne for zero dollars; BankTwo for zero dollars; and BankThree for zero dollars.

205. The foreclosure sale terminates Debtor's property interest in the dental equipment, as well as the security interest(s) claimed by

(A) BankTwo and BankThree only.

(B) BankTwo only.

(C) BankOne, BankTwo, and BankThree.

(D) BankOne and BankTwo only.

206. What makes a disposition of collateral a "public disposition"?

ANSWER:

207. Give two reasons why a secured party needs to know the difference between a public disposition of collateral, and a private disposition of collateral.

ANSWER:

208. Assume that a secured party intends to dispose of the collateral. Briefly state the four situations in which the secured party need not send the disposition notice to the debtor.

ANSWER:

209. Two years ago, Dealer sold a car on credit to Bruce, who used the car primarily for personal and family use. Dealer retained an enforceable PMSI in the car and timely perfected its security interest.

A few weeks ago, Dealer peaceably repossessed the car following Bruce's payment default. Dealer intends to sell the car and apply the proceeds to the unpaid debt. The inside of the car could use some general cleaning, and the exterior could use a gentle wash.

Which of the following statements is true?

(A) Dealer has no obligation to clean the inside or outside of the car before disposing of it.

(B) Dealer can use an Internet auction site to dispose of the car.

(C) Dealer makes no warranties when it disposes of the car.

(D) Because Bruce used the car as a consumer good, Dealer must dispose of the car at a public, rather than a private, disposition.

210. Lender has an enforceable security interest in Debtor's current and (when Debtor acquires rights in them) future accounts. Debtor recently triggered a default when it failed to make a required loan payment. Lender wants to contact the account debtors (Debtor's customers who are obligated to pay the accounts) and direct those customers to remit their payments to Lender (rather than to Debtor). Lender will apply any customer payments it receives against Debtor's unpaid secured debt.

Lender can contact the account debtors and seek their direct payment if

(A) Lender and Debtor agreed to that action in the security agreement.

(B) Lender proceeds in a commercially reasonable manner.

(C) Debtor has been in default for at least 10 business days.

(D) Lender notifies the account debtors in writing and timely sends a copy of each writing to Debtor.

211. Five weeks ago, following a payment default on a secured loan, Dealer peaceably repossessed four photocopiers (the collateral) from BizCorp. Dealer opted to sell the photocopiers at a public disposition. It gave timely and appropriate notice to BizCorp of the proposed disposition.

Immediately prior to the auction, BizCorp owed $15,000 to Dealer. Following the auction, which yielded an aggregate sales price of $11,000, Dealer initiated a deficiency action for $4,000. BizCorp responded with convincing proof that several aspects of the auction were not commercially reasonable. Furthermore, BizCorp's expert testified that the photocopiers had an aggregate fair market value of $12,500 at disposition (but offered no specific testimony as to what price could be obtained at a commercially reasonable sale). Dealer responded with credible and convincing proof that, even if all aspects of the sale had been commercially reasonable, the photocopiers would have sold for no more than $11,300.

Based on this evidence, the court should enter a deficiency judgment against BizCorp for

(A) $0.

(B) $2,500.

(C) $3,700.

(D) $4,000.

212.   Three years ago, MusiCorp sold a harp on credit to Emily. Emily uses the harp for personal (non-business) reasons. MusiCorp retained a PMSI in the harp to secure repayment of the purchase price.

Three weeks ago, following Emily's payment default, MusiCorp peaceably repossessed the harp. MusiCorp opted to sell the harp at a public disposition.

Immediately prior to the auction, Emily owed $15,000 to MusiCorp. Following the auction, which yielded a sales price of $11,000, MusiCorp initiated a deficiency action for $4,000. MusiCorp has acknowledged its failure to send timely notice of the disposition to Emily. Emily's expert testified that the harp had a fair market value of $12,500 at disposition (but she offered no evidence that she — or anyone she might have brought to the sale if she had been given notice of it — would have offered a bid any higher than the actual sale price of $11,000).

The court should enter a deficiency judgment against Emily for what amount?

ANSWER:

Bankruptcy (Excluding Voidable Preferences)

213. JeeHee, Inc., makes cookie molds. It has significant inventory and equipment to produce these molds. FirstBanc has lent $5,000,000 to JeeHee, and has a valid and perfected security interest in all of JeeHee's inventory and equipment. On June 1, FirstBanc validly notifies JeeHee of a default. On June 15, JeeHee agrees to turn over some of its equipment to FirstBanc in a transaction that does not qualify as an acceptance under Section 9-620. FirstBanc schedules a foreclosure sale for July 15, and JeeHee agrees to that date.

    On July 15, however, five minutes before the scheduled foreclosure sale, JeeHee files a chapter 7 bankruptcy petition.

    At this point, FirstBanc should

    (A)   conduct the foreclosure sale because JeeHee had consented to the repossession and the time of the sale.

    (B)   conduct the foreclosure sale but only if it notifies all potential bidders of the bankruptcy.

    (C)   conduct the sale unless JeeHee can produce written evidence that it has filed a bankruptcy petition.

    (D)   postpone the sale.

214. Same facts as Question 213. FirstBanc did postpone the sale. Now JeeHee's bankruptcy trustee wants the equipment back in order to sell it to a third party. The trustee offers to pay to FirstBanc a monthly amount equal to the monthly depreciation on the equipment until the trustee is able to sell the equipment.

    FirstBanc should

    (A)   keep the equipment, otherwise it will lose its security interest.

    (B)   keep the equipment, discover who the third party is, and sell it to them.

    (C)   take the deal offered by the trustee, and return the equipment.

    (D)   return the equipment without any understanding regarding monthly payment.

215. Karen recently filed a Chapter 7 bankruptcy petition. BigBank holds a perfected purchase-money security interest in her 2017 Lexus sport utility vehicle to secure an unpaid debt of

$38,000. Appraisers and online services estimate the fair market value of the vehicle as low as $36,500 and as high as $39,000. BigBank intends immediately to file a motion to lift the automatic stay, hoping that it can take possession of the vehicle and conduct a non-judicial foreclosure as permitted by Article 9.

With respect to any motion to seek relief from stay that BigBank files,

(A)   BigBank has the burden of proof on the issue of Karen's equity in the vehicle, and Karen has the burden of proof on the issue of adequate protection.

(B)   BigBank has the burden of proof on the issues of adequate protection and Karen's equity in the vehicle.

(C)   Karen has the burden of proof on the issue of her equity in the vehicle, and Big-Bank has the burden of proof on the issue of adequate protection.

(D)   Karen has the burden of proof on the issues of adequate protection and her equity in the vehicle.

216.   Henry borrowed $1 million from Lost Bank. The loan agreement provides that Henry will use the loan proceeds in his business, Sock-o-Rama, LLC. Henry secures the loan with a security interest in all of his deposit accounts held at Lost Bank (they do this because the state in which Henry resides does not recognize common law liens in deposit accounts). Beset by bad business, Sock-o-Rama files a Chapter 11 bankruptcy petition; Henry also files a Chapter 11 bankruptcy petition. Henry's lawyers make a mistake in noticing creditors in Henry's case. Although they listed Lost Bank as a creditor in Sock-o-Rama's bankruptcy, they neglected to do so in Henry's. As a result, Lost Bank receives notice of Sock-o-Rama's bankruptcy only.

One week after the two filings, Lost Bank applies all of the funds in Henry's Lost Bank deposit accounts to reduce the balance of Henry's loan to Lost Bank. Henry finds all this out when he is buying groceries, and his debit card is declined. Incensed, he immediately calls Lost Bank, tells it of his filing and demands that Lost Bank credit his account with its previous balance. Lost Bank's representative simply hangs up the phone and does nothing.

In Henry's action for violation of the automatic stay, a well-informed court will most likely

(A)   rule in Lost Bank's favor, because they did not receive proper notice and thus did not violate any stay of which it was aware.

(B)   rule in Henry's favor, because consumer deposit accounts are outside the scope of Article 9.

(C)   rule in Henry's favor and award damages to Henry because the stay of 11 U.S.C. § 362(a) is automatic, and is effective without notice.

(D)   rule in Henry's favor and award damages incurred from and after Henry's phone call caused by Lost Bank's refusal to restore Henry's deposit account to its previous balance.

217. On July 1, Bank made a $150,000 loan to Clinic, repayment of which was secured by an enforceable security interest in all of Clinic's equipment, whether then owned or thereafter acquired. Bank perfected its interest on July 7 by filing a proper financing statement with the appropriate authority.

On August 1, MedCo sold a $100,000 kidney dialysis machine on credit to Clinic under a retail installment contract. MedCo retained an enforceable security interest in the machine. MedCo delivered the machine to Clinic on August 9 and filed a proper financing statement in the proper place on August 25.

On December 1, Clinic filed a Chapter 7 bankruptcy petition. As of that date, Clinic owed $120,000 to Bank and $80,000 to MedCo (all loan repayments on both loans were made outside the preference period). As of December 1, Clinic's equipment had a fair market value of $140,000 (which included $90,000 attributable to the kidney dialysis machine sold to Clinic by MedCo).

If the bankruptcy trustee cannot set aside or otherwise avoid the two creditors' security interests, which of the following statements best states their respective claims to Clinic's equipment?

(A) Bank has a $90,000 secured claim and a $30,000 unsecured claim, and MedCo has a $50,000 secured claim and a $30,000 unsecured claim.

(B) Bank has a $60,000 secured claim and a $60,000 unsecured claim, and MedCo has an $80,000 secured claim.

(C) Bank has a $120,000 secured claim and MedCo has an $80,000 secured claim.

(D) Bank has a $120,000 secured claim, and MedCo has a $20,000 secured claim and a $60,000 unsecured claim.

218. On June 1, Dealer sold a freezer on credit to Restaurant Corp. Under terms of the contract executed by both parties on that date, Dealer retained an enforceable security interest in the freezer to secure repayment of the purchase price. Dealer delivered the freezer to Restaurant on June 10. Dealer filed a proper financing statement with the appropriate official on June 18. Unknown to Dealer, Restaurant had filed a Chapter 7 bankruptcy petition on June 12.

Which of the following statements is true?

(A) Dealer's interest in the freezer was automatically perfected as a purchase-money security interest.

(B) The freezer may be "exempt property" in the bankruptcy, and thus not subject to Dealer's security interest.

(C) Dealer did not violate the automatic stay by filing a post-petition financing statement.

(D) The trustee's strong-arm power under 11 U.S.C. § 544(a) freezes creditors' interests as of the date the bankruptcy case commenced, and so Dealer could not perfect its interest.

219. Bank made a $2 million loan to Debtor on February 1. To secure repayment of the loan, Bank obtained an enforceable and perfected security interest in Debtor's inventory and accounts. The security agreement, also dated February 1, included an after-acquired property clause. Bank filed a proper financing statement with the appropriate official on February 10.

Debtor filed a Chapter 11 bankruptcy petition on July 1. On that date, Debtor owed $1 million to Bank. On August 1, Debtor still owed $1 million to Bank. Information on Debtor's inventory and accounts as of that date follows:

Inventory:	
Existed as of July 1	$300,000
Purchased after July 1 with cash received from:	
accounts existing as of July 1	$100,000
accounts generated after July 1	$50,000
sale on July 15 of Google stock purchased last year	$50,000
Total Value of Inventory	$500,000
Accounts:	
Existed as of July 1	$250,000
Generated after July 1 from credit sales of:	
inventory existing as of July 1	$100,000
inventory acquired after July 1	$50,000
equipment donated to Debtor last year	$50,000
Total Value of Accounts	$450,000

Ignoring voidable preference or fraudulent conveyance concerns, Bank can claim a perfected security interest in collateral worth

(A) $550,000.

(B) $750,000.

(C) $750,000—$850,000.

(D) $800,000—$900,000.

220. The "strong-arm clause" of Section 544 of the Bankruptcy Code permits the bankruptcy trustee to avoid

(A) an unperfected security interest.

(B) a property transfer made by the debtor "with actual intent to hinder, delay, or defraud" a creditor.

(C) a security interest for which a financing statement was filed 10 seconds before the filing of the debtor's bankruptcy petition.

(D) a judicial lien that impairs an exemption.

221. Henry gives his daughter a birthday gift of a new car on his daughter's sixteenth birthday. Two weeks later, when one of Henry's judgment creditors seeks to levy execution on the car to satisfy that creditor's judgment,

    (A) Henry's daughter will retain possession of the car so long as it is titled in her name.

    (B) Henry's daughter will retain possession of the car if she (the daughter) can prove that she is solvent.

    (C) the judgment creditor will prevail if he can show that Henry was not generally paying his debts as they become due, and Henry offers no additional evidence at trial.

    (D) the judgment creditor will prevail only if Henry did not file a financing statement against his daughter describing the car as collateral.

222. Fred is the sole owner of all of the common stock issued by Gadgets, Inc., a Delaware corporation ("GI"). GI is a family business physically located in Kentucky that Fred incorporated for tax reasons several years ago. GI's general manager, Alice, knows that Fred wants to retire, and that Fred has no sons or daughters who want to continue the business. Alice approaches Fred and offers to buy the business for $350,000. Fred agrees, and Alice and Fred agree that the purchase price will be paid by a downpayment of $50,000 at the closing on March 1, and then by the payment of four equal installments of $75,000 on each July 1 following the sale. Alice will sign a note to evidence the deferred portion of the purchase price.

    Fred also wants collateral for the note. To accommodate his desires, at the closing, simultaneously with the transfer of the stock in GI from Fred to Alice, Alice (as the new GI chairperson of the board and president) will sign a security agreement on behalf of GI under which GI will grant an interest in "all inventory, accounts, equipment, general intangibles, instruments, investment securities, and deposit accounts, in each case whether now owned or hereafter acquired." The security agreement will secure the note and all of Fred's enforcement costs under the security agreement.

    The closing goes as planned, and Fred files an accurate and complete financing statement with the Delaware Secretary of State that describes the collateral as "all assets."

    Running the business, however, does not go as planned. It is a disaster. Alice tries to raise new equity capital, but she cannot do so. She tries to borrow money but is told that the presence of Fred's senior security interest makes any loan to GI too risky. Both Alice and GI file a Chapter 7 bankruptcy petition on June 30.

    Fred claims a security interest in all of GI's assets to secure the unpaid portion of the note. You represent GI's trustee in bankruptcy.

    Your best option to obtain any recovery for GI's numerous unsecured creditors is

(A)   do nothing; Fred is right and should get all the assets.

(B)   bring an action against Fred alleging that the grant of the security interest in the assets of the business was an avoidable preference.

(C)   bring an action against Fred alleging that the grant of the security interest in the assets of the business was a fraudulent transfer.

(D)   bring an action against Fred alleging that the grant of the security interest in the assets of the business was both an avoidable preference and a fraudulent transfer.

223.   Darlene Debtor, a lifelong resident of Butte, Montana, runs a printing business. On June 1, Darlene entered into negotiations with First Bank for a loan of $5,000,000. When Darlene signed the letter of intent for the loan, First Bank had Darlene sign the following: "I authorize First Bank to file an 'all assets' financing statement with the Montana Secretary of State." First Bank then filed an otherwise accurate and complete financing statement with the Montana Secretary of State naming Darlene as the debtor and describing the collateral as "all assets." On June 15, Darlene signed a security agreement granting a security interest to First Bank. The collateral description in the security agreement is stated as "all equipment." The security agreement described the secured obligation as "that certain loan in the amount of $5,000,000 made by First Bank to Darlene Debtor, all obligations under this security agreement (including all attorneys' fees), and all advances made by First Bank to Darlene Debtor hereafter."

After the security agreement is signed, First Bank lends Darlene $5,000,000. First Bank does not amend its financing statement.

On July 1, as anticipated in the security agreement with First Bank, Darlene purchased a new printing press for $1,000,000, using a portion of the $5,000,000 loan proceeds. On August 15, Darlene sells some surplus ink and paper to Seraph Printing, Inc. ("SPI"), another printing business. SPI gives Darlene a check for the purchase price of $5,000. On September 30, Darlene sells a used printing press to SPI for $500,000, with SPI giving Darlene a check for $100,000, and its written promise to pay the balance by December 1.

Darlene defaulted under the security agreement on October 1 and filed a Chapter 11 bankruptcy petition on October 15. It is now October 16. No purchases or sales of any of Darlene's property other than completed printing jobs occurred between June 15 and October 15 except as stated above. Darlene has not cashed, and still holds, the $5,000 and the $100,000 checks from SPI.

If the bankruptcy court determines that the value of all collateral in which First Bank has a perfected security interest is $6,000,000, the amount of First Bank's secured claim in bankruptcy is

(A)   less than $5,000,000.

(B) $5,000,000.

(C) $5,000,000 plus any of First Bank's attorneys' fees, but in no event more than $6,000,000.

(D) $6,000,000.

224. Same facts as Question 223, but change the following: If the bankruptcy court determines that the value of all collateral in which First Bank has a perfected security interest is $4,000,000, the amount of First Bank's secured claim in bankruptcy is

(A) less than $5,000,000.

(B) $5,000,000.

(C) $5,000,000 plus any of First Bank's attorneys' fees, but in no event more than $6,000,000.

(D) $6,000,000.

225. Lucy owns all of the membership interests in Lucy's, LLC, a restaurant. Beelzebub Bank has lent Lucy's, LLC, $1 million, and has a perfected and enforceable security interest in all of its equipment and inventory. It does not have a security interest in any of Lucy's, LLC's intangibles, and thus does not have a security interest in any of Lucy's, LLC's accounts or bank accounts. Lucy owns the land on which the restaurant operates, and leases it to Lucy's, LLC, at a market rate.

Lucy's, LLC, owes more than $250,000 to its unsecured creditors. Its total assets are probably worth no more than $1 million. Many of the unsecured creditors are in the process of obtaining judgments against Lucy's, LLC.

Lucy devises the following plan, with the assistance of Beelzebub. Lucy will incorporate Lucy's, Inc. On Friday, Lucy's, LLC will acknowledge default, and, with Lucy's assistance, Beelzebub will foreclose on all of its collateral at Lucy's, LLC. Beelzebub will sell the collateral at a UCC foreclosure sale (to which Lucy will consent on behalf of Lucy's, LLC in all respects, after acknowledging default) to Lucy's, Inc. Lucy's, Inc. will then borrow the necessary money from Beelzebub to pay the price at foreclosure (which will be the appraised value of the assets). Beelzebub will then take a security interest in all of Lucy, Inc.'s personal property (Lucy will also contribute $500 to Lucy's, Inc., which will be sufficient to make it just barely solvent) to secure the loan. Lucy will terminate the lease with Lucy's, LLC, and re-lease the property to Lucy's, Inc. on the same terms. The transfers are made right after Lucy closes the restaurant on Friday night.

The result is that when Lucy unlocks the doors on Saturday morning, she will be doing so for Lucy's, Inc., and not Lucy's, LLC. To the public, nothing will have changed. The creditors of Lucy's, LLC, however, will have only an assetless shell against which to pursue their claims.

Lucy's, Inc., has no better luck than Lucy's, LLC. Eighteen months later, Lucy files bankruptcy for Lucy's, Inc.

Without consideration of any state law successor liability theories, does Beelzebub have anything to fear from Lucy's, Inc.'s bankruptcy trustee?

(A)   No, because more than one year has passed since the transaction.

(B)   No, because Beelzebub did not intend to defraud any of Lucy's, LLC's creditors.

(C)   No, because Lucy's, Inc., was solvent after the transaction.

(D)   Yes, if Lucy and Beelzebub intended to hinder or delay the creditors of Lucy's, LLC, through the transaction with Beelzebub.

Bankruptcy (Voidable Preferences)

226. Lima Bank lends $1 million to SpotCo on July 1. The loan is unsecured. SpotCo makes no effort to repay this loan until December 1, at which time it pays SpotCo $1.1 million, representing all principal and accrued interest. On December 2, SpotCo files a chapter 7 bankruptcy petition.

   Which of the following amounts is SpotCo's bankruptcy trustee ultimately likely to recover?

   (A) $100,000, representing the interest but not the principal on the loan.

   (B) $1 million, representing the principal but not the interest on the loan.

   (C) $1.1 million, representing the principal and the interest on the loan.

   (D)   Nothing.

227. Same facts as Question 226, except now assume that Lima Bean took and properly perfected a security interest in collateral worth $2 million when it made the loan, and further assume that the collateral held its value throughout.

   Which of the following amounts is SpotCo's bankruptcy trustee ultimately likely to recover?

   (A) $100,000, representing the interest but not the principal on the loan.

   (B) $1 million, representing the principal but not the interest on the loan.

   (C) $1.1 million, representing the principal and the interest on the loan.

   (D)   Nothing.

228. Same facts as Question 227, but now assume that the collateral was worth $500,000 when the loan was made and at all times thereafter.

   Which of the following amounts is SpotCo's bankruptcy trustee ultimately likely to recover?

   (A) $100,000.

   (B) $600,000.

   (C) $1 million.

   (D) $1.1 million.

229. Same facts as Question 228, but now assume that the collateral, although worth $500,000 at all times, was not granted and perfected until November 15.

Which of the following amounts is SpotCo's bankruptcy trustee ultimately likely to recover?

(A) $100,000.

(B) $600,000.

(C) $1 million.

(D) $1.1 million.

230.   Same facts as Question 229, but now assume that SpotCo granted the security interest when the loan was made in July (that's when the security agreement was signed). Also assume that the collateral was worth $500,000 when the loan was made and at all times thereafter. Assume, finally, that Lima Bank forgot to perfect its interest until November 15.

Which of the following amounts is SpotCo's bankruptcy trustee likely to recover?

(A) $100,000.

(B) $600,000.

(C) $1 million.

(D) $1.1 million.

231.   Debtor borrowed $100,000 from Bank on June 1. To secure repayment of the loan, Debtor granted to Bank a security interest in its current and future equipment. The security agreement was executed on June 1. On June 4, Bank filed a proper financing statement against Debtor's equipment with the appropriate filing officer. On June 8, Debtor used its own funds to buy a new piece of equipment (the "Item") from Seller, who placed a "sold" sticker on the Item. At Debtor's request, Seller did not deliver and install the Item at Debtor's office until June 12.

Debtor fell on hard times and filed a bankruptcy petition in late August. The bankruptcy trustee has challenged Bank's property interest in the Item as a voidable preference.

Under applicable bankruptcy law, the "transfer" took place on

(A)   June 1.

(B)   June 4.

(C)   June 8.

(D)   June 12.

232.   On March 1, Kirk borrowed $5,000 from a co-worker, Robert. Kirk executed an unsecured promissory note with a maturity date of June 30. Kirk was unable to pay the note at maturity and requested a six-month extension. Robert agreed, provided that Angela (Kirk's sister) guarantee repayment of the loan and Elliott (Kirk's brother) collateralize the loan with a security interest in his investment portfolio. Angela obliged by executing a guaranty on July 10. Elliott obliged by creating an enforceable security interest in the investment portfolio on July 12. Robert perfected the security interest on July 25.

Alas, Kirk's financial situation did not improve, and he filed a Chapter 7 bankruptcy petition on October 15. On that date, he owed $4,500 to Robert. Angela had paid $500 to Robert on the debt just three days before the bankruptcy petition was filed.

Evidence reveals that Kirk has been insolvent for five months, and his unsecured creditors will not be paid in full in the bankruptcy.

Ignoring any possible defenses, the bankruptcy trustee can attack as voidable preferences

(A)   neither the $500 payment nor the security interest.

(B)   the $500 payment and the security interest.

(C)   the $500 payment but not the security interest.

(D)   the security interest but not the $500 payment.

233.   In a voidable preference action, the bankruptcy trustee

(A)   enjoys an irrebuttable presumption of insolvency during the 90-day preference period.

(B)   bears the burden of proving nonavoidability of the transfer under any exception found in 11 U.S.C. § 547(c).

(C)   can never prove that a security interest transfer was made for antecedent debt if the security interest is perfected within 30 days of attachment.

(D)   cannot recover loan repayments made to a non-insider creditor that were received by that creditor outside the 90-day preference period, even if the one-year preference period applies (e.g., when the debt is guaranteed by an insider).

234.   Which of the following voidable preference exceptions preserves only payment transfers?

(A)   The "substantially contemporaneous exchange" exception.

(B)   The "ordinary course of business" exception.

(C)   The "enabling loan" exception.

(D)   The "floating lien" exception.

235.   Bank loaned $2 million to Debtor on July 16. To secure repayment of the loan, Bank obtained a non-purchase-money security interest in Debtor's existing and future inventory under a security agreement executed by Debtor at the time of the loan. Bank filed a proper financing statement in the right place on July 18. Debtor filed a bankruptcy petition on October 1. Debtor had not repaid any of the loan, and its inventory (which turns over every 15 days) had the following value on the stated dates:

July 1	$2.1 million
July 16	$1.7 million
August 1	$1.6 million

August 16	$1.5 million
September 1	$1.5 million
September 16	$1.6 million
October 1	$1.8 million

The bankruptcy trustee has attacked Bank's security interest in each item of inventory as a voidable preference and has proven all elements of its case under Bankruptcy Code § 547(b).

Under the "floating lien" exception, Bank can preserve its security interest in inventory worth

(A) $1.5 million.

(B) $1.6 million.

(C) $1.7 million.

(D) $1.8 million.

236.   Susan borrows $5,000 from Friendly Bank on January 1. She also signs a valid security agreement granting Friendly a security interest in her existing television set, a 105", flat-screen wonder. She uses the loan funds to take a trip to Bermuda. Friendly Bank does not file any financing statement.

Susan defaults on her loan on May 1, and Friendly accelerates the debt. Friendly sends one of its collection agents to Susan's house on May 15 to repossess the television set. Susan allows the person to come into her house to take the set. She does not object to the repossession in any way.

The next day, on May 16, Friendly forecloses upon the television set by selling it to one of its tellers for $2,500, which is the fair market value of the used set.

On May 17, Susan files a Chapter 7 bankruptcy petition. Susan's trustee in bankruptcy demands that Friendly Bank give the trustee the $2,500 proceeds of sale.

Friendly Bank

(A)   can keep the $2,500.

(B)   must pay the trustee the $2,500 because the trustee has the status of a lien creditor under state law.

(C)   must pay the trustee the $2,500 because Friendly's repossession of the television set was a preference.

(D)   must pay the trustee the $2,500 because it breached the peace by entering Susan's house to repossess the set.

237.   Soup Bowls, Inc., borrowed $100,000 from Ladle Bank. It is secured by Soup Bowls' accounts receivable. There was nothing unremarkable about the loan. Ladle is known,

however, for its quick collection practices. Six months after the loan is made, Soup Bowls is two days late with its monthly $5,000 payment. Ladle sends its burliest collector out to Soup Bowls. He is nothing but polite and soft-spoken, but does request the payment due. The scrawny accounts payable clerk, intimidated by the mere size of the collector, pays the amount owing with a regular company check. Soup Bowls files a Chapter 11 bankruptcy petition the next day; its accounts receivable are only $20,000, and have only been $20,000 for the last month.

When the bankruptcy trustee sues to recover the $5,000 payment as preferential, the most likely outcome is

(A)   the trustee will lose, because Ladle was secured.

(B)   the trustee will win, because the accounts payable clerk was forced to make the payment.

(C)   the trustee will lose, because all Ladle collected was what it was owed.

(D)   the trustee will win, because Ladle's quick collection procedures are not within industry standards.

Practice Final Exam: Questions

Questions

Practice Final Exam

This "practice final exam" consists of approximately 40 questions (including several short-answer questions). Try to complete it within 3.5 hours.

238. A few months ago, Dave borrowed $1,000 from Laura. Because Dave and Laura were friends, Laura did not insist on any collateral.

    In recent days, Dave has defaulted on the loan by failing to pay the balance due ($650). Despite their friendship, Laura is rather annoyed and is insisting on collateral (in exchange for her willingness to extend the maturity date of the loan by 30 days). Dave offers as collateral the $700 sales commission that his employer is expected to pay him in two weeks. Laura agrees, and she and Dave then execute paperwork to memorialize their understanding.

    Does the secured loan fall within the scope of Article 9?

    ANSWER:

239. BizCorp and Lender are negotiating the terms of a $2 million secured loan. BizCorp is offering some traditional forms of collateral (e.g., inventory and accounts receivable). But BizCorp also is offering some nontraditional forms of collateral.

    Which of the following, being offered by BizCorp as collateral, falls within the scope of Article 9?

    (A) Monthly rental income from an office building that BizCorp owns.

    (B) A negotiable promissory note, payable to the order of BizCorp, and itself secured by a real estate mortgage.

    (C) $75,000 judgment against a supplier for breach of contract.

    (D) Contingent death-benefits claim under a "key person" life insurance policy issued to BizCorp on the life of its founder (who is still living).

240. Last week, Meredith borrowed $10,000 from Bank to remodel the kitchen in her home (which she shares with two dogs and a cat). Meredith has a poor credit history, so Meredith's parents (Tim and Lisa) joined Meredith in signing the promissory note. Meredith's sister, Grace, agreed to guaranty the loan. And Meredith's aunt, Diana, delivered to Bank eight pieces of jewelry to serve as collateral for the loan.

    Which of the following statements is true?

    (A)   Meredith and her parents are primary obligors.

    (B)   Grace is the only secondary obligor in the transaction.

    (C)   Diana is the only debtor in the transaction.

    (D)   Meredith and Grace are each a primary obligor.

241.   Bank intends to make a $350,000 secured loan to Law Firm. The collateral description in the security agreement will include a reference to current and after-acquired "inventory."

The "inventory" reference will capture Law Firm's

    (A)   receivables due from its clients for legal services rendered.

    (B)   two photocopiers.

    (C)   coins and bills in the petty cash drawer.

    (D)   letterhead stationery.

242.   Which of the following organizations is *not* a "registered organization" (assuming that the letters appearing at the end are accurate representations of the type of entity that they are)?

    (A)   Bruce A. Markell, L.L.C.

    (B)   ZinnMark, Inc.

    (C)   Markell & Zinnecker, L.L.P.

    (D)   Zinnecker and Markell, L.P.

243.   Lender is making a $1 million secured loan to BAMCO. Part of the collateral offered by BAMCO will include its investment portfolio of stocks, bonds, and mutual funds in an account managed by its broker, The ZinnVestments Group. At the present time, that account includes 300 shares of Facebook stock, 400 shares of Amazon stock, 500 shares of Netflix stock, 600 shares of Google stock, and 3,000 shares of the Puritan International Stock Fund.

Which of the following statements is true?

    (A)   The ZinnVestments Group is an entitlement holder.

    (B)   BAMCO is a securities intermediary.

    (C)   The Amazon shares represent one or more security entitlements.

    (D)   Lender (the secured party) is not a purchaser of the collateral.

244.   Lender has agreed to make a $50 million secured loan to TZCorp, a corporation that sells furniture through several retail stores primarily, but not exclusively, to consumer customers. Lender's lawyer has drafted the security agreement, which describes the collateral as:

Debtor's rights, whether now owned or hereafter acquired or created, in each of the following: accounts, chattel paper, commercial tort claims, deposit accounts, documents, equipment, farm products, general intangibles, instruments, inventory, investment property, letter-of-credit rights, and money.

Which observation voiced by Lender should cause its lawyer the greatest concern?

(A)   The description inadequately describes "commercial tort claims."

(B)   The description includes "deposit accounts," which cannot serve as Article 9 collateral.

(C)   The description omits "consumer goods."

(D)   The description fails to mention "fixtures."

245.   Two years ago, Trent borrowed $20,000 from his father, Richard, and used the money to purchase a car. At Richard's insistence, Trent executed a security agreement, which created an enforceable purchase-money security interest in the car. Richard, being unfamiliar with Article 9, filed no paperwork to perfect his security interest.

Last week, Trent sold the car for $13,000. He still holds the purchaser's check. Richard has asked Trent to deliver the check to him (to apply against the unpaid debt of $14,200), insisting that the check represents Richard's collateral.

Which of the following statements is true?

(A)   Richard has no security interest in the check unless the security agreement included a "proceeds" reference in the collateral description.

(B)   Richard has no security interest in the check because his security interest in the car was unperfected.

(C)   Richard has an enforceable security interest in the check, but only for 20 days from the date when Trent receives the check.

(D)   Richard has an enforceable, but unperfected, security interest in the check.

246.   In February, Templeton Finance loaned $5 million to Clinic. To secure repayment of the loan, Clinic granted to Templeton Finance a security interest in its medical equipment. During the year, Templeton Finance funded additional advances to Clinic. Also during the year, Clinic bought additional medical equipment. A summary of the activity follows:

February 1	Parties execute security agreement and other loan papers
	Templeton Finance advances $5 million
	Value of existing medical equipment is $4.6 million
April 10	Templeton Finance advances $1 million
May 20	Clinic buys scanning equipment for $1.2 million
June 25	Clinic buys radiology equipment for $1.4 million
August 15	Templeton Finance advances $1.5 million

In November, Clinic defaulted on its obligations to Templeton Finance, having repaid none of the loans.

Ignore any market changes or depreciation in the value of the equipment. Assume that the security agreement included an after-acquired property clause, but not a future advance clause.

Calculate the amount of Templeton Finance's *secured* claim.

ANSWER:

247. Ignore any market changes or depreciation in the value of the equipment. Assume that the security agreement included a future advance clause, but not an after-acquired property clause.

Calculate the amount of Templeton Finance's *unsecured* claim.

ANSWER:

248. Bank makes a $25,000 loan to BAM Corp. (a Delaware corporation) in January. The loan is secured by an enforceable security interest in BAM's accounts, inventory, and equipment, and the security agreement includes an after-acquired property clause. Bank promptly files a proper financing statement with the appropriate Delaware filing office.

BAM Corp. changes its name to "ZinnCo" on March 15. Bank knows of the name change, but takes no action in response. Thereafter, ZinnCo acquires three pieces of equipment (Item #1 in May, Item #2 in July, and Item #3 in September).

As of November 1, Bank has

(A) no security interest in Items #1, #2, and #3.

(B) unperfected security interests in each of the three items.

(C) unperfected security interests in Items #2 and #3.

(D) a perfected security interest in Item #1.

249. Assume that BAM Corp. does not change its name. Instead, in March, and without Bank's knowledge or permission, BAM sells a piece of equipment (the "Item") to Purchaser.

As of November 1, Bank's security interest in the Item

(A) no longer exists.

(B) remains perfected, but only if the Item remains located in Delaware.

(C) remains perfected, regardless of where Purchaser is located.

(D) remains perfected, but only if Purchaser is located in Delaware.

250. Bob's Furniture Store (BFS) sells furniture to consumers. Its standard form contract gives consumers up to one year to pay the balance in installments, and states "BFS retains title

to the furniture sold under this contract until the full balance hereunder is paid in full." BFS only lends to consumers for their personal use, and their form contract contains a warranty that "Customer hereby warrants that the furniture bought under this contract is being bought, and will be used for, personal, family or household purposes only."

Xbank wants to lend money to BFS based on BFS's customer contracts. It is impractical for Xbank to take delivery each day of the contracts. Describe what Xbank should do to ensure perfection in the contracts and in all customer payments made with respect to those contracts.

ANSWER:

251. MediCorp is a Delaware corporation that owns and operates hospitals and clinics in San Francisco, Los Angeles, and San Diego. A few months ago, BAM Technologies sold three pieces of medical equipment to MediCorp on credit, retaining an enforceable security interest in the equipment to secure the aggregate purchase price. BAM Technologies filed its financing statement with California's central filing office.

Yesterday, without the knowledge or consent of BAM Technologies, MediCorp sold one of the three pieces of equipment to HealthNet for $1.5 million. HealthNet paid $500,000 in cash and executed and delivered a short-term $1 million negotiable promissory note for the balance.

If BAM Technologies can satisfy its tracing burden, BAM Technologies has

(A) no security interest in either the cash or the note.

(B) an unperfected security interest in both the cash and the note.

(C) a perfected security interest in both the cash and the note, but only if BAM Technologies filed its financing statement within 20 days after MediCorp took possession of the equipment.

(D) a perfected security interest in both the cash and the note.

252. SteamBroom makes cleaning devices, and sells them wholesale to retail stores. First Bank has a perfected security interest in all of SteamBroom's "inventory, now owned or hereafter acquired." It filed its UCC-1 financing statement on June 1. Second Bank has a perfected security interest in all of SteamBroom's "accounts, now owned or hereafter aquired." It filed its UCC-1 financing statement on July 1.

SteamBroom sells $50,000 worth of inventory to Cleaner, Inc. on credit on August 1. On August 15, Cleaner pays that amount by check to SteamBroom. SteamBroom deposits the check into its only bank account at Third Bank. Before the deposit, the account had a $5,000 balance. Thirty days after the check clears, SteamBroom defaults to both First Bank and Second Bank, and owes more than $100,000 to each. There were no deposits or withdrawals to the Third Bank account during this period.

As between First Bank and Second Bank, which bank has priority in the deposit account balance of $55,000, and why?

ANSWER:

253.   Briefly state four differences between a standard financing statement and a fixture filing.

ANSWER:

254.   Meredith, a resident of Boston, has hired Quality Contractors to install granite counter-tops and new cabinets and lighting in the kitchen of her vacation home near San Francisco. Quality Contractors is financing the remodeling on a secured basis. The countertops, cabinets, and lights will serve as collateral. Once installed, all of these items will be "fixtures" under local law.

Quality Contractors

(A)   has no reason to file a fixture filing because its PMSI is automatically perfected in the consumer goods.

(B)   has no reason to file a fixture filing because Article 9 excludes from its scope a security interest in consumer goods that are, or will become, fixtures.

(C)   should file a fixture filing in the appropriate Massachusetts county.

(D)   should file a fixture filing in the appropriate California county.

255.   MegaHealth is a Delaware corporation with a chief executive office in the Seattle area, from which it operates three local hospitals.

In April, First Bank obtained an enforceable security interest in MegaHealth's "equipment." First Bank promptly filed its financing statement (with the same collateral description) in Delaware.

In September, Second Bank obtained an enforceable security interest in MegaHealth's "equipment, whether now owned or hereafter acquired." Second Bank promptly filed its financing statement (with the same collateral description) in Washington.

In December, MegaHealth defaulted on its material contracts. A priority dispute soon erupted between First Bank and Second Bank over an item of equipment (the "Item") that MegaHealth had acquired in February with its own funds.

First Bank will

(A)   win the priority dispute because its security interest in the Item is perfected, and Second Bank's security interest is unperfected.

(B)   win the priority dispute because Second Bank has no security interest in the Item.

(C)   lose the priority dispute because its security interest in the Item is unperfected, and Second Bank's security interest is perfected.

(D)   neither win nor lose the priority dispute, but instead will share priority with Second Bank because both security interests in the Item are unperfected.

256.   First Bank and Second Bank also are involved in a priority dispute over a second piece of equipment (the "Item") that MegaHealth had acquired in July with its own funds (which are not proceeds of any collateral).

First Bank will

(A)   win the priority dispute in the Item because it filed its financing statement before Second Bank filed its financing statement.

(B)   win the priority dispute because its security interest in the Item attached before Second Bank's security interest attached.

(C)   lose the priority dispute because it has no security interest in the Item, and Second Bank has an enforceable security interest in the Item.

(D)   lose the priority dispute because its security interest in the Item is unperfected, and Second Bank's security interest is perfected.

257.   In 2016, Esther borrowed $10,000 from Matthew, her brother. To secure repayment of the loan, Esther authenticated a security agreement that created an enforceable security interest in her collection of chess sets. Matthew perfected his security interest by filing a financing statement in Texas, as Esther lived in San Antonio.

On November 20, 2017, Esther moved to Phoenix. Matthew knew that his sister had left Texas, but he took no filing action.

In January 2018, Esther borrowed $8,000 from Shelby, her sister. To secure repayment of the loan, Esther authenticated a security agreement that created an enforceable security interest in the same collection of chess sets. Shelby perfected her security interest by filing a financing statement in Arizona. Shelby knew of Matthew's earlier loan so she ordered a UCC search report in Texas, which disclosed Matthew's filing.

Thereafter, following several financial setbacks, Esther filed a bankruptcy petition. Matthew and Shelby are fighting over Esther's collection of chess sets. They have asked the bankruptcy court to resolve their priority dispute as of the petition date.

How should the court resolve the dispute, if Esther filed her petition on (i) March 1, 2018, or (ii) April 1, 2018? (Ignore any possible avoidance actions by the bankruptcy trustee.)

ANSWER:

258. Bank made a $2 million loan to Texas Avionics, Inc. (a Delaware corporation) in January. The loan was secured by a security interest in Texas Avionics's accounts, inventory, and equipment, and the security agreement included an after-acquired property clause. Bank promptly filed its financing statement in the correct place.

     Texas Avionics changed its name to "Southwest Avionics, Inc." on May 1. Bank knew of the name change, but it took no action in response.

     Lender made a $1 million loan to Southwest Avionics in July. The loan was secured by a security interest in Southwest Avionics's accounts, inventory, and equipment, and the security agreement included an after-acquired property clause. Lender filed its financing statement with the correct filing office on July 8. Lender was aware of Bank's security interest in the collateral, but the UCC search report that Lender ordered against "Southwest Avionics, Inc." did not disclose Bank's filing.

     Southwest Avionics defaulted on both loans in December. A priority dispute in four particular pieces of equipment has erupted. Evidence reveals that the debtor used its own funds during the year to acquire Item #1 on February 10, Item #2 on June 10, Item #3 on August 10, and Item #4 on October 10.

     As of December 15, Lender has priority in

     (A)   all four Items.

     (B)   Items #2, #3, and #4 only.

     (C)   Items #3 and #4 only.

     (D)   Item #4 only.

259. Last year, Debtor borrowed $1 million from Lender. The loan is secured by an enforceable security interest in Debtor's equipment. The security agreement included an after-acquired property clause. Lender perfected its security interest by filing a financing statement shortly after extending credit.

     On June 1 of this year, Debtor bought a new piece of equipment on credit from Dealer. Dealer retained an enforceable security interest in the item to secure repayment of its purchase price. Dealer delivered and installed the item at Debtor's plant on June 5 and filed its financing statement on June 29.

     As of July 1,

     (A)   Dealer has a perfected PMSI that enjoys priority.

     (B)   Dealer has a perfected PMSI that does not enjoy priority.

     (C)   Dealer has a perfected non-PMSI that does not enjoy priority.

     (D)   Dealer has an unperfected non-PMSI that does not enjoy priority.

260. On March 1, Midtown Bank made a $5 million loan to Hooks & Slices, Inc. ("HSI"), a corporate entity that sells golf clubs through retail stores located throughout the country. To secure repayment of the loan, HSI granted to Midtown Bank a security interest in its inventory, equipment, and accounts. The security agreement included an after-acquired property clause. Midtown Bank filed its financing statement, proper in all respects, against the collateral on March 10.

On August 1, HSI purchased 2,000 sets of golf clubs from Kirkland Corporation. The sale was on credit, with payment due no later than one year later. To secure payment, Kirkland retained an enforceable security interest in the 2,000 sets. HSI executed the security agreement on August 5. Kirkland delivered the 2,000 sets to HSI on three different dates: 800 sets on August 10, 700 sets on August 20, and 500 sets on August 30. Kirkland filed its financing statement, proper in all respects, against the golf clubs on August 15. On August 18, Kirkland sent a written notice of its security interest in the 2,000 sets of golf clubs to Midtown Bank; the contents of the notice satisfied the statutory requirements of UCC Article 9. Midtown Bank received the notice on August 22.

HSI defaulted on its obligations to both creditors in December. Each creditor asserts priority in the golf clubs sold by Kirkland that HSI has not yet sold (300 from the first shipment; 200 from the second shipment, and 250 from the third shipment).

In how many sets of golf clubs does Kirkland have priority?

(A) Zero.

(B) 250.

(C) 450.

(D) 750.

261. Markers is a Texas corporation that operates a high-end camera equipment store in Houston. Last year, Markers borrowed $500,000 from ZinnBank. The loan was secured by an enforceable security interest in Markers' inventory, equipment, and accounts. The security agreement included an after-acquired property clause and authorized collateral dispositions in the ordinary course of business. ZinnBank perfected its security interest by filing in Texas.

Two months ago, Markers sold camera equipment valued at $4,000 to Gwen (an amateur photographer), who sells photocopiers. The parties agreed that Gwen would pay the purchase price by delivering and installing a photocopier of comparable value at Markers' store. Gwen did so.

Last month, Gwen gave a $2,200 DigiCon camera to her favorite nephew, Ethan, as a birthday present. The DigiCon camera was part of the camera equipment sold by Markers to Gwen.

A priority dispute now exists between ZinnBank and Ethan over the DigiCon camera.

How should the dispute be resolved?

ANSWER:

262. Assume that Markers later sold Gwen's photocopier to BizSmart (an entity that sells office equipment), which then sold it for cash to a customer, Ashley.

    If ZinnBank sues Ashley for conversion of the photocopier,

    (A)   Ashley should lose.

    (B)   Ashley should win if she uses the photocopier primarily as a consumer good.

    (C)   Ashley should win because she was a buyer in the ordinary course of business.

    (D)   Ashley should win because she paid cash, and ZinnBank can claim a perfected security interest in the cash if it remains identifiable.

263. In early June, Mockingbird Industries and Fidelity Bank began negotiating the terms of a $250,000 secured loan. With Mockingbird's consent, on June 15, Fidelity Bank filed a financing statement against Mockingbird, describing the collateral as "all assets."

    The parties concluded their negotiations on July 1, when the parties executed several agreements, documents, and instruments, including:

    > a loan agreement under which Fidelity Bank agreed to consider lending up to $250,000 to Mockingbird in one or more advances; and

    > a security agreement that described the collateral as "all inventory, equipment, and accounts, in each case whether now owned or existing or hereafter acquired or created."

    The parties also approved a UCC-3 amendment that changed the collateral description in its original filing to mirror the collateral description found in the security agreement.

    On July 7, Fidelity advanced $85,000 pursuant to Mockingbird's initial borrowing request. On July 10, Fidelity filed the UCC-3 amendment.

    Unknown to Fidelity Bank, a court official had validly levied on a significant part of Mockingbird's inventory and equipment on July 5, at which time Heather Finch became a "lien creditor" under UCC Article 9.

    In a priority dispute between Fidelity Bank and Heather over the seized assets,

    (A)   Fidelity Bank will win because Mockingbird had signed a security agreement and because Fidelity Bank's financing statement covered inventory and equipment when Heather became a lien creditor.

    (B)   Heather will win because she became a lien creditor before Fidelity Bank's security interest attached.

(C) Heather will win because an "all assets" collateral description in a financing statement is ineffective.

(D) Heather will win if Fidelity Bank cannot claim a PMSI in the seized assets.

264. Would your answer to Question 263 change if Heather Finch had levied on June 28, making that date the date she became a lien creditor?

ANSWER:

265. Ten days after Tim defaults on his secured car loan, Dealer sends its agent (Repo Company) to Tim's house in the early morning hours to seize the car. Repo Company finds the car locked and parked on Tim's driveway. Repo Company notices a laptop computer on the front passenger seat and correctly assumes that the computer is not part of Dealer's collateral.

Which of the following statements is true?

(A) Repo Company cannot repossess Tim's car at this time because the car is parked on private property.

(B) Repo Company cannot repossess Tim's car at this time because its contents include a computer that is not part of Dealer's collateral.

(C) Repo Company can repossess the car at this time and can refuse to return the computer until Tim pays all past-due amounts on the car note.

(D) Repo Company can repossess the car at this time but must make the computer available to Tim as soon as reasonably possible following the completion of the repossession.

266. Three days ago, AutoMart peaceably repossessed Meredith's car, which she had always driven primarily for personal use. The default that prompted AutoMart's repossession was Meredith's failure to make a $550 monthly payment. The loan papers included an acceleration clause. AutoMart has taken all steps necessary to trigger the acceleration clause. As a result, Meredith now owes $8,750. Meredith's sister, Grace, had guaranteed repayment of the debt. Grace has contacted AutoMart to discuss the possibility of redeeming the car for her sister.

Which of the following statements is true?

(A) Article 9 permits Meredith (the debtor), but not Grace (a secondary obligor), to redeem the car.

(B) Article 9 permits Grace to redeem the car, but AutoMart can refuse to accept Grace's check for $550 (representing Grace's attempt to cure the missed payment) and insist that she pay $8,750.

(C) Article 9 usually permits Grace to redeem the car, but an exception bars Grace from exercising any redemption right because Meredith used the car for personal use and the accelerated debt exceeds $7,500.

(D) Article 9 usually permits Grace to redeem the car, but Grace will be contractually barred from exercising her redemption rights if she waived those rights when she executed her guaranty.

267. Two years ago, Dealer sold a grand piano on credit to the ZinnMark Resort for use at various functions. Dealer timely perfected its PMSI in the piano.

Following the Resort's payment default a few weeks ago, Dealer peaceably repossessed the piano.

Dealer intends to sell the piano, either to a private buyer or at a public auction. Once it makes a final decision on how to proceed, it will send a disposition notice to the Resort.

To be effective under Article 9, Dealer's notice must

(A) be sent to, but need not be received by, the Resort.

(B) be written, and cannot be electronic or oral.

(C) be sent at least 10 days before the earliest date of disposition.

(D) include a reference to the filing number of the relevant UCC-1 filing.

268. Should Dealer request a UCC search report against the Resort before it sells the piano?

ANSWER:

269. On March 1, Remington Farms sold a horse to Simon Webster for $100,000. Simon delivered a personal check for $40,000, and Remington Farms agreed to finance the $60,000 balance. Remington Farms retained an enforceable security interest in the horse to secure repayment of the unpaid purchase price, but Remington Farms never filed a financing statement. Simon and his family use the horse for recreational pleasure.

On July 1, Simon granted an enforceable security interest in the horse to First Bank to secure a $20,000 personal loan made the same day. First Bank perfected its security interest by filing a financing statement that day with the proper official. Simon's sister, Rachel, guaranteed repayment of the loan.

On August 15, Simon granted an enforceable security interest in the horse to Second Bank to secure a $10,000 personal loan made the same day. Second Bank perfected its security interest by filing a financing statement that day with the proper official.

For reasons beyond his control, Simon defaulted on the loan from First Bank on September 1. The default to First Bank also triggered a cross-default on the loans from Remington Farms and Second Bank.

Shortly thereafter, First Bank possessed the horse with Simon's consent.

First Bank intends to sell the horse at a public sale. Remington Farms has provided First Bank with written notice of its security interest, but Second Bank has not. First Bank has ordered, and received, a UCC search report reflecting all financing statements filed against Simon and the horse through September 15.

In order to comply with the requirements of Article 9, First Bank must send its notice of sale to

(A) Simon only.

(B) Simon and Rachel only.

(C) Simon, Rachel, and Remington Farms only.

(D) Simon, Rachel, Remington Farms, and Second Bank.

270. After sending proper notice to the required party (or parties), First Bank sells the horse for $78,000 at a public sale (all aspects of which are commercially reasonable) to Purchaser. First Bank has received a timely written demand for proceeds from Remington Farms but no demand from Second Bank. At the time of the sale, Simon owes $45,000 to Remington Farms, $15,000 to First Bank, and $7,000 to Second Bank. Throughout the disposition process, First Bank has acted in good faith with no knowledge that its conduct violates the rights of any other party.

After deducting $3,000 to cover its reasonable costs of repossessing and feeding the horse, to which parties should First Bank distribute the remaining $75,000?

ANSWER:

271. A week before the sale, Purchaser had the horse appraised at $120,000. Having purchased the horse for only $78,000, Purchaser is quite pleased with the "great deal" on the purchase.

Explain to Purchaser why the "great deal" may not be so "great."

ANSWER:

272. Debtor, a Delaware corporation, filed a Chapter 11 bankruptcy petition on September 13. Under which of the following situations is Secured Party most vulnerable to an attack by the bankruptcy trustee under 11 U.S.C. § 544(a), the "strong-arm clause"?

(A) Secured Party's security interest in Debtor's equipment (located at a Delaware plant) attached on February 1, and Secured Party filed a financing statement covering equipment with the appropriate Delaware official on February 7. On May 1, Debtor closed the Delaware plant and relocated the equipment to an Illinois plant. Secured Party never refiled a financing statement in Illinois.

(B) Secured Party's security interest in Debtor's investment property (a stock certificate held by Debtor in a safety deposit box in Atlanta) attached on July 2. None of Secured

Party's then-existing financing statements covered this type of collateral, and so on July 6 Secured Party filed its financing statement with the appropriate Georgia official.

(C) Secured Party's purchase-money security interest in Debtor's inventory (located in Texas) attached on September 8; on that date there was no financing statement covering such inventory. Secured Party never filed a financing statement in Texas, and did not file a financing statement with the appropriate Delaware official until three days after the petition date.

(D) Secured Party's security interest in Debtor's bank account (maintained with Secured Party) attached on July 20; Secured Party took no action to perfect its security interest.

273. Sinister Bank lends to high-risk businesses. Billy's Bird House, LLC (BBH) is one such business. It builds birdhouses and sells them to various home improvement stores. Sinister has lent $1 million to BBH, secured by "all of BBH's inventory, equipment, accounts, general intangibles, instruments, deposit accounts, chattel paper, and investment securities, now owned or hereafter acquired." Sinister properly perfects a security interest in this collateral.

Sinister has concluded that BBH is not a "viable" loan. It is, however, worried that the value of BBH's collateral is not sufficient to cover its loan. It starts to squeeze BBH with respect to its day-to-day expenditures, micro-managing BBH from afar, and trying to get it to conserve Sinister's collateral. When the lumber suppliers to BBH notice this, they call Sinister and ask what's going on. Sinister tell the callers that Sinister has no present intention to stop lending (which is technically true — it intends very shortly to stop lending, but not presently). It believes that this answer will cause the lumber suppliers to continue to ship lumber to BBH, which will increase the value of Sinister's collateral without Sinister having to advance any more funds. It then tells BBH it should order more lumber on credit which it does, because the lumber suppliers have relied on Sinister's representations. After all the new lumber is delivered, and BBH has taken title, Sinister ceases lending and, in compliance with Article 9, begins to foreclose on all the newly arrived lumber, along with other collateral. BBH responds by filing a chapter 11 bankruptcy.

In BBH's bankruptcy, Sinister

(A) Need not worry about its claim because BBH did not complain.

(B) Needs to worry about its security interest, but not its claim.

(C) Need not worry about its claim because it had a properly perfected security interest and was following all relevant provisions of Article 9 with respect to the foreclosure.

(D) Needs to worry about both its claim and its security interest.

274. Which of the following situations creates a voidable preference? (Assume that unsecured claims will not be paid in full and no creditor is an insider.)

(A) On May 1, Debtor borrows $1,000 from Lender. The loan is unsecured. Debtor's brother repays the loan on June 1. Prior to that time, Debtor did not owe her brother anything. Debtor files a bankruptcy petition on July 1.

(B) On June 1, Debtor buys a piece of equipment for $100,000 from Dealer. Debtor makes a $20,000 cash payment and finances the $80,000 balance with Dealer, who retains a security interest in the equipment. Dealer files its financing statement against the equipment on June 8. Debtor makes a $35,000 loan repayment to Dealer on July 15 and files a bankruptcy petition on August 7. At all relevant times the equipment had a value of at least $80,000.

(C) On April 1, Debtor borrows $50,000 from Bank. The loan is unsecured. Debtor repays the loan on May 1 and files a bankruptcy petition on August 15.

(D) On February 1, Debtor borrowed $10,000 from Finance Company. The loan is unsecured. On February 5, after Debtor releases a poor earnings report, Finance Company insists on collateral. On February 8, Debtor granted to Finance Company a security interest in its existing inventory and equipment (which at all relevant times had a value of at least $20,000). Finance Company filed its financing statement on February 9. Debtor filed a bankruptcy petition on April 25.

275. BankOne has lent $1 million to Construction, Inc., secured by a perfected security interest in a special purpose dump truck that Construction, Inc. bought for $2 million originally. BankOne obtained a valid appraisal on the truck before lending, which confirmed that the truck was worth at least $2 million. BankOne has no other loans out to Construction, Inc.

Unfortunately, the day after the loan a meteor hit the truck, destroying it. The fragments of the truck are worth maybe $1,000. To make matters worse, Construction, Inc.'s insurance policy excludes casualties caused by anything falling from the sky.

BankOne presses for repayment of the loan, and receives a lump sum payment of $1 million one month later. Five weeks after that, Construction, Inc. files for chapter 7 bankruptcy. The bankruptcy trustee sues BankOne to recover the $1 million payment. Who wins?

ANSWER:

Answers

Scope

1. **Answer (D) is the correct answer.** Section 9-109 is the scope provision of Article 9. Section 9-109(a) states that Article 9 applies to "(3) a sale of accounts, chattel paper, payment intangibles, or promissory notes." (But note that Section 9-109(d) excludes from the scope of Article 9 certain assignments and sales of payment receivables. *See* § 9-109(d)(4), (5), and (7).) Accounts are expressly mentioned within the quoted scope provision, **making Answer (A) an incorrect answer.** Equipment lease contracts are examples of "chattel paper" under Section 9-102(a)(11) (i.e., a record that evidences a monetary obligation [the periodic lease payments] and a lease in specific goods [one or more pieces of equipment]), **making Answer (B) an incorrect answer.** Sales of promissory notes also fall within the language of Section 9-109(a)(3), regardless of dollar amount and whether executed by consumer obligors. Therefore, **Answer (C) is incorrect.** Customer lists can serve as Article 9 collateral (the lists will be a general intangible), but the *sale* of the lists does not by itself trigger application of Article 9, **making Answer (D) the correct answer.**

2. **Answer (B) is the correct answer.** The scope provision of Article 9 is Section 9-109. Subsection (a) states: "Except as otherwise provided in subsections (c) and (d), this article applies to: (1) a transaction . . . that creates a security interest in personal property or fixtures by contract. . . ." As a general rule, then, Article 9 applies to any voluntary transaction in which the collateral is not real estate (unless the real estate qualifies as a fixture). Under this general rule, Article 9 covers all three items, each an example of "personal property."

   The lottery tickets represent a claim against a particular entity and are an example of a general intangible. (A ticket that later generates "winnings" may become an "account" under Section 9-102(a)(2)(viii).) Therefore, Article 9 will cover Meredith's interest in the tickets.

   The bottles of wine are moveable and, therefore, "goods" under Section 9-102(a)(44) (and probably "consumer goods" under Section 9-102(a)(23) if Meredith claims them primarily for personal, family, or household purposes). Meredith may use them as Article 9 collateral.

   As noted above, the scope provision of Section 9-109(a) is subject to exclusions in subsection (d). Subsection (d)(3) expressly excludes from Article 9 coverage "an assignment of a claim for wages, salary, or other compensation of any employee." Therefore, the assignment by Meredith of her claim for next week's wages falls outside the scope of Article 9.

In summary, then, the lottery tickets and the bottles of wine, but not the assignment of wages, may serve as Article 9 collateral. Therefore, **Answer (B) is the correct answer.**

Answer (A) is incorrect because Article 9 excludes from its coverage Meredith's assignment of her claim for wages.

Answer (C) is incorrect because it omits the bottles of wine (covered by Article 9) and it includes Meredith's assignment of her claim for wages (not covered by Article 9).

Answer (D) is incorrect because it omits the lottery tickets (covered by Article 9) and it includes Meredith's assignment of her claim for wages (not covered by Article 9).

3. **Answer (A) is the correct answer.** As a general rule, Article 9 covers any transaction "that creates a security interest in personal property or fixtures by contract." § 9-109(a)(1). But Section 9-109(a) is expressly subject to exclusions stated in subsection (d). Subsection (d)(11) excludes from the scope of Article 9 "the creation or transfer of an interest in or lien on real property" (subject to some inapplicable exceptions). The condominium is real property, so it will not be Article 9 collateral. The condominium may be used as collateral, but the parties must comply with law other than Article 9, such as by obtaining a mortgage or a deed of trust under local real estate law.

The other two items of collateral also raise concerns under subsection (d), which expressly excludes certain types of property from the scope of Article 9. Subsection (d)(8) excludes any transfer by BizCorp of its rights as beneficiary under a life insurance policy. Therefore, BizCorp's rights under the life insurance policy may not serve as Article 9 collateral. (Those rights may be used as collateral, but the parties must comply with law other than Article 9. The parties should consult with the insurance company and follow its instructions on how to effectively assign BizCorp's rights as beneficiary to Lender.)

Section 9-109(d)(12) excludes tort claims, other than "commercial tort claims." The term is defined in Section 9-102(a)(13) and picks up BizCorp's claim because BizCorp is an organization (defined in Article 1 as a party other than a human), and the trademark infringement action is typically classified as a cause of action or claim for relief arising under tort law. *See Alitalia-Linee Aeree Italiane S.p.A. v. Casinoalitalia.com*, 128 F.Supp.2d 340 (E.D. Va. 2001) ("[T]rademark infringement is a tort."). So the trademark infringement claim will serve as Article 9 collateral.

In summary, then, Article 9 will apply to the trademark infringement claim, but not to the condominium or the life insurance policy. Therefore, **Answer (A) is the correct answer.**

Answer (B) is incorrect for two reasons. First, it erroneously suggests that BizCorp's rights under the life insurance policy may serve as Article 9 collateral (but it cannot). Second, it erroneously suggests that BizCorp's trademark infringement claim may not serve as Article 9 collateral (but it can).

Answer (C) is incorrect. True, the trademark infringement claim can serve as Article 9 collateral. But the condominium cannot.

Answer (D) is incorrect because the trademark infringement claim can serve as Article 9 collateral.

4. It depends. Section 9-109(d)(13) excludes from Article 9 coverage "an assignment of a deposit account in a consumer transaction[.]" Section 9-102(a)(26) defines "consumer transaction" in a manner that requires Ingrid to incur the obligation "primarily for personal, family, or household purposes" and to hold the deposit account "primarily for personal, family, or household purposes." The facts do not indicate why Ingrid borrowed the money. Did she use the funds to buy office equipment, or remodel the kitchen in her home? Also, the facts do not indicate the primary purpose of the bank account. Does Ingrid use it primarily for business reasons, or personal reasons? If the purpose of the loan *and* the bank account *both* meet the "primarily for personal, family, or household purposes" test, then the transaction is a "consumer transaction," the exclusion in Section 9-109(d)(13) applies, and Matt will not have an Article 9 security interest in the bank account. But if the purpose of the loan *and/or* the bank account do *not* meet the "primarily for personal, family, or household purposes" test, then the transaction is *not* a "consumer transaction," the exclusion in Section 9-109(d)(13) does not apply, and Matt will have an Article 9 security interest in the bank account.

5. **Answer (D) is the correct answer.** Section 9-109(a)(4) states that Article 9 applies to "a consignment." Therefore, **Answer (B) is incorrect.** This question focuses attention on the meaning of "consignment."

   Article 9 defines "consignment" in Section 9-102(a)(20), which provides a four-part test. The first part requires the merchant to meet certain conditions. Joe's Bike Shop may or may not meet these conditions, but we will assume that it does. Second, the aggregate value of the goods must be at least $1,000 when delivered. These three bikes have an aggregate value of $600-$900, so this transaction is not an Article 9 "consignment." Therefore, Article 9 does not cover the transaction, **making Answer (D) correct and Answer (A) incorrect.** The third part of the definition excludes consumer goods from coverage. The facts indicate that Lisa's daughters used the bikes for recreational purposes, making them "consumer goods" under the definition found at Section 9-102(a)(23). This is a second reason why the transaction is not an Article 9 "consignment" (**and another reason why Answer (A) is incorrect**). And the fourth part of the test is that the transaction itself does not create a security interest. This part of the definition seems to be met, but the second and third parts are not met, so the transaction falls outside the definition of "consignment" and, accordingly, does not fall within the scope of Article 9.

   Answer (C) is incorrect. Whether a transaction is an Article 9 "consignment" does not turn on the amount of the commission to be retained by the merchant.

6. **Answer (D) is the correct answer.** Section 9-109(a)(1) states that Article 9 applies to "a transaction, regardless of its form, that creates a security interest in personal property or fixtures by contract." This question focuses attention on two requirements. First, the property interest must arise contractually (consensually). Second, the property interest must be in personal property or fixtures (and not real estate).

The dealer's interest in the car (personal property) arises contractually. The contract is labeled "Promissory Note" and not "Security Agreement," but the statutory language quoted above reveals that substance trumps form. The contract includes "title retention" language, which effectively gives the dealer a "security interest" in the vehicle. *See* § 1-201(b)(35) (stating, in the penultimate sentence of the definition of "security interest," that "[t]he retention or reservation of title by a seller of goods notwithstanding shipment or delivery to the buyer under Section 2-401 is limited in effect to a reservation of a 'security interest'"). Because the dealer's interest in the car is a "security interest" that arises contractually, Article 9 applies.

Boats and jewelry can serve as collateral under Article 9. But the county assessor's interest in the boat arises statutorily, and the neighbor's interest in the jewelry is created by judicial process. Neither creditor's interest in the personal property arises contractually, so Article 9 does not apply.

Unlike the county assessor and the dealer, the mortgage bank has a property interest that arises contractually. But the property interest is in Erin's residence, which is real estate (rather than personal property). Therefore, Article 9 does not apply. *See* § 9-109(d)(11).

Because Article 9 applies only to the car dealer's interest, but not to the interests claimed by the county assessor, the neighbor, or the mortgage bank, **Answer (D) is the correct answer.**

Answer (A) is incorrect because the neighbor's judicial lien on Erin's jewelry, and the bank's interest in Erin's residence, are not covered by Article 9.

Answer (B) is incorrect because the county assessor's statutory lien on Erin's boat, and the bank's interest in Erin's residence, are not covered by Article 9.

Answer (C) is incorrect because the county assessor's statutory lien on Erin's boat, and the neighbor's judicial lien on Erin's jewelry, are not covered by Article 9.

7. The president's note, although itself secured by real estate, can serve as Article 9 collateral. The original transaction between ZinnCo (presumably the lender) and its president (presumably the borrower) is not covered by Article 9 because, as a general rule, Article 9 excludes from its scope the creation of an interest in real property (such as a collateral interest in a residence or a building contractually created by a mortgage or a deed of trust). *See* § 9-109(d)(11). But ZinnCo can offer the president's note as Article 9 collateral to Bank, even though the note itself is secured by non-Article 9 collateral. Authority for this conclusion is found in Section 9-109(b) and cmt. 7 (Example 1).

Definitions

8. **Answer (A) is the correct answer.** Section 9-102(a)(23) defines "consumer goods" as "goods that are used or bought for use primarily for personal, family, or household purposes." A "good," defined in Section 9-102(a)(44), is something that is moveable when the security interest becomes enforceable. Of the four possibilities, only the two cats and the laptop computer are moveable and, therefore, goods. To be a "consumer good," the asset must be a good that is used by Sarah *primarily* for personal, family, or household reasons. Nothing in the question suggests that Sarah's two cats serve any purpose other than a personal, family, or household purpose, so the cats fall within the definition of "consumer good," **making Answer (A) the correct answer.**

    Answer (C) is incorrect. The laptop is a good, but it is a good that is equipment, rather than a consumer good. Sarah uses the laptop computer for equal purposes, neither of which is primary. If Sarah used the laptop more than 50% of the time for personal matters, the laptop computer would be a "consumer good." But because Sarah's personal use is not dominant, or primary, the laptop computer is deemed "equipment" — the residual classification of "goods." *See* § 9-102(a)(33) (defining "equipment" in the negative). Therefore, **Answer (C) is incorrect.**

    Answer (B) is incorrect because Sarah's checking account (regardless of its primary use) is an intangible "deposit account" under Section 9-102(a)(29). Deposit accounts are expressly excluded from the definition of "goods." *See* § 9-109(a)(44) (last sentence). Because a deposit account is not a "good," it cannot be a "consumer good."

    Answer (D) is incorrect. Sarah's claim is not a good (it is not movable within the meaning of that term). Instead, her claim against a client for unpaid services rendered is an "account" under Section 9-102(a)(2)(ii), unless the claim is evidenced by "chattel paper" or an "instrument" (see clause (i) of the last sentence of the definition of "account").

9. **Answer (B) is the correct answer.** "Investment property" is defined in Section 9-102(a)(49) and includes "a security, whether certificated or uncertificated, security entitlement, [and] securities account[.]" The terms "certificated security," "securities account," "security entitlement," and "uncertificated security" are defined in UCC Article 8. Typical examples of investment property are stocks, bonds, and mutual fund shares that are traded on the securities exchanges. Answer (B) describes shares of capital stock. The fact that the market value is considerably less than Rebecca's original purchase price is irrelevant, a red herring. Without getting bogged down in the intricate definitions of Article 8, it appears that the shares may be a "certificated security" or an "uncertificated security" (depending

on how Myspace originally issued them, and how they are currently held) or perhaps a "securities entitlement" (if the shares were purchased at Rebecca's request by her broker, who manages Rebecca's investment portfolio). Both an "uncertificated security" and a "security entitlement" are examples of investment property, **so Answer (B) is the correct answer.**

Many investors purchase certificates of deposit as an investment. The annual rate of return may not be high, but many investors take comfort in knowing that the investment may be covered by FDIC insurance. Even so, certificates of deposit are not "investment property" as defined by Article 9, but instead are either "instruments" or "deposit accounts" (see Section 9-102, cmt. 12, for further discussion). Therefore, **Answer (A) is incorrect.**

Many individuals buy antiques, figurines, baseball cards, stamps, coins, and other collectibles as an "investment," hopeful that the market value of the items will increase with the passage of time. Perhaps those hopes come true. But the collector's motive, even if investment-driven and realized, does not convert these "goods" into "investment property" as defined by Article 9. Therefore, the baseball autographed by legendary pitcher Sandy Koufax is not "investment property," **so Answer (C) is incorrect.**

As with collectibles, a party may buy real estate as an investment. Rebecca has made a wise investment, based on the considerable appreciation in market value. But Article 9 does not apply to real estate collateral (see Section 9-109(d)(11)), so Sarah's cabin cannot be "investment property," at least within the meaning of Article 9. **Answer (D), then, is incorrect.**

10. **Answer (C) is the correct answer.** Article 9 defines "general intangible" in a negative manner ("... any personal property ... other than ..."), making it the catch-all classification for collateral that does not fall within any of the other Article 9 classifications. A payment right arising from a winning lottery ticket is an "account" under Section 9-102(a)(2)(viii), unless the claim is evidenced by a writing that falls within the definition of "chattel paper" or "instrument." But each of those three terms are excluded from the definition of "general intangible." For this reason, **Answer (C) is the correct answer** (because the question asks you to identify which asset is *not* a "general intangible").

Ellen's claim against the IRS for an unpaid federal tax refund is a "general intangible" because it does not fit within any other type of collateral. **Therefore, Answer (A) is incorrect.** Hopefully, Ellen's claim will ripen into a check (an "instrument" under Section 9-102(a)(47)) or an electronic credit to her bank account ("a deposit account" under Section 9-102(a)(29)). But until the IRS pays the claim, the claim is a general intangible.

Patents, trademarks, and copyrights (even if not registered) are examples of "general intangibles." *See* § 9-102, cmt. 5.d. **Therefore, Answer (B) is incorrect.**

A claim held by a debtor that represents a third party's obligation to repay funds borrowed from the debtor might appear to be an "account." But that term expressly excludes from its definition "rights to payment for money or funds advanced or sold." *See* § 9-102(a)(2) (clause (vi) of last sentence). So Ellen's claim against her brother is not an "account." And because Ellen's claim arises from her brother's oral (rather than written or electronic) promise, her claim cannot be "chattel paper" or an "instrument." By default, then, the claim falls within the definition of "payment intangible," a term defined in Section 9-102(a)(61). Because "payment intangibles" by definition are "general intangibles," **Answer (D) is an incorrect answer.**

11. A "debtor" is the party who has rights, and is granting a security interest, in the collateral. *See* §9-102(a)(28)(A). An "obligor" is the party who is personally liable on the secured debt. *See* §9-102(a)(59)(i). In many secured transactions, a party is both an "obligor" and a "debtor." For example, Tim borrows $10,000 from Bank and signs a promissory note, evidencing his obligation to repay the loan, which is secured by an enforceable security interest granted by Tim in his baseball card collection. Tim is the debtor, and the obligor. On occasion, however, a single party in a secured transaction may not fit both labels. For example, Tim borrows $10,000 from Bank and signs a promissory note, evidencing his obligation to repay the loan. Tim offers no collateral. Bank insists on collateral, however. Tim's friend, Bruce, comes to the rescue and grants to Bank a security interest in Bruce's baseball card collection as collateral for the loan. Bank and Bruce agree that Bruce has no personal liability to repay the loan; only his baseball card collection is at risk. Tim is an obligor, but he is not the debtor (he has no property rights in the collateral). Bruce is the debtor (he is offering the collateral), but he is not an obligor (he has no personal liability).

12. **Answer (B) is the correct answer.** Article 9 defines "registered organization" in Section 9-102(a)(71) as "an organization organized solely under the law of a single State . . . and as to which the State . . . must maintain a public record showing the organization to have been organized." Examples include a limited partnership (Answer (A)), a limited liability company (Answer (C)), and a corporation (Answer (D)). *See* §9-102, cmt. 11 (fifth paragraph). The fact that the entity may be delinquent in paying its property taxes (Answer C)) or in bankruptcy proceedings (Answer (D)) is irrelevant, the proverbial "red herring." So **Answers (A), (C), and (D) are incorrect,** as the question asks you to identify which entity is *not* a registered organization. A sole proprietorship, even one that has complied with any "d/b/a" filing requirements, is not a registered organization (the law does not sever a proprietor's personal identity from the business identity), so **Answer (B) is the correct answer.**

     Also be aware that a general partnership is *not* a registered organization.

13. **Answer (D) is the correct answer.** Section 9-102(a)(9) defines "cash proceeds" as "proceeds that are money, checks, deposit accounts, or the like." The term "proceeds" includes "whatever is acquired upon the sale . . . of collateral." §9-102(a)(64)(A). BizCorp acquired "proceeds" when it sold the unit of inventory to Jessalyn. The proceeds will be "cash proceeds" if Jessalyn purchased the item by paying with money, a check, etc.

     Answer (A) is incorrect. Checks are expressly mentioned as a form of cash proceeds.

     Answer (B) is incorrect. Money is expressly mentioned as a form of cash proceeds, and Article 1 defines "money" in a manner that includes foreign currency.

Answer (C) is incorrect. Checks (whether personal, teller's, or cashier's) are a form of cash proceeds.

Answer (D) is correct. An oral promise to pay for goods sold creates an "account" under Section 9-102(a)(2), a type of collateral that is not mentioned in the definition of "cash proceeds" (nor does it fall within the "or the like" language).

Why is the classification important? Perhaps the most important reason is found in Section 9-315(d)(2), which automatically extends the temporary 20-day perfection period applicable to proceeds if those proceeds are "identifiable cash proceeds." No such automatic extension applies to noncash proceeds.

14. A review of Section 9-102(a)(24) (which defines "consumer-goods transaction") and Section 9-102(a)(26) (which defines "consumer transaction") reveals significant overlap between the two terms. Indeed, the last sentence of the definition of "consumer transaction" states that "[t]he term includes consumer-goods transactions." Both definitions require that the individual incur the secured obligation "primarily for personal, family, or household purposes." Also, both definitions require the presence of collateral. A consumer-goods transaction requires consumer goods as collateral, whereas a consumer transaction requires collateral that "is held or acquired primarily for personal, family, or household purposes." This language is quite similar to the definition of "consumer goods" found in Section 9-102(a)(23) ("goods that are used or bought for use primarily for personal, family, or household purposes"). While consumer goods can serve as collateral in a consumer transaction, the collateral need not be consumer goods. But the non-consumer goods must be "held or acquired primarily for personal, family, or household purposes." What might a consumer debtor offer as collateral that is not a consumer good, and yet be "held or acquired primarily for personal, family, or household purposes"? One example is investment property, such as stocks purchased with personal funds for personal investment. So an example of a consumer transaction that is not a consumer-goods transaction arises if Tim borrows $10,000 to remodel his kitchen and grants a security interest in all of his Netflix stock (held in a personal trading account) to secure repayment of the loan. Another example might be a promissory note secured by real property, held by the consumer for investment purposes.

15. **Answer (A) is the correct answer.** Section 9-102(a)(3) defines "account debtor" as "a person obligated on an account, chattel paper, or general intangible" but does not include a person "obligated to pay a negotiable instrument." The question tests your ability to review ZinnCorp's obligation and determine whether that obligation is an account, chattel paper, a general intangible, or a negotiable instrument (a term defined in UCC Article 3).

Answer (A) states that the promissory note is negotiable. The note is unsecured, which prevents it from being chattel paper. **Answer (A), then, is correct** because the question asks you to identify an obligation on which ZinnCorp will *not* be an "account debtor," and that term excludes obligations evidenced by a negotiable instrument.

Answer (B) is incorrect because the sales contract is chattel paper. The contract evidences not only ZinnCorp's monetary obligation, but also creates in favor of the seller a security interest in the shipment of copier paper. *See* § 9-102(a)(11) (defining "chattel paper"). Therefore, ZinnCorp is an "account debtor."

Answers (C) and (D) are incorrect because both answers describe an "account" under Section 9-102(a)(2)(i). One concern might be that ZinnCorp's payment obligation could be evidenced by a writing that qualifies as chattel paper or an instrument. But Answer (C) refers to an oral agreement, so it remains an "account." And Answer (D) refers to a *non-negotiable, non-transferable* writing, so the writing will not be an "instrument" under Section 9-102(a)(47) and the obligation is *unsecured*, so the writing cannot be "chattel paper" under Section 9-102(a)(11). Because Answers (C) and (D) describe an "account," ZinnCorp is an "account debtor" and **both answers are incorrect.**

16. Section 9-104(a) provides three ways in which Secured Party can achieve "control" of Debtor's deposit account maintained with Bank. The first option, which gives "control" to a secured party that is also the financial institution that maintains the account, is not available to Secured Party because a third party—Bank—maintains the deposit account. The second option is available to Secured Party, though. It requires Secured Party, Debtor, and Bank to authenticate a record in which Bank agrees to honor Secured Party's instructions to liquidate the deposit account without Debtor's further consent. The third option provides Secured Party with "control" if it becomes Bank's "customer" on the deposit account. Section 9-102(b) incorporates the definition of "customer" found in UCC Article 4. Under the definition, Secured Party can become Bank's "customer" (and thereby achieve "control") if the account records at Bank are revised in a manner that names Secured Party as the owner (or perhaps co-owner with Debtor) of the deposit account.

Appreciate that Secured Party can achieve "control" even if Debtor "retains the right to direct the disposition of funds from the deposit account." *See* § 9-104(b). Secured Party should consider under what conditions, if any, Debtor may access the account. For example, may Debtor continue to make deposits, but not make any future withdrawals?

Why does "control" matter? You will find an explanation in Section 9-104, cmt. 2. Essentially, control can be a substitute for authentication under Section 9-203(b), and control is the only way to perfect a security interest in a deposit account (absent a proceeds argument). *See* §§ 9-203(b)(3)(D), 9-312(b)(1). *See also* § 9-327(1) (stating that a security interest in a deposit account subject to control enjoys priority over a security interest in a deposit account not subject to control).

17. **Answer (B) is the correct answer.** Section 9-102(a)(44) defines "goods" as "all things that are movable when a security interest attaches." The last sentence of the definition of "goods" expressly excludes "money" (defined in Section 1-201 in a manner that includes U.S. coins and currency). Therefore, the money in the petty cash drawer is not a "good," **making Answer (B) the correct answer.**

Answer (A) is incorrect. The definition of "goods" expressly includes fixtures. Therefore, a microwave oven—even one that has become a fixture—is a "good." **Answer (A), then, is incorrect** (the question asks you to identify an asset that is *not* a "good").

Answer (C) is incorrect. A person sometimes buys baseball cards, rare books, glassware, and other collectibles for investment reasons. But the investment purpose will not convert these "goods" into "investment property" as defined by Article 9. The rare baseball card remains a "good," regardless of the owner's purpose in purchasing and holding it.

Answer (D) is incorrect. The definition of "goods" expressly includes "the unborn young of animals."

18. **Answer (B) is the correct answer.** Section 9-102(a)(48) defines "inventory," in part, as "goods, other than farm products[.]" The term "farm products" is defined in Section 9-102(a)(34) and will include unpicked tomatoes. At some point, the tomatoes will be picked and then used by the debtor in manufacturing its prize-winning pasta sauce. Sometime after the tomatoes are picked they will become "inventory." But prior to severance from the plants, the tomatoes will be "farm products" (and, therefore, not "inventory"). Thus, **Answer (B) is the correct answer.**

   Answer (A) is incorrect. Section 9-102(a)(48)(A) defines "inventory" to include goods leased by the debtor as lessor. Therefore, vehicles leased by the debtor to customers at an airport site are "inventory," **making Answer (A) incorrect** (the question asks you to identify assets that are *not* "inventory").

   Answer (C) is incorrect. Section 9-102(a)(48)(D) defines "inventory" to include "materials used [up] or consumed in a business." This language will cover office supplies used by faculty and staff at an elementary school.

   Answer (D) is incorrect. Section 9-102(a)(48)(D) defines "inventory" to include "raw materials." This language picks up ingredients (e.g., sugar and chocolate) used by a debtor to make its products (e.g., cookies).

19. Section 9-106(a) states that a person has "control of a certificated security . . . as provided in Section 8-106." Because the facts indicate that the stock certificate is registered in Debtor's name, Section 8-106(b) applies. Secured Party must satisfy two requirements. First, it must take "delivery" of the certificate, a term that is defined in Section 8-301(a) (e.g., Secured Party can take delivery by taking possession of the certificate). Second, Debtor must indorse the certificate (either to Secured Party, or in blank), or the certificate must be registered by the issuer in Secured Party's name (upon either issuance of a new certificate to Secured Party or registration of transfer by Debtor to Secured Party). The goal is to put Secured Party in a position "where it can have the securities sold, without further action by the owner." *See* § 8-106, cmt. 1 (last sentence).

   Why should Secured Party strive to achieve "control" of the stock certificate? The reason is found in Section 9-338(1): a security interest in investment property that is perfected by control enjoys priority over a competing security interest that is not perfected by control (e.g., perfected merely by filing), regardless of the timing of the creation or the perfection of the competing security interest. (Note that the stock certificate is a "certificated security" under Article 8 and, therefore, a form of "investment property" under

Section 9-102(a)(49). Thus, a security interest in the stock certificate may be perfected by filing as well as by control.)

20. **Answer (C) is the correct answer.** Section 9-102(a)(61) defines "payment intangible" as "a general intangible under which the account debtor's principal obligation is a monetary obligation." Notice that a "payment intangible" is a special form of "general intangible." Section 9-102(a)(42) defines "general intangible" in the negative: personal property that is *not*, among other types of collateral, an account, chattel paper, or an instrument. Meredith's one-sentence writing, which evidences her obligation to pay Grace for borrowed money, has created a payment intangible if it has not created an account, instrument, or chattel paper. The writing cannot be an account because Section 9-102(a)(2) excludes from its definition "rights to payment for money or funds advanced." The writing is not an instrument under Section 9-102(a)(47) because (i) it is not a "negotiable instrument" under UCC § 3-104, as it fails to include the so-called words of negotiability required by subsection (a)(1), and (ii) it is not the "type [of writing] that in ordinary course of business is transferred by delivery with any necessary indorsement or assignment." Finally, the writing is not chattel paper because the writing (which is the only writing executed by Meredith) does not evidence a lease obligation or a secured obligation. Absent being an account, an instrument, or chattel paper, the one-sentence writing has created a "payment intangible," **making Answer (C) the correct answer.**

Answer (A) is incorrect. Meredith's oral promise to pay $500 to purchase Grace's sofa has created an "account" under Section 9-102(a)(2). The definition of "general intangible" excludes accounts, so the oral promise has not created a payment intangible.

Answer (B) is incorrect. The negotiable promissory note that Meredith executed to evidence her obligation to pay for the puppy is an "instrument" under Section 9-102(a)(47) (assuming that a "negotiable promissory note" is a "negotiable instrument"). The definition of "general intangible" excludes instruments, so Meredith's writing has not created a payment intangible.

Answer (D) is incorrect. The lease that Meredith executed to evidence her payment obligations arising from her use of Grace's riding lawnmower has created "chattel paper" under Section 9-102(a)(11) (in short, and using these specific facts, a writing that evidences a monetary obligation [the monthly $100 payments] and a lease of goods [the lawnmower]). The definition of "general intangible" excludes chattel paper, so Meredith's writing has not created a payment intangible.

21. Section 9-102(a)(78) defines "supporting obligation" as "a letter-of-credit right or secondary obligation that supports the payment or performance of an account, chattel paper, a document, a general intangible, an instrument, or investment property." An example of such a "secondary obligation" is a third-party guaranty of an account, or a third-party pledge of collateral to secure payment of an instrument. With respect to such secondary obligations, Section 9-203(f) indicates that a secured party's interest in collateral also gives that party "attachment of a security interest in a supporting obligation for the collateral." Assume that Bank obtains an enforceable security interest in a promissory note executed

by Tim and payable to the order of Bruce (the debtor). When Tim executed the note, his parents also executed a guaranty on the note. The note itself is an account, chattel paper, a general intangible, or an instrument. The guaranty, a secondary obligation that supports payment of a payment obligation, is a "supporting obligation." When Bank's security interest attaches to the promissory note, it also attaches to the supporting obligation (the guaranty) for the note.

22. The "lowest intermediate balance rule" is a tracing mechanism used to determine the extent to which a creditor's security interest extends to the balance in a debtor's deposit account that holds both proceeds and non-proceeds. The rule requires a review of the activity (debits and credits) in the deposit account. Under the rule, the debtor is presumed to spend its own money (non-proceeds) first. If, under the rule, the debtor is deemed to have spent some of the creditor's proceeds, the creditor can "recover" those proceeds through subsequent deposits if, but only if, those subsequent deposits themselves represent proceeds.

One or more examples elsewhere in this study guide offer you the opportunity to apply the rule to a fact pattern.

23. **Answer (C) is the correct answer.** Article 8 offers a definition of "entitlement holder." *See* § 8-102(a)(7). Reading that definition, together with the companion definitions of "security entitlement" and "securities intermediary," reveals that the entitlement holder can be viewed as a broker's customer. In this question, MegaCorp is ZinnMark's customer. As the customer on a broker-managed investment portfolio account, MegaCorp is the entitlement holder on that account, **making Answer (C) the correct answer.**

SubCorp is nothing more than the issuer of the certificate evidencing 1,000 shares of its capital stock.

ZinnMark is the securities intermediary, as discussed in the answer to the next question.

Answer (A) is incorrect. SubCorp is an issuer, but the facts do not suggest that SubCorp is the customer on any broker-managed investment account. Therefore, it is not an entitlement holder.

Answer (B) is incorrect. ZinnMark is the broker on a broker-managed investment account, making it a securities intermediary, rather than the entitlement holder.

Answer (D) is incorrect for the same reasons that Answers (A) and (B) are incorrect.

24. **Answer (C) is the correct answer.** Article 8 offers a definition of "securities intermediary." *See* § 8-102(a)(14). Reading that definition, together with the companion definitions of "entitlement holder" and security entitlement," reveals that the securities intermediary can be viewed as the broker on a broker-managed investment portfolio account. In this question, then, ZinnMark is the securities intermediary, **making Answer (C) the correct answer.**

Answer (A) is incorrect. SubCorp is an issuer, but the facts do not suggest that SubCorp is the broker on any broker-managed investment account. Therefore, it is not a securities intermediary.

Answer (B) is incorrect. MegaCorp is the customer on a broker-managed investment account, making it an entitlement holder, rather than a securities intermediary.

Answer (D) is incorrect for the same reason that Answer (B) is incorrect.

25. A "strict foreclosure" is a colloquial term given to the post-default remedy that allows a secured party to propose to the debtor that the secured party will keep all or some of the collateral and forgive all or part of the unpaid secured debt. The technical term under article 9 is "acceptance." The governing statutes are Sections 9-620, 9-621, and 9-622.

26. The term "recognized market" may arise in an Article 9 context after the debtor has defaulted. Article 9 permits a secured party to dispose of the collateral after the debtor has defaulted. *See* § 9-610(a). Generally, the secured party must give notice of the intended disposition to the debtor (and perhaps others). *See* § 9-611(b). However, notice is excused if the collateral "is of a type customarily sold on a recognized market." *See* § 9-611(b). Guidance on the meaning of the term, and an example, are found in Section 9-610, cmt. 9.

27. **Answer (A) is the correct answer.** Section 9-109(a)(2) brings "agricultural liens" within the scope of Article 9. Section 9-102(a)(34) defines the term, in relevant part, as "an interest in farm products."

Answer (B) is incorrect because Section 9-102(a)(44) defines "goods" in a manner that includes more than just farm products (e.g., equipment).

Answer (C) is incorrect. Crops can be a farm product, but farm products include more than just crops. *See* § 9-102(a)(34) (defining "farm products").

Answer (D) is incorrect. Livestock can be a farm product, but farm products include more than just livestock. *See* § 9-102(a)(34) (defining "farm products").

Attachment

28. **Answer (B) is the correct answer.** Article 9 uses "attachment" (or variations of that word) as a synonym for enforceability. *See* § 9-203(a), (b).

     Answer (A) is incorrect. A security interest can be enforceable and yet be unperfected.

     Answer (C) is incorrect. The enforceability of a security interest does not turn on its priority (over a lien creditor, or any other party).

     Answer (D) is incorrect. Many security interests will be memorialized in writing, but that is not a requirement for enforceability/attachment. For example, the parties may create an enforceable security interest under an oral agreement if the secured party takes possession of the collateral. *See* § 9-203(b)(3)(B). Furthermore, even if the parties memorialize their agreement in writing, the security interest will not attach at the moment of written memorialization if the other two attachment conditions have not yet been satisfied. *See* § 9-203(b)(1), (2).

29. **Answer (C) is the correct answer.** A "security interest" is defined as "an interest in personal property or fixtures[.]" § 1-201(b)(35) (first sentence).

     Answer (A) is incorrect. Section 9-203(b)(1) requires value to be given. In many transactions, the secured party will give value to the debtor, the party offering the collateral. But the secured party can give value to a non-debtor (and not give any value to the debtor). For example, Tim borrows money from Bank. Tim offers no collateral. Tim's friend, Bruce, offers collateral. Bank gave value (the loan proceeds) to Tim (the non-debtor), rather than to Bruce (the debtor). *See also* § 9-102, cmt. 2.a.

     Answer (B) is incorrect. In many transactions, the debtor will own the collateral. But Section 9-203(b)(2) does not require the debtor to own the collateral. That Section merely requires the debtor to have "rights in the collateral or the power to transfer rights in the collateral[.]" For example, assume that Tim is leasing a piano from Dealer. Tim offers his rights in the piano to secure a loan from Bruce. Tim, as lessee, does not own the piano (Dealer continues to own the piano). But Tim's leasehold interest gives him a sufficient property interest in the piano to allow it to serve as collateral. (By offering the piano as collateral, however, Tim may be violating the lease agreement with Dealer.)

     Answer (D) is incorrect. In many transactions, the debtor will authenticate a security agreement that adequately describes the collateral, satisfying the "agreement" requirement of Section 9-203(b)(3). *See* § 9-203(b)(3)(A). But the parties can satisfy the "agreement" prong of attachment by taking other action mentioned in Section 9-203(b)(3)(B), (C), or (D).

30. **Answer (D) is the correct answer.** Section 9-203(b)(3)(A) requires the parties to include only two pieces of information in the written security agreement: the debtor's authentication (*see* Section 9-102(a)(7), defining "authenticate" to include a signature), and a description of the collateral. The written security agreement need not state any final payment date, regardless of the contractual length of the loan. **Therefore Answer (D) is the correct answer.**

    Answer (A) is incorrect. Section 9-108 addresses acceptable descriptions of collateral. Section 9-108(c) condemns a "supergeneric" description, such as the one posed in Answer (A). (Note, however, that "supergeneric" collateral descriptions *are* permitted in financing statements. *See* § 9-504(2).)

    Answer (B) is incorrect. Section 9-203(b)(3)(A) does not require the security agreement to provide the location of tangible assets (although the statute does require "a description of the land concerned" if the collateral includes "timber to be cut"). At least two problems might arise if the statute did require the agreement to provide locations. First, mistakes in the location (e.g., a transposition error in a street address) might trigger attachment challenges. Second, any relocation of collateral to previously unmentioned locations might place on the secured party a duty to monitor collateral locations (and then . . . amend the security agreement?).

    Answer (C) is incorrect. Section 9-203(b)(3)(A) does not require the security agreement to mention the amount of original principal, the interest rate, any scheduled payment dates, or any other details of the secured debt. The parties can include such details, but their omission does not prevent the security interest from becoming enforceable and attaching.

31. **Answer (D) is the correct answer.** For attachment, Section 9-203(b)(3)(A) requires the debtor, and only the debtor, to authenticate (e.g., sign) the security agreement. ZinnCorp is the only party offering collateral, making it the only "debtor." Therefore, only ZinnCorp must sign the security agreement for purposes of attachment, **making Answer (D) the correct answer.**

    BigBank and Smith *may* authenticate the security agreement (particularly if the agreement obligates BigBank or Smith to take, or refrain from taking, certain action), but authentication by the secured party or a guarantor is not necessary for attachment. Therefore, **Answers (A), (B), and (C) are incorrect answers** because they include in their responses BigBank, Smith, or both.

32. **Answer (C) is the correct answer.** Section 9-203(b)(3)(A) states that a written security agreement must provide "a description of the collateral." That statute offers no other guidance on the quoted language. Guidance, though, is found elsewhere. Section 9-108

("Sufficiency of Description") offers the general rule that the collateral description is "sufficient . . . if it reasonably identifies what is described." § 9-108(a). Therefore, **Answer (C) is correct** because it adopts the "reasonably identifies" standard, and **Answers (A), (B), and (D) are incorrect** because they adopt some other erroneous standard.

Answer (B) also is incorrect because Section 9-108 states that a description of the collateral can be "sufficient, whether or not it is specific[.]" § 9-108(a).

Answer (D) suggests that the parties must utilize Article 9's defined terms, such as "inventory" and "equipment." Section 9-108(b)(3) *permits* the parties to use those terms (with few exceptions), but the statute *does not require* the parties to do so, offering another reason why **Answer (D) is incorrect**.

33. **Answer (A) is the correct answer.** Section 9-108(a) states that a collateral description is sufficient if it "reasonably identifies what is described." Section 9-108(b) gives examples of reasonable identification, permitting descriptions by type of collateral, "except as otherwise provided in subsection (e)." Subsection (e) states: "A description only by type of collateral defined in [the Uniform Commercial Code] is an insufficient description of: (1) a commercial tort claim[.]" Thus, **Answer (A) is the correct answer.** The policy is explained in cmt. 5: "Subsection (e) requires greater specificity of description in order to prevent debtors from inadvertently encumbering certain property." Comment 5 also offers an example of an acceptable description of a commercial tort claim.

The limitation in Section 9-108(e) does not apply to security entitlements (except in a consumer transaction, which this is not because the debtor is not a consumer), negotiable instruments, or general intangibles, so **Answers (B), (C), and (D) are incorrect answers.**

34. **Answer (C) is the correct answer.** Section 9-204(a) approves the use of an after-acquired property clause, which negates any need for the parties to negotiate or authenticate a security agreement each and every time the debtor buys more inventory or equipment, generates new accounts, etc. The statute does not expressly state the date to which the "after" in "after-acquired property clause" refers. But the general understanding is that the "after" refers to any time after the moment when the debtor executes, or otherwise authenticates, the security agreement. That understanding makes sense, given that the clause cannot exist apart from the security agreement itself, and it is the security agreement that initially specifies the collateral. Section 9-204, cmt. 4 also supports that understanding. Therefore, **Answer (C) is correct** because it refers to the date on which ZinnCorp authenticates the security agreement. **Answers (A), (B), and (D) are incorrect** because they refer to some other date.

35. **Answer (A) is the correct answer.** Section 9-203(b)(3)(B) permits oral security agreements, but only if the secured party takes possession of the collateral (or, under clause (C), the secured party takes delivery of a certificated security).

Answer (D) is incorrect because it suggests that oral security agreements frustrate attachment. But that is false. Oral security agreements are permissible if the secured party takes possession of the collateral. § 9-203(b)(3)(B).

Answers (B) and (C) are incorrect because they suggest that oral security agreements are permissible even if the collateral is intangible. That is false. The collateral must be tangible, and the secured party must take possession or delivery of it. § 9-203(b)(3)(B), (C).

Answer (C) also is incorrect because it suggests that oral security agreements will not cover after-acquired property. Neither Section 9-203(b)(3)(B) nor Section 9-204 include any such limitation. But the secured party must remember to take possession or delivery of the collateral.

One might ask why this matters, if both BigBank and ZinnCorp agree that security was granted. One key situation in which this would matter is if ZinnCorp would file bankruptcy. The bankruptcy trustee would not be bound by ZinnCorp's consent.

36. Grace will have an enforceable security interest in all of the household furnishings, other than the sofa.

   As a general rule, Article 9 permits a debtor to grant a security interest in collateral that the debtor acquires after it authenticates the security agreement, by including in the agreement an after-acquired property clause. *See* § 9-204(a). But in an effort to discourage a creditor's predatory practices, Article 9 renders ineffective an after-acquired property clause that attempts to encumber consumer goods acquired by the debtor more than 10 days after the creditor has given value. *See* §§ 9-204(a), (b).

   Meredith's household furnishings are consumer goods as defined in Section 9-102(a)(23) (goods that she has acquired primarily for a "personal, family, or household" purpose). Grace made the $3,000 loan on July 4, when she delivered the check to Meredith, so the after-acquired property clause will not encumber furnishings that Meredith acquired after July 14 (notice that the 10-day period commences when Grace gives value, not when Meredith authenticates the security agreement). The first four purchases are timely, each having occurred no later than July 14, so Grace will have an enforceable security interest in those furnishings. But the final purchase, which fell on July 15, is untimely (having occurred after July 14), so Grace will not have an enforceable security interest in the sofa.

37. Because the security agreement failed to include a future advance clause, Hoover Finance will have a secured claim no greater than the initial loan of $2 million. The security agreement did include an after-acquired property clause, so the value of the collateral is $2.25 million. Because the value of the available collateral meets or exceeds the unpaid initial $2 million loan, Hoover Finance has a fully secured claim for that amount, but no more. Hoover Finance also has an unsecured claim of $600,000 (the sum of the April and August advances). The surplus collateral value of $250,000 does *not* secure Hoover Finance's two unsecured loans because the parties failed to include a future advance clause in their contract.

38. The security agreement included a future advance clause, so Hoover Finance might have a secured claim equal to the sum of all advances: $2.6 million. But the security agreement failed to include an after-acquired property clause, so the collateral is limited to the

equipment owned by ZeeCo on the date of the agreement: $1.7 million. Therefore, Hoover Finance has a secured claim of $1.7 million, and an unsecured claim of $900,000 (total debt of $2.6 million, minus the secured claim of $1.7 million). Hoover Finance has no security interest in the road grader or the bulldozer acquired by ZeeCo in May and June, respectively, because the parties failed to include an after-acquired property clause in the contract.

39.   **Answer (C) is the correct answer.** Sarah has given value of $5,000, and Helen has rights in the jewelry, so Sarah will have an enforceable security interest in the jewelry if the parties satisfy one of the four "security agreement" conditions of Section 9-203(b)(3). The third and fourth options (Sections 9-203(b)(3)(C) and (D)) are inapplicable because the jewelry is not a deposit account, electronic chattel paper, investment property, or a letter-of-credit right, and the first option (Section 9-203(b)(3)(A)) is not met because the parties are relying on an oral agreement rather than an authenticated agreement. The parties can rely on an oral security agreement under Section 9-203(b)(3)(B) if the jewelry "is in the possession of the secured party[.]" Therefore, **Answer (C) is the correct answer.**

Answer (A) is incorrect because Section 9-203(b)(3)(B) does not condition the permissibility of oral security agreements on the amount of debt.

Answer (B) is incorrect because Section 9-203(b)(3)(B) permits oral security agreements even if the collateral consists of consumer goods.

Answer (D) is incorrect because Section 9-109, the "scope" provision of Article 9, does not include any dollar threshold test. Nor does Section 9-203 include any such test.

40.   **Answer (D) is the correct answer.** Article 9 permits a debtor to offer a deposit account as collateral, subject to the notable exception found in Section 9-109(d)(13): the transaction cannot be a "consumer transaction." (The policy for the exception is probably rooted in a concern that most humans need unfettered access to a deposit account to buy food and clothing, to pay bills, and to otherwise function in society on a daily basis.) Section 9-102(a)(26) defines "consumer transaction" in a manner that requires the consumer debtor to (i) incur the secured debt primarily for a personal, family, or household reason *and* (ii) hold or acquire the collateral primarily for a personal, family, or household reason. Helen is using the loan proceeds for a business purpose in Answer (D), so the transaction contemplated by Answer (D) is not a "consumer transaction." In the absence of a "consumer transaction," the prohibition found in Section 9-109(d)(13) does not apply. Even so, the oral understanding must satisfy one of the four "security agreement" options of Section 9-203(b)(3). Because Helen maintains her personal checking account (a "deposit account" under Section 9-102(a)(29)) with Puritan Bank, the secured party, Puritan Bank has "control" of the checking account under Section 9-104(a)(1). Because Puritan Bank has control of Helen's checking account, their oral understanding suffices as the security agreement under Section 9-203(b)(3)(D). Therefore, Puritan Bank has an enforceable security interest in Helen's checking account if Helen uses the loan proceeds for a business purpose (regardless of the primary use of the checking account itself), **making Answer (D) the correct answer.**

Answer (A) is incorrect because Article 9 does not always require a written security agreement when the collateral is a deposit account. As noted in the preceding paragraph, an oral understanding can suffice in certain situations.

Answer (B) is incorrect because Article 9 permits a deposit account to serve as collateral if the transaction is *not* a consumer transaction. *See* § 9-109(d)(13).

Answer (C) is incorrect because Section 9-203(b)(3) nowhere conditions the effectiveness of an oral security agreement on the type of debtor.

41. **Answer (B) is the correct answer.** The collateral description turns on the *debtor's* use. The use of the debtor's *customers* is irrelevant. The debtor is BAMCO, a corporation. In its hands, the musical instruments are inventory under Section 9-102(a)(48)(B) (goods held for sale). Therefore, **Answer (B) is correct.**

It is irrelevant that BAMCO sells the musical instruments to customers who may use them as equipment or consumer goods. Therefore, **Answer (C) is incorrect.**

The inventory is "goods," but "goods" is a much broader term. *See* § 9-102(a)(44). For example, describing the collateral as "goods" will include BAMCO's equipment as collateral, perhaps a result not intended by BAMCO. Therefore, **Answer (D) is incorrect.**

A piano, a guitar, a trombone, etc., are all examples of an "instrument" as that term is used in everyday conversation (e.g., "What instrument do you play?"). But "instrument" has a completely different meaning under Article 9, most often referring to payment rights evidenced by promissory notes and checks (and certainly not musical instruments). *See* § 9-102(a)(47). For this reason, **Answer (A) is incorrect.** (But describing the collateral as "musical instruments" is acceptable.)

42. **Answer (C) is the correct answer.** Section 9-204(b) offers two cases in which an after-acquired property clause is ineffective. In one case, the clause will not reach out and encumber consumer goods (which is inapplicable to this question, as it involves a corporate debtor). *See* § 9-204(b)(1). In the other case, the clause will not encumber future commercial tort claims. *See* § 9-204(b)(2). Section 9-204(b) renders the after-acquired property clause ineffective only in these two cases. Answer (C) references commercial tort claims, **making Answer (C) the correct answer.**

Answer (A) is incorrect because Section 9-204(b) does not render ineffective an after-acquired property clause to letter-of-credit rights.

Answer (B) is incorrect because Section 9-204(b) does not render ineffective an after-acquired property clause to money.

Answer (D) is incorrect because Section 9-204(b) does not render ineffective an after-acquired property clause to deposit accounts.

43. **Answer (D) is the correct answer.** Bank had an enforceable security interest in the jewelry, so Section 9-203(f) extends the security interest to proceeds, if provided by Section 9-315. Section 9-315(a)(2) extends Bank's security interest "to any identifiable proceeds." Section 9-102(a)(64) defines "proceeds" to include claims for loss of collateral, and insurance payable for loss of the collateral, in each instance capped at the value of the collateral. § 9-102(a)(64(D), (E). The value of the stolen collateral in this question is $8,000, which is the highest amount in the checking account that Bank can claim. The challenge for Bank is to "identify" that portion of the total balance of $21,500, which represents its $8,000 claim. Section 9-315(b)(2) informs Bank that the mere act of commingling proceeds and non-proceeds in the checking account does not automatically frustrate Bank's ability to identify a particular piece of the checking account as its proceeds. But the statute does place on Bank the burden of identifiability through an appropriate tracing mechanism (e.g., lowest intermediate balance rule, first-in-first-out, last-in-first-out, etc.). In a "best case" scenario, Bank may have an enforceable security interest in the checking account, capped at no more than $8,000 (the amount of the insurance claim and check attributable to stolen jewelry collateral). Therefore, **Answer (D) is the correct answer.** Appreciate, however, that the amount could be less than $8,000, depending on the equitable rule adopted by the court, further activity in the account, the timing of the determination, etc.

Answer (A) is an incorrect answer. Section 9-315(b)(2) permits a security interest to attach to commingled proceeds if the secured party meets its burden of proof on identifiability through an appropriate tracing method.

Answer (B) is incorrect. Section 9-109(d)(8) excludes from Article 9 coverage "a transfer of an interest in or an assignment of a claim under a policy of insurance," but the statute retains jurisdiction over insurance-related collateral premised on a "proceeds" theory (which is Bank's argument).

Answer (C) is incorrect for two reasons. First, there is no assurance that Bank "has" any security interest in any part of the checking account. The statute requires Bank to satisfy a tracing duty, which remains questionable. Second, even if Bank does satisfy its tracing duty, its security interest is capped at the amount traceable to its collateral ($8,000); its interest will not extend to the entire $21,500 in the checking account.

Perfection

44.   **Answer (A) is the correct answer.** Unlike the filing rules under pre-2001 Article 9, the current version of Article 9 adopts a "single filing" rule for non-fixtures. The place to search, then, is the same place to file. Section 9-301(1) states that BigBanc, the secured party, should file its financing statement in the jurisdiction where Friendly Furniture Corp., the debtor, is located. Section 9-307 states where a debtor is located, and generally classifies debtors by their form of organization. Friendly is a corporation, so it is a "registered organization" under Section 9-102(a)(71). Under the 2010 amendments to Article 9, an organization is a registered organization if it is formed or organized under the law of a state by the filing of a public record with the state (this is slightly different from the 2001 Version of Article 9, which defined a registered organization as one in which a state was merely being required to maintain a public record showing that the organization has been organized).

Under Section 9-307(e), a registered organization is located in its state of incorporation. Friendly is organized under California law by the filing of articles of incorporation there, so BigBanc will file—and need only search—in California. Therefore, **Answer (A) is the correct answer.** BigBanc need not search in Nevada or Arizona (because a registered organization only has one location), **making Answer (B) incorrect.** The location of a debtor's chief executive office may be relevant if the debtor is not a registered organization (see Section 9-307(b)(3)), but Friendly is a registered organization, so **Answer (C) is incorrect.** In addition, the location of a corporate debtor's operations is irrelevant when the debtor is a registered organization, **making Answer (D) incorrect.**

Among other things, BigBanc is taking a security interest in Friendly's equipment. Equipment can be a "fixture" as that term is defined in Section 9-102(a)(41). If BigBanc is concerned about possible priority disputes with Friendly's real estate creditors, it should file (and, therefore, also search) for fixture filings, which are recorded in the county where the relevant real estate is located. *See* §§ 9-501(a)(1), 9-334. For this reason, BigBanc may wish to search the county records in counties where Friendly has physical operations in California, Nevada, and Arizona. But the facts of this question focus attention on non-fixture encumbrances.

45.   **Answer (A) is the correct answer.** Section 9-523 addresses search inquiries. Subsection (c) obligates the filing officer to provide particular information, and subsection (e) requires the filing officer to respond "not later than two business days after the filing office receives the request." In this question, the filing officer received the lawyer's request on Wednesday, July 22. Therefore, the filing officer must communicate the results of its search to the lawyer no later than two business days later, or Friday, July 24. For this reason, **Answer**

(A) is correct, and the other suggested dates, all erroneous, **make Answers (B), (C), and (D) incorrect.**

46.   **Answer (C) is the correct answer.** A searcher wants timely information. Information that is stale exposes the searcher to the risk that another creditor has filed (or may file) a financing statement after the date of the report (which may prevent the searcher, who has yet to file, from enjoying priority). Section 9-523(c) addresses this concern by requiring the filing office to provide a report that is current as of a date "not . . . earlier than three business days before the filing office receives the request[.]" In this question, the filing officer received the lawyer's request on Wednesday, July 22, so the search report must provide information through a date no earlier than three business days before that date, or Friday, July 17. For this reason, **Answer (C) is correct,** and the other suggested dates, all erroneous, **make Answers (A), (B), and (D) incorrect.**

47.   **Answer (C) is the correct answer.** Sometimes filings are innocently recorded against the wrong entity (this could result, for example, if the preparer used an incorrect name, which happened to be the name of a third party). And sometimes filings are intentionally, but fraudulently or maliciously, filed against a particular party. Section 9-518 addresses inaccurate or wrongfully filed financing statements and permits the affected party to file an "information statement." The statement must cross-reference the filing number of the filing to which it relates, state that it is being filed as an information statement, and offer an explanation of the problem. A party named in a record filed with the filing office (such as a debtor or a secured party) can file the information statement unilaterally, **making Answer (C) the correct answer and Answer (B) an incorrect answer.** The information statement need not be executed or otherwise authenticated by a different party (such as the party whose name is reflected as "debtor" on the earlier filing), **making Answer (D) an incorrect answer.** And the affected party does not file a "termination statement" (a filing addressed by Section 9-513 and reserved for a different matter), **making Answer (A) an incorrect answer.**

Friendly's general counsel should note that an information statement does not remove the other filings from the public records or otherwise terminate their effectiveness. *See* § 9-518(e). It merely permits the general counsel to explain the alleged problem in the public records. As noted in Section 9-518, cmt. 3, though, the general counsel may resort to other law for further redress as needed.

Note also that the 2010 amendments to Article 9 changed the name of the document referred to in Section 9-518. Before 2010 it was called a "correction statement;" after 2010, it is called an "information statement."

48.   **Answer (B) is the correct answer.** After-acquired property clauses (and future advance clauses) permitted by Section 9-204 should be written into the security agreement, but need not be referenced in the financing statement. *See* §§ 9-204, cmt. 7; 9-502, cmt. 2 (last paragraph). Therefore, **Answer (B) is the correct answer.**

Section 9-501 permits a secured party to perfect its security interest in fixtures by filing its financing statement either centrally (subsection (a)(2)), or locally (subsection (a)(1)).

Therefore **Answer (A) is incorrect.** As you may discover later, however, a secured party that relies on a central, rather than a local, filing may not enjoy priority in fixtures if the competing claimant is a real estate creditor. *See generally* § 9-334 (sometimes awarding priority to a secured party that has timely filed a "fixture filing," which — under Section 9-501(a)(1) — is filed locally in the county where the affected real estate is located, rather than centrally).

Under Section 9-509(a), Friendly (as the debtor) must *authorize* the financing statement. But in an effort to accommodate electronic filing, the current version of Article 9 departs from the predecessor statute and no longer requires Friendly, as the debtor, to sign, execute, or otherwise *authenticate* the financing statement. *See* § 9-502, cmt. 3. Therefore, **Answer (C) is incorrect.**

The secured party may file its financing statement before the debtor authenticates the security agreement. *See* § 9-502(d). So **Answer (D) is incorrect.** This act (sometimes referred to as "pre-filing") cannot perfect a security interest prior to its attachment because perfection requires attachment. *See* § 9-308(a). Also, the debtor must authorize any pre-filing, which may raise concerns if the parties are squabbling over what will serve as collateral or the debtor has yet to authenticate the security agreement. *See* §§ 9-509(a) (requiring the debtor to authorize any filing), 9-509(b) (providing such authorization through the debtor's authentication of the security agreement).

49. **Answer (B) is the correct answer.** Section 9-502(a) requires a financing statement to include the names of both the debtor and the secured party (or, if applicable, the secured party's agent). Therefore, **Answer (B) is correct.** The same statute also requires the financing statement to include a collateral description. Unlike the description that must be found in the security agreement, however, the description in the financing statement may be supergeneric, such as "all assets" or "all of the debtor's personal property." *See* § 9-504 and cmt. 2. Therefore **Answer (C) is incorrect.** As to the amount of any debt secured, the financing statement does not need to describe the secured debt (and the parties may have legitimate reasons for not disclosing the terms in the public records), so **Answer (A) is incorrect.** Indeed, there is no blank or box on the official form for such information. Finally, as previously noted, BigBanc must file its financing statement against Friendly, which is a corporation (and thus a registered organization), only in the state of Friendly's incorporation (California), rather than in any (or every) state in which it or the collateral has a physical presence. *See* §§ 9-301(1), 9-307(e). For this reason, **Answer (D) is incorrect.**

50. **Answer (C) is the correct answer.** While it is accurate that Section 9-509 requires that all financing statements be authorized, Section 9-509(b) states that "[b]y authenticating or becoming bound as debtor by a security agreement, a debtor . . . authorizes the filing of an initial financing statement . . . covering: [¶] (1) the collateral described in the security agreement. . . ." So when Friendly signed the loan and security agreement, that act of authentication (the signing) authorized the previously filed financing statement, regardless of Friendly's stated position (until that signing, however, the filing was unauthorized). This ipso facto authorization-by-authentication means that **Answer (A) and Answer (B) are**

not correct. Section 9-509's authorization, however, only extends as far as the collateral actually specified in the security agreement. It is like having two filters, and the filter with the smallest holes (here, inventory as opposed to all assets) will describe the scope of authorization. As a result, **Answer (D) is incorrect** as it is too broad. *See* § 9-509, cmt. 4 (Examples 1 & 2).

51. A filing officer does not have unfettered discretion when deciding whether to accept or reject a financing statement. Section 9-520(a) says that a "filing office *shall* refuse to accept a record for filing for a reason set forth in Section 9-516(b) and may refuse to accept a record for filing *only* for a reason set forth in Section 9-516(b)." This somewhat ungainly language seeks to bind a filing officer to check the proffered filing to see if it complies with Section 9-516(b). If it does, the filing officer must accept it; if not, the filing officer must reject it.

The primary reasons listed in Section 9-516(b) for rejection of an initial financing statement include:

- The financing statement is sent by a method not authorized by the filing office (if, for example, BigBanc tried to send in a financing statement by email attachment when the filing office had not authorized email filing) — § 9-516(b)(1)

- The filer fails to tender the appropriate filing fee — § 9-516(b)(2)

- The financing statement fails to provide the debtor's name — § 9-516(b)(3)(A)

- The financing statement lists a debtor as an individual, but does not provide that individual's surname — § 9-516(b)(3)(C)

- The financing statement does not give both the name of the secured party and the secured party's mailing address — § 9-516(b)(4)

- The financing statement does not provide the mailing address of the debtor — § 9-516(b)(5)(A)

- The financing statement fails to indicate whether the named debtor is an individual or an organization — § 9-516(b)(5)(B)

Any three of these reasons would be responsive to the question posed. But the following four remarks should be kept in mind — acceptance or rejection has limitations and various consequences:

- First, the rejection rules generally focus attention on the complete omission of information, rather than the inclusion of incorrect information.

- Second, notwithstanding the filing officer's mandate to reject a filing for a *proper* reason, Section 9-520(c) says that if the filing officer accepts such a filing, then the filing is "effective" (that is, if it otherwise meets the requirements of Section 9-502(a) by stating the name of the debtor and the name of the secured party, and identifying the collateral).

- Third, Section 9-516(d) states that if the filing officer rejects a filing for an *improper* reason, then the rejected filing "is effective as a filed record except as against a purchaser of the collateral which gives value in reasonable reliance upon the absence of the record from the files."

- And fourth, whenever the filing officer rejects (properly or wrongfully) a filing, the officer must timely communicate the rejection to the filing party no later than two business days after rejection. *See* § 9-520(b).

52. **Answer (D) is the correct answer.** Article 9 takes the position that a financing statement is more than just the first piece of paper filed. Section 9-102(a)(39) states that "'Financing statement' means a record or records composed of an initial financing statement and any filed record relating to the initial financing statement." Two things are noteworthy here. First, the definition refers to "record or records," meaning that despite the usual of the singular "statement," a "financing *statement*" can consist of many documents. Second, the financing statement includes any record "related to the initial financing statement," meaning that the list of documents that may be included is not limited to the official forms that appear in Section 9-521. The all-inclusive definition thus means that **Answers (A), (B), and (C) are each incorrect**, as each one of them excludes different records filed that relate to the initial financing statement.

53. **Answer (B) is the correct answer.** As a general rule, a financing statement will perfect a security interest in all collateral. *See* § 9-310(a). There are notable exceptions, however. These include:

- collateral, such as an airplane or a ship, that is subject to federal registration (*see* § 9-311(a)(1));

- vehicles that are *not* held by the debtor as inventory and are otherwise subject to certificate-of-title laws (*see* §§ 9-311(a)(2) and 9-311(d));

- deposit accounts (as original collateral) and letter-of-credit rights, which require "control" (*see* § 9-312(b)(1), (2)); and

- money (as original collateral), which requires possession by the creditor (*see* § 9-312(b)(3)).

Friendly's fleet of delivery trucks will be equipment, rather than inventory. So BigBanc must comply with applicable certificate-of-title laws to obtain perfection; its financing statement will not suffice. Therefore, **Answer (B) is the correct answer.**

A domain name is an example of a "general intangible" as defined in Section 9-102(a)(42). A filing will perfect a security interest in general intangibles. Therefore, BigBanc's filing will perfect its security interest in Friendly's domain name, **making Answer (A) an incorrect answer.**

As noted in the first paragraph above, a security interest in a bank account (a "deposit account" under Article 9 terminology) as original collateral can be perfected *only* by control. *See* § 9-312(b)(1). The statutory language does not turn on the presence or absence of FDIC insurance coverage. **Therefore, Answer (C) is incorrect.**

A security interest in investment property (whether or not subject to federal or state regulatory oversight) may be perfected by filing. *See* § 9-312(a). Under Section 9-102(a)(49), "'[i]nvestment property' means a security, whether certificated or uncertificated, security entitlement, [or] securities account . . ." Therefore, **Answer (D) is incorrect** (because the question asks you to identify collateral in which a security interest *cannot* be perfected by filing).

54. **Answer (D) is the correct answer.** Receivables owed by customers for goods bought are an example of an "account" under Section 9-102(a)(2). Sometimes a writing is produced at the close of the transaction, but that writing is merely evidence of the obligation; it cannot be an "instrument" or "chattel paper" as those terms are defined in Sections 9-102(a)(47) and 9-102(a)(11), respectively, because no security interest is taken or retained (thus eliminating classification as an instrument), and the writing contains more than just a simple promise to pay (thus eliminating classification as an instrument). Therefore, Big-Banc cannot perfect its security interest in the receivables by possessing the writings (as it could if the obligations were chattel paper or instruments), leaving its financing statement as the sole method of perfection. For this reason, **Answer (D) is the correct answer.**

Cash (paper money and coins, *but not checks*) is "money" under Section 1-201(b)(24) (incorporated by reference into Article 9 via Section 9-102(c)). A secured party can perfect a security interest in money as original collateral only by taking possession of it. Filing is ineffective. *See* § 9-312(b)(3). Therefore, **Answer (A) is incorrect.**

Article 9 does not apply to the assignment of a beneficiary's payment rights under a life insurance policy. *See* § 9-109(d)(8). Therefore, BigBanc's filing will not perfect any property interest that it can claim in Friendly's rights under the policy, **making Answer (B) an incorrect answer.**

The lease contracts, which most likely evidence the lessee's monetary obligation and describe the furniture being leased, are "chattel paper" as defined in Section 9-102(a)(11). A security interest in chattel paper can indeed be perfected by filing. *See* § 9-312(a). But filing is not the *exclusive* method. BigBanc also can perfect its security interest by taking possession of the contracts. *See* § 9-313(a). Therefore, **Answer (C) is incorrect.**

55. **Answer (C) is the correct answer.** Subject to rare exceptions (which are inapplicable to our questions), a financing statement is effective for five years. *See* § 9-515(a). The effectiveness of the original filing (usually a UCC-1 form) can be extended for an additional five-year period by the timely filing of a continuation statement (usually a UCC-3 form, with the "continuation" box checked). To be timely, the continuation statement must be filed "within six months before the expiration of the five-year period." § 9-515(d). The filing officer recorded BigBanc's financing statement on November 1, 2018, so the filing is effective for the five-year period thereafter (concluding on October 31, 2023). The six-month period runs from April 30 through October 31, 2023, so the correct answer must be a date that falls within that period. The date of June 1, 2023, is such a date, so **Answer (C) is correct.** Filing dates after November, 2023 are too late, so **Answer (B) is incorrect.** In addition, a continuation statement filed before the six-month period (that is, during

the first 4½ years after the initial filing) is ineffective (see § 9-510(c)), so the November 2, 2018 filing, found in **Answer (A), is incorrect**. Finally, the filing period for continuation statements does not turn on the amount of principal outstanding on any particular date, so **Answer (D) is incorrect.**

56. **Answer (C) is the correct answer.** A continuation statement that is not filed within the six-month period provided by Section 9-515 "is ineffective." *See* § 9-510(c). This is so, even though the "notice" function is served by the original filing and the tardy continuation statement. Because BigBanc has not timely filed its continuation statement, the effectiveness of BigBanc's original filing has lapsed. *See* § 9-515(c). This leaves BigBanc unperfected (absent perfection by a non-filing method, such as possession or control) prospectively. Because its other options (see below) do nothing for its position, BigBanc should immediately file a new financing statement.

Filing a continuation statement is not an option. Article 9 provides no "grace period" for continuation statements filed outside the six-month window, no matter how close to the window the filing falls. Section 9-510(c) states that "A continuation statement that is not filed within the six-month period prescribed by Section 9-515(d) is ineffective." Moreover, a filing officer would be required to reject the filing. § 9-516(b)(7). As a consequence, any presentation of a continuation statement would be rejected and, even if improperly accepted, would be ineffective. Therefore, **Answer (A) is incorrect.**

Filing an amendment will also not help. Section 9-312(b) provides that "the filing of an amendment does not extend the period of effectiveness of the financing statement." Therefore, **Answer (B) is incorrect.**

Doing nothing, as shown above, will leave BigBanc unperfected with respect to future actions by other creditors. For that reason alone, **Answer (D) is incorrect**. In addition, contrary to the assumption embedded in Answer (D), BigBanc has lost some priority. Section 9-515(c) provides that BigBanc's initial financing statement "cease[d] to be effective and any security interest . . . that was perfected by the financing statement becomes unperfected, unless the security interest is perfected otherwise. If the security interest . . . becomes unperfected upon lapse, it is deemed never to have been perfected as against a purchaser of the collateral for value." The other filing creditor, inasmuch as it gave credit to enable Friendly to acquire the copier, will be a purchaser for value (*see* § 1-201(b)(29)/(30), which defines secured creditors as "purchasers," and Section 1-204 regarding value). BigBanc will now be junior to the creditor who sold the copier to Friendly, and who was named on the other filing. *See* § 9-515, cmt. 3 (Ex. 1).

BigBanc will not, however, be junior to the judicial lien creditor, as lien creditors are not purchasers. *See* § 9-515, cmt 3 (Ex. 2). But, if that creditor renews its levy or otherwise obtains new property interests to satisfy its judgment, failure to file a new financing statement will further subordinate BigBanc.

57. Once the transaction has concluded and Friendly has honored all of its payment and other obligations, BigBanc can, on its own volition, file a termination statement (usually a UCC-3

form with the "termination" box checked). Section 9-513(c) is phrased, however, in a manner that permits BigBanc to remain passive until it receives from Friendly an authenticated demand for a termination statement. Within 20 days following receipt of Friendly's demand, BigBanc must file a termination statement or, alternatively, prepare and send the termination statement to Friendly (who presumably will file it).

If BigBanc breaches its duty to timely respond, Section 9-509(d) permits Friendly to unilaterally file a termination statement (which must indicate why Friendly, rather than Big-Banc, is filing the statement). Section 9-625(b) permits Friendly to recover damages caused by BigBanc's breach (e.g., Friendly's "inability to obtain, or increased costs of, alternative financing" triggered by the delay in filing the termination statement and the resulting questionable cloud on Friendly's assets). Furthermore, Section 9-625(e)(4) imposes an automatic statutory penalty of $500 for BigBanc's breach, whether or not the breach caused loss or harm to Friendly.

The rules are different if the debtor is a consumer and the collateral includes consumer goods. In that case, the secured party cannot remain passive and wait for the debtor's request for a termination statement. Instead, the secured party must timely take the lead in preparing and filing the termination statement itself. *See* § 9-513(a), (b).

58. **Answer (D) is the correct answer.** This question is based on a real-life problem. Chump was JPMorgan Chase Bank; Gasoline Motors was General Motors; the inventory loan was a loan secured by synthetic leases; and the equipment loan was, well, an equipment loan. The eye-catching aspect was that the collateral for the equipment loan was worth about $1.5 billion (that's $1,500,000,000 of equipment).

Chase raised the arguments that it did not authorize the errant filing, and that no one—either Chase or GM—subjectively intended to terminate the equipment loan. The dispute quickly rose from the bankruptcy court to the Second Circuit Court of Appeals, who promptly certified the legal questions to the Delaware Supreme Court (after all, Article 9 is part of state law). The Delaware Supreme Court responded:

> [I]t is enough that the secured party authorizes the filing to be made, which is all that § 9-510 requires. The Delaware UCC contains no requirement that a secured party that authorizes a filing subjectively intends or otherwise understands the effect of the plain terms of its own filing.

Official Comm. of Unsecured Creditors of Motors Liquidation Co. v. JPMorgan Chase Bank, N.A., 103 A.3d 1010, 1018 (Del. 2014). Taking this statement of law and applying it to the facts, the Second Circuit concluded that the undisputed facts

> show that JPMorgan and its counsel knew that, upon the closing of the Synthetic Lease transaction, [GM's counsel] was going to file the termination statement that identified the [Equipment] Loan UCC-1 for termination and that JPMorgan reviewed and assented to the filing of that statement. Nothing more is needed.

Official Comm. of Unsecured Creditors of Motors Liquidation Co. v. JPMorgan Chase Bank, N.A. (In re Motors Liquidation Co.), 777 F.3d 100, 105 (2d Cir. 2015). For these reasons, **Answer (A) is incorrect** (the act of permitting the document to be filed after review was authority to file) and **Answer (B) is incorrect** (subjective intention does not matter for authority if external actions provide the authority).

Given that the bankruptcy was filed before the mistake was known, there was no correcting it by filing a new financing statement. The automatic stay of Section 362(a)(4) of the Bankruptcy Code precluded that; there is no grace period tied to the date a bankruptcy is commenced. As a result, **Answer (C) is incorrect**.

59. **Answer (C) is the correct answer.** The only instance in which a secured party should file its financing statement at the county level (rather than in the state's central filing office) is if the financing statement will serve as a fixture filing. *See* § 9-501(a). Miguel is offering both personal and business assets as collateral. Miguel intends to use the loan proceeds to open a restaurant. Presumably, then, some of the business assets will include restaurant equipment, such as ovens or built-in refrigerators. Some of that equipment may be affixed to the walls and floors in such a manner that it becomes a "fixture" as that term is defined in Section 9-102(a)(41). Therefore, Friendly Financing should file a fixture filing (at the local county level) to better protect itself against competing claims (in the fixtures) that might be asserted by Miguel's real estate creditors. *See* § 9-334. For this reason, **Answer (C) is the correct answer.**

Answer (A) is incorrect because the nature of the debtor (human versus entity) is irrelevant; whether the debtor is a human or an organization does not dictate the filing office.

Answer (B) is incorrect because neither the marital status of a human debtor, nor the property laws of the state in which the human debtor resides, dictates the filing office.

Answer (D) is incorrect because a security interest in Miguel's personal automobile cannot be perfected by filing (in any office). Instead, Friendly Financing must comply with relevant certificate-of-title laws in order to perfect its security interest in the vehicle.

60. **The correct response is Answer (A).** The 2010 Amendments to Article 9 attempted to resolve issues regarding the correct name of an individual (that is, a flesh and blood human being). This is more difficult than it might first appear, given the reluctance of Americans to agree or to adopt a system that uniquely identifies every citizen (and even when they do, such as with the Social Security system, the legitimate and authorized uses of that identifier are significantly limited). At common law, the "correct" or "legal" name of an individual was the name by which the person was generally known for non-fraudulent purposes. *See* Petition of Dengler, 246 N.W.2d 758 (N.D. 1976) (in which the court struggles with what a "name" is in the context of a name change petition that sought to change the plaintiff's name from Michael Herbert Dengler to "1069"). *See also* Smith v. United States Casualty Co., 197 N.Y. 420, 90 N.E. 947 (NY. 1910).

Indeed, the name given at birth to the eighteenth president of the United States was Hiram Ulysses, not Ulysses S. Grant (his name was mistakenly changed when he entered West Point, and he never corrected it thereafter), and the name given at birth to the twenty-second and twenty-fourth president was Stephen G. Cleveland, not Grover Cleveland. *Smith*, 197 N.Y. at 429, 90 N.E. at 949.

The 2010 Amendments did not uniformly address this issue. They contained two solutions to the problem, imaginatively named "Alternative A" and "Alternative B." Alternative A, which has been adopted by nearly 40 states, is generally described as the "only if" approach. Under this approach, as set forth in Sections 9-503(a)(4) and (5), a financing statement filed against an individual with an unexpired driver's license is effective *only if* filed against the name indicated on such license. Here, the relevant driver's license says "Jim F. Lump." That is thus the only correct name, making **Answer (A) the correct answer.**

The fact that other authoritative documents may differ is irrelevant. As Comment 2.d. to Section 9-503 states, "A financing statement does not 'provide the name of the individual which is indicated' on the debtor's driver's license unless the name it provides is the same as the name indicated on the license. This is the case even if the name indicated on the debtor's driver's license contains an error." This is re-emphasized in ¶ 11 of Comment 2.d., which states that "a court should not assume that the name as presented on an individual's birth certificate is necessarily the individual's current name."

Each of Answers (B), (C), and (D) lists a name that varies, and is different, from the relevant driver's license. Under Alternative A, then, **Answers (B), (C), and (D) are incorrect.**

61.   **The correct answer is (B).** Because the debtor does not have a driver's license, it does not matter whether Alternative A or Alternative B is chosen. Under Alternative A, Section 9-503(a)(5) provides that the financing statement uses the debtor's correct name "only if the financing statement provides the individual name of the debtor or the surname and first personal name of the debtor." Alternative B — the minority rule — takes a so-called "safe harbor" approach. This approach provides, in Section 9-503(a)(4)(A)–(C), three choices for the name to include in a financing statement filed against an individual debtor: (1) the "individual name" of the debtor, (2) the "surname and first personal name" of the debtor, or (3) as in Alternative A, the name on the debtor's unexpired driver's license. The first two of these correspond exactly to Alternative A's options if the debtor has no driver's license, and the last does not apply here.

So the test is whether any of the choices provide (1) the "individual name" of the debtor or (2) the "surname and first personal name" of the debtor. As the comments to Section 9-503 point out, "Article 9 does not determine the 'individual name' of a debtor. Nor does it determine which element or elements in a debtor's name constitute the surname. . . . In disputes as to whether a financing statement sufficiently provides the 'individual name' of a debtor, a court should refer to any non-UCC law concerning names." §9-503, cmt. 2.d (¶¶ 8, 10).

As indicated in Question 60, at common law, the "correct" or "legal" name of an individual was the name by which the person was generally known for non-fraudulent purposes. Here, we are told that "all her friends" and her employer used "Jill Smith." That would indicate that **the correct answer is Answer (B)**.

Answer (A) uses the birth certificate name, but because that name is not generally used, it is likely not her common law name, making **Answer (A) incorrect**.

A name used only occasionally and then for whimsy is certainly not used generally to refer to the debtor, disqualifying it from being an "individual name," and making **Answer (C) incorrect**.

Finally, no one apparently uses "Jillian Smith," or calls the debtor "Jillian." This indicates that "Jillian" is not the "first personal name" required by the statute. This makes **Answer (D) incorrect**.

62. **Answer (A) is correct.** This question asks for the "best practices" in an uncertain area, and the almost-always correct answer is to provide as many variants as possible. This approach is anticipated in the comments to Section 9-503, which say "If there is any doubt about an individual debtor's name, a secured party may choose to file one or more financing statements that provide a number of possible names for the debtor and a searcher may similarly choose to search under a number of possible names." § 9-503, cmt. 2.d. (¶ 14). The official UCC-1 form (see § 9-521) allows for this practice.

Any other answer is fraught with peril that a court will not accept the Hispanic naming convention. The comments to Section 9-503 attempt to anticipate this:

> Names can take many forms in the United States. For example, whereas a surname is often colloquially referred to as a "last name," the sequence in which the elements of a name are presented is not determinative. In some cultures, the surname appears first, while in others it may appear in a location that is neither first nor last. In addition, some surnames are composed of multiple elements that, taken together, constitute a single surname. These elements may or may not be separated by a space or connected by a hyphen, "i," or "y." In other instances, some or all of the same elements may not be part of the surname. In some cases, a debtor's entire name might be composed of only a single element, which should be provided in the part of the financing statement designated for the surname.

§ 9-503, cmt. 2.d. (¶ 9). Because Answer (A) uses all possible permutations of the two *apellidos*, it is the best choice for a filer. **Answer (A) is thus correct**.

As a consequence, any effort to use something less than all possible combinations will not be optimal. This makes **Answer (B), Answer (C), and Answer (D) incorrect**.

Note: This confusion is partly caused by Section 9-516(b)'s requirement that a filer designate some part of an individual debtor's name as a "surname" (this is for indexing purposes). If no name or part of a name is designated as a surname, the filing officer may rightfully reject any proffered financing statement. *See* § 9-516(b)(3)(C).

63. **Answer (D) is correct.** The debtor here is Jim's corporation. Corporations, as well as all other legal entities, have different rules for names than do individuals. For certain entities, which Article 9 calls "registered organizations" (see § 9-102(a)(71)), Section 9-503(a)(1) states the following rule:

> A financing statement sufficiently provides the name of the debtor . . . if the debtor is a registered organization . . . only if the financing statement provides the name that is stated to be the registered organization's name on the public organic record most recently filed with or issued or enacted by the registered organization's jurisdiction of organization which purports to state, amend, or restate the registered organization's name.

So the rule is that the only correct name is the name that appears on the most recent "public organic record." This odd term, "public organic record," is defined in Section 9-102(a)(68), as:

> [A] record that is available to the public for inspection and is: [¶] (A) a record consisting of the record initially filed with or issued by a State or the United States to form or organize an organization and any record filed with or issued by the State or the United States which amends or restates the initial record . . .

For corporations, the "public organic record" includes the original articles of incorporation, as that was the document that was used to form and create the entity (such documents are often called an entity's "birth certificate"). If there have been no amendments, and the fact pattern indicates that there were not, then the name shown on the articles of incorporation is the "correct" name. As a result, **Answer (D) is correct.**

Answer (A) uses the name the business is generally known by in the public. This is often referred to as a trade name, or a "dba" — "doing business as." Such names are not correct names for registered organizations. Section 9-503(c) states that "A financing statement that provides only the debtor's trade name does not sufficiently provide the name of the debtor." As a result, **Answer (A) is incorrect.** As Answer (C) is just a variation of Answer (A) and is thus also a trade name, **Answer (C) is also incorrect.**

Answer (B) states a correct legal conclusion, but not a correct name. When indexed, the portion that begins with "dba . . ." will be indexed as part of the name. Under normal rules of indexing, then, Answer (B) will look like "JAMESSFOODDRINKDBAJIMSBARGRILL" (because spaces and connectors such as "and" are omitted, noise endings such as "Inc." or "LLC" are dropped, and all letters capitalized). That string of letters will be much different from the string for the correct name, "JAMESSFOODDRINK," So Answer (B) not only provides the incorrect name, but is also seriously misleading. As a result, **Answer (B) is incorrect.**

64. Article 9 has, as we have seen, many rules regarding what an entity's "correct" name is. But it does not have a rule that says the use of a name that is not correct automatically invalidates a financing statement that uses it. Rather, the rule is stated in Section 9-506(a) as "A financing statement substantially satisfying the requirements of this part is

effective, even if it has minor errors or omissions, unless the errors or omissions make the financing statement seriously misleading."

This is incomplete; it does not define "seriously misleading." That is the province of Section 9-506(c), which states:

> If a search of the records of the filing office under the debtor's correct name, using the filing office's standard search logic, if any, would disclose a financing statement that fails sufficiently to provide the name of the debtor in accordance with Section 9-503(a), the name provided does not make the financing statement seriously misleading.

This statute requires knowledge of the filing office's "standard search logic." Most filing offices publish these rules. In addition, most filing offices adopt the model search office rules drafted and promulgated by the International Association of Commercial Administrators (IACA) (this organization is referred to in Section 9-526).

These rules manipulate the name given in the financing statement for the debtor to create a unique string of letters and characters. Under the IACA manipulations,

- No distinction is made between upper and lower case letters.

- Punctuation marks and accents are disregarded.

- Ending words and abbreviations that indicate the existence or nature of an organization are disregarded. ("Inc.," "Corp." "LLC," etc.)

- The word "the" at the beginning of the search criteria is disregarded.

- All spaces are disregarded.

If this manipulation means that a financing statement with an incorrect name (as judged by Section 9-503) is manipulated so that the resulting string of characters is the same as the string returned by the correct name, the financing statement is not seriously misleading.

Start first with the observation that the name Swoop used on the financing statement is not the correct name of the debtor. A limited liability company is a registered organization; that is, one that is "organized solely under the law of a single State or the United States by the filing of a public organic record with, the issuance of a public organic record by, or the enactment of legislation by the State or the United States." § 9-102(a)(71). An LLC is formed (typically) by the filing of its articles of organization with a central authority, such as a secretary of state. As a registered organization, its correct name is the name on those articles of organization (or the latest amendment to them).

But as in Question 63, a financing statement is not invalid if it does not contain the correct name; it is invalid only if the name used is "seriously misleading." Under Section 9-506(c), a name is seriously misleading if a search under the correct name would not return or reveal the name used in the challenged financing statement.

So here the test would be if the financing statement filed — using Acme Paints, Inc. — would be found in a search under the correct name — Acme Paints!, LLC.

It would. Why? Search logic is not full text searching; that was not widespread when the 2001 amendments were considered. Rather, a financing statement is indexed under a string of letters obtained by applying certain rules to the name submitted. The key here is that under IACA standard search logic (see Question 63), punctuation is dropped, spaces are omitted, and noise endings such as "LLC" and "Inc." are tossed. So "Acme Paints!, LLC" would be indexed as "ACMEPAINTS."

A financing statement filed under "Acme Paints, Inc." would be manipulated by dropping spaces and noise words to be "ACMEPAINTS." That result is the same as the result when the correct name is used. So a computer would find Swoop's financing statement because its manipulated name is the same as the manipulated correct name.

65. The result here would be different from Question 64. A financing statement is seriously misleading, and hence ineffective, if a search under the correct name would not, using the filing office's standard search logic, return or find the financing statement in question. Here, there would be no match. As seen before, the debtor's correct name reduces to ACMEPAINTS. The name on the financing statement in this question, however, would reduce to ACMEPAINTERS. The two extra letters will cause the computer to not match the two names. As a result, because of the lack of a match, a search under Acme Paints!, LLC, would not return a financing statement that named the debtor as Acme Painters, LLC. The filing under Acme Painters, LLC, is thus seriously misleading and ineffective to perfect any security interest.

66. No, the filing is sufficient to perfect security interests claimed by BigBank (and MidBank and SmallBank). There are two potential issues here: the misspelling of the agent bank's name — Bigbanc instead of the correct BigBank (the last letter differs), and the listing of the bank's syndicate's agent only.

As to the misspelling, it will be rare when an error in a secured party's name will render a financing statement seriously misleading or invalid. The reason for this is that filing offices do not index by secured party's name. As stated in Comment 2 to Section 9-506: "Inasmuch as searches are not conducted under the secured party's name, and no filing is needed to continue the perfected status of security interest after it is assigned, an error in the name of the secured party or its representative will not be seriously misleading." As a consequence, the misspelling of the agent bank's name will not render the financing statement seriously misleading.

The second issue arises from the use of only the syndicate's agent's name. To be effective, a financing statement must provide "the name of the secured party or a representative of the secured party." § 9-502(a)(2). The filing identifies BigBank as a representative ("AS AGENT"). Even so, BigBank and its fellow syndicate members may be concerned that the filing fails to identify for whom BigBank is acting as agent. This concern is addressed in Section 9-503(d), which states: "Failure to indicate the representative capacity of a secured party or representative of a secured party does not affect the sufficiency of a financing statement." Further discussion (including an example similar to the fact pattern posed in the question) is found in Section 9-503, cmt. 3, and indicates that each syndicate bank is protected by the filing, whether or not specifically identified as "secured party" on the filing (and even if the words "AS AGENT" fail to accompany BigBank's name).

67. **Answer (C) is the correct answer.** The initial issue is to identify whether Robert Zimmer, or RWZ Consulting, is the debtor. (Unlike the situation where Zimmer operates the business as a sole proprietorship and the law treats the two as the same legal entity, Zimmer in this question has incorporated his business as a separate entity.) The computer system is serving as collateral. Zimmer bought the computer system, but the facts state that he did so as an agent (e.g., executive officer) of the consulting service. Therefore RWZ Consulting is the debtor, **eliminating Answer (A) and Answer (B)** (both of which erroneously suggest that Zimmer himself is the debtor). Under Section 9-301(1), BCC should file its financing statement in the jurisdiction where the debtor is located. The debtor, RWZ Consulting, is a corporation incorporated under Delaware law. A corporation is an example of a "registered organization" as defined in Section 9-102(a)(71). Section 9-307(e) states that a registered organization is located in the state of its incorporation. RWZ Consulting, then, is located in Delaware, and the central filing office in that state is where BCC should file its financing statement. For this reason, **Answer (C) is the correct answer. Answer (D) is incorrect** because the location of a corporate debtor's operations does not dictate the filing office.

68. Section 9-309 provides a list of situations in which a security interest is automatically perfected at the moment of attachment. Perhaps the best-known example appears first on the list: a purchase-money security interest (PMSI) in consumer goods (excluding vehicles subject to certificate-of-title laws). BCC has a PMSI in the computer system because it provided seller financing for the object serving as collateral. *See* §9-103(a), (b)(1). But the computer system is being used by the debtor—RWZ Consulting—as equipment in its business. It is not being used (nor could it be used, because it is a corporation) for personal, family, or household purposes, so it is not a "consumer good" as defined in Section 9-102(a)(23). (The foregoing conclusion remains true even if Zimmer operates his business as a sole proprietorship and he uses the computer system at least 50% of the time for business purposes.) Therefore, notwithstanding the purchase-money nature of its security interest, BCC cannot rely on automatic perfection, but instead must perfect its PMSI by other means (in this instance, filing).

69. A contract in which a seller retains title to goods sold on credit until the buyer has fulfilled all payment obligations creates, under the UCC, a security interest in the seller's favor in those goods. *See* §§ 1-201(b)(35), 2-401(1). That means that, contrary to the contract's terms, title will pass immediately to the buyer, leaving the seller with only a security interest. This characterization means that BizCorp's contracts, then, are "chattel paper" as defined in Section 9-102(a)(11), because they evidence both the buyer's monetary obligation (the promise to pay the full purchase price) and a security interest in the goods being purchased by the buyer (which is the consequence of application of the UCC Section cited above to the title retention language).

The first proposed structure is nothing more than a traditional secured transaction: Biz-Corp is offering its contracts as collateral to secure a loan. Lender can perfect its security interest in the contracts—chattel paper—by either filing a financing statement in the appropriate office (*see* § 9-312(a)) or, alternatively, by taking possession of the contracts (*see* § 9-313(a)).

The second proposed structure—in which BizCorp will *sell* the contracts to Lender for a discounted price—is not a traditional secured transaction. Nevertheless, Article 9 does apply to certain sales transactions, including sales of chattel paper. *See* §§ 9-109(a)(3) and cmt. 4; 9-102(a)(28)(B) (defining "debtor" to include BizCorp as the seller of chattel paper); 9-102(a)(73)(D) (defining "secured party" to include Lender as the buyer of chattel paper). Lender should take the same action mentioned above to perfect its property interest: file a financing statement or take possession of the contracts.

70.   The analysis would change in two respects. First, because the negotiable promissory notes are unsecured (that is, they neither create nor refer to any security interests), they are no longer "chattel paper." Instead, they are "promissory notes" and "instruments" as those terms are defined in Sections 9-102(a)(65) and 9-102(a)(47), respectively. Second, Lender's property interest in the promissory notes that it *purchases* from BizCorp is automatically perfected, obviating the need to file a financing statement to perfect its interest. *See* § 9-309(4). Other than these two modifications, the previous analysis remains unchanged.

71.   **Answer (B) is the correct answer.** A security interest becomes perfected "if it has attached and all of the applicable requirements for perfection [e.g., filing a financing statement] . . . have been satisfied. A security interest is perfected when it attaches if the applicable requirements are satisfied before the security interest attaches." § 9-308(a). So Bank's security interest became perfected upon filing, if the interest had previously attached; but Bank's security interest became perfected on attachment, if filing had previously occurred. Under Section 9-203(a) and (b), Bank's interest attached on July 7. The security agreement was in place on July 1. Debtor acquired rights in the computer system as early as July 3, when it purchased the system. *See* §§ 2-401 (absent contrary agreement, title passes upon identification to contract); 2-501 (defining when identification to contract occurs). And Bank gave value under Section 1-204(1) as early as July 7 when it entered into a binding commitment to make a loan. The date on which the last of those three events occurred—July 7—is the date of attachment. As Bank had previously filed its financing statement on July 4, attachment and perfection occurred simultaneously on July 7, **making Answer (B) the correct answer.**

Answer (A) is incorrect because the filing date of July 4 cannot be the perfection date of a security interest that does not attach until a later date (in this case, July 7).

Answer (C) is incorrect because BizCorp acquired rights in the computer system on the purchase date of July 3. BizCorp need not take possession of the system as a predicate to acquiring rights in the system.

Bank did indeed give value on July 12 when it funded the $100,000 loan request. But Bank also gave value on the earlier date of July 7, when it contractually agreed to make the loan. Because value was given at an earlier date, **Answer (D) is incorrect.**

72. Never. Bank cannot perfect a security interest that never attaches. TBN authenticated a security agreement that described the collateral as "equipment." But TBN is a retail bookseller, and thus it will hold the shipment of children's books for sale in its ordinary course of business. That makes them "inventory" under Section 9-102(a)(48)(B). Bank's security interest is limited to the collateral description in the security agreement, which does not include "inventory" or any other language that would reasonably identify these books. Therefore, Bank has no security interest in the shipment because it is not "equipment." And absent attachment, perfection is a moot point.

73. **Answer (D) is the correct answer.** Section 9-301 provides rules that "determine the law governing perfection," but those rules are subject to Sections 9-303 through 9-306. Because the collateral is investment property (§ 9-102(a)(49)), one of the referenced Sections— Section 9-305—applies. Section 9-305(a) provides general rules governing perfection, but subsection (a) is subject to subsection (c). And subsection (c) states: "The local law of the jurisdiction in which the debtor is located governs . . . perfection of a security interest in investment property by filing." Under Section 9-307(b)(1), a debtor who is an individual is located at her principal residence. Because Maria is a Dallas resident, Texas law governs perfection by filing and is the state in which SmallBank should file its financing statement. SmallBank will not file a fixture filing—the only filing contemplated by Article 9 that is recorded locally, usually in the county records. So **Answer (A) and Answer (B) are incorrect.** Instead SmallBank will file a standard financing statement with the central filing office in Texas. *See* § 9-501(a). Therefore, **Answer (D) is the correct answer.** The law under which an investment is created, the law under which her brokerage manager is organized, and the law that governs Maria's investment contracts are all irrelevant and have no bearing on where SmallBank should file its financing statement. Therefore, **Answer (B) and Answer (C) are incorrect.**

74. SmallBank should file a financing statement identifying the collateral against Arturo in the central filing office of New York. Under Article 9, a security interest such as Small-Bank's survives any unauthorized disposition. *See* § 9-315(a)(1). By taking title and possession of the stock, Arturo has become a "debtor" as defined in Section 9-102(a)(28)(A). This change in debtor does not immediately affect SmallBank; as a general rule, Small-Bank's filing against Maria remains effective to perfect its security interest in the shares of stock now owned by Arturo. *See* § 9-507(a). But an exception to this general rule arises because Arturo lives in New York, rather than in Texas (where SmallBank filed its financing statement). Section 9-316(a)(3) addresses this change of ownership (resulting in an additional debtor with respect to the collateral transferred) when the new debtor is located in a different state from the original debtor (here, the change is from Texas to New York). Section 9-316(a)(3) continues the effectiveness of SmallBank's original filing for one year from the date on which Maria sold the shares to her father. In order to avoid any lapse in

perfection, Section 9-316(b) requires SmallBank to file a financing statement against Arturo in New York before that one-year period expires.

(Observe that the one-year grace period is not absolute. It can be shorter if the five-year period of the filing's effectiveness will conclude within that one-year period. *See* § 9-316(a)(1).)

75. SmallBank should file a financing statement against Maria in the central filing office of New Mexico. Appreciate that Maria's creditors may be misled because SmallBank's filing (in Texas) will not be discovered by a search against Maria where she is now "located" — New Mexico. Section 9-316(a)(2) addresses this change in jurisdiction of the original debtor (from Texas to New Mexico) by continuing the effectiveness of SmallBank's original filing in Texas for four months from the date on which Maria relocated from Texas to New Mexico. In order to avoid any lapse in perfection, Section 9-316(b) requires SmallBank to file a financing statement against Maria in New Mexico before that four-month period expires.

(Observe, again, that the four-month grace period is not absolute. It can be shorter if the five-year period of the filing's effectiveness will conclude within that four-month period. *See* § 9-316(a)(1).)

76. The statement, taken as a whole, is false (because part of it is false). Section 9-301(1) requires financing statements to be filed where the debtor — here BAMCO — is located. If BAMCO is a corporation, then it is a "registered organization" as defined in Section 9-102(a)(71). Under Section 9-307(e), a debtor that is a registered organization is located in the state of its creation. If BAMCO is a Delaware corporation, then Chi-Town Bank should file its financing statement in the central filing office of Delaware. The location of BAMCO's business operations, chief executive office, books and records, and collateral is irrelevant. Chi-Town Bank needs to file only one financing statement, in only one place: Delaware. The statement erroneously suggests that Chi-Town Bank must file in multiple jurisdictions, making the statement false.

77. The statement, taken as a whole, is false (because part of it is false). If BAMCO is a general partnership, then it is *not* a "registered organization" as defined in Section 9-102(a)(71). *See* § 9-102, cmt. 11. As noted earlier, Section 9-301(1) informs Chi-Town Bank that it should file its financing statement where BAMCO is "located." Under Section 9-307(b)(3), a debtor that is an organization (other than a registered organization) with multiple locations is deemed located at its chief executive office. From Question 76, we know that BAMCO's chief executive office is in Las Vegas, so Chi-Town Bank should file its financing statement in the central filing office of Nevada. The location of collateral is irrelevant. Chi-Town Bank needs to file only one financing statement, in only one place: Nevada. The statement erroneously suggests that Chi-Town Bank must file in multiple jurisdictions, making the statement false.

78. The statement is true. As noted earlier, Section 9-301(1) informs Chi-Town Bank that it should file its financing statement where BAMCO is "located." If BAMCO is a

corporation, then it also is a registered organization. A registered organization is located in the state of its formation. BAMCO can move its chief executive office from Las Vegas (Nevada) to Denver (Colorado), without re-incorporating or otherwise changing its "location" under Article 9. Therefore, the original filing (presumably in the state under which BAMCO is incorporated) remains effective for the duration of its five-year term (and thereafter, if timely continued), and BAMCO's relocation of its chief executive office from Nevada to Colorado imposes no filing duty on Chi-Town Bank.

(Observe, though, that a debtor's relocation of its chief executive office to a different state can have adverse consequences if the debtor is *not* a registered organization. *See* § 9-316(a)(2), (b) (giving the secured party a four-month grace period in which to refile in the new state when a debtor changes its location to a new jurisdiction.)

79. Foreign debtors cause problems. The rule is laid out in Section 9-307(b)(3)—a debtor that is an organization with multiple locations is located at its chief executive office. (The special rule in Section 9-307(e) for registered organizations only applies to registered organizations organized under the laws of a state in the United States.) So here, the United Kingdom corporation is an "organization," and thus you would file centrally in Colorado, the new location of the chief executive office. Section 9-316(a)(2) would apply to give you a four-month grace period in which to make the filing.

Subsection (c) of Section 9-307 does refer to filing in the District of Columbia, however. When is that appropriate? Subsection (c) singles out those countries that "generally require[] information concerning the existence of a nonpossessory security interest to be made generally available in a filing, recording, or registration system as a condition or result of the security interest's obtaining priority over the rights of a lien creditor with respect to the collateral." If that is the case—that is, if there is a public filing system—then there is no change from the location specified by Section 9-307(b). Here, you are told that the United Kingdom's system is substantially similar to the United States. As a result, there is no change from the location rule found in Section 9-307(b)(3): you file where the chief executive office is located.

A filing in the District of Columbia is required only if the country under which the debtor is organized does not maintain a public filing system as described in Section 9-307(c).

If interested, you can ascertain the status of many countries' filing systems under Article 9 by reference to these articles: Arnold S. Rosenberg, *Where to File Against Non-U.S. Debtors: Applying UCC § 9-307(c)[Rev] to Foreign Filing, Recording, and Registration Systems*, 39 U.C.C.L.J. 109 (2006) (canvasses 72 countries' systems); Arnold S. Rosenberg, *Foreign Filing Systems: A Seven-Country Study*, 66 Consumer Fin. L.Q Rep. 303 (2012) (article studies the filing and registration systems for secured transactions in seven countries: Brazil, China, England and Wales, France, Japan, Mexico, and Spain).

80. **Answer (A) is the correct answer.** The collateral is a certificated security, a form of "investment property" under Section 9-102(a)(49). Section 9-313(a) permits Bank to perfect its security interest in a certificated security by taking "delivery" of the certificate under

Section 8-301. Bank has taken "delivery" under that Section because it has taken possession of the certificate. Therefore Bank is perfected, **making Answer (A) the correct answer.** (Because the certificate is issued in Meredith's name, the absence of her indorsement may prevent Bank from having "control" of the shares under Section 8-106(b), but the indorsement is not necessary for "delivery" and perfection.)

Bank has a perfected security interest in Tom's boat if Bank has a PMSI and the boat is a consumer good. *See* §9-309(1). The facts state that Bank holds a PMSI in the boat. The boat is a consumer good under Section 9-102(a)(23) if Tom uses the boat *primarily* for personal, family, or household purposes. He uses the boat equally for personal and business purposes, so neither purpose is primary (more than 50%). Therefore, the boat is not a consumer good. Instead, it is "equipment" as defined in Section 9-102(a)(33) (a good that is not a consumer good, inventory, or a farm product). Bank cannot claim automatic perfection of its PMSI in equipment, so the absence of a financing statement leaves Bank unperfected. Therefore, **Answer (B) is incorrect.**

Normally, Bank must comply with certificate-of-title laws in order to perfect its security interest in a debtor's motor vehicles. An exception exists under Section 9-311(d) if the motor vehicles are "inventory held for sale or lease by a person or leased by that person as lessor and that person is in the business of selling goods of that kind," in which case Bank can perfect its security interest in the motor vehicles by filing a financing statement. Zippy Rental Agency falls within the first half of the quoted language. But Zippy is in the business of leasing, rather than selling, its motor vehicles. Perhaps it is true that Zippy typically sells a motor vehicle when it reaches a certain mileage or age. Even so, these ultimate sales do not convert Zippy into an entity "in the business of selling goods of that kind." *See* §9-311, cmt. 4 (second paragraph). Because the filing exception does not apply, Bank can perfect its security interest in Zippy's fleet of vehicles only by complying with certificate of title laws. It has failed to do so, leaving it unperfected, and **making Answer (C) an incorrect answer.**

The only method by which Bank can perfect a security interest in BizCorp's deposit accounts as original collateral is by control. *See* §9-312(b)(1). A financing statement is ineffective, and BizCorp is unperfected. It is true that control is automatic if the debtor maintains the deposit accounts with the secured party. *See* §9-104(a)(1). But in this transaction, BizCorp does not maintain the deposit accounts at Bank, but with other financial institutions. For these reasons, **Answer (D) is an incorrect answer.**

81. **Answer (C) is the correct answer.** Section 9-109(c)(1) states that Article 9 "does not apply to the extent that . . . a statute, regulation, or treaty of the United States preempts this article." Therefore, the secured party must be concerned that federal law may require it to record its security interest in a debtor's registered copyrights, trademarks, and patents with the applicable national registry. Under existing case law, a secured party must record its security interest in a debtor's registered copyrights in the national registry (**making Answers (B) and (D) incorrect answers**), but may perfect its security interest in a debtor's

registered patents and registered trademarks by filing a financing statement in the appropriate state filing office (**making Answer (C) the correct answer** and **making Answer (A) an incomplete and incorrect answer**). The leading cases in this area are *In re Peregrine Entertainment, Ltd.,* 116 B.R. 194 (C.D. Cal. 1990) (registered copyrights); *In re World Auxiliary Power Co.,* 303 F.3d 1120 (9th Cir. 2002) (unregistered copyrights); *Trimarchi v. Together Development Corp.,* 255 B.R. 606 (D. Mass. 2000) (trademarks); and *In re Cybernetic Services, Inc.,* 252 F.3d 1039 (9th Cir. 2001) (patents).

82. Article 9 provides four methods of perfection: filing, possession (or delivery), control, and automatic. Filing works on almost all types of collateral. Possession is limited to collateral with a tangible quality. Control is unique to deposit accounts, electronic chattel paper, investment property, letter-of-credit rights, and electronic documents. Automatic perfection arises in limited situations (see Section 9-309), the most common of which is when the secured party has a PMSI in a consumer good.

    A certificated security (a form of investment property) is an example of collateral in which a security interest can be perfected in three different ways. The secured party may file a financing statement, obtain control of the certificate, or take delivery (possession) of the certificate (which also will constitute control if the certificate is in bearer form).

    A secured party can perfect its security interest in consumer goods (excluding motor vehicles subject to certificate-of-title laws) by filing a financing statement or taking possession. If the secured party can claim a PMSI, it also can enjoy automatic perfection.

    Perhaps you can come up with other examples.

83. **Answer (D) is the correct answer. Answer (A) is incorrect** because financing statements (but not security agreements) can use supergeneric descriptions such as "all assets" or "all personal property." *See* § 9-504(2). (Appreciate, though, that the supergeneric description in the financing statement will not perfect a security interest in collateral that falls outside the collateral description found in the security agreement.) The remainder of the question requires an examination of the use of definitions in Article 9.

    The security agreement covers "accounts, equipment, and general intangibles." "Equipment," as defined in Section 9-102(a)(33), means "goods other than inventory, farm products, or consumer goods." It is a definition by exclusion, which is intended; "equipment" is the residual or default classification of goods. If it is tangible, and it is not something else, it is likely equipment. In the question, the computers, photocopiers, and office furniture are equipment. They are not inventory because GetSmart! uses the items internally; they are neither held by GetSmart! for sale in the ordinary course of its business, nor are they consumable supplies (e.g., pencils, tablets, paper clips, etc.) used in the business. And for rather obvious reasons, they are not farm products or consumer goods (the customers may be consumers, but the debtor is a business entity). The security agreement and the financing statement both cover equipment, so Omega Bank has (or will have) a perfected security interest in the office furniture, computers, and photocopiers.

Cash — presumably bills of various denominations, and pennies, nickels, dimes, and quarters — is "money" as defined in Section 1-201(b)(24). Money is not an "account." The security agreement fails to mention "money," and the supergeneric collateral description in the financing statement cannot expand the pool of collateral beyond the contours of the security agreement. Therefore, Omega Bank has no security interest in the cash. (Even if Omega Bank had an enforceable security interest in the cash, the only way to perfect a security interest in money as original collateral is by possession (by the secured party or its agent). *See* § 9-312(a)(3).)

The checks are not "money," nor are they "accounts." Instead, they are an example of an "instrument" as defined in Section 9-102(a)(47). The security agreement fails to mention "instruments," and the supergeneric collateral description in the financing statement cannot expand the pool of collateral beyond the contours of the security agreement. Therefore, Omega Bank has no security interest in the checks.

Credit card receivables for merchants are payment intangibles, a subset of "general intangibles." *See* § 9-102, cmts. 5.a. and 5.d. (the merchant is owed an obligation from the credit card issuer, not from the customer (unless it is a "house" or proprietary credit card), and typically this payment is on a different schedule from the one applicable to the customer's payments to the credit card company). Both the security agreement and the financing statement cover general intangibles, so Bank has (or will have) a perfected security interest in the credit card receivables.

What is the customer list? A customer list can be tangible (e.g., evidenced by one or more sheets of paper, or stored on a computer disk), and intangible (a collection of names that has value). If the list has a tangible quality, it may be equipment. But because the inherent value of the list is not found in the manner in which the information is stored, but in the information itself, the list also could be deemed a general intangible. Either way, Omega Bank is, or will be, perfected because its security agreement and financing statement cover both equipment and general intangibles.

In summary, then, Omega Bank has a perfected security interest in all the specific assets mentioned, other than the cash and the checks. For this reason, **Answer (D) is correct and Answer (B) and Answer (C) are incorrect.**

Proceeds

84. **Answer (D) is the correct answer.** This entire transaction is governed by Section 9-315. With respect to the forklift traded away, Section 9-315(a)(1) states that "a security interest . . . continues in collateral notwithstanding sale, lease, license, exchange, or other disposition thereof unless the secured party authorized the disposition free of the security interest. . . ." The basic notion here is that a debtor cannot destroy a lender's security interest by merely selling the collateral to another. Here, the facts state that ZinnBank did not give permission for the sale, so Section 9-315(a)(1) provides that ZinnBank's security interest stays with the forklift. Because Answer (A) states that the forklift is not subject to the security interest, **Answer (A) is incorrect.**

With respect to the check and the pallets, Section 9-315(a)(2) controls. It provides that "a security interest attaches to any identifiable proceeds of collateral." Proceeds is an extremely broad concept. Under Section 9-102(a)(64), proceeds are defined as

(A)   whatever is acquired upon the sale, lease, license, exchange, or other disposition of collateral;

(B)   whatever is collected on, or distributed on account of, collateral;

(C)   rights arising out of collateral;

(D)   to the extent of the value of collateral, claims arising out of the loss, nonconformity, or interference with the use of, defects or infringement of rights in, or damage to, the collateral; or

(E)   to the extent of the value of collateral and to the extent payable to the debtor or the secured party, insurance payable by reason of the loss or nonconformity of, defects or infringement of rights in, or damage to, the collateral.

A lender's security interest automatically attaches to proceeds, both under Section 9-315(a)(2) and Section 9-203(f).

Section 9-315(a)(2), however, requires that the proceeds be "identifiable." That is easily met here because the check and the pallets were what BAM received in the trade. As such, they are each identifiable for purposes of Section 9-315(a)(2).

There are no distinctions made between negotiable instruments (such as the check) and regular goods (such as the pallets). They both are proceeds, and ZinnBank's security interest will automatically attach to each item. As a result, **both Answer (B) and Answer (C) are incorrect.**

85. **Answer (D) is the correct answer.** This question differs from Question 84 in that it asks whether the security interests are *perfected*, not just *attached*. With respect to the forklift traded away, ZinnBank retains a perfected security interest in the forklift by virtue of Section 9-507(a). That Section provides that "[a] filed financing statement remains effective with respect to collateral that is sold, exchanged, leased, licensed, or otherwise disposed of and in which a security interest or agricultural lien continues, even if the secured party knows of or consents to the disposition." Although ZinnBank could file a financing statement naming Sadie as debtor, Section 9-507(a) releases it from any obligation to do so. (Note that this rule has an exception if Sadie is located in a different state from BAM— under Section 9-316(a)(3), ZinnBank would then have to file a financing statement in the state where Sadie is located, but would have a one-year grace period to do so.) Because the forklift remains perfected, **Answer (A) is incorrect.**

The remaining issues are controlled by Section 9-315. Section 9-315(c) says that "[a] security interest in proceeds is a perfected security interest if the security interest in the original collateral was perfected." Because, from Question 84, we know that ZinnBank took all necessary steps to perfect its security interest in the forklift originally, we know that its security interest in proceeds is automatically perfected as well.

This perfection, however, is not without limits. Section 9-315(d) terminates perfection in proceeds on the twenty-first day after attachment *unless* one of three conditions is met. Section 9-315(d) describes them as follows:

(1)   the following conditions are satisfied:

    (A)   a filed financing statement covers the original collateral;

    (B)   the proceeds are collateral in which a security interest may be perfected by filing in the office in which the financing statement has been filed; and

    (C)   the proceeds are not acquired with cash proceeds;

(2)   the proceeds are identifiable cash proceeds; or

(3)   the security interest in the proceeds is perfected other than under subsection (c) when the security interest attaches to the proceeds or within 20 days thereafter.

Paragraph (1) is often referred to as the "same office rule." It requires three things:

- that a financing statement be filed against the original collateral (so it will not apply to collateral which is perfected automatically—such as purchase-money security interests in consumer goods—or by control—such as deposit accounts and investment property);

- that the proceeds *could be* perfected by filing a financing statement in the same office where the financing statement covering the original collateral *was filed*; and

- the proceeds were not acquired with cash proceeds; that is, they were bartered for (when good are exchanged for goods) or were intangibles given as consideration (such as when a buyer gives its promise to pay the purchase price at a later time—referred to in Article 9 as an account).

Here, the pallets would be covered by the same office rule; that is, perfection in the pallets would extend beyond 20 days. The first condition is met: the original collateral—a forklift—was perfected by the filing of a financing statement. The second condition is also met. The pallets are equipment, and thus a security interest in them could be perfected by filing in the same filing office where the financing statement for the forklift was filed. Finally, the third condition is met—the pallets were acquired as part of a trade or barter; no cash proceeds were given by Sadie. As a result, **Answer (B) is incorrect.**

ZinnBank's perfection in the check rests on paragraph (2) of Section 9-315(d). That paragraph continues perfection beyond 20 days in "identifiable cash proceeds." With a check, the identification process is fairly simply as the delivery of the check can be directly traced to the transaction under which the collateral, the forklift, was traded. But the proceeds must also be "cash proceeds." That term is defined in Section 9-102(a)(9) as "proceeds that are money, checks, deposit accounts, or the like." Because a check qualifies as "cash proceeds," and because the check is traceable to the transaction in which the forklift was sold, it is identifiable cash proceeds, and under Section 9-315(d)(2) perfection continued beyond the twentieth day. As a result, **Answer (C) is incorrect.**

86. **Answer (C) is correct.** As to the display racks, they are proceeds of proceeds. The first "generation" of proceeds was the cash paid by Hank. So long as the 10 100-dollar bills were segregated (which the question indicates they were), the bills were "identifiable." They also fit the definition of "cash proceeds." So Sturm was perfected in the cash. When the cash was used as partial payment for the display racks, the racks became proceeds of the cash proceeds—although there is some minor disagreement, most courts hold that if any of the consideration given for an item was collateral, the entire item is proceeds (so it doesn't matter if only half of the value of the display racks was acquired with collateral, the entirety of the racks are collateral). Article 9 covers this by defining "collateral" in Section 9-102(a)(12)(A) as including "proceeds to which a security interest attaches."

So the interest in the racks attached, but is it perfected? Yes. Although the racks are not "cash proceeds"—thereby disqualifying use of Section 9-315(d)(2)—and were acquired with cash proceeds (the cash paid by Hank)—thereby disqualifying the use of the same office rule of Section 9-315(d)(1)—there is still Section 9-315(d)(3). That Section requires that "the security interest in the proceeds is perfected other than under subsection (c) when the security interest attaches to the proceeds or within 20 days thereafter." Thus, Sturm could have filed a financing statement indicating the display racks as collateral within 20 days, and have been perfected. But it did not have to do that. Its original financing statement indicated that the collateral was "all assets." The display racks would be "equipment" in Larabie's hands, and so could be perfected by the generic "all assets" description. As such, Sturm was perfected from the moment of attachment. Accordingly, **Answer (A) is incorrect.** In addition, because Answer (D) also assumes no perfected security interest in the display racks, **Answer (D) is also incorrect.**

What about Hank's check? It is also proceeds of proceeds. Hank's contractual obligation to pay the purchase price of the air conditioning unit is an account under Article 9. It was given in exchange for the unit, and thus Hank's promise—the account—was proceeds of inventory. It was also perfected under the same office rule, and under the "all assets" filing. When the check was tendered in satisfaction of the obligations in the account, the check was also proceeds; it was "collected on, or distributed on account of, collateral" within the meaning of Section 9-102(a)(64)(B). Although perfection would be automatic and continuous for at least 20 days (the 20-day period of Section 9-315(d) starts anew with each new item of proceeds), it would continue beyond that period if the check was not cashed (as "cash proceeds" under Section 9-315(d)(2) or under the "all assets" description and Section 9-315(d)(3)). Accordingly, **Answer (B)** (**and derivatively, Answer (D)**) **are both incorrect.**

87.   **Answer (D) is the correct answer.** The check represents "proceeds" under Section 9-102(a)(64)(A) ("whatever is acquired upon the sale . . . of collateral"). Under Section 9-203(f), Omega Bank's enforceable security interest in BizCorp's inventory of photocopiers gives it "rights to proceeds provided by Section 9-315." Under that Section, Omega Bank's security interest attaches to the check if it is "identifiable" proceeds (i.e., proceeds that can be traced to a unit of inventory). Under Section 9-315(c), the security interest in the check (the "proceeds" of the inventory) is perfected initially because the security interest in the photocopier (the original collateral) was perfected (by a financing statement). This automatic perfection is only temporary for 20 days, however, and terminates thereafter unless perfection continues under subsection (d). Omega Bank enjoys continued perfection under (d)(2) because the check is an example of "cash proceeds" as defined in Section 9-102(a)(9). Therefore, assuming that the check is traceable to a unit of inventory (the photocopier), then Omega Bank has a perfected security interest in the check, **making Answer (D) the correct answer.**

The failure to include an after-acquired property clause in the security agreement could be fatal, especially if the collateral is not of a type that constantly changes in composition (e.g., inventory and accounts). (Appreciate that the after-acquired property clause need not be repeated in the financing statement. *See* §§ 9-204, cmt. 7; 9-502, cmt. 2.) This would include things such as equipment, or general intangibles. When dealing with inventory and accounts, however, many courts have inferred the existence of an after-acquired property clause when the security agreement is silent, on the plausible assumption that no secured party in its right mind lending on collateral that changes constantly—such as inventory or accounts—would intend to limit its interest to just the inventory and accounts on hand when the debtor authenticated the security agreement. *See In re Filtercorp, Inc.*, 163 F.3d 570 (9th Cir. 1998). But this is not universal, even with the same type of constantly changing collateral. *Compare Van Hattem v. Dublin Nat'l Bank*, 47 U.C.C. Rep. Serv. 2d 1171, 1172 (N.D. Tex. 2002) ("a security agreement covering livestock does not reach after-acquired livestock unless the security agreement expressly so provides") *with Peoples Bank v. Bryan Bros. Cattle Co.*, 504 F.3d 549 (5th Cir. 2007) (a security interest in a cattle dealer's livestock presumptively includes after-acquired property).

More important, because we are talking about transferring property interests, the implication of an after-acquired property clause for ongoing inventory and accounts simply confirms what the debtor likely assumed, especially if the loan agreement had a term longer than the "turn" of the inventory. As a result, courts interpret the contract between the debtor and the secured party sensibly in the context of ever-changing collateral, and generally imply an after-acquired property clause when there is ongoing financing of inventory or accounts.

It does not matter that BizCorp did not acquire rights in the check until June. But no proceeds-related provision of Article 9 conditions attachment or perfection of a security interest therein on the presence of an after-acquired property clause in the security agreement. **For these reasons, Answer (A) is incorrect.**

Also, no proceeds-related provision of Article 9 conditions attachment or perfection of a security interest therein on the presence of magical words—such as "proceeds" or "cash proceeds"—in the collateral description of any loan paper. Therefore, **Answer (B) is incorrect.**

As the photocopier is a unit of BizCorp's inventory, it is highly likely that the sale of the photocopier to the law firm terminated Omega Bank's security interest therein, because either Omega Bank authorized BizCorp to sell its inventory free and clear of the security interest (*see* § 9-315(a)(1)) or the law firm can invoke the protections afforded to a buyer in the ordinary course of business (*see* § 9-320(a)). But Omega Bank's loss of its security interest in the photocopier (which it has to anticipate) does not mean that Omega Bank has abandoned, or Article 9 has terminated, any possible security interest in proceeds that Omega Bank may claim. Therefore, **Answer (C) is incorrect.**

88. **Answer (B) is the correct answer.** This question deals with accessions, defined in Section 9-102(a)(1) as "goods that are physically united with other goods in such a manner that the identity of the original goods is not lost." Here, the memory chips are "accessions;" while they are an integral part of the computer (and the computer will not work without them), the identity of both the chips and the computer is not altered by their installation.

Accessions are not proceeds. The substitution of the new for the old memory chips is not a disposition of the old chips that would give rise to proceeds. Put another way, the addition of the memory chips to Frank's computer does not make the chips proceeds of the computer. Similarly, the attaching of the chips to the computer does not make the computer proceeds of the chips; again there is no disposition.

Section 9-335 deals with accessions. Subsection (a) of Section 9-335 states that "A security interest may be created in an accession and continues in collateral that becomes an accession." The first part of this subsection essentially means that Wolf can have a security interest in an accession (such as the chips); the second part means that if collateral (such as the new chips) become an accession, the security interest is not destroyed or otherwise terminated. (Recall that Article 9 does not respect reservation of title language, and converts it into a conveyance to the debtor of title with a retention of only a security interest — §§ 1-201(b)(35); 2-401.)

Section 9-335 is clear that other provisions of Article 9 govern attachment and perfection of interests in accessions. Section 9-335(c) states that "[e]xcept as otherwise provided in subsection (d) [covering collateral subject to certificate of title statutes such as cars], the other provisions of this part determine the priority of a security interest in an accession." So we look to the basic requirements of attachment and perfection here to determine the answer.

The facts state that Frank bought the computer for use in his work. That makes the computer equipment under Article 9. Equipment is perfected by filing a financing statement (it can also be perfected by possession, but that is not indicated on the facts).

Mark's Memory's security interest may be attached (through its reservation of title language), but it never filed a financing statement. It thus has an attached, but unperfected, security interest in the new chips. This makes **both Answer (C) and Answer (D) incorrect**, because both incorrectly state that Mark's Memory has a perfected security interest in the new chips.

Because Frank has title, he has rights in the collateral. Value exists in the original loan. The facts state that the security agreement was valid. The security agreement specifically covers "accessions," and thus Wolf has satisfied all three requirements of Section 9-203(b) to have an attached security interest in the new chips.

It is also perfected in those chips. The chips, being used for Frank's business purposes, are equipment, and thus picked up by the indication of collateral in the filed financing statement. Because Wolf thus has a perfected security interest in accessions, it has a perfected security interest in the new chips (which are both equipment and accessions), **making Answer (A) incorrect**, and **making Answer (B) the correct answer**.

89. **Answer (D) is the correct answer.** Section 9-315(a)(2) states that "a security interest attaches to any *identifiable* proceeds of collateral." Section 9-315 thus generally requires that proceeds can be *identified* — that, for example, the secured party can isolate and identify what check was given in payment for inventory or in satisfaction of an account, or what equipment was bartered or traded for other collateral.

Sometimes, however, you can't. When collateral is so commingled with other property that it no longer retains a separate existence, the security interest in the lost collateral is similarly lost — with two exceptions. One exception is commingled intangible property — usually deposit accounts (which are no more than a bank's unsecured promise to pay its depositor's check or other demands to the extent of the relevant account balance). Section 9-315(b)(2) extends the security interest to such intangible property, and is the subject of some later questions.

This question deals with commingled *tangible* goods. The cakes are no longer eggs, flour, sugar or dairy products. The original ingredients have lost their identity. In such case, identification is no longer possible. Section 9-315(b)(1), however, extends identification to such cases "to the extent provided by Section 9-336." Section 9-336(a) starts by defining commingled goods. It states that "'commingled goods' means goods that are physically united with other goods in such a manner that their identity is lost in a product or mass." That is the case here; the identities of the cake's ingredients have been lost in the cake.

Is the security interest thus lost? No. That's where Section 9-336 comes in. It states that "[i]f collateral becomes commingled goods, a security interest attaches to the product or mass." Given the extension of a security interest into commingled goods, this makes **Answer (A) incorrect.**

Section 9-336 carries forward attachment, but what about perfection? That is covered by Section 9-336. It states: "If a security interest in collateral is perfected before the collateral becomes commingled goods, the security interest that attaches to the product or mass under subsection (c) is perfected." This means that each of B1, B2, and B3's perfected security interest in the ingredients are now attached and perfected in the cakes, the "product or mass" of the ingredients. Because all secured parties are perfected in the cakes, this makes **Answer (B) incorrect.**

Each secured creditor is perfected in the cakes, but in what order of priority? That is the province of Section 9-336(f), which covers cases in which each ingredient of a product or mass was subject to a perfected security interest before their collateral was commingled. Section 9-336(f)(2) states that "[i]f more than one security interest is perfected under subsection (d), the security interests rank equally in proportion to the value of the collateral at the time it became commingled goods." There is no provision for the allowance of any labor used to combine or commingle the goods, making **Answer (C) incorrect.**

Because Answer (D) states the correct formula for allocating the security interests, **Answer (D) is the correct answer.** Under Section 9-336(f)(2), the security interests will rank equally, and share in the ratio of 2:3:1 (that is, B1's collateral was worth $20 at the time the cakes were baked (the time the collateral became commingled), B2's was worth $30, and B3's was worth $10). That ratio of 20:30:10 reduces to 2:3:1. This means that you divide the value of the commingled collateral (the cakes) into six parts (the sum of 2+3+1). B1 gets 2/6, or 1/3, B2 get 3/6, or 1/2, and B3 gets 1/6 of the value of the cakes. This means that as between the secured creditors, the $120 in sales revenues would be split $40 to B1, $60 to B2, and $20 to B3 (but in no event more than the remaining unpaid debt owed to the creditor).

90. **Answer (C) is the correct answer.** The bookstore's insurance claim arises from damage to, or loss or destruction of, the inventory in which Trinity Finance has a perfected security interest. The insurance claim falls within the definition of "proceeds" either under Section 9-102(a)(64)(D) ("claims arising out of the loss . . . or damage to . . . the collateral") or Section 9-102(a)(64)(E) ("insurance payable by reason of the loss . . . or damage to . . . the collateral"). Sections 9-203(f) and 9-315(a) permit Trinity Finance to claim an interest in the insurance policy claim as an "identifiable" proceed of its perfected security

interest in the inventory. Perfection of its security interest in the insurance claim is automatic for 20 days under Section 9-315(c). Perfection continues thereafter because Trinity Finance can satisfy all three conditions of Section 9-315(d)(1): Trinity Finance perfected its security interest in the original collateral (the inventory) by filing a financing statement; a filing in the same office will perfect a security interest in the insurance claim (either an "account" or a "general intangible"); and the bookstore's insurance claim was not acquired with cash proceeds. Therefore, **Answer (C) is the correct answer.**

Answer (A) is incorrect because Trinity Finance has a perfected security interest in the insurance claim.

Answer (B) is incorrect because, as discussed in the preceding paragraph, the perfection of Trinity Finance's security interest in the insurance claim extends beyond the automatic, but temporary, 20-day period of Section 9-315(c).

Answer (D) is incorrect because the broad exclusion of a debtor's interest in an insurance policy from the scope of Article 9 includes an exception for insurance claims that represent proceeds of collateral. *See* § 9-109(d)(8) (the "but" clause at the end).

91. **Answer (D) is the correct answer.** The $1 million check is identifiable as proceeds of the inventory. Because there is an intervening insurance claim, the check is what might be termed "second generation proceeds" or "proceeds of proceeds." Article 9 does not limit proceeds to "first generation proceeds," but also includes second, third, and other generations. *See* § 9-102, cmt. 13.c. At some point, however, the secured party's tracing duty will become difficult, if not impossible. That is not the case here, though, as the check can be easily traced back to the insurance claim, which arises from hurricane damage to the bookstore's inventory. A check is a form of "cash proceeds" as defined in Section 9-102(a)(9). Therefore, Trinity Finance's perfection is not limited to the automatic, but temporary, 20-day period of Section 9-315(c), but extends beyond that period under Section 9-315(d)(2). **For these reasons, Answer (D) is the correct answer.**

Answer (A) is incorrect for two reasons. First, a check is not "money" as defined in Section 1-201. Second, Article 9 does not exclude "money" from its scope of coverage. *See, e.g.,* § 9-312(b)(3) (discussing how a security interest in money may be perfected).

Answer (B) is incorrect for two reasons. First, as already explained, Trinity Finance's perfection extends beyond the 20-day period of Section 9-315(c). Second, a check is an "instrument" under Section 9-102(a)(47). A security interest in an instrument can be perfected by possession (*see* § 9-313(a)), but it also can be perfected by filing (*see* § 9-312(a)).

Answer (C) is incorrect because Trinity Finance has a perfected security interest in the check. Absent indorsement and delivery, Trinity Finance may not have enforcement rights in the check under UCC Article 3. But Trinity Finance's perfected status does not turn on whether it can enforce the check.

92. **Answer (A) is the correct answer.** The bookstore's general operating bank account is a "deposit account" as defined in Section 9-102(a)(29), and a deposit account (like a check) is an example of "cash proceeds" as defined in Section 9-102(a)(9). Therefore, assuming that Trinity Finance can satisfy its tracing burden (which could be a challenge, with the passage of time, as the account is not a segregated "proceeds only" account), Trinity Finance has a perfected security interest in the deposit account for 20 days and beyond, as explained more fully in the preceding answer. **For these reasons, Answer (A) is the correct answer.**

    Answer (B) is incorrect for two reasons. First, as already explained, Trinity Finance is perfected beyond the 20-day period of Section 9-315(c). Second, while Section 9-312(b)(1) does state that a security interest in a deposit account can be perfected only by control, the opening language of Section 9-312(b) defers and makes an exception to this rule for the proceeds-related provisions in Sections 9-315(c) and (d). For this reason, **Answer (C) is also incorrect.**

    Answer (D) is incorrect and is a nonsense answer. Article 9 applies to security interests in deposit accounts (subject to a consumer-related exception found in Section 9-109(d)(13)), regardless of how funds are deposited (e.g., cash, check, wire transfer, etc.) into the deposit account.

93. As of December 1, Omega Bank has a perfected security interest in the photocopier. Gershwin received the photocopier as payment for a piano (a unit of inventory), making it "proceeds" under Section 9-102(a)(64). Omega Bank should be able to prove that Gershwin acquired a property interest in the photocopier by bartering it from Lauren as payment for a piano (a unit of inventory), making the photocopier "identifiable" proceeds. Therefore, Omega Bank has an attached security interest in the photocopier under Section 9-315(a)(2). Because Omega Bank had a perfected security interest in the piano, its security interest in the photocopier is perfected for at least 20 days under Section 9-315(c). Perfection continues thereafter because Omega Bank can satisfy the three conditions of Section 9-315(d)(1) (the "same office" rule): a filed financing statement covers the piano, a filing in the same office as the financing statement covering the inventory will perfect a security interest in the photocopier (equipment in the debtor's hands), and there are no intervening cash proceeds. Therefore, as of December 1, Omega Bank has a perfected security interest in the photocopier.

94. As of December 1, Omega Bank would likely have an unperfected security interest in the photocopier. The analysis tracks the previous answer, until the 20-day perfection period of Section 9-315(c) expires.

    As to attachment, the check was proceeds of the piano, as was the bank account into which the check was deposited—given the lowest intermediate balance test and the relatively low amount in the account at the time of deposit. A check drawn on that account was then used to buy the photocopier. The photocopier was thus proceeds of the deposit account, given the amount of the purchase (the price was greater than the balance of the account when Lauren's check was deposited, meaning that some of the funds used to honor the check were proceeds of the check that paid for the piano originally). This is an application of Section 9-315(b)(2), which permits identification of intangible proceeds by any method of tracing permitted under non-Article 9 law. Here, the Lowest Intermediate Balance Test (sometimes referred to as the "LIBR Rule") would identify the proceeds paying for the photocopier as coming at least partly from the funds used to honor Lauren's check to Gershwin. Most courts would hold that this is sufficient to attach Omega Bank's security interest in the entire photocopier.

Perfection of Omega Bank's security interest in the photocopier lapses on November 21 (the twenty-first day after the security interest attached to the photocopier on November 1) because Omega Bank is unable to extend perfection under Section 9-315(d). It cannot satisfy subsection (d)(1) because Gershwin acquired the photocopier with cash proceeds — the check (notice that subsection (d)(1) has three subparts, all of which must be met). Subsection (d)(2) does not apply because the photocopier is not "cash proceeds." And subsection (d)(3) offers no help because Omega Bank has failed to take any other action to perfect its interest in the photocopier (i.e., amending its original financing statement to mention the photocopier or filing a new financing statement against the photocopier). Because Omega Bank is unable to extend perfection under Section 9-315(d), it does not have a perfected security interest in the photocopier as of December 1.

95. **Answer (C) is the correct answer.** The act of commingling proceeds with non-proceeds does not automatically destroy a secured party's ability to "identify" some or all of the assets as its collateral. Article 9 permits the secured party to identify the proceeds "by a method of tracing, including application of equitable principles, that is permitted under law other than this article with respect to commingled property of the type involved." § 9-315(b)(2). A common "equitable principle" is the "lowest intermediate balance rule." § 9-315, cmt. 3. Under the lowest intermediate balance rule, (i) the creditor can claim an interest in commingled assets identified as proceeds, (ii) non-proceeds are considered used by the debtor before proceeds, and (iii) proceeds that are used by the debtor are not deemed replenished with subsequently commingled non-proceeds.

When the problem involves a bank account, it is helpful to run a daily balance and identify the part of the total balance that represents proceeds. The following is a summary of the bank activity (with deposits of proceeds in bold):

Date	Begin Balance	Deposit/ (Withdrawal)	End Balance		Proceeds
4/1	8,000				2,000
4/5	8,000	**6,000**	14,000		8,000
4/7	14,000	(7,000)	7,000		7,000
4/15	7,000	4,000	11,000		7,000
4/20	11,000	(5,000)	6,000		6,000
4/24	6,000	**3,000**	9,000		9,000
4/28	9,000	2,000	11,000		9,000

Because the ending number in the "proceeds" column is $9,000, **Answer (C) is the correct answer** and **Answers (A), (B), and (D) are incorrect answers.**

96. As of April 30, under the lowest intermediate balance rule, Lender can claim a security interest in $5,000, calculated as follows:

Date	Begin Balance	Deposit/ (Withdrawal)	End Balance		Proceeds
4/1	8,000				2,000
4/5	8,000	**6,000**	14,000		8,000
4/7	14,000	(7,000)	7,000		7,000
4/12	7,000	**4,000**	11,000		11,000
4/15	11,000	4,000	15,000		11,000
4/17	15,000	8,000	7,000		7,000
4/20	7,000	(5,000)	2,000		2,000
4/22	2,000	2,000	4,000		2,000
4/24	4,000	**3,000**	7,000		5,000
4/28	7,000	2,000	9,000		5,000

97. **Answer (B) is the correct answer.** Under the facts, Tim gave his parents a security interest in all chess sets with an after-acquired property clause as permitted by Section 9-204. In October 2018, his parents' interest in the newly acquired chess set was perfected by the Ohio filing. Tim then received the baseballs as payment for the chess set, so the baseballs represent proceeds under Section 9-102(a)(64). The baseballs are rather special, and not generic, facilitating the ability of Tim's parents to satisfy their tracing burden, making the baseballs "identifiable proceeds" in which Tim's parents can claim an enforceable security interest under Section 9-315(a)(2). Therefore, **Answer (A) is incorrect.**

Normally a security interest in proceeds is automatically (albeit temporarily) perfected for 20 days under Section 9-315(c). But that brief period of perfection is available only if the security interest in the original collateral was perfected. Tim's parents did file a financing statement against Tim and the chess set in Ohio, where Tim (at the time) was "located" under Section 9-307(b)(1). But Tim later moved to New York, a different state. This change in jurisdiction required the parents to file a new financing statement in New York within four months after the relocation if they wanted to maintain continuous and uninterrupted perfection. *See* § 9-316(a)(2). The facts do not indicate that the parents took any filing action in response to Tim's relocation, leaving them unperfected both prospectively and retroactively. *See* § 9-316(b). This means that Tim's parents cannot invoke Section 9-315(c), leaving them with an unperfected security interest in the baseballs. **For these reasons, Answer (B) is the correct answer and Answer (D) is an incorrect answer.**

Answer (C) suggests that the label assigned to the chess set may be relevant to the analysis. That might be true, if Tim's parents could claim automatic perfection in the chess set. They can do so under Section 9-309(1) *if* their security interest qualified as a PMSI, *and* if Tim used or acquired the chess set as a consumer good. If both conditions are met, Tim's relocation may have an impact on the continued effectiveness of the Ohio filing, but Tim's parents could rely on the alternative method of automatic perfection, which would not be adversely affected by Tim's relocation to New York. The problem, though, is that even if Tim uses the chess set as a consumer good (which is not likely because he bought it for his part-time professional chess endeavors), the parents do not have a PMSI in the chess set. Tim used their money to take a vacation and pay off credit cards; he used his own money to purchase the chess set. Therefore, the parents cannot prove (under Section 9-103(a)(2)) that they hold a "purchase-money obligation" and, accordingly, do not have a PMSI that may be eligible for automatic perfection. This means that the label assigned to the chess set (e.g., consumer good, inventory, or equipment [we will safely assume the set is not a farm product]) is irrelevant. **For these reasons, Answer (C) is incorrect.**

98.   **The correct answer is Answer (C).** BankOne has a perfected interest in inventory, such as the luggage sold to Harold. When Harold gives Frank a check in exchange for the luggage, the check is proceeds of the inventory—it is something that was "acquired upon the sale, lease, license, exchange, or other disposition of collateral," thus meeting the definition of Section 9-102(a)(64)(A). BankOne's security interest thus attaches to the check upon Harold's delivery of it to Frank. BankOne's security interest in the check is perfected because a check is a form of "cash proceeds," and Section 9-315(d)(2) extends indefinitely the 20-day period of automatic perfection in Section 9-315(c) for proceeds that are identifiable "cash proceeds."

When Frank takes the check and deposits it into the deposit account at BankTwo, the nature of the asset changes. The check is paid, and the value is transferred to Frank's deposit account, making the deposit account "proceeds," either because the funds obtained by the check's payment were in "exchange" for the check, § 9-102(a)(64)(A), or such funds were what was "collected on" the check, § 9-102(a)(64)(B). In either case, because the balance in the account reflects the amount of funds paid on the check, there is a proceeds argument so long as the increase in balance can be identified. As in previous questions, Section 9-315(b)(2) allows courts to use tracing methods such as the lowest intermediate balance rule to "identify" what portion of the account's balance is identifiable as BankOne's collateral.

We are asked to make determinations as of the time Harold's check clears, at which time the lowest intermediate balance rule would find that the increase in the amount of the bank account (assuming a positive balance at the time of deposit) was traceable to BankOne's collateral, and thus BankOne has a "proceeds of proceeds" claim to the account. Because BankOne has an interest, **Answer (A) is incorrect.**

Further, because the deposit account is "cash proceeds," BankOne's interest will be perfected not only for the 20-day automatic perfection period of Section 9-315(c), but also for such time after that period that the LIBR will identify the proceeds. As a result, BankOne's interest is perfected, **making Answer (B) incorrect.**

As a matter of priority (not requested by the question), BankTwo will have priority under Section 9-327. The bank maintaining the deposit account always has priority over a proceeds interest of another secured party because it will always (unless it has agreed otherwise) have control over the deposit account, and under Section 9-327(1), control beats filing, regardless of when attachment or perfection occurred.

No provision of Article 9 requires a bank's consent for a security interest in a bank account to attach, making **Answer (D) incorrect**—although such attachment might be a default under BankTwo's agreement with Frank. But a contractual default will not prevent the property interest from arising and attaching to the account.

99. **The correct answer is Answer (D).** We know from the last question that BankOne had a perfected security interest in the deposit account maintained at BankTwo, at least to the extent that it can identify its proceeds under the lowest intermediate balance rule. We also know that Frank granted an original security interest in the same account to BankTwo. Direct interests in deposit accounts (as opposed to interests claimed as proceeds) can be perfected only by control, § 9-312(b)(1), and control here arises from the fact that the account is maintained at BankTwo, § 9-104(a)(1).

When Frank buys new inventory with a check drawn on the deposit account at BankTwo, the new inventory is proceeds of the deposit account—it is received on disposition of a portion of the account balance represented by the check Harold wrote. As a result, Bank-Two has a security interest in the new inventory—the new luggage—**making both Answer (A) and Answer (B) incorrect**, because they both assume BankTwo has no interest in the luggage.

Does BankOne have an interest? The answer is yes. There are two arguments, each sufficient, for BankOne's interest. First, Question 98 stated that BankOne's security agreement had an after-acquired property clause. Thus, when Frank acquired the new luggage for resale, he acquired new inventory subject to the after-acquired property clause. As a consequence, BankOne has an interest in the luggage, **making Answer (C) incorrect**.

The second and independently sufficient argument is that the new inventory is *proceeds* of the deposit account (which Question 98 established was at least partially proceeds of BankOne's collateral to the extent the LIBR could "identify" a portion). The issue is whether the funds used to honor Harold's check given in exchange for the luggage can be identified; if so, then the new luggage is proceeds. Here, we know that the deposit account had a balance of $500 before the deposit of Harold's check, and $1,500 afterward. Of that $1,500, at least $1,000 (the last $1,000 to be spent) was identifiable proceeds under the LIBR. When Harold wrote a check on the account for $1,000, he reduced the balance from $1,500 to $500, and used at least $500 of proceeds in the account to acquire the new luggage. Most courts would hold that the luggage in its entirety (without taking into account any proportionality) was thus proceeds, because proceeds were used to acquired it. That makes the new luggage proceeds of proceeds of proceeds (luggage < deposit account < check). As an aside, application of the LIBR also means that the remaining $500 in the deposit account is all proceeds of BankOne's collateral as well.

As a result, both BankOne and BankTwo have a proceeds interest in the luggage, making **Answer (D) correct.**

100.   Under Section 9-315(c), both security interests are perfected for at least 20 days. But after that 20-day period ends, BankOne has a perfected security interest in the new luggage. BankTwo has an unperfected security interest. As established in Question 99, BankOne has a security interest in the luggage either under its after-acquired property clause or as proceeds of the sale of its collateral. BankOne's security interest continues after the initial 20 days because it has a financing statement on file that indicates inventory, thus satisfying the third paragraph of Section 9-315(d).

BankTwo took no action with respect to its security interest in the deposit account. It is thus unperfected as to the luggage as it has neither filed a financing statement nor taken possession of the luggage.

101.   **The correct answer is Answer (A).** The facts lead to the conclusion that BankOne has a perfected security interest in all of Lucent's chattel paper, now owned or later-acquired. Here, the contract between Lucent and Balrog is chattel paper as defined in Section 9-102(a)(11): it states a monetary obligation (Balrog's obligation to pay) and a property interest in favor of Lucent (the reservation of title is converted into a security interest in Lucent's favor by virtue of Sections 1-201(b)(35) and 2-401). As a consequence of BankOne's after-acquired property clause, BankOne has a security interest in the chattel paper once it is delivered (in the legal sense) by both parties.

That security interest is perfected because BankOne's financing statement specifically covers chattel paper.

The facts indicate that BankOne neither consented nor knew about the transfer to HEFI. As a result, BankOne's interest continues in the chattel paper under Section 9-315(a)(1). It also continues as a perfected security interest as the original filing against Lucent suffices to continue perfection against HEFI under Section 9-507(a). As BankOne has a perfected security interest in the chattel paper (the Lucent/Balrog contract), **Answer (C) and Answer (D) are incorrect.**

As to HEFI's deposit account, we are told that payments on the Balrog contract were deposited in the account, and they represent the only amounts on deposit. The checks sent to HEFI were identifiable proceeds of the chattel paper, representing amounts "collected on" the chattel paper under Section 9-102(a)(64)(B). The deposit account is thus "proceeds of proceeds" as the entire balance can be traced to Balrog's two checks. BankOne thus has a perfected security interest in the deposit account that will endure beyond the 20-day period of Section 9-315(c) as identifiable cash proceeds of its collateral. § 9-315(d)(2). As a result, **Answer (B) is incorrect, and Answer (A) is correct.**

102.   As established in Question 101, the Balrog contract is chattel paper as to Lucent. The sale to HEFI does not cut off BankOne's security interest as BankOne was perfected before the sale. Sales of chattel paper, however, are subject to Article 9 under Section 9-109(a)

(3). In this "sale" transaction then, Lucent thus became a debtor as to the chattel paper, § 9-102(a)(28)(B), and HEFI became a secured party, § 9-102(a)(73)(D). As a secured party, it became perfected when it took possession of the chattel paper, as chattel paper may be perfected by possession as well as filing under § 9-313(a).

As to the chattel paper itself, then, there are two perfected secured parties who have a perfected security interest. Normally, such disputes are resolved under the first-to-file-or-perfect rule of Section 9-322(a). If that were the rule, BankOne would prevail because its filing date precedes BankTwo's possession/perfection date. But Section 9-322(a) by its own language is subject to other subsections of Section 9-322. One of these subsections—subsection (f)—refers to priority rules found elsewhere in "this part," which refers to part 3 of Article 9; that is, any section of the form "9-3xx."

Part 3 contains Section 9-330(b), which is relevant here. It provides for an exception from the first-to-file-or-perfect rule for certain types of chattel paper. It provides that a "purchaser" of chattel paper has priority in chattel paper already subject to a security interest if that purchaser "gives new value and takes possession of the chattel paper . . . in good faith, in the ordinary course of the purchaser's business, and without knowledge that the purchase violates the rights of the secured party."

Here, HEFI gave new value (the purchase price) and took possession. Whether it is in good faith is an open question given its refusal to search the records. A party cannot be in good faith if it turns a blind eye to records that might give it disqualifying information. On the other hand, if BankOne did not require Lucent to place a legend on its contract indicating BankOne's interest, or require a particular form of contract (as, for example, when the bank specifies or provides the form (noting its interest)—this is, by the way, what most banks that finance car dealers require), then perhaps the trade usage is different. This aspect is discussed in cmt 5. to Section 9-331. (Interpretation of Section 9-331 is relevant under Section 9-330 as Section 9-331 is referred to in the second paragraph of cmt. 6 to Section 9-330, and in the last paragraph of comment 7 to Section 9-330.) If we assume HEFI was in good faith, it is senior to BankOne with respect to the Balrog contract; if not in good faith, it is junior.

As to the deposit account, Question 101 also established that it is proceeds of the chattel paper. Section 9-330(c) deals with proceeds of chattel paper, and generally gives priority to the person entitled to priority under Section 9-322—which contains the first-to-file-or-perfect rule (the only exception being whether the proceeds are returned or repossessed collateral). This temporal priority rule is carried forward in Section 9-322(d) for proceeds of certain collateral—including chattel paper—but *only* if the proceeds are *not* cash proceeds. § 9-322(e).

Here, of course, the proceeds are cash proceeds. In that case, Section 9-327 gives priority to the secured party with control. HEFI, as the customer of the deposit account into which the Balrog checks were deposited, has control under Section 9-104(a)(3), and thus would have priority as to the deposit account as well.

103.   The answer would change as to the contract itself. Section 9-330(b) only applies when the chattel paper purchaser takes possession. That did not occur here, leaving HEFI as an unperfected secured creditor. Under Section 9-322(a)(2), a perfected security interest defeats an unperfected security interest in the same collateral, and so BankOne would have priority as to the contract.

Somewhat paradoxically, there is no difference as to the deposit account. HEFI may be unperfected as to the contract, but once it takes possession of Balrog's checks, it became perfected in those instruments by possession, §9-313(a). When deposited in HEFI's account, the perfection continued as the account was "cash proceeds" as defined in Section 9-102(a)(9). As to priority between the two perfected secured creditors, Section 9-327 still governs, and it holds that, regardless of when perfection occurred, a secured party perfected by control over a deposit account has seniority over any other security interest in that account which is perfected by a method other than control (such as filing).

So while HEFI would lose priority as to the contract, it would retain priority as to all payments received and deposited in its bank account.

Fixtures

104. **Answer (D) is the correct answer.** The definition of "fixtures" references "goods." *See* § 9-102(41). Goods include consumer goods, equipment, farm products, and inventory. TZ Farms is a corporate debtor, so it has no rights in any consumer goods, but it could have rights in equipment, farm products, and inventory. Certainly one or more pieces of its equipment, and its farm products (the strawberry plants), could be "so related to particular real property that an interest in them arises under real property law." And if TZ Farms has rights in farm products (the strawberry plants), those farm products (such as strawberries, once picked) could become subject to a manufacturing process, after which they can become inventory. *See* § 9-102 cmt. 4.a. Bank should be concerned that another entity has filed against any of these goods, including any good that is, will be, or was, a possible fixture (although under Section 9-334(i) a security interest under Article 9 in growing crops has priority over the same crops if local real estate law includes them in real estate, and thus subject to a real estate mortgage or deed of trust). Therefore, Bank should search for fixture filings against any of TZ Farms's goods, whether the goods are equipment, or farm products, or inventory. For this reason, **Answer (D) is the correct answer.**

      Answers (A), (B), and (C) are incorrect answers because each answer is too narrow, omitting two other types of goods that may merit a fixture filing search.

105. The collateral description may mention "fixtures," but the description can be effective without doing so. Fixtures are goods. TZ Farms has rights in goods that may be equipment, farm products, or inventory. A "fixture" is not a separate and independent type of good. It is a label that can be applied to equipment, farm products, or inventory (or, if the debtor is a consumer, perhaps a consumer good). Perhaps rephrased, an asset that is "equipment" bears that label regardless of whether it is a fixture. Therefore, if the collateral description mentions "equipment" and "farm products" and "inventory," then the description covers any fixtures that also fall within those types of collateral—even if the collateral description omits any reference to "fixtures."

106. Bank's belief may rest on a faulty assumption: all of Tim's "consumer goods" are readily movable, therefore negating any concern that any of the collateral might be a "fixture." But the collateral in this question is located at Tim's primary residence, and some of Tim's consumer goods may be affixed with such a degree of permanence to the dwelling structure (or the land) that the goods may fall within the definition of "fixtures" in Section 9-102(a). Examples that come to mind include: a built-in microwave oven and stove, an expensive chandelier, the heating and air conditioning system, security cameras, a

basketball pole, a landscape fountain, etc. Because some of Tim's consumer goods might be a fixture, Bank should conduct a fixture filing search as part of its due diligence and not rely solely on a general UCC search against Tim in the state's central filing office.

107.   Lauren is correct (but the authors have an uneasy sense that Brenda's view is shared by many practitioners). Readers are aware of the four basic methods of perfection: filing/recording, possession, control, and automatic. Fixtures must be goods. As control does not apply to goods, then control will not work as a method of perfecting a security interest in fixtures. Possession is not likely to work as a method of perfecting a security interest in fixtures because the secured party (or its agent) will not be inclined to take up occupancy on the land to which the good is affixed, claiming "possession" of the good. Brenda and Lauren agree that a fixture filing will perfect a security interest in a fixture. They disagree on whether a generic financing statement can perfect the interest, and they disagree on whether the secured party can claim automatic perfection of a PMSI in a consumer good (that is a fixture). Lauren should refer Brenda to at least three different Article 9 provisions to support her view. First, Section 9-501(a)(2) indicates that a secured party can file a financing statement against fixtures in the central filing office (although the filing will not qualify as a fixture filing). Second, Section 9-334 (which addresses priority of security interests in fixtures) mentions, in subsection (e)(3), a security interest in a fixture "perfected by any method permitted by this article[.]" And third, the last paragraph of Official Comment 8 to Section 9-334 acknowledges that "perfection without any filing will be possible" if the secured party is claiming a PMSI in a consumer good.

Brenda does have the law on her side if she asserts that a secured party who relies on a generic financing statement in the central records, or automatic perfection, is less likely to enjoy priority than a secured party who files a fixture filing. *See, e.g.*, § 9-334(d)(3) (referring to perfection by a fixture filing), (e)(1)(A) (same). *But cf.* § 9-334(i) (giving priority to Article 9 interests in crops over interests claimed under local real estate law through a mortgage or deed of trust). But if Brenda and Lauren are discussing perfection, rather than priority, then Lauren's view should carry the day.

108.   **Answer (A) is the correct answer.** Section 9-102(a)(41) defines "fixtures" as "goods that have become so related to particular real property that an interest in them arises under real property." A large video monitor, almost certainly bolted or otherwise affixed to the ceiling of the university auditorium, and thus connected by structural and electrical connections, could be a fixture, **making Answer (A) the correct answer.**

Answer (B) is incorrect. The mirror is affixed to a motor vehicle, which may make the mirror or the motor vehicle, or both, an "accession" as defined in Section 9-102(a)(1). But neither the mirror nor the motor vehicle has triggered an interest in them under real estate law, so there is no fixture. Therefore, **Answer (B) is incorrect.**

Answer (C) is incorrect. Notice that a fixture, by definition, must be a "good," a term defined in Section 9-102(a)(44). The definition of "goods" excludes "oil, gas, or other minerals before extraction," so oil reserves not yet extracted from the ground are not fixtures, **making Answer (C) incorrect.**

Answer (D) is incorrect. A revenue stream from "greens fees" is not "goods," but is something else (e.g., money, instruments, accounts, etc.). Therefore, **Answer (D) is incorrect.**

109.   **Answer (A) is the correct answer.** The contents of an effective fixture filing are summarized in Section 9-502(b). A fixture filing must include the same information as a regular financing statement. It also must (i) state that it covers fixtures, (ii) state that it is to be filed in the real estate records, (iii) provide a description of the real estate, and (iv) provide the name of the record owner of the real estate if the debtor does not have a recorded interest. Only Answer (A) mentions information that the statute requires, so **Answer (A) is the correct answer.**

   Answer (B) is incorrect. While timely filing may enhance priority (*see, e.g.,* § 9-334(d)(3)), the effectiveness of the filing is not dictated by its timeliness.

   Answer (C) is incorrect. As with a generic financing statement, a fixture filing need not be authenticated (by the debtor or, in the case of a fixture filing, the record owner) in order to be effective.

   Answer (D) is incorrect. Section 9-501(a) indicates that a party can file against fixtures by filing locally (county office) or centrally (e.g., the Secretary of State's office). But only a filing at the local level will be treated as a fixture filing. *See* § 9-501(a)(1)(B), (2).

110.   **Answer (C) is the correct answer.** The priority rules concerning fixture disputes are found in Section 9-334. The default rule is found in subsection (c), which awards priority to Bay Area Bank (the real estate encumbrancer) unless BAMCO can claim priority under another subsection. BAMCO has engaged in seller financing to enable CG to acquire the tanks, so it can claim a purchase-money security interest in the tanks under Sections 9-103(a) and (b)(1). And Bay Area Bank's interest in the real estate arose in February, before the tanks became fixtures in August. The only way, then, that BAMCO can enjoy priority is if there is a statute allows BAMCO to "prime" or subordinate Bay Area Bank's interest — and there is: Section 9-334. That Section provides that BAMCO's security interest in the tanks enjoys priority if BAMCO files a fixture filing with respect to that security interest no later than the twentieth day "after the goods become fixtures." § 9-334(d). The date that the tanks became fixtures (the date which starts the running of the 20 days) is August 15, not July 20 (the purchase date), because it is only on the later date that the tanks became so affixed to the real estate that they became subject to local real estate law. So BAMCO's fixture filing is timely if it is filed on or before September 4. A fixture filing on September 1, then, is timely, and BAMCO can claim priority. Therefore, **Answer (C) is the correct answer.**

   Answer (A) is incorrect. Even though the tanks are fixtures, BAMCO can perfect its security interest by filing a standard financing statement in the central filing office of the state where the debtor (GC) is located. *See* §§ 9-501(a)(2); 9-301(1). GC, a corporation, is a "registered organization" under Section 9-102(a)(71). A registered organization is deemed located in the state of its creation (*see* § 9-307(e)), so BAMCO should file its standard financing statement in Delaware, the state in which BAMCO is incorporated, rather than in California, (the location of business operations). For this reason, **Answer (A) is incorrect.**

Answer (B) is incorrect. Absent a fixture filing, BAMCO cannot claim priority over Bay Area Bank under any other subsection of 9-334 (subsection (e)(1) requires a fixture filing, subsection (e)(2) is inapplicable because the tanks are not readily removable, and no other subsection applies). BAMCO can rely on a standard financing statement to perfect its security interest, but that filing is of little comfort in a priority dispute with a real estate claimant. Therefore, **Answer (B) is incorrect.**

Answer (D) is incorrect. The tanks are being offered as collateral by GC, a corporation. Therefore, the tanks are not consumer goods (but instead are equipment). This means that BAMCO's seller-financed PMSI is not eligible for automatic perfection under Section 9-309(1) (or any other Section), so **Answer (D) is incorrect.**

111.   **Answer (C) is the correct answer.** Section 9-604 provides the fixture creditor with a choice: it can exercise its rights and remedies afforded by Part 6 of Article 9, or it can elect to pursue its rights and remedies under the relevant real estate law. *See* § 9-604(b). If BAMCO decides to pursue its rights and remedies under Article 9, it can remove the fixtures—but only if its security interest enjoys priority. *See* § 9-604(c). Therefore, **Answer (C) is the correct answer.**

Answer (A) is incorrect because it erroneously suggests that BAMCO is governed exclusively by real estate law. As noted above, BAMCO has the option to pursue its rights and remedies under Part 6 of Article 9.

Answer (B) is incorrect because Section 9-604(c) does not condition BAMCO's removal on GC's consent (although BAMCO cannot breach the peace).

Answer (D) is incorrect because neither Section 9-604(c) (nor any other provision of Article 9) prohibits BAMCO from removing fixtures if GC has paid off a certain percentage of the debt.

112.   **Answer (B) is the correct answer.** Section 9-604(d) states that BAMCO "need not reimburse the encumbrancer [Bay Area Bank] or owner [GC] for any diminution in value of the real property caused by the absence of the goods removed [the tanks] or by any necessity of replacing them." Therefore, neither Bay Area Bank nor GC is entitled to $15,000 (or $20,000), so **Answer (A) and Answer (C) are incorrect answers.** BAMCO is liable for damage that it causes during removal—but to whom? Section 9-604(d) states that BAMCO "shall promptly reimburse any encumbrancer or owner of the real property, other than the debtor, for the cost of repair of any physical injury caused by the removal." This means that BAMCO must pay $5,000 to Bay Area Bank rather than to GC, **making Answer (B) the correct answer and Answer (D) an incorrect answer.**

113.   **Answer (A) is the correct answer.** This question seems to involve fixtures, but it does not. The three appliances have yet to be installed, so they have not become fixtures. Until they

become fixtures, Fidelity Finance has no interest in them (at least through its mortgage). The appliances retain their character as personal property (equipment) covered solely by Article 9. This is a one-party dispute, easy to resolve in favor of KAI under Section 9-201(a), **making Answer (A) the correct answer.** Fidelity Finance cannot win a priority dispute unless it has an enforceable interest in the collateral—and it does not, prior to installation. Therefore, **Answers (B), (C), and (D) are incorrect.** As we will see in the next question and answer, however, the analysis changes if the units become fixtures before Tasty Treats files its bankruptcy petition.

114. Fidelity Finance enjoys priority in the three appliances, which became fixtures upon their installation. Section 9-334(h) awards priority to Fidelity Finance because its interest arises in the units under a construction mortgage that was recorded in the real property records before the appliances became fixtures (and the appliances became fixtures before construction had been completed). KAI cannot invoke the exceptions found in Sections 9-334(d) and (e)(1) because it never filed a fixture filing. Nor can KAI invoke the exception found in Section 9-334(e)(2) because the appliances, under the facts, are not readily removable. No other exception in Section 9-334 is available. Therefore, Fidelity Finance, as a construction mortgagee, enjoys priority in the three appliances.

115. No, the bankruptcy trustee will not be successful in its attempt to convert KAI's secured claim into an unsecured claim by avoiding KAI's security interest under the strong-arm clause of the Bankruptcy Code. The strong-arm clause (11 U.S.C. § 544(a)(1)) effectively permits the trustee to avoid any security interest that is unperfected, or would otherwise be subordinate to the interest of a hypothetical lien creditor arising as of the filing of a bankruptcy case (perhaps an oversimplification, but one that suffices for this question). KAI filed a standard financing statement, which perfected its security interest in the three appliances under Section 9-501(a)(2). Therefore, under Section 9-334(e)(3), KAI's security interest is senior to the trustee's hypothetical lien ("obtained by legal or equitable proceedings"), which arose (hypothetically) on the petition date after KAI perfected its security interest by a central filing (a "method permitted by this article," particularly Section 9-501(a)(2)). In summary, then, KAI's perfected security interest in the appliances cannot be avoided by the bankruptcy trustee under the strong-arm clause (notwithstanding the absence of a fixture filing). *See* § 9-334, cmt. 9.

116. **Answer (A) is the correct answer.** The chandelier has been installed at Grace's home, making it a consumer good. ZinnCo has provided seller financing, so its PMSI (in a consumer good) is eligible for automatic perfection under Section 9-309(1). A purchase-money security interest in a fixture is senior to an existing encumbrance of fixtures so long as the secured party properly files a fixture filing by the twentieth day after the goods become a fixture. § 9-334(d). This provision is broad enough to cover purchase-money security interests in consumer goods perfected automatically by Section 9-309(1) (such as the chandelier). *See* § 9-334, cmt. 8 (last paragraph).

Answer (B) is incorrect. No provision of Article 9 terminates automatic perfection of a PMSI when the consumer good becomes a fixture.

Answer (C) is incorrect. The priority rules concerning fixture disputes are found in Section 9-334. The default rule is found in subsection (c), which awards priority to Friendly Finance (the real estate encumbrancer) unless ZinnCo can claim priority under another subsection. ZinnCo has engaged in seller financing, so it can claim a purchase-money security interest in the chandelier under Sections 9-103(a) and (b)(1). And Fidelity Finance's interest in the real estate arose in March, before the chandelier became a fixture in August. Therefore, ZinnCo's security interest in the chandelier enjoys priority if, but only if, it files a fixture filing no later than the twentieth day "after the goods become fixtures." § 9-334(d). **Answer (C) is incorrect** because it suggests that ZinnCo can enjoy priority, even if it fails to timely file a fixture filing.

Answer (D) is incorrect (at least in an absolute sense). The chandelier became a fixture on August 7. As noted above, to enjoy priority, ZinnCo must file its fixture filing no later than the twentieth day thereafter. A fixture filing in August might, or might not, be timely. The timeliness turns on *when* in August the filing is recorded. A fixture filing on or before August 27 is timely, but a fixture filing on any of the last four days in August is not timely. Therefore, **Answer (D) is incorrect (at least in an absolute sense).** More information (the filing date in August) is necessary.

117. ZinnCo's security interest in the chandelier enjoys priority over the competing claim asserted by Nancy Neighbor. Section 9-334(e) awards priority to a "perfected security interest in fixtures" over "a conflicting interest of an encumbrancer" if "(3) the conflicting interest is a lien on the real property obtained by legal or equitable proceedings after the security interest was perfected by any method permitted by this article." ZinnCo can satisfy the three conditions of this priority rule. First, the chandelier is installed in Grace's residence, so the chandelier is a consumer good; and ZinnCo provided seller financing, so ZinnCo is a purchase-money creditor. Therefore, ZinnCo's PMSI in the chandelier (a consumer good) is automatically perfected (a "method permitted by this article") under Section 9-309(1). Second, Nancy's lien on the residence and chandelier arose from her successful lawsuit, a "legal proceeding." And third, Nancy's lien arose on September 1, after ZinnCo's security interest attached and became automatically perfected in August. Therefore, notwithstanding the absence of any standard filing or fixture filing, ZinnCo's automatically perfected PMSI in the chandelier enjoys priority over Nancy's competing judgment lien.

118. **Answer (B) is the correct answer.** This three-party dispute can be broken down into three separate two-party disputes (Dealer v. Bank, Bank v. Big Tex, and Big Tex v. Bank). As the following analysis reveals, no clear winner emerges. Instead, the facts illustrate the "circular priority" conundrum, where each party enjoys priority over one other party but does not enjoy priority over the other party (think "rock, paper, scissors").

Dealer's standard financing statement perfected its security interest under Section 9-501(a)(2). Big Tex perfected its security interest under Section 9-501(a)(1) by filing a fixture filing. And Bank's interest arose from the mortgage that it recorded.

The competing property interests of Dealer and Big Tex arose under Article 9, rather than real estate law. Therefore, the applicable priority rule is not found in Section 9-334, but in Section 9-322(a). Dealer filed and perfected its interest earlier than did Big Tex, so Dealer wins this two-party dispute.

Bank's interest arose under its mortgage, so Section 9-334 will resolve its disputes with Dealer and Big Tex. Bank enjoys priority over Dealer under Section 9-334(c) because Bank is a real estate encumbrancer and Dealer is claiming an interest in fixtures. No exception applies (Dealer never filed a fixture filing, and the fixture is not readily removable). But because Big Tex filed a fixture filing that perfected its security interest before Bank recorded its mortgage, Big Tex enjoys priority over Bank under Section 9-334(e)(1).

In summary, then, Dealer beats Big Tex, Big Tex defeats Bank, and Bank enjoys priority over Dealer. Everyone is a winner. But everyone is a loser, too. We are not quite sure how a court will resolve this dilemma. But the correct answer among the four options is the answer that recognizes no party will lose to, or have priority over, the other two parties. Answer (B) is the only answer that does so, so **Answer (B) is the correct answer.** The other three answers erroneously suggest that a party suffers two defeats or enjoys two victories—neither of which is true—**making Answers (A), (C), and (D) incorrect answers.**

Priority (Secured Party v. Secured Party; No PMSI)

119.   **Answer (D) is the correct answer.** The first step is to determine whether (or the extent to which) Meredith and Ethan have an enforceable security interest in any of Grace's jewelry. As a general rule (subject to exceptions not applicable here), Section 9-203(b) requires the debtor (Grace) to authenticate a written security agreement in order to create an enforceable security interest in the collateral, unless the secured party (Meredith or Ethan) takes possession of agreed-upon collateral. Grace and Meredith never memorialized their agreement in writing, so Meredith has no enforceable security interest in any of Grace's jewelry, except for the diamond necklace in her possession. And because Meredith has possession, a valid form of perfection under Section 9-313, Meredith's enforceable security interest in the diamond necklace is also perfected. Ethan and Grace memorialized their agreement in writing, so Ethan has an enforceable security interest in all of Grace's jewelry, including the diamond necklace. But Ethan did not take possession of any jewelry, and he did not file a financing statement. Therefore, he has an enforceable, but unperfected, security interest in Grace's jewelry.

Meredith's perfected security interest in the diamond necklace enjoys priority over Ethan's unperfected security interest in the diamond necklace. *See* §9-322(a)(2). Ethan's unperfected security interest in all of the remaining jewelry enjoys priority over Meredith's unsecured claim (she has no enforceable security interest in the remaining jewelry). *See* §9-201(a). Answer (D) reflects these two conclusions, **making Answer (D) the correct answer.**

Answer (A) is incorrect. Meredith and Ethan do not have coequal claims to any of the jewelry. Meredith has an enforceable security interest only in the diamond necklace in her possession, and that security interest (which is perfected) has priority. Ethan has the only enforceable security interest in all of the remaining jewelry. Therefore, he has priority in it.

Answer (B) is incorrect. Meredith has an enforceable (and perfected) security interest in the diamond necklace in her possession (but the statement is otherwise true, as to all other jewelry).

Answer (C) is incorrect. Ethan's failure to take possession of any jewelry or file a financing statement does not frustrate enforceability, but merely perfection. Ethan and Grace memorialized their agreement in writing, so Ethan has an enforceable (albeit unperfected) security interest in all of Grace's jewelry.

120.   **Answer (B) is the correct answer.** As noted in the previous discussion, Ethan has an enforceable security interest in all of the jewelry. If Meredith and Grace timely memorialize their understanding in writing (by "timely" we will assume that the agreement was memorialized before Ethan and Grace entered into their agreement), then Meredith now has an enforceable security interest in all of the jewelry. Both Meredith and Ethan have enforceable security interests in the jewelry in Grace's possession. But neither creditor filed a financing statement, and they do not have possession if Grace has possession. Therefore, each of them has an enforceable, but unperfected, security interest in the jewelry that Grace possesses. Section 9-322(a)(3) resolves a priority dispute between two secured but unperfected security interests in favor of the creditor whose interest attached first. That creditor is Meredith, whose security interest attached to all of the jewelry (none of which has been acquired by Grace in recent months) when Meredith and Grace memorialized their agreement in writing, which, if "timely," was before Ethan's security interest attached two months later. Therefore, **Answer (B) is the correct answer.**

   Answer (A) is incorrect because Meredith's interest attached before Ethan's interest attached. If both interests attached at the same time (which could happen if we were dealing with jewelry that Grace acquired after Ethan and Grace memorialized their agreement), then we would have a "tie." But no such "tie" exists under these facts; there is no after-acquired property.

   Answer (C) is incorrect. Meredith's security interest has priority for reasons stated above.

   Answer (D) is incorrect. Both Meredith and Ethan have enforceable security interests for reasons stated above.

121.   **Answer (B) is the correct answer.** Meredith has a perfected security interest in the diamond necklace in her possession, for reasons previously stated. Now Ethan, as a result of his filing, also has a perfected security interest in the same necklace (and all other jewelry in Grace's possession). When a priority dispute arises between two perfected secured parties, the dispute is resolved in favor of the party who filed or perfected first (whichever is earlier, and assuming no lapse of both filing and perfection thereafter). *See* § 9-322(a)(1). Meredith never filed, but she perfected her security interest in the diamond necklace when she took possession of it. At that time, Ethan had yet to become a secured party, so his filing and perfection date are sometime later. Because Meredith has the earliest of the possible filing or perfection dates, her perfected security interest in the diamond necklace in her possession enjoys priority, **making Answer (B) the correct answer.**

   Answer (A) and Answer (D) are incorrect answers because Meredith has priority over, rather than shared priority with, Ethan's security interest.

   Answer (C) is incorrect because Meredith's perfected security interest, not Ethan's perfected security interest, enjoys priority.

122.   **Answer (C) is the correct answer.** By October, when the priority dispute erupts, both First Bank and Second Bank can claim a perfected security interest in the piece of equipment.

When a priority dispute arises between two perfected secured parties, the dispute is resolved in favor of the party who filed or perfected first (whichever is earlier, and assuming no lapse of both filing and perfection thereafter). *See* § 9-322(a)(1). Thorough analysis requires the reader to determine First Bank's filing date and perfection date, and Second Bank's filing date and perfection date. The earliest of these four possible dates will dictate which bank has priority. First Bank's filing date is February 20, and its perfection date is April 10 (when the last of the attachment steps is satisfied). Second Bank's filing date is March 23, which is also its perfection date (as ZinnCorp had already acquired the piece of equipment). Second Bank has the earlier perfection date (March 23 versus April 10), but First Bank has an even earlier filing date (February 20). Therefore, First Bank has priority because of its filing date, **making Answer (C) the correct answer.**

Answer (A) is incorrect. First Bank was the first creditor to file, but it was the second creditor to perfect.

Answer (B) is incorrect. Second Bank was the first creditor to both file and perfect, but it did so in March after First Bank had already filed in February. Therefore, Second Bank loses the priority battle.

Answer (D) is incorrect. Second Bank is the first creditor to perfect its security interest, but it loses priority because First Bank has an earlier filing date.

123. The result is the same: First Bank has priority. The analysis remains the same, except in determining each creditor's perfection date. ZinnCorp does not acquire rights in the piece of equipment until July 1, a necessary step for attachment under Section 9-203(b)(2). For each creditor, that is the date of both attachment and perfection. Despite the "tie" as to attachment and perfection, First Bank continues to win under Section 9-322(a)(1) because it has a filing date (February 23) earlier than Second Bank's filing date (March 23) and perfection date (July 1).

124. Without an after-acquired property clause, First Bank has no enforceable security interest in equipment purchased after ZinnCorp has authenticated its security agreement. ZinnCorp authenticated its security agreement with First Bank on April 10, and ZinnCorp acquired the piece of equipment at a later date (July 1). Therefore, First Bank has no enforceable security interest in the piece of equipment acquired by ZinnCorp on July 1. Second Bank has a perfected security interest in it, however, by operation of the after-acquired property clause in its security agreement. Second Bank has priority because it has a security interest in the piece of equipment, whereas First Bank does not. *See* § 9-201(a).

125. First Bank will have priority in the piece of equipment. The amended security agreement allows First Bank's security interest to attach to the piece of equipment (not on the purchase date of July 1, but on the security agreement amendment date of August 1). Its interest is perfected on August 1 (the date of attachment) by its earlier filing in February. And because its filing date in February is earlier than any filing date or perfection date claimed by Second Bank, First Bank has priority (as of the date of its security agreement amendment) in the piece of equipment acquired by ZinnCorp on July 1.

126.   **Answer (C) is the correct answer.** A security interest in investment property can be perfected by filing. *See* § 9-312(a). Therefore, **Answer (D) can be eliminated as an incorrect answer.**

The general rule on filing location is found in Section 9-301(1), which directs the secured party to file its financing statement where the debtor is located. But the opening language of Section 9-301(1) defers to rules found in Sections 9-303 through 9-306, if applicable. Section 9-305 applies to this question because the collateral (in particular, the LCI stock certificate) is investment property (as defined in Section 9-102(a)(49)). Subsection (c)(1) of Section 9-305 states the same filing rule found in Section 9-301(1): file where the debtor is located. In this question, MegaCorp is the debtor. It is a corporate entity and, therefore, a registered organization under Section 9-102(a)(71). A registered organization is located in its state of creation. *See* § 9-307(e). MegaCorp is incorporated under Delaware law, so it is deemed located in Delaware. Therefore, a secured party seeking to perfect its security interest in MegaCorp's investment property by filing must file its financing statement in Delaware. **Answer (A) is incorrect**, then, because it erroneously suggests that a filing in Texas (the state in which LCI, the issuer of the investment property, is located) is effective.

Answer (B) correctly identifies Delaware as the place to file. But if First Bank does not file in Delaware until April 15, it will lose the priority dispute to an earlier filer under the general "first to file or perfect" rule of Section 9-322(a)(1). Second Bank did file its financing statement earlier, on April 13. So **Answer (B) is an incorrect answer.**

Answer (C) implicitly, but correctly, suggests that Second Bank can perfect its security interest in the LCI stock certificate by taking delivery of it. *See* § 9-313(a). If the stock certificate was issued in bearer form (issued to "bearer" or in blank), then Second Bank will have "control" of the certificate under Section 8-106(a) by taking delivery of it. Perfection by control trumps perfection by filing. *See* § 9-328(1). But the facts state that the certificate is in registered form. Taking delivery of a certificate in registered form, without more, does not give Second Bank control. *See* § 8-106(b) (requiring delivery *plus* either indorsement or registration). So it is possible, without knowing more facts, that Second Bank does not have control of the LCI stock certificate even though it has taken delivery. And without control, it cannot invoke the priority rule of Section 9-328(1). Even so, though, there is another way in which Second Bank can claim priority. Second Bank enjoys priority under Section 9-328(5). That section states: "A security interest in a certificated security in registered form which is perfected by taking delivery . . . and not by control . . . has priority over a conflicting security interest perfected by a method other than control." First Bank perfected by filing, not control. Therefore, the rule applies and Second Bank's possession gives it priority, **making Answer (C) the correct answer.**

127.   **Answer (B) is the correct answer.** A financing statement is effective for five years. *See* § 9-515(a). A secured party can extend the life of its filing by timely filing a UCC-3 continuation statement within the last six months of that five-year period. *See* § 9-515(c), (d). Both banks did so. Therefore, the basic "first to file or perfect" rule of Section 9-322(a)(1) applies. Alpha Bank's original filing date of August 1, 2013, is earlier than (i) Omega Bank's

filing date of October 1, 2013, and (ii) its own and Omega Bank's perfection dates of February 1, 2017, and November 1, 2018 (the two attachment and perfection dates in the after-acquired equipment). Because Alpha Bank's filing date is earlier than any other relevant date, it has priority in both pieces of equipment, **making Answer (B) the correct answer.**

Answer (A) is incorrect. Yes, Alpha Bank does have priority in Item #1, but it also has priority in Item #2 (and Omega Bank does not).

Answer (C) is incorrect because Alpha Bank, rather than Omega Bank, has priority in Item #1 and Item #2.

Answer (D) is incorrect because the priority in Item #2 does not ebb and flow, depending on the filing dates of the UCC-3 continuation statements (assuming, as under these facts, that both continuation statements are timely filed).

128.   Yes, the analysis will change, as will the result. To be effective, a continuation statement must be filed within the last six months of the five-year life of the UCC-1 financing statement. *See* § 9-515(d). A continuation statement filed early (before the six-month period starts running) is *ineffective* (even if it slips past the clerk and is recorded). *See* §§ 9-510(c); 9-516(b)(7); 9-520(a), (c). Alpha Bank filed its financing statement on August 1, 2013, so its five-year life expired on or about August 1, 2018. The preceding six months started running on or about February 1, 2018. If Alpha Bank files its UCC-3 continuation statement on January 15, 2018, the filing is premature and ineffective. *See* § 9-510(c). Absent a timely continuation statement, Alpha Bank's security interest will become unperfected prospectively when its filing lapses on or about August 1, 2018, and, as against Omega Bank as "a purchaser of the collateral for value," retroactively. *See* § 9-515(c). After the lapse, Omega Bank has priority in both pieces of equipment under Section 9-322(a)(2), which states that a perfected security interest (held by Omega Bank) has priority over an unperfected security interest (held by Alpha Bank).

129.   **Answer (D) is the correct answer.** The $40,000 check represents identifiable proceeds of the inventory. The hotel delivered the check at the time of purchase, so there was never any intervening account. Midway Bank is the only party to have a security interest in the inventory, so it is the only party to have a security interest in the $40,000 check. (First Finance cannot claim an interest in the check as "proceeds" of an account because the transaction was a cash sale. There is no intervening account. Nor can First Finance argue that the check may have been "proceeds" of inventory that was itself "proceeds" of an account. This particular inventory has been owned by the debtor since February, before First Finance became a secured party.) The $50,000 check also represents identifiable proceeds of the inventory. But the college delivered the check sometime after purchasing the furniture, creating an intervening account. First Finance has an interest in accounts, creating a two-party dispute in the check (First Finance claiming it as first-generation proceeds of an account, and Midway Bank claiming it as second-generation proceeds of inventory). The basic first-to-file-or-perfect rule resolves the two-party dispute in favor of First Finance because its filing date (March 1) is earlier than any filing date (June 4) or

perfection date (no earlier than June 4) claimed by Midway Bank. In summary, then, Midway Bank has priority in the $50,000 check (as the only creditor with an interest), and First Finance has priority in the $40,000 check (as the earlier filer), **making Answer (D) the correct answer.**

Answer (A) is incorrect. First Finance has priority in one, but not both, of the checks.

Answer (B) is incorrect. Midway Bank has priority in one, but not both, of the checks.

Answer (C) is incorrect. Each creditor has priority in one check, but the checks (or the priority) should be reversed.

130.   **Answer (B) is the correct answer.** As between First Finance and Midway Bank, the priority remains the same as discussed in the previous answer. The issue in this question is whether Paragon Bank might have priority in the two credits after Odyssey Furniture deposits the two checks. It does. The facts state that Paragon Bank has a security interest in the deposit account (and, therefore, in the part of the deposit account created by the two credits arising from the two check deposits). Its enforceable security interest is perfected by "control" under Section 9-104(a)(1), as Paragon Bank is the financial institution that maintains the deposit account (and its failure to file a financing statement is a red herring, because Section 9-312(b)(1) states that "a security interest in a deposit account [as original collateral] may be perfected only by control"). All three creditors are now claiming a perfected security interest in two particular credit entries to the deposit account. Under Section 9-327(1), Paragon Bank has priority because, with respect to conflicting security interests in a deposit account, a security interest perfected by control enjoys priority over a competing security interest not perfected by control (e.g., filing). **For these reasons, Answer (B) is the correct answer.**

Answer (A) and Answer (D) are incorrect. Rarely does Article 9 provide a priority rule that results in "shared" priority, and no such rule applies here. (For such a rule, see Section 9-322(a)(3), which could create "shared" priority between two unperfected security interests that attach simultaneously.)

Answer (C) is incorrect. As between just First Finance and Midway Bank, the answer states the correct priority. But Paragon Bank has priority over both First Finance and Midway Bank in the two credits arising from the two check deposits under Section 9-327(1).

131.   **Answer (A) is the correct answer.** The accounts and chattel paper contracts resulted from inventory sales, so Metro Bank can claim an enforceable security interest in them as proceeds under Sections 9-203(f) and 9-315(a)(2). The security interest in each is perfected for 20 days under Section 9-315(c) and thereafter under Section 9-315(d)(1). ZeeCorp's sale of accounts and chattel paper falls within the scope of Article 9 (*see* § 9-109(a)(3)), making ZeeCorp a debtor and Friendly Finance a secured party (*see* §§ 9-102(a)(28)(B) (defining "debtor"); 9-102(a)(73)(D) (defining "secured party"). Friendly Finance has a security interest in the accounts and chattel paper that it has purchased. *See* § 1-201(b) (35) (defining "security interest"). Metro Bank's perfected security interest in the accounts

enjoys priority over Friendly Finance's unperfected security interest under Section 9-322(a)(2) (Friendly Finance, which never filed a financing statement, also loses even if its security interest in the accounts is automatically perfected under Section 9-309(2) because Metro Bank's filing date of February 15 is earlier than Friendly Finance's perfection date in June.) But under Section 9-330(a), Friendly Finance, a purchaser of the chattel paper contracts, has priority over Metro Bank's perfected security interest in chattel paper claimed merely as proceeds of inventory. Friendly Finance acquired the contracts in the ordinary course of its business, took possession of the contracts, and gave "new value" under Section 9-102(a)(57) in the form of $35,000. Furthermore, the facts do not indicate that the contracts included any type of legend indicating they had been assigned to Metro Bank or any other party, and its knowledge of Metro Bank's filed financing statement should not preclude Friendly Finance from satisfying the requirement of good faith as defined in Section 1-201(b)(20) (*see* § 9-330, cmt. 6). In summary, then, Metro Bank enjoys priority in the accounts, and Friendly Finance has priority in the chattel paper contracts. Therefore, **Answer (A) is the correct answer. Answers (B), (C), and (D) are incorrect** because they misstate one or both priority dispute results.

132.   **Answer (C) is the correct answer.** Fidelity Finance's security interest in the Item became perfected on November 1, when Clinic acquired the Item (the security agreement was in place on September 1, Fidelity Finance had given value on September 1, and Fidelity Finance had filed its financing statement on September 12). Bluebird Bank's security interest in the deposit account was perfected by control under Section 9-104(a)(1) on May 1. It can claim an enforceable security interest in the Item under Section 9-315(a)(2) as an "identifiable proceed" of the funds in the deposit account. Therefore, **Answer (A) is incorrect.** Fidelity Bank's security interest in the Item is perfected for at least 20 days from the date of attachment under Section 9-315(c), which runs through the dispute resolution date of November 15. Therefore, **Answer (B) is incorrect.** So as of November 15, both Fidelity Finance and Bluebird Bank have a perfected security interest in the Item. Under the general "first to file or perfect" rule of Section 9-322(a)(1), Bluebird Bank has priority because its perfection date of May 1 (which is the appropriate date under Section 9-322(b) because Bluebird Bank is asserting an interest in the Item as a "proceed" of the deposit account) is earlier than Fidelity Finance's filing date of September 12 and perfection date of November 1. But by its own opening language, Section 9-322(a) is subject to other priority rules. The rule that applies to this dispute is found in Section 9-322(d). Under that provision, a creditor's security interest in proceeds of a deposit account does not enjoy priority if another creditor filed first against those proceeds. This means that Bluebird Bank's security interest in the Item (claimed as a proceed of Clinic's deposit account) is junior to the competing security interest claimed by Fidelity Finance, which filed first against Clinic's equipment. Therefore, **Answer (C) is the correct answer and Answer (D) is an incorrect answer.**

133.   **Answer (D) is the correct answer.** Bluebird Bank's filing on November 18 extends its automatic perfection beyond the 20-day period of Section 9-315(c) to the dispute resolution date of December 1. *See* § 9-315(d)(3). But Fidelity Finance continues to enjoy priority under Section 9-322(d) for reasons explained in the previous answer. Therefore, **Answer (D) is correct and Answer (C) is incorrect.**

Fidelity Finance has an enforceable security interest in the current and after-acquired equipment. Its financing statement describes the collateral in a manner that omits any reference to after-acquired equipment. This is a red herring, though, as the after-acquired property clause need not be mentioned in the financing statement. *See* §§ 9-204, cmt. 7; 9-502, cmt. 2. Therefore, **Answer (A) is incorrect.**

Article 9 makes clear that a secured party can have "control" over the deposit account, even if the debtor continues to enjoy access to the funds therein. *See* § 9-104(b). Therefore, **Answer (B) is incorrect.**

134.   **Answer (A) is the correct answer.** If the judge relies on the general priority rule of Section 9-322(a)(1), then she should rule in favor of Beta Bank because its filing date (2015) is earlier than Alpha Bank's filing date (2016). But if she does so, she would be wrong. Section 9-322(a) is subject to Section 9-322(f), which states that priority rules found elsewhere in Sections 9-301 through 9-342 (part 3 of Article 9, or "this part") may control. One of those rules is Section 9-325(a), which states: "[A] security interest created by a debtor [BetaTech] is subordinate to a security interest in the same collateral created by another person [AlphaTech] if: (1) the debtor [BetaTech] acquired the collateral subject to the security interest created by the other person [AlphaTech]; (2) the security interest created by the other person [AlphaTech] was perfected when the debtor [BetaTech] acquired the collateral; and (3) there is no period thereafter when the security interest is unperfected." Clause (1) is satisfied because Alpha Bank's security interest survived the unauthorized sale under Sections 9-201 and 9-315(a), and BetaTech's acquisition does not terminate the security interest under Section 9-320(a) (BetaTech is not a buyer in the ordinary course of business because the Item in AlphaTech's hands is equipment, not inventory) or Section 9-320(b) (neither AlphaTech nor BetaTech hold the Item as a consumer good, and Alpha Bank has filed a financing statement). Therefore, **Answer (D) is incorrect.** Clause (2) is met because Alpha Bank's financing statement remained effective at the time of sale and, under Section 9-507(a), thereafter. Therefore, **Answer (C) is incorrect.** In addition, clause (3) is met (no filing lapse, and no known change in jurisdiction which might otherwise trigger concerns under Section 9-316). Finally, Section 9-325(b) applies to subordinate the security interest of Beta Bank to the security interest of Alpha Bank because otherwise Beta Bank would enjoy priority under Section 9-322(a). For these reasons, **Answer (A) is the correct answer and Answer (B) is an incorrect answer.**

The result should not be surprising. If BetaTech acquires the Item subject to the security interest held by Alpha Bank, then BetaTech's creditors (e.g., Beta Bank) also take the Item subject to the security interest held by Alpha Bank. Perhaps rephrased, a secured party can only take a security interest in the limited, and possibly encumbered, rights held by its debtor.

135.   Beta Bank enjoys priority under the revised facts. Under the original facts, both AlphaTech (the selling debtor) and BetaTech (the buying debtor) were located in Delaware, the state in which their respective creditors filed financing statements. Under the revised facts,

AlphaTech is a Texas corporation and, therefore, deemed located in that state for filing purposes. *See* §§ 9-301(1), 9-307(e). Alpha Bank must be concerned, then, with what effect this difference in jurisdiction might have on its continued perfection. The answer is found in Section 9-316(a)(3), which continues Alpha Bank's perfected status for one year from the transfer date (unless the five-year effectiveness period of the original financing statement is scheduled to lapse in a shorter period). AlphaTech sold the Item to BetaTech on August 10, 2017, more than a year before the dispute resolution date of September 1, 2018. The facts do not suggest that Alpha Bank filed a new financing statement in Delaware, so its security interest in the Item has become unperfected prospectively and, as against Beta Bank as "a purchaser of the collateral for value," retroactively. *See* § 9-316(b). Alpha Bank can no longer navigate Section 9-325(a)(3), so the protections afforded by Section 9-325 (as under the original facts) are no longer available. BetaTech can now invoke Section 9-317(b), under which it acquires the Item free and clear of Alpha Bank's security interest (it gave value as a buyer, and took delivery of the Item presumably without knowledge of Alpha Bank's security interest). *See also* 9-316, cmt. 3 (example 5).

136.   **Answer (D) is the correct answer.** Section 9-316(a) addresses the continued perfection of Karen's security interest after Tim moves from Texas to North Carolina. Karen remains perfected for the shorter of two periods: four months, or the remaining life of her Texas filing. *See* § 9-316(a)(1), (2). Under the facts, four months is the shorter of the two periods. Therefore, Karen's security interest remains perfected until July 15 (four months after the relocation date of March 15). The dispute resolution date is July 1, a date on which both sisters are perfected. Karen enjoys priority under the basic first-to-file-or-perfect rule in Section 9-322(a)(1). Answer (D) captures the correct status and priority, **making Answer (D) the correct answer.**

Answer (A) is incorrect. Diana does have the only North Carolina filing on July 1, but Karen remains perfected (and therefore enjoys priority) for four months after Tim's relocation.

Answer (B) is incorrect. Karen's interest remains perfected for four months after Tim's relocation.

Answer (C) is incorrect. Tim's relocation did not terminate Karen's security interest, which remains perfected for four months thereafter.

137.   **Answer (D) is the correct answer.** To avoid any break in her perfection, Karen must file a new financing statement against Tim within the four-month period, which ends on or about July 15. Karen filed a financing statement in North Carolina, but she waited until July 20 to do so. Her filing is untimely, and her perfection lapsed on or about July 15. *See* § 9-316(b). She re-perfects on July 20, but the break in her perfection prevents her from using her Texas filing date in the priority dispute. Both Karen and Diana have perfected security interests in the grand piano in November 2018. Diana wins under the first-to-file-or-perfect rule of Section 9-322(a)(1) because her filing and perfection date of May 10,

2018, is earlier than Karen's filing and perfection date of July 20, 2018. **Answer (D) is the correct answer.**

Answer (A) is incorrect. Diana did file first in North Carolina, but she enjoys priority because Karen failed to file in North Carolina within the four-month period. Diana can be the first filer in North Carolina and, under revised facts, still lose a priority dispute if Karen files after Diana files but within the four-month period. In effect, Diana cannot be assured of priority until the four-month period expires and she determines whether Karen filed in North Carolina prior to the expiration of that period.

Answer (B) is incorrect. Karen had priority until the four-month period expired. Because she failed to file a financing statement in North Carolina within that period, her perfection ceased. As a result, Karen lost priority thereafter.

Answer (C) is incorrect. Karen does not regain priority when she files in North Carolina on July 20. She does become re-perfected, but she lost priority to Diana when the four-month period ended, and Diana retains priority even after Karen refiles (albeit untimely) in North Carolina.

138. **Answer (B) is the correct answer.** Lender's search against the debtor's current legal name of "Houston Healthcare Corp." has failed to reveal Bank's previous filing against "Health-Net Corp." Therefore, under Section 9-506(c), the debtor's name change has caused Bank's financing statement to become seriously misleading. Nevertheless, the filing against "HealthNet Corp." remains effective to perfect a security interest in equipment acquired by the debtor (i) prior to the name change and (ii) within four months after the name change (*see* § 9-507(c)) — even if the perfected or unperfected status is examined (as in this question) on a date long after the four-month period has concluded. The debtor acquired Item #1 on May 10, within four months after the name change on March 15, so Bank's filing remains effective to perfect its security interest in Item #1. The debtor acquired Item #2 on July 20 and Item #3 on September 18. These two dates fall outside the four-month period that concluded on or about July 15. Therefore, Bank's filing does not perfect its security interest in those two items. Bank remains perfected in Item #1 by its filing, so it has priority in Item #1 under the "first to file or perfect" rule of Section 9-322(a)(1) because it filed in January, and Lender filed in July. But Lender has priority in Items #2 and #3 under the "perfected beats unperfected" rule of Section 9-322(a)(2), because Lender's filing perfected its security interest in all of the equipment, and Bank's filing is not effective to perfect its security interest in Items #2 and #3. The debtor's name change has rendered Bank's filing seriously misleading and Items #2 and #3 were acquired by the debtor more than four months after the name change. These priority results are correctly stated in Answer (B), **making Answer (B) the correct answer and Answers (A), (C), and (D) incorrect answers.**

139. The analysis changes slightly, but the result remains the same. Bank never lost perfection in Item #1, so it continues to enjoy priority. Bank filed its UCC-3 on August 1, more than four months after the name change on March 15. Therefore, there is a break in Bank's

perfection as to collateral acquired by the debtor after the four-month period expired. Bank's filing on August 1 allows it to re-perfect its security interest in collateral acquired more than four months after the name change, so the status of its security interest in Items #2 and #3 changes from unperfected to perfected. Even so, Lender continues to have priority in those two items under the "first to file or perfect" rule of Section 9-322(a)(1). Lender has a filing date in July, which is earlier than Bank's UCC-3 filing date of August 1 and its perfection dates of August 1 (Item #2) and September 18 (Item #3).

140. **Answer (C) is the correct answer.** The first step is to identify what types of collateral are evidenced, or have been created, by the writings. The choices are accounts, instruments, chattel paper, and general intangibles. The Customer Contracts, which evidence BizCorp's right to receive payment for inventory sold on credit, could be accounts. But because these contract rights are evidenced by writings, they may be excluded from the definition of "accounts" if the writings are "instruments" or "chattel paper." *See* § 9-102(a)(2) (inclusion under clause (i) of the first sentence, and exclusion under clause (i) of the second sentence). We are not provided with the full text of the Customer Contracts, so we can conclude only that the Customer Contracts might have created contract rights that are (i) accounts, or (ii) might be evidenced by writings that are instruments or chattel paper. The same conclusion can be reached on the IP Contracts. The Officer Contracts evidence corporate loans and terms of repayment. The definition of "accounts" excludes "rights to payment for money or funds advanced or sold." *See* § 9-102(a)(2) (clause (vi) of second sentence). The Officer Contracts might be instruments, and they might be chattel paper (if the loan is secured). But it is possible that they are neither type of collateral, leaving open the possibility that the Officer Contracts have created a contract right that is a "general intangible" (or a subset thereof, a "payment intangible"). In summary, then, the contract rights may have created accounts or general intangibles, or be evidenced by writings that are instruments or chattel paper. Lender is perfected in the contract rights regardless of label because it can perfect a security interest in all four types of collateral by filing. But Bank is relying on possession as its method of perfection. A secured party cannot perfect a security interest in accounts or general intangibles by possession (notwithstanding, as in this case, the presence of a tangible writing). Therefore, Bank will have an unperfected security interest in any contract rights evidenced by writings that have created accounts or general intangibles. Bank will be perfected in contract rights evidenced by writings that are instruments and chattel paper, and it will enjoy priority in those contract rights under the "first to file or perfect" rule of Section 9-322(a)(1). But Lender will have priority in contract rights evidenced by writings that have created accounts or general intangibles because it is perfected in those contract rights, and Bank is not. This result is found in Answer (C), **making Answer (C) the correct answer.**

Answer (A) is incorrect. Bank's security interest in contract rights evidenced by writings that have created accounts or general intangibles is unperfected and will not have priority.

Answer (B) is incorrect. Bank will have priority in contract rights evidenced by writings that are instruments and chattel paper, but it will not have priority in contract rights evidenced by writings that have created accounts (because its interest in those contract rights is unperfected, and Lender's interest in those contract rights is perfected).

Answer (D) is incorrect. Bank has a perfected interest in contract rights that are evidenced by writings that are instruments or chattel paper, but it has an unperfected interest in contract rights evidenced by writings that have created accounts or general intangibles.

Priority (Secured Party v. Secured Party; PMSI)

141. **Answer (C) is the correct answer.** Because the second piano is used by Jennifer's family for personal use more than 50% of the time, the piano is a consumer good under Section 9-102(a)(23). Her parents can attempt to claim an enforceable security interest in the second piano through the after-acquired property clause in their security agreement. But Section 9-204(b)(1) negates the reach of an after-acquired property clause to a consumer good unless the debtor acquires the consumer good within 10 days after the secured party has given any value. (Presumably the limitation has the intended purpose, at least in part, of discouraging overreaching, or possible predatory practices, by a secured party who seeks to claim a property interest in a consumer's goods against which the secured party advanced no funds and that have little value to anyone other than the consumer (think "hostage value" rather than "commercial value")). Under the facts, Jennifer's parents funded the $6,000 loan 15 months ago, but Jennifer did not acquire the second piano until about nine months later, creating more than a 10-day gap between the purchase date of the second piano and the funding date of the loan (and the facts do not suggest that Jennifer's parents have given any other value). This means that Jennifer's parents cannot rely on the after-acquired property clause, without which they cannot claim an enforceable security interest in the second piano. The facts state that Dealer retained an enforceable purchase-money security interest in the piano, so Dealer wins this one-party dispute, **making Answer (C) the correct answer.**

     Answer (A) is incorrect. Dealer's PMSI in the piano, a consumer good, is automatically perfected. (Perfection of a PMSI in the consumer good is automatic under Section 9-309(1), so Dealer's error in describing the debtor on the filing by using the studio's name, rather than Jennifer's individual name, has no adverse consequences.) And Dealer's PMSI has priority. But the answer gives the wrong reason for Dealer's priority. Dealer has priority because the parents have no security interest (rather than an enforceable but unperfected security interest) in the piano.

     Answer (B) is incorrect. Dealer's security interest is perfected. The parents have no security interest in the second piano.

     Answer (D) is incorrect. The parents have no security interest in the second piano.

142. **Answer (D) is the correct answer.** If the percentage breakdown between personal use and business use changes from 60:40 to 35:65, then the piano becomes equipment under

Section 9-102(a)(33)—it is a good that is not something else. Because the piano is equipment (rather than a consumer good), Jennifer's parents need not worry about Section 9-204(b) and now can rely on the after-acquired property clause (and their financing statement) to claim an enforceable (and perfected) security interest in the second piano. But switching the label on the second piano from "consumer good" to "equipment" also means that Dealer cannot rely on automatic perfection of its PMSI under Section 9-309(1). Dealer's security interest is unperfected. It no longer has possession of the piano, so it must rely on its filing to claim perfection. But its filing is defective. It used the studio's trade name as the debtor's name. However, the studio is not a separate legal entity; the only "entity" is Jennifer. As a result, Dealer should have used Jennifer's name on the filing (to be indexed under her surname, "Jacklin"). Because a search against Jennifer's surname is not likely to reveal a filing under the studio's name, the filing fails to accomplish its desired notice function and is not effective to perfect the security interest. Absent possession and an effective filing, Dealer's PMSI is unperfected. The parents have priority under the general priority rule of Section 9-322(a)(2), which states that perfected security interests have priority over unperfected security interests. Answer (D) captures this result, **making Answer (D) the correct answer.**

Answer (A) is incorrect. Absent possession or an effective filing, Dealer's PMSI is unperfected (rather than perfected). Furthermore, the parents have a perfected (rather than unperfected) security interest. As a result, the parents have priority.

Answer (B) is incorrect. The parents have a perfected security interest, which enjoys priority over Dealer's unperfected security interest.

Answer (C) is incorrect. The parents also have a perfected security interest in the second piano, as it has become equipment under the revised facts. This change in use will negate the concern over the reach of the after-acquired property clause under Section 9-204(b), which applies only if the collateral is a consumer good.

143.   Omitting the after-acquired property clause from the financing statement has no impact on the effectiveness of the filing to perfect the parents' security interest. As noted in Sections 9-204 (cmt. 7) and 9-502 (cmt. 2), the after-acquired property clause must be included in the security agreement to be effective, but it does not need to be included or referenced in the financing statement. Therefore, the parents' filing remains effective to perfect their security interest in the second piano, giving them priority over Dealer's unperfected PMSI.

144.   **Answer (D) is the correct answer.** Under the general first-to-file-or-perfect rule of Section 9-322(a)(2), the parents can argue priority because their filing date (15 months ago) precedes Dealer's filing and perfection date (six months ago). But Section 9-322 defers to other priority rules within that Section. And Section 9-322(f) mentions that those other superpriority rules may be found elsewhere in "this part" of Article 9. The quoted phrase— "this part"—is a reference to the other priority rules found in Part 3 of Article 9 (rules with a Section number of 9-3xx). One such superpriority rule is found in Section 9-324(a). That rule favors purchase-money creditors who claim an interest in non-inventory and who perfect by filing no later than the twentieth day following the date on which the debtor

took possession of the collateral. Dealer can satisfy each element of the rule and can claim superpriority. It has a PMSI in the piano, as stated in the facts. It properly used Jennifer's name on her driver's license as the name on the financing statement. *See* §§ 9-503(b)(4) [Alternative A]; 9-503(b)(4)(C) [Alternative B]. Jennifer is using the piano as equipment, rather than inventory (she uses it in giving piano and voice lessons; she is not in the business of selling pianos). Dealer delivered the piano six days after the purchase date, and it filed its financing statement 25 days after the purchase date. This means that Dealer filed its financing statement 19 days after the delivery date, making the filing timely (by one day) under the superpriority rule of Section 9-324(a). As a result, Dealer's perfected PMSI in the piano enjoys priority over the parents' perfected security interest, **making Answer (D) the correct answer.**

Answers (A), (B), and (C) are each incorrect because Dealer's filing was timely and complete under Section 9-324(a). The reader may think otherwise, by concluding that a filing 25 days after the purchase date is untimely. But the statute starts the running of the 20-day period on the date of delivery, not the date of purchase (which could be the date of attachment, if Jennifer acquired rights in the piano on the purchase date). Under the facts, Dealer filed on the nineteenth day following the delivery date, so its filing was timely (for the purpose of asserting PMSI superpriority). Furthermore, the first two answers suggest that an untimely filing can adversely affect the purchase-money nature of the security interest or the perfected status of the security interest. Any such suggestion is untrue. Section 9-324(a) is a priority statute. Noncompliance does not affect enforceability, purchase-money status, or perfection (assuming that the secured party filed on some date, even a date after the 20-day period has run its course).

145. **Answer (D) is the correct answer.** BizCorp can claim the superpriority afforded to equipment sellers by Section 9-324(a) if, and only if, its security interest is perfected no later than 20 days after ZinnCo took possession of the photocopiers. BizCorp filed its financing statement on March 30, within 20 days after delivering the photocopiers to ZinnCo on March 12 (a difference of 18 days). Therefore, it has a perfected PMSI in the photocopiers (equipment, rather than inventory, as used by ZinnCo), which enjoys superpriority over Alpha Bank's perfected security interest under Section 9-324(a), **making Answer (D) the correct answer.**

Answers (A) and (B) are incorrect. True, Alpha Bank filed last year, before BizCorp filed in March of this year. And true, Alpha Bank's security interest in the five photocopiers became perfected on or about March 5 of this year (the purchase date, when ZinnCo acquired rights in the photocopiers), before BizCorp's PMSI became perfected by its filing thereafter on March 30 of this year. So Alpha Bank may, in reliance on Section 9-322(a), contend that its security interest enjoys priority under the first-to-file-or-perfect rule. But the superpriority rule of Section 9-324(a) overrides the basic first-to-file-or-perfect rule of Section 9-322(a)(1) under the latter statute's introductory clause, together with Section 9-322(f) (which refers the reader to other priority rules in the 9-300 series).

Answer (C) is incorrect. The reader may observe that BizCorp's filing date of March 30 is more than 20 days after ZinnCo's purchase date of March 5. Therefore, the reader may conclude that BizCorp's filing under Section 9-324(a) is untimely, costing it superpriority. But the timeliness of BizCorp's filing under the statute is measured by comparing the filing date to the delivery date, not the purchase date (or the attachment date). BizCorp delivered the photocopiers on March 12, making its filing 18 days later, on March 30, timely.

146. Alpha Bank will win the priority dispute in the photocopiers under the baseline first-to-file-or-perfect rule of Section 9-322(a). BizCorp did file a financing statement (March 30), within 20 days after delivery (March 12), in Alabama. But ZinnCo is a corporation, an example of a registered organization. *See* § 9-102, cmt. 11 (fifth paragraph). Section 9-307(1) tells BizCorp to file its financing statement where its debtor is located. ZinnCo, as a corporation and a registered organization, is located in its state of incorporation — Delaware — under Section 9-307(e). BizCorp filed its original filing in the wrong state (Alabama). Implicit in the priority rules is the assumption that any reference to a filing is a reference to a filing recorded in the proper jurisdiction. And because BizCorp did not file its original financing statement in Delaware, it cannot rely on this mis-filed filing in Alabama for perfection or priority of its PMSI. BizCorp discovers its error and files a new filing in Delaware, but that filing is on April 17, more than 20 days after it delivered the photocopiers to ZinnCo on March 12. Therefore, while the Delaware filing does perfect BizCorp's PMSI, the filing does not allow BizCorp to successfully invoke the superiority rule of Section 9-324(a). As a result, BizCorp's perfected PMSI loses the priority battle to Alpha Bank and its perfected security interest.

147. **Answer (A) is the correct answer.** ZinnCo took delivery of the photocopiers in January, long before BizCorp filed its financing statement in August. It appears, then, that BizCorp's filing is untimely and it cannot invoke the superpriority afforded by Section 9-324(a). But as illustrated by the last paragraph of Official Comment 3 to Section 9-324, the 20-day period did not commence in this transaction until the photocopiers became "collateral." That occurred in August, when the parties terminated the lease and entered into a secured transaction. Therefore, the filing is timely (**making Answer (C) an incorrect answer**). As the filing is timely, BizCorp's PMSI enjoys superpriority under Section 9-324(a), **making Answer (A) the correct answer.**

Answer (B) is incorrect. Unlike the superpriority rule of Section 9-324(b), applicable to purchase-money security interests in inventory, the superpriority afforded by Section 9-324(a) does not impose any notice duty on the purchase-money creditor. Therefore, BizCorp's failure to provide Alpha Bank with notice of its security interest is irrelevant.

Answer (D) is incorrect. Article 9 does not state any such rule.

148. **Answer (A) is the correct answer.** Dealer has a PMSI in the machine. Dealer perfected its PMSI by filing a financing statement 18 days after the possession date (which was 10 days after the attachment date). Remember that Section 9-324(a) uses the possession date, rather than the attachment date, as the commencement of the 20-day period (perhaps because the former is easier to determine and subject to less debate and potentially misleading manipulation). Therefore, Dealer's filing is timely, and it enjoyed superpriority in the

machine under Section 9-324(a) (**making Answer (C) an incorrect answer**). That Section also extends the superpriority to identifiable proceeds (**making Answer (D) an incorrect answer**). Therefore, assuming that the $150,000 check remains identifiable as proceeds from the sale of the machine, Dealer has the senior claim, **making Answer (A) the correct answer.**

Exhaustive analysis will include a discussion of the perfected (or unperfected) security interests in the check. Section 9-315(c) provides 20 days of automatic perfection if the security interest in the underlying collateral (here, the machine) was perfected (it was). That 20-day period has not yet expired. If it had expired, the perfection would extend beyond the 20-day period under Section 9-315(d)(2), as the check is an example of "cash proceeds" as defined in Section 9-102(a)(9).

Answer (B) is an incorrect answer because the basic first-to-file-or-perfect rule of Section 9-322(a), by its own terms, defers to other priority rules, including the superpriority rule in Section 9-324(a).

149.   Bank has priority in the $150,000 deposit made into the deposit account, which it maintains for Clinic. The facts stipulate that both Lender and Dealer can satisfy any tracing burden. To that extent, then, they have an enforceable security interest under Section 9-315(a)(2) that remains perfected for 20 days under Section 9-315(c), and beyond under Section 9-315(d)(2). Although Bank has never filed a financing statement against Clinic or the deposit account, it has perfected its security interest in the deposit account by control under Section 9-104(a)(1) (Bank is both the secured party, and the bank that maintains the deposit account for the customer). Therefore, all three creditors can claim a perfected security interest in the $150,000 deposit. The previous answer concluded that Dealer's interest in the check enjoys priority over Lender's interest, and that priority does not change after the check has been deposited. But Bank enjoys superpriority over both Dealer and Lender under Section 9-327(1), which favors creditors perfected by control (e.g., Bank) over creditors who are perfected by a method other than control, such as by filing (e.g., Dealer and Lender). In summary, then, Bank has priority, followed by Dealer and then Lender.

150.   **Answer (B) is the correct answer.** For 20 days from the date of purchase, both Lender and Dealer can claim a perfected security interest in the new equipment under Section 9-315(c). During that 20-day period, Dealer has superpriority under Section 9-324(b). After that 20-day period expires, however, so, too, does Dealer's perfection. Perfection will not extend under Section 9-315(d)(1) because its financing statement described the collateral as the original machine sold by Dealer. That description of collateral will not capture the new equipment, so the filing is ineffective to perfect the security interest in the new equipment. Furthermore, the check represents intervening cash proceeds, precluding application of Section 9-315(d)(1). Perfection will not extend under Section 9-315(d)(2) because the new equipment is not "cash proceeds." And unless Dealer has filed a second UCC-1, or a UCC-3, that will capture the new equipment in the collateral description, and further assuming that Dealer has not taken possession of the new equipment, then Dealer cannot extend perfection under Section 9-315(d)(3). Therefore, its perfection will cease

on the twenty-first day following Clinic's purchase of the new equipment. Lender has none of these worries, as it does not need to rely on a "proceeds" argument. Its security agreement (which includes an after-acquired property clause) and financing statement cover Clinic's equipment in general, picking up the new equipment (through the after-acquired property clause) acquired by Clinic in exchange for the $150,000 check. In two months (actually, earlier), Lender's perfected security interest will start to enjoy priority over Dealer's unperfected security interest. In summary, then, Dealer has the initial priority in the new equipment, but Lender will soon enjoy priority in the new equipment (absent timely action by Dealer). Answer (B) captures this result, **making Answer (B) the correct answer.**

Answer (A) is incorrect. Yes, Dealer has the initial priority, but it will not have priority in two months (absent timely corrective action).

Answer (C) is incorrect. Yes, Dealer has the initial priority, but only Dealer (and not Lender) will become unperfected within two months (actually, in 19 days). Lender will be perfected in two months, and its perfected security interest will enjoy priority over (rather than share priority with) Dealer's soon-to-be unperfected security interest.

Answer (D) is incorrect. Dealer (rather than Lender) has the initial priority. But Lender, rather than Dealer, will have priority in about 20 days.

151.   **Answer (D) is the correct answer.** Section 9-103 addresses purchase-money security interests, limiting them to collateral that is goods or software. The MegaCorp shares are investment property, not goods or software, so Lauren cannot claim a PMSI in the shares. Therefore, **Answer (A) is an incorrect answer.** A secured party can perfect a security interest in investment property (whether certificated or not, and whether managed by the customer or the broker) by filing a financing statement. *See* § 9-312(a). Both Luke and Lauren have filed effective financing statements, perfecting their respective security interest. **Therefore, Answer (C) is incorrect.** Section 9-204 addresses the reach of an after-acquired property clause. It raises concerns if the collateral includes consumer goods or commercial tort claims. The MegaCorp shares are investment property, not consumer goods or commercial tort claims. Therefore, Luke's security interest, through the after-acquired property clause, captures the MegaCorp shares. As a result, **Answer (B) is incorrect.** (Under Section 9-108(e), the defined term "investment property" is insufficient to describe collateral only if: the underlying transaction is a "consumer transaction" and if there are no further descriptive terms used. Here, although the original transaction was likely a "consumer transaction" (unless the car was used in business), the specification of an account number and the broker provide the additional information necessary to validate the description. *See* § 9-108, cmt. 5.) In summary, then, both Luke and Lauren have a perfected security interest in the MegaCorp shares. Both are relying on filing, rather than any sort of control. Luke's security interest in the shares enjoys priority under the basic first-to-file-or-perfect rule of Section 9-322(a)(1) (his filing date from two years ago precedes Heather's filing and perfection dates in a subsequent year). No other priority rule overrides the result under Section 9-322(a)(1). Therefore, **Answer (D) is the correct answer.**

152. **Answer (B) is the correct answer.** Under the first-to-file-or-perfect rule of Section 9-322(a)(1), FW will lose a priority dispute because Lender's filing date will precede FW's filing and perfection date. But FW can enjoy priority if it successfully navigates Sections 9-324(b) and (c), which afford superpriority to purchase-money security interests in inventory. One condition is that the purchase-money creditor must file its financing statement before the debtor-buyer takes possession of the inventory. Answer (B) states that requirement, **making Answer (B) the correct answer.**

Answer (A) is incorrect. Including a "title retention" clause in the security agreement (e.g., "Seller retains title to the goods being sold until Buyer has completed all of its payment and performance obligations under this contract.") does not negate FW's need to timely file a financing statement.

Answer (C) is incorrect. Unlike Section 9-324(a), which affords superpriority to non-inventory creditors, Sections 9-324(b) and (c) afford no post-delivery grace period for inventory creditors.

Answer (D) is incorrect for the same reason that Answer (C) is incorrect. **Answer (D) is further incorrect** because Article 9 requires FW to file in the single state where ToyCo, a corporation and a registered organization, is located (Delaware, under Section 9-307(e)), not also in each state where the inventory may be located.

153. **Answer (B) is the correct answer.** As noted in the previous answer, if FW wants to enjoy superpriority over a competing claim asserted by Lender, an earlier filer, then FW must comply with the requirements of Sections 9-324(b) and (c). Section 9-324(b)(2) obligates FW, the purchase-money creditor, to send notice of its PMSI to a previous filer (Lender), **making Answer (D) an incorrect answer.** Additionally, Section 9-324(b)(3) offers superpriority only if the previous filer (Lender) receives the notice before the debtor (Toyco) receives possession of the goods. Therefore, to enjoy superpriority, FW will enjoy priority over Lender only if Lender receives FW's notice before ToyCo receives the shipment, **making Answer (B) the correct answer.** Note that under Section 1-202(c) (applicable in Article 9 transactions under Section 9-102(c)), "receipt" requires that any notice either come to the attention of the recipient or be "duly delivered" to the recipient.

Answer (A) is incorrect because it fails to recognize that Lender must timely *receive* FW's notice.

Answer (C) is incorrect because Lender must receive FW's notice before FW delivers the shipment to ToyCo; there is no post-delivery grace period.

154. **Answer (B) is the correct answer.** If FW satisfied its filing and notice duties and enjoyed superpriority in the FidgetyWidgets, then Section 9-324(b) extends its superpriority to "identifiable cash proceeds [that] are received [by the debtor] on or before the delivery of the inventory to a buyer." Cash, and checks, are examples of "cash proceeds" under Section 9-102(a)(9). None of the other forms of payment create cash proceeds at the checkout counter (although with the passing of time, they are likely to generate cash proceeds).

Therefore, FW's superpriority will extend to customer payments, at the checkout counter, in the form of cash and checks, but nothing more. FW, and Lender, will be perfected in these other identifiable proceeds under Section 9-315(c) (for 20 days) and (d)(1) (thereafter). Lender will have priority under the first-to-file-or-perfect rule of 9-322(a)(1) as its filing date precedes FW's filing and perfection dates. For these reasons, **Answer (B) is the correct answer, and Answers (A), (C), and (D) are incorrect answers.**

155. **Answer (A) is the correct answer.** Both Dealer and Emily can claim a purchase-money security interest in the freezers under Sections 9-103(a) and (b)(1). Dealer has a PMSI for the $70,000 (seller financing), and Emily has a PMSI for the remaining $30,000 (third-party financing). In the hands of BAM, Inc., the freezers are equipment. And both Dealer (August 5) and Emily (August 1) perfected their security interests in the freezers by filing financing statements no later than 20 days after the restaurant took possession of the freezers (July 20). As between Dealer and Emily, Dealer's security interest enjoys priority under Section 9-324(g)(1), which favors the seller over a third-party financer. *See* § 9-324, cmt. 13. So Dealer's unpaid debt is repaid first ($60,000), leaving no remaining proceeds for Emily. This result is found in Answer (A), **making Answer (A) the correct answer and Answers (B), (C), and (D) incorrect answers.**

156. As in the previous question, this fact pattern involves competing purchase-money security interests. Fidelity Bank, regardless of whether it files on July 30 or August 7, joins Emily (August 1) as a party entitled to superpriority under Section 9-324(a), as both parties filed financing statements no later than the twentieth day following the delivery date of July 20. Neither purchase-money creditor is the seller, however, so Section 9-324(g)(1) does not apply. Instead, subsection (g)(2) applies and directs the reader to the general priority rule of Section 9-322(a). Under Section 9-322(a)(1), Fidelity Bank enjoys priority if its filing date is July 30 (earlier than Emily's filing date of August 1), but Emily enjoys priority if Fidelity Bank does not file until August 7 (later than Emily's filing date of August 1). Under the first scenario, the liquidator should distribute the first $60,000 to Fidelity Bank, leaving nothing for Emily. But under the second scenario, the liquidator should distribute the first $20,000 to Emily and remaining $40,000 to Fidelity Bank.

157. **Answer (D) is the correct answer.** BigBank has an enforceable security interest in the furnishings through its after-acquired property clause. That interest is perfected by BigBank's filing. Because BigBank filed its financing statement two years ago, long before Upscale Furnishings filed this year, Upscale Furnishings will not enjoy priority in any of the furnishings or proceeds therefrom unless its security interest is a purchase-money security interest that qualifies for superpriority. Prior to the enactment of revised Article 9, some courts held that the inclusion of after-acquired property clauses and future advance clauses destroyed, or transformed, a PMSI into a non-PMSI because cross-collateralization upset the traditional one-to-one relationship between a unit of collateral and its unpaid purchase price. Some courts disagreed, concluding that a security interest could be both a PMSI and a non-PMSI. As revised, Article 9 adopts this latter approach, often referred to as the "dual status rule." *See* § 9-103(f) and cmt. 7.

Under the dual status rule, all of the furnishings secure Upscale Furnishings' unpaid debt of $60,000. Because the contract requires application of payments to oldest debts first (enforceable under Section 9-103(e)(1)), the $60,000 represents $25,000 unpaid on the chairs and lamps, and $35,000 unpaid on the mirrors and pictures. (The aggregate purchase price of all three items is $180,000. At the time of default, BCI owes $60,000 to Upscale Furnishings, indicating that BCI has repaid $120,000. Under the contract terms, that $120,000 repaid the entire purchase price of the beds [$100,000] and part of the purchase price of the chairs and lamps [$20,000].) To the extent that an item secures repayment of its own purchase price, the security interest is a PMSI. But because the purchase price of the beds has been paid in full, the security interest in the beds is not a PMSI. So Upscale Furnishings cannot claim any superpriority in the beds under Section 9-324(a). Instead, Upscale Furnishings receives $0 and BigBank is entitled to the entire $80,000 under Section 9-322(a)(1) because BigBank's filing date precedes Upscale Furnishings' filing and perfection dates. This result is found in Answer (D), **making Answer (D) the correct answer and Answers (A), (B), and (C) incorrect answers.**

158. **Answer (B) is the correct answer.** Under the dual status rule, the chairs and lamps secure Upscale Furnishings' unpaid debt of $60,000. As noted in the previous answer, the $60,000 represents $25,000 unpaid on the chairs and lamps, and $35,000 unpaid on the mirrors and pictures. To the extent that an item secures repayment of its own purchase price, the security interest is a PMSI. So Upscale Furnishings can claim a PMSI in the beds for $25,000. And Upscale Furnishings' PMSI enjoys priority over BigBank's security interest under Section 9-324(a). Upscale Furnishings cannot claim a PMSI in the extra $5,000. BigBank receives that $5,000 under Section 9-322(a)(1) because its filing date precedes Upscale Furnishings' filing and perfection dates. Therefore, the liquidator should pay $25,000 to Upscale Furnishings and $5,000 to BigBank. This result is found in Answer (B), **making it the correct answer and Answers (A), (C), and (D) incorrect answers.**

159. **Answer (A) is the correct answer.** Under the dual status rule, the mirrors and pictures secure Upscale Furnishings' unpaid debt of $60,000. As noted in the previous answer, the $60,000 represents $25,000 unpaid on the lamps and chairs, and $35,000 unpaid on the mirrors and pictures. To the extent that an item secures repayment of its own purchase price, the security interest is a PMSI. So Upscale Furnishings can claim a PMSI in the mirrors and pictures for $35,000. And Upscale Furnishings' PMSI enjoys priority over Big-Bank's security interest under Section 9-324(a). The liquidator should pay the entire $15,000 to Upscale Furnishings, **making Answer (A) the correct answer and Answers (B), (C), and (D) incorrect answers.**

160. The transformation rule "transforms" what might originally have been a purchase-money security interest into a generic (or non-purchase money) security interest if (i) the security agreement includes an after-acquired property clause or a future advance clause or (ii) the purchase-money debt is later refinanced, restructured, etc. Courts used this rule when (i) purchase-money debt was secured by more than its related purchase-money collateral and (ii) purchase-money collateral secured more than its related purchase-money

debt. Left with no PMSI (at least according to the court), the secured party could not seek superpriority, resulting in its priority loss to an earlier filer. For the most part, Article 9 now rejects the transformation rule and adopts the dual-status rule. *See* § 9-103(f) and cmt. 7. But a court can still apply the transformation rule in a "consumer-goods transaction" (defined in Section 9-102(a)(24)). *See* § 9-103(f) (introductory carve-out language), (h).

161. **Answer (B) is the correct answer.** The absence of the after-acquired property clause from TNB's financing statement is a red herring. That clause must appear in the security agreement, but it need not appear in the financing statement. *See* §§ 9-204, cmt. 7; 9-502, cmt. 2. Therefore, **Answer (C) is incorrect.**

Both TNB and Keyboard Corporation have perfected security interests in the musical instruments sold by Keyboard to MusicLand. TNB filed its financing statement on February 10, and Keyboard filed its financing statement on July 15. Therefore, under the general priority rule of Section 9-322(a)(1), TNB will enjoy priority because its filing date is earlier than Keyboard's filing and perfection dates. By its own language, however, the general priority rule is subject to other applicable priority rules found in Section 9-322 and elsewhere in Part 3 (e.g., the 9-300 series), one of which is Section 9-324, which affords superpriority to purchase-money creditors. Keyboard Corporation provided seller financing and retained a security interest in the instruments to secure the unpaid purchase price, so it has a PMSI. MusicLand operates two retail stores, so the instruments are inventory. Section 9-324(b) and (c) address the superpriority available to secured parties with a PMSI in inventory. Parsing the statute reveals that Keyboard Corporation must satisfy four requirements in order to achieve superpriority. First, its security interest must be perfected when MusicLand receives the pianos and electric keyboards. *See* § 9-324(b)(1). Keyboard Corporation perfected its security interest by filing a financing statement on July 15. MusicLand received the pianos on July 10 and the electric keyboards on July 20. Therefore, Keyboard Corporation cannot claim superpriority in the pianos (**making Answer (A) an incorrect answer**) but might be able to claim superpriority in the electric keyboards. Second, Keyboard Corporation must send notice of its PMSI to TNB (a previous filer entitled to such notice under Section 9-324(c)) before MusicLand receives the electric keyboards. *See* § 9-324(b)(2). Keyboard sent notice on July 13, before MusicLand received the electric keyboards on July 20. Third, TNB must receive Keyboard Corporation's notice before MusicLand receives the electric keyboards. *See* § 9-324(b)(3). TNB received the notice on July 17, before MusicLand received the electric keyboards on July 20. Fourth, Keyboard Corporation's notice must state that it "has or expects to acquire a purchase-money security interest in inventory of [MusicLand] and describe the inventory." *See* § 9-324(b)(4). The facts state that the notice satisfied these requirements. Keyboard Corporation can satisfy all four of the statutory requirements, so it enjoys superpriority in the electric keyboards. It does not have superpriority in the pianos (failing the opening requirement), so TNB claims priority in them under the general "first to file or perfect" rule of Section 9-322(a). These results are correctly stated in Answer (B), **making Answer (B) the correct answer and Answer (D) an incorrect answer.**

162. **Answer (B) is the correct answer.** First, Section 9-324(b) extends superpriority to proceeds of inventory sales if the purchase-money creditor had superpriority in the inventory itself. The previous answer revealed that Keyboard Corporation had superpriority in the electric keyboards. Therefore, Section 9-324(b) extends the superpriority to "identifiable cash proceeds [that] are received [by MusicLand] on or before the delivery of the inventory to a buyer." A check is an example of "cash proceeds" under Section 9-102(a)(9), so Keyboard Corporation has priority in Meredith's check. The retail installment contracts, which include a title-retention clause, are probably chattel paper (a writing that evidences First Church's monetary obligation and, under Section 1-201(b)(35), creates a security interest in the electric keyboards via the title-retention clause). Section 9-324(b) does extend superpriority to chattel paper, but only if the creditor claiming superpriority can navigate Section 9-330. Keyboard Corporation cannot do so because MusicLand, rather than KeyBoard Corporation, possesses the contracts. Therefore, Keyboard Corporation does not have priority in the two contracts executed by First Church. In summary, then, Keyboard Corporation has priority in the check, but not in the two contracts. This conclusion appears in Answer (B), **making Answer (B) the correct answer and Answers (A), (C), and (D) incorrect answers.**

163. **Answer (A) is the correct answer.** The judge may be tempted to award priority to Bank-Two under Section 9-324(a). BankTwo seems to satisfy all requirements. It has a PMSI in the Items (which are neither inventory nor livestock), which was perfected by a financing statement filed on February 23, 2018, within 20 days of February 5, 2018, when Omega took possession of the Items. The judge should resist this temptation and instead rule in favor of BankOne, relying on Section 9-325(a). That provision states: "[A] security interest created by a debtor [Omega] is subordinate to a security interest in the same collateral created by another person [Alpha] if: (1) the debtor [Omega] acquired the collateral subject to the security interest created by the other person [Alpha]; (2) the security interest created by the other person [Alpha] was perfected when the debtor [Omega] acquired the collateral; and (3) there is no period thereafter when the security interest is unperfected."

    Clause (1) is satisfied because BankOne's security interest in the Items survived the unauthorized sale under Sections 9-201 and 9-315(a), and Omega's acquisition does not terminate the security interest under Section 9-320(a) (Omega is not a buyer in the ordinary course of business because the Items in Alpha's hands are equipment, not inventory) or Section 9-320(b) (neither Alpha nor Omega hold the Items as consumer goods, and BankOne has filed a financing statement). Therefore, **Answer (C) is incorrect.** Clause (2) is met because BankOne's financing statement remained effective at the time of sale and, under Section 9-507(a), thereafter. Therefore, **Answer (D) is incorrect.** Also, clause (3) is met (no filing lapse, and no known change in jurisdiction that might otherwise trigger concerns under Section 9-316). Finally, Section 9-325(b) applies to subordinate the security interest of BankTwo to the security interest of BankOne because otherwise BankTwo would enjoy priority under Section 9-324(a). For these reasons, **Answer (A) is the correct answer and Answer (B) is an incorrect answer.**

The result should not be surprising. If Omega acquires the Items subject to the security interest held by BankOne, then Omega's creditors (e.g., BankTwo) also take the Items subject to the security interest held by BankOne. Perhaps rephrased, a secured party can only take a security interest in the limited, and possibly encumbered, rights held by its debtor.

Priority (Secured Party v. Buyer of Collateral)

164. **Answer (D) is the correct answer.** The baseline rule in any priority dispute between the secured party and a buyer of collateral is this: the secured party wins. Section 9-201(a) says as much by stating that "a security agreement is effective according to its terms between the parties, *against purchasers of the collateral*, and against creditors." Although this is tempered by the introductory caveat, "Except as otherwise provided in [the Uniform Commercial Code]," Section 9-315(a)(1) reaffirms that "a security interest or agricultural lien continues in collateral notwithstanding sale, lease, license, exchange, or other disposition thereof. . . ." This rule, however applies only if the secured party is perfected, *see* Section 9-317(b), which the facts of this question state is the case.

    Combined, these two Sections make a lack of knowledge of the secured party's interest irrelevant. **This makes Answer (A) incorrect.** It also does not matter that the secured party received the benefit of the proceeds of a sale (so long as there is still some debt outstanding that is secured by the collateral). **That makes Answer (B) incorrect.** The purpose of the purchase is also irrelevant to the durability of the security interest (although we'll see an exception for this for sales of inventory when we look at buyers in the ordinary course of business and Section 9-320). **This makes Answer (C) incorrect.**

165. **Answer (A) is the correct answer.** Although both Sections 9-201 and 9-315(a) provide that a security interest continues in collateral even though it is bought or sold, Section 9-315(a) qualifies this by indicating that this continuation of the security interest only happens "unless the secured party authorized the disposition free of the security interest. . . ." Here, the secured party has, in the agreement, authorized the disposition in advance of minor amounts of collateral without consent, subject to the condition of notice. Answer (A) incorporates that condition, and thus is consistent with consent. **Answer (C) is incorrect because it does not reference the condition to the consent.**

    Answer (B) is incorrect because the consent can be given in advance, and does not need to be given for each individual transaction.

    Answer (D) is incorrect because the employees' knowledge is irrelevant to the applicable rule; the only relevant facts are those related to the issue of whether HedgeBanc consented generally or specifically to the transaction.

166. **Answer (D) is the correct answer.** As indicated in the previous question, although both Sections 9-201 and 9-315(a) provide that a security interest continues in collateral even

though it is bought or sold, Section 9-315(a) qualifies this by indicating that this continuation of the security interest only happens "unless the secured party authorized the disposition free of the security interest . . . ." In Question 165, the consent was explicit. This question raises the issue of whether explicit consent is required. It is not. Courts have uniformly held that consent can be given implicitly. In addition, cases also hold that a lender can waive its right to consent, or a lender can be estopped to withhold consent. Here, the lender allowed the donations to continue for 12 months, once a week. Such continuous acquiescence has sometimes been equated with the intentional relinquishment of a known right (the definition of a waiver). If the charity has distributed the eggs to the needy, it also can argue that it detrimentally relied on the inaction of anyone who knew it was receiving the eggs (the definition of estoppel). In either case (and the detrimental reliance of a charity makes the estoppel argument more plausible), BankOne's consent will be implied given its lack of action despite notice.

The foodbank was a donee; that is a recipient of a gift, and thus cannot be a "buyer" in the ordinary course of business. This makes **Answer (A) incorrect**.

Answer (B) is incorrect because the eggs are "farm products" (the description used in the security agreement) because Trevor is in the farming business, and his eggs are "products of crops or livestock in their unmanufactured states. . . ." § 9-102(a)(34)(D). The coverage of eggs as farm products thus makes **Answer (B) incorrect**.

Answer (C) is incorrect because secured parties do not have to consent on a transaction-by-transaction basis; they may consent in advance, and by reference to the types of items subject to the consent.

167. **Answer (D) is the correct answer.** Although the baseline rule in any priority dispute between the secured party and a buyer of collateral is that the secured party wins, *see* Sections 9-201(a) and 9-315(a)(1), there is a large and common-sense exception for retail sales. Section 9-320(a) provides that "a buyer in ordinary course of business, other than a person buying farm products from a person engaged in farming operations, *takes free of a security interest* created by the buyer's seller, even if the security interest is perfected and the buyer knows of its existence."

To understand this exception, you must understand the concept of a "buyer in the ordinary course of business." That concept is defined, albeit in Article 1 (incorporated into Article 9 by Section 9-102(c)). Section 1-201(b)(9) defines a "buyer in the ordinary course of business" as a:

person that buys goods in good faith, without knowledge that the sale violates the rights of another person in the goods, and in the ordinary course from a person, other than a pawnbroker, in the business of selling goods of that kind.

Here, the security interest was created by the law firm's seller, so that part of Section 9-320(a) is met. There is also no indication that the law firm was not in good faith or had any knowledge regarding any violation of the secured party's rights. Section 1-201(b)(9) states that "[a] person buys goods in the ordinary course if the sale to the person comports with the usual or customary practices in the kind of business in which the seller is engaged or with the seller's own usual or customary practices." The question states that ZinnMark sells office equipment, so a "routine cash sale of three photocopiers" is, presumably, a transaction in the ordinary course of ZinnMark's business. In effect, then, ZinnMark's sale of the photocopiers to the law firm has terminated MegaBank's security interest in the photocopiers, **making Answer (D) the correct answer.**

Answers (A) and (B) are incorrect because MegaBank's security interest is terminated at the point of sale, regardless of what knowledge (if any) the law firm had about MegaBank's security interest or filing. Recall that knowledge is subjective (not objective), under Section 1-202(b), and thus knowing of a filing cannot be knowledge of a security interest (as it might be a filing before attachment as permitted by Section 9-502(d)). The fact of a routine sale without any knowledge of a violation or other skullduggery likely establishes good faith—defined in Section 1-201(b)(20) as *"honesty in fact and the observance of reasonable commercial standards of fair dealing."*[1]

Answer (C) is incorrect not because MegaBank will not lose, but because MegaBank will lose for reasons discussed above. Whether it has a duty to file against the law firm is irrelevant under the facts of this transaction.

168.   Under the revised facts, MegaBank will probably lose. Because the sale was not permitted by the security agreement, MegaBank's security interest survives the disposition under Section 9-315(a)(1). The law firm, however, will invoke the protection afforded by Section 9-320(a), which states: "a buyer in the ordinary course of business . . . takes free of a security interest created by the buyer's seller, even if the security interest is perfected and the buyer knows of its existence."

With respect to this definition, the transaction meets all of the requirements of Section 9-320(a). The security interest was indeed created by the law firm's seller—ZinnMark—so the law firm can win the priority dispute if it is a "buyer in the ordinary course of business," a term defined in Section 1-201(b)(9). In comparing the transaction with that definition, the law firm

- bought (the UCC does not define "buy" as opposed to "purchase," but at a minimum "buying" includes an exchange of goods for a price, as contrasted with "purchasing," which under Section 1-201(b)(29) includes taking by gift, for example),

- goods (the photocopiers),

- in good faith and without knowledge that the sale violates MegaBank's rights (probably, but fact-sensitive), and

---

1. We use the Article 1 definition of good faith because we are interpreting how that word is used in the Article 1 definition of "buyer in the ordinary course of business." Even if we were to use the Article 9 definition, found in Section 9-102(b)(43), the result would not change, as the text of the definition of good faith in that Section is virtually identical to the text used in Section 1-201(b)(20).

- in the ordinary course of the seller's business (ZinnMark is in the business of selling photocopiers).

The definition also states: "A person buys goods in the ordinary course if the sale to the person comports with the usual or customary practices in the kind of business in which the seller is engaged or with the seller's own usual or customary practices." Therefore, the fact that the law firm executed a note — the standard form used by ZinnMark, and a form that comports with industry-wide standards — will not preclude the law firm from being a buyer in the ordinary course. And if the law firm does meet the definition of a buyer in the ordinary course of business, it will win the priority dispute.

169.   **Answer (D) is the correct answer.** A cashier's check is an example of "cash proceeds" under Section 9-102(a)(9), as is a deposit account. Therefore, assuming MegaBank can satisfy its tracing burden, it has a perfected security interest in the $30,000 for 20 days under Section 9-315(c), and for all periods thereafter during which it remains "identifiable" under Section 9-315(d)(2). **Therefore, Answer (D) is the correct answer, and Answer (C) is an incorrect answer.**

Answer (A) is incorrect because MegaBank can claim a security interest in proceeds that are identifiable, whether or not the collateral description mentions "proceeds" or any derivation thereof. *See* §§ 9-203(f); 9-315(a)(2).

Answer (B) is incorrect because MegaBank can release (or otherwise lose) its security interest in the photocopiers, without abandoning its claim to identifiable proceeds. *See* § 9-315, cmt. 2 (second paragraph).

170.   **Answer (D) is the correct answer.** Here, the key fact is that Hank filed in the wrong place, leaving his security interest unperfected. Because Erewhon is a Delaware limited liability company, the only proper place to file a financing statement was Delaware. *See* §§ 9-301(1); 9-307(e). The Nevada filing was thus ineffective to perfect a security interest in Hank's collateral.

Because Hank was unperfected, the governing rule is found in Section 9-317(b). That provision states that:

> a buyer, other than a secured party, of ... goods ... takes free of a security interest ... if the buyer gives value and receives delivery of the collateral without knowledge of the security interest or agricultural lien and before it is perfected.

Here, EOR took delivery and gave value (its check) while Hank's interest was unperfected. Because knowledge is subjective, *see* Section 1-202(b), EOR is without knowledge of Hank's interest because Erewhon did not tell it, and EOR had no other way to know of it. As a result, EOR took delivery free of Hank's interest.

Answer (A) is incorrect because there is no duty to check the filing records for evidence of perfection (in part because even a positive response would not provide knowledge of the interest given that financing statements can be filed before attachment under Section 9-502(d)).

EOR is not a buyer in the ordinary course, because buying more than one-half of someone's inventory is a sale "in bulk" and thus not within the definition of "ordinary" under Section 1-201(b)(9). That renders Section 9-320(a) inapplicable, but has no bearing on the applicability of Section 9-317(b); they are independent grounds for severing a security interest. Accordingly, **Answer (B) is incorrect.**

Under either Section 9-320(a) or 9-317(b), the consent of the secured party is irrelevant. The termination of the security interest occurs under each of these Sections despite a lack of consent. As a result, **Answer (C) is incorrect.**

171.   **The correct answer is Answer (C).** This question is a variation of the last set of facts. Investment property, such as interests in stocks traded on exchanges, is not "goods" covered by Section 9-317(b). Investment property is, however, covered by Section 9-317(d)—along with any other collateral that is not "tangible chattel paper, tangible documents, goods, instruments, or a certificated security." The rule for such collateral is that a buyer takes free of a security interest if the buyer "gives value without knowledge of the security interest and before it is perfected." This is almost the same test as in Section 9-317(b), except it omits the requirement of the buyer's good faith. Here, by facilitating the trade, the broker provided value, and nothing in the facts indicates subjective knowledge of BankOne's security interest. As BankOne did not file against investment property or take control of GoGetter's brokerage account, it was unperfected. As a result, the sale was free of BankOne's security interest under Section 9-317(d), **making Answer (C) the correct answer.**

Answers (A) and (B) are incorrect because neither lists all the requirements of Section 9-317(d). Thus, they are incomplete, and inferior to Answer (C).

Answer (D) is incorrect because Section 9-317(d) applies, and conversion will not lie against any party if the disposition is rightful. (If you are wondering about whether the broker could be liable in conversion, you should wonder no more. "Agents such [as brokers] selling collateral are generally held to the same standards for conversion as their principal, [even though] they frequently have no knowledge that the sale is wrongful. Agents claim only a right to sell the property, not title or a right to proceeds." Russell A. Hakes, *A Quest for Justice in the Conversion of Security Interests*, 82 Ky. L.J. 837, 896 (1993).

172.   **The correct response is Answer (D).** Initially, you could be forgiven for thinking that the security interest in the equipment was not affected by the two transfers. After all, Section 9-315(a)(1) says that a security interest is unaffected by any sale or other disposition. But the lead-in to that language says that the survival rule is always applicable "[e]xcept as otherwise provided in this article *and in Section 2-403(2)*."

That brings us to the wacky world of Section 2-403(2). Under that Section, any "entrustment" of property to a "merchant who deals in goods of that kind" gives the merchant "power to transfer all rights of the entruster to a buyer in the ordinary course of business."

Before getting to the status of the seller and buyer, was there "entrusting" here? Under Section 2-403(3), "'[e]ntrusting' includes any delivery and any acquiescence in retention of possession regardless of any condition expressed between the parties to the delivery or acquiescence." Was Lender's failure to act (its acquiescence) when it learned of the sale of the collateral to Dealer, and Dealer's holding out the collateral for sale, "entrustment"? The comments to the UCC say yes: "Lender's acquiescence constitutes an 'entrusting' of the goods to Dealer within the meaning of Section 2-403(3)." [This question is taken directly from Example 2 in Comment 3 to Section 9-320.]

If there is entrusting, then are the other requirements met? Yes. The facts tell us that Dealer "is in the business of buying and selling used equipment." Dealer thus is a "merchant who deals in goods of that kind," that is, the equipment. Was Buyer a "buyer in the ordinary course"? Here again, yes. Buyer bought for cash, which the question says was the primary manner in which Dealer got paid. There are no facts to call into question Buyer's good faith, and we are told Buyer knows nothing of Lender's interest. As summarized in the comment to Section 9-320, "Buyer takes free of Lender's security interest under Section 2-403(2) if Buyer qualifies as a buyer in ordinary course of business." § 9-320, cmt 3, ex. 2.

Answers (A) and (B) are incorrect because Section 2-403 does not require or mention the consent of any party. **Answer (C) is incorrect** because of the exception in Section 9-315(a)(1) for entrustment under Section 2-403.

173. **Answer (C) is the correct answer.** Friendly Furniture's security interest survives the sale under Section 9-315(a)(1) because the sale was unauthorized. Nevertheless, the buyer can win the lawsuit if the buyer can navigate the protection afforded by Section 9-320(b) (often referred to as the "garage sale" provision). To do so, the dining room suite must be a consumer good in the hands of both the seller and the buyer, the buyer must purchase the goods without knowledge of the security interest, and the sale must precede any filing by the creditor. Answer (C) offers an answer that meets all conditions, so **Answer (C) is the correct answer.**

Friendly Furniture engaged in seller financing with Sandra and can claim a PMSI in the furniture under Sections 9-103(a) and (b)(1). In Sandra's hands, the furniture was a consumer good. Because Friendly Furniture has a PMSI in consumer goods, its security interest is automatically perfected under Section 9-309(1). **Therefore, Answer (A) is incorrect.**

Just because the sale generated identifiable cash proceeds—in which Friendly Furniture has a continuing perfected security interest—does not necessarily mean that Friendly Furniture loses any priority dispute in the original collateral itself. **Therefore, Answer (B) is incorrect.**

Friendly Furniture may win the lawsuit. But it also may lose the lawsuit, as suggested by facts found in Answer (C). Without more information, the absolute truth of Answer (D) remains unknown, **making Answer (D) an incorrect answer.**

174. Because Section 9-320(b) requires that the collateral be consumer goods in both the buyer's and seller's hands, the result would change. Under these facts, Fred is buying the furniture as inventory, not as consumer goods. As such, Section 9-320(b) does not provide Fred with any protection. Fred also cannot claim the protection afforded by Section 9-320(a) to buyers in the ordinary course of business because Sandra, the seller, is not in the business of selling dining room suites.

175. Friendly Furniture wins the conversion lawsuit under these revised facts. Its security interest is effective against all buyers under Section 9-201(a), unless an exception applies. Because Sandra's sale was not authorized, Friendly Furniture's security interest survives the sale under Section 9-315(a)(1). The buyer cannot claim the protection afforded by Section 9-320(a) to buyers in the ordinary course of business because Sandra, the seller, is not in the business of selling dining room suites. Nor can Sandra's buyer—even one who uses the furniture as a consumer good and who purchases the furniture with no knowledge of Friendly Furniture's security interest claim the protection afforded by Section 9-320(b). Why? Because Friendly Furniture filed a financing statement against Sandra and the dining room suite under the revised facts, blocking the buyer from successfully navigating through Section 9-320(b)(4). (One could criticize this statutory hurdle, given that most buyers of consumer goods rarely, if ever, request a UCC search report before buying the goods.) Finally, Friendly Furniture's security interest is perfected at the time of sale (automatically, and by filing), and also when the buyer takes possession, so the buyer cannot invoke Section 9-317(b). No other exception to the general rule applies to these facts, so Friendly Furniture will win its conversion lawsuit.

176. **Answer (B) is the correct answer.** Omega Bank's security agreement prohibits AMC from selling its inventory on credit. Therefore, Omega Bank may argue that its security interest survived AMC's sale of the harp to Ima, invoking Section 9-315(a)(1). That Section, however, opens with the phrase "Except as otherwise provided in this article . . . ." And Ima will rely on Section 9-320(a), which states: "a buyer in the ordinary course of business . . . takes free of a security interest created by the buyer's seller, even if the security interest is perfected and the buyer knows of its existence." The security interest was indeed created by Ima's seller (AMC), and Ima had no knowledge of the business relationship between AMC and Omega Bank. Therefore, Ima will win the priority dispute if she is a "buyer in the ordinary course of business," a term defined in Section 1-201(b)(9). The only concern is that she executed a promissory note as her form of payment, which was not authorized by Omega Bank's security agreement. Nevertheless, the facts indicate that promissory notes are an "industry practice" for expensive items, permitting Ima to meet this language from the definition: "A person buys goods in the ordinary course if the sale to the person comports with the usual or customary practices in the kind of business in which the seller is engaged or with the seller's own usual or customary practices." Ima

can successfully invoke the protections of Section 9-320(a), **making Answer (B) the correct answer.**

Even though Omega Bank did not consent to AMC's credit sale of the harp to Ima, Omega Bank does not necessarily win the priority dispute under Section 9-315(a)(1). That Section is subject to other rules, one of which is Section 9-320(a). And in this question, that Section favors Ima, **making Answer (A) an incorrect answer.**

The fact that Ima is using the harp as equipment, rather than a consumer good, prevents her from claiming priority under Section 9-320(b) (which will not apply for other reasons, as well). But her use is irrelevant under Section 9-320(a), the conditions of which she satisfies. Therefore, **Answer (C) is an incorrect answer.**

If Omega Bank's security interest in the harp survives the sale by AMC to Ima, it also remains perfected by Omega Bank's original filing. *See* § 9-507(a). Ima and AMC are both located in Texas, so Omega Bank need not worry about any change in jurisdiction that might trigger an additional filing under Section 9-316(a). Therefore, Ima cannot claim priority under Section 9-317(b) or otherwise, on the theory that Omega Bank's security interest is not perfected after the sale. Ima does enjoy priority (under Section 9-320(a)), but for reasons different from those stated in Answer (D), **making Answer (D) an incorrect answer.**

177. **Answer (B) is the correct answer.** AMC is in the business of selling musical instruments and related items. Therefore, AMC used the computer equipment as "equipment," rather than "inventory." Omega Bank's security interest extends to equipment, and its security agreement prohibits AMC from selling its equipment. Omega Bank, then, can recover the equipment from Hewey under Section 9-201(a) and Section 9-315(a), unless some other provision favors Hewey. He cannot invoke the protection afforded to buyers under Section 9-320(a). Hewey is not a "buyer in ordinary course of business" as defined in Section 1-201(b)(9) because AMC does not sell computer equipment in the ordinary course of its business. **Therefore, Answer (C) is incorrect.** In addition, Hewey cannot invoke the protection afforded to buyers under Section 9-320(b) because the computer equipment is not a consumer good in the hands of AMC (and Omega Bank had filed a financing statement against the equipment). **Therefore, Answer (A) is incorrect.** No provision that might favor Hewey turns on whether he is or is not an employee of the debtor, **making Answer (D) an incorrect answer.** (If Hewey was an in-house lawyer who negotiated the transaction with Omega Bank, then perhaps he would fail a "good faith" or "no knowledge" requirement, but those facts are not present in this question.) Hewey cannot successfully invoke any buyer-protection statute, so Omega Bank wins the priority dispute in reliance on Section 9-201(a) and Section 9-315(a), **making Answer (B) the correct answer.**

178. **Answer (D) is the correct answer.** The term "buyer in ordinary course of business" is defined in Section 1-201(b)(9). The phrase "ordinary course of business" refers to the seller's course of business, not the buyer's course of business. Dealer is in the business of selling sports memorabilia, so Mickey may meet the definition, regardless of what business he is in, and no matter how he intends to use the baseballs. **Therefore, Answer (B) is**

incorrect. To qualify as a buyer in the ordinary course of Dealer's business, Mickey must purchase the baseballs "without knowledge that the sale violates the rights of [Redbird Bank] in the goods." Mickey's mere knowledge of an existing security interest and awareness of an accompanying filing is acceptable. *See* § 9-320(a) (last clause) and cmt. 3. **Therefore, Answer (C) is incorrect.** Because the terms of sale violated Omega Bank's security agreement, Omega Bank's security interest may survive the disposition under Section 9-315(a). But that contract breach does not, by itself, preclude Mickey from qualifying as a buyer in the ordinary course of Dealer's business. **Therefore, Answer (A) is incorrect.** Payment terms can pose a problem, though, as the definition states: "A person buys goods in the ordinary course if the sale to the person comports with the usual or customary practices in the kind of business in which the seller is engaged or with the seller's own usual or customary practices." Here, Mickey paid by executing a negotiable, unsecured promissory note. Unless that payment device is customary for either Dealer or the sports memorabilia industry, Mickey will not be a buyer in the ordinary course of business. Answer (D) raises that possibility, **making Answer (D) the correct answer.**

Priority (Secured Party v. Lien Creditor)

179.   **Answer (D) is the correct answer.** Section 9-317(a) states the general rule that resolves priority disputes between secured parties and "lien creditors" (as that term is defined in Section 9-102(a)(52)). That Section states: "A security interest . . . is subordinate [i.e., junior, inferior, etc.] to the rights of . . . (2) a person that becomes a lien creditor before . . . (A) the security interest is perfected." Observe that the lien creditor's interest must arise "before" the secured party is perfected. MegaBank will be perfected in collateral when it files its financing statement, if ZinnCorp then has rights in the collateral (assuming previous value, and a security agreement is in place). MegaBank will be perfected in subsequent collateral when ZinnCorp acquires rights in it (assuming previous value, a security agreement is in place, and a previous filing). MegaBank's security agreement includes an after-acquired property clause, and it filed its financing statement long before BAMCO became a lien creditor. BAMCO's lien cannot encumber ZinnCorp's assets until ZinnCorp acquires rights in those assets. But at that very moment, MegaBank's security interest will become perfected in those same assets (by the earlier filing). In that case, there is a "tie" between the moment of MegaBank's perfection and BAMCO's lien. Because the statute uses the word "before," it resolves any temporal "tie" in favor of the secured party. Therefore, BAMCO's lien in any seized asset will never arise earlier than ("before") MegaBank's moment of perfection in that asset. This leaves MegaBank with priority in all of the seized collateral (whether "pre-lawsuit" or "post-lawsuit"), **making Answer (D) the correct answer and Answer (A) and Answer (B) incorrect answers.**

       Answer (B) also is incorrect because it erroneously suggests that priority turns on what happens during a specific 45-day period. No such period is mentioned in Section 9-317(a).

       Answer (C) is incorrect because Section 9-317(a) does not distinguish between involuntary and voluntary lien creditors, and no other Article 9 priority rule does so, either.

180.   **Answer (D) is the correct answer.** Under Section 9-317(a)(2), the general rule used to resolve priority disputes between lien creditors and secured parties, Ima's lien will enjoy priority if AMC's security interest was unperfected on September 10, when Ima's lien encumbered the violin. AMC provided seller financing, and the violin secures repayment of its purchase price, so AMC's security interest is a purchase-money security interest (PMSI) under Section 9-103. Timmy Zee, however, has bought the violin to learn how to play it for noncommercial purposes. This qualifies the violin as a "consumer good." As such, AMC's PMSI is automatically perfected at the moment of attachment. *See* § 9-309(1). Therefore, AMC has priority in the violin with no regard to if or when it filed a financing statement. Answer (D) contemplates this situation, **making Answer (D) the correct answer.**

Answers (A) and (B) are incorrect because they each erroneously require that AMC file a financing statement in order to have priority in the violin. As shown above, however, if the violin is a consumer good, AMC need not file at all because Article 9 provides for automatic perfection of purchase-money security interests in consumer goods.

Answer (B) raises an issue of collateral description. Under Section 9-108(e)(2), the term "consumer good" is insufficient to describe an interest in collateral for a consumer transaction. Section 9-504 provides that the rules of identification in Section 9-108 control the sufficiency of identification for financing statements. As a result, a description insufficient for a security agreement under Section 9-108 is also insufficient under Section 9-504 (with the sole exception that a description of "all assets," inapplicable here, would be permissible). But because a financing statement is unnecessary here to perfect, the point is moot.

Answer (C) is incorrect because AMC was perfected at the time that Ima became a lien creditor. Under Section 9-317(a)(2), a perfected security interest is superior to a later-arising interest of a lien creditor.

181.   If Timmy Zee is a professional musician, the violin would then be described as "equipment" under Article 9. In that case, AMC will still enjoy purchase-money status, but its security interest would not be automatically perfected upon attachment. Instead, absent possession of the violin, AMC will have to perfect its interest by filing a financing statement. Under the baseline priority rule, Ima's lien has priority if AMC has not filed its financing statement by September 10, the date of Ima's lien.

Mindful, though, that purchase-money sellers "sell today and file tomorrow," the drafters of Article 9 offered some protection against the risk that a "lien" will encumber the collateral after the security interest attaches but before the secured party files. Section 9-317(a)(2) defers to this purchase-money exception by directing the reader to subsection (e), which awards priority to a security interest that (i) attaches before the lien arises, (ii) enjoys purchase-money status, and (iii) is perfected by a financing statement filed no later than 20 days after the debtor receives delivery of the collateral.

The question states that AMC retained an enforceable security interest in the violin in the contract of purchase, so attachment occurred no later than September 5 (and perhaps as early as September 1), before Ima's lien arose on September 10. And AMC's security interest is a PMSI, as already noted. If AMC files a financing statement by September 26—that is, within 20 days after delivery of the violin to the debtor—Section 9-317(e) will give AMC's security interest retroactive priority, so long as the description in the financing statement meets the requirements of Section 9-108 and avoids a generic description such as "consumer goods." The conclusion would be that the answer would change from Answer (D) to Answer (B).

182.   **The correct answer is Answer (C).** The relationship between RI and Clueless historically has been referred to as consignment. It is an agency relationship in which the owner of goods leaves the goods with another with the power to transfer title to a buyer, usually within an agreed price range. It is a form of bailment.

Article 9 saw the relationship as potentially harboring hidden liens. People buying goods from vendors don't usually inquire into the title of their seller; when was the last time you asked a grocery store clerk if the supermarket really owned the milk on its shelves? This had consequences not only for buyers, but for other lenders. How do you know if the debtor has rights in the collateral sufficient for attachment? The result was to bring most large-scale consignments into Article 9. Section 9-109(a)(4) states that Article 9 covers a "consignment."

Section 9-102(a)(20) then defines "consignment" in a manner that varies significantly from the common law understanding. The definition is:

"Consignment" means a transaction, regardless of its form, in which a person delivers goods to a merchant for the purpose of sale and:

(A)   the merchant:

    (i)   deals in goods of that kind under a name other than the name of the person making delivery;

    (ii)   is not an auctioneer; and

    (iii)   is not generally known by its creditors to be substantially engaged in selling the goods of others;

(B)   with respect to each delivery, the aggregate value of the goods is $1,000 or more at the time of delivery;

(C)   the goods are not consumer goods immediately before delivery; and

(D)   the transaction does not create a security interest that secures an obligation.

The relationship between RI and Clueless meets these requirements. RI is a merchant selling vases without notice that Clueless is retaining title to them, and without notice that RI is selling the goods of another. The amounts are certainly in excess of $1,000 (or at least most of them should be—it would take more than 1000 separate deliveries to exempt all the shipments). The other requirements are met or inapplicable.

This means that the consignment is subject to Article 9. Indeed, Section 9-102(a)(73)(C), a "consignor"—here, Clueless—is defined as a secured party. Section 9-102(a)(28)(C), a "consignee"—here, RI—is defined as a debtor. That means that Clueless's agreement to retain title is treated as a transaction under Article 9. *See also* § 1-201(b)(35) (defining "security interest"). That being the case, any dispute between an Article 9 secured creditor such as Clueless and a lien creditor such as TIG is resolved by Article 9, specifically Section 9-317(a)(2)(A). That Section provides that an unperfected security interest is junior to the interest of a lien creditor. Because Clueless did not take any action—such as filing a financing statement—its security interest was unperfected, and thus would lose to a lien creditor such as TIG. **That makes Answer (C) correct.**

Answer (D) is incorrect, although it reaches the correct result, because the triggering condition it identifies is wrong. A lien creditor's interest priority is determined at the time it becomes a lien creditor, not at the time the rights vested that enabled it to apply to become a lien creditor.

Answer (B) is incorrect because, as set forth above, consignments of this type are within Article 9.

Answer (A) is incorrect because both Section 1-201(b)(35) and Section 2-401 specifically provide that retention of title to ensure repayment of an obligation is treated as a passage of title from the previous owner to the new owner, with the property rights being converted from title to a security interest.

183. **The correct answer is Answer (D).** As in Question 182, the correct answer to this question turns on the inclusion within Article 9 of transactions other than transactions strictly for security. Here, the inclusion is the "sale of accounts, chattel paper, payment intangibles, or promissory notes." § 9-109(a)(3).

As with consignments, the seller and buyer of such payment obligations are denominated as debtor and secured party. Section 9-102(a)(73)(D) defines "secured party" as including "a person to which accounts, chattel paper, payment intangibles, or promissory notes have been sold"; Section 9-102(a)(28)(B) defines "debtor" as including "a seller of accounts, chattel paper, payment intangibles, or promissory notes."

Are the receivables "accounts, chattel paper, payment intangibles, or promissory notes" so as to bring the transaction with Factors into Article 9? Yes. The amounts owed to SOI are most likely accounts, defined in Section 9-102(a)(3) as a "right to payment of a monetary obligation . . . for services rendered." Here, the services would be the glazing of the pottery. The receivables are not chattel paper because there is no indication that SOI took a security interest from any of its customers to secure payment and there is no other indication of any property interest taken or retained. The payments relate to a service — the glazing — and thus not to an intangible. Finally, they are not promissory notes as the invoices do not have the signature of the customer as would be required if they were to be characterized as a note.

Article 9 thus applies, making **Answer (B) incorrect**. The fact that the sale was an absolute assignment does not matter, because Section 9-109(a)(3) refers to a sale. **That makes Answer (A) incorrect.**

Answer (C) is incorrect because the relevant rule under Article 9 for determining the priority between a lien creditor such as Fred is Section 9-317(a)(2)(A) (under Section 9-102(a)(52), Fred became a lien creditor upon service of the writ of garnishment because that is when he acquired a property interest in RI's obligation to pay SOI). As in Question 182, that Section essentially states that an unperfected security interest loses to a lien creditor.

The key question, then, is whether Factors perfected its interest. We know that it did not file a financing statement, so it is unperfected unless another avenue of perfection exists. For example, with respect to some payment obligations, perfection is automatic upon attachment; that applies to sales of payment intangibles or promissory notes. § 9-309(3), (4).

But it is not automatic as to all accounts. Section 9-309(2) states that perfection is automatic only if it is "an assignment of accounts or payment intangibles which does not by itself or in conjunction with other assignments to the same assignee transfer *a significant part* of the assignor's outstanding accounts or payment intangibles"

What constitutes "a significant part"? That is a factual issue and can be open to dispute in some cases, but not when the transaction involves 75% of the debtor's accounts, as does this transaction. Because more than a significant part were sold (or assigned, same thing here, see cmt. 11 to Section 9-102), Factors was unperfected, and thus loses to Fred. As a result, **Answer (D) is correct.**

184.   **Answer (D) is the correct answer.** This again turns on Section 9-317(a)(2)(A): a lien creditor's interest is superior to an unperfected security interest. Here, GeeHard is a lien creditor. Service of its writ creates all the necessary elements for a lien creditor under Section 9-102(a)(52).

Both SC1 and SC2 possess security interests. But are they perfected? Most all courts follow *National Peregrine, Inc. v. Capitol Federal Savings & Loan Association (In re Peregrine Entertainment, Ltd.)*, 116 B.R. 194 (C.D. Cal. 1990) (holding specifically adopted in *In re World Auxiliary Power Co.*, 303 F.3d 1120, 1125 (9th Cir. 2002)), which holds that the only place to perfect a security interest in a registered copyright is with the United States Copyright Office. Filings with local UCC filing offices are insufficient (note that this applies to the copyright itself). Contractual rights to receive royalties are payment intangibles under Article 9, and an interest in those payment obligations must comply with Article 9). Neither SC1 nor SC2 filed with the Copyright Office, so their interests are unperfected. Under Section 9-317(a)(2)(A), their interests will be subordinate to GeeHard's, making **Answer (D) correct, and Answer (C) incorrect.**

Answer (A) and Answer (B) are each incorrect for the same reason: Section 9-317(a)(2)(A) makes no distinction as to when the debt behind the lien creditor's lien arose. All that matters is the timing of the creation of the property interest that will secure that debt. Here that was when the writ was served upon Software.

185.   **The correct answer is Answer (D)**, for much the same reasons as in Question 184. Under Article 9, the assignee of an assignment for the benefit of creditors has the status of a lien creditor. Specifically, Section 9-102(a)(52)(B) provides that "Lien creditor" means: . . . (B) an assignee for benefit of creditors from the time of assignment." Here, Alice has that status, and because (under the logic of Question 184), both SC1 and SC2 were unperfected at the time Alice became an assignee, her interest is superior.

Answer (A) is incorrect because assignments for the benefit of creditors are covered in Article 9, as shown by the reference to them in the definition of "lien creditor." (An assignment for the benefit of creditors is a common law (and sometimes statutory) collective remedy similar to a bankruptcy.)

Answer (B) is incorrect because under Article 9 an assignee for the benefit of creditors has the status of a lien creditor from the moment the assignment is effective.

Answer (C) is incorrect because such financing statements are irrelevant for the perfection of federal property interests such as copyrights. SC1 and SC2 are thus unperfected.

186. The answer to this question turns on the type of receiver that was appointed. If SC2 obtained a receiver as part of its rights as a secured creditor—a so-called "rents and profits" receiver—then the receiver should lose. That is because the appointment of a "rents and profits" receiver simply gives the receiver the ability to collect assets from the debtor, and then administer them for the benefit of the secured party. It is *not* perfection—the only exception might be if under local law the appointment of a receiver constitutes constructive possession of the intangible copyright (and thus the secured creditor would thereby be perfected by possession). This is not likely to be the case because you cannot physically possess an intangible—it would be like trying to grab air with your hand.

As a consequence, the rule of priority here is the rule between two unperfected secured creditors found in Section 9-322(a)(3); that is, the first to attach has priority. Because SC1's interests attached earlier, it would have priority.

If, however, the receiver appointed was an "equity receiver," then the result changes. Unlike a "rents and profits receiver," an equity receiver is not an agent for any party. An equity receiver has the duty to wind up the debtor's affairs for the benefit of *all* creditors, not just the creditor or party who petitioned for the receiver's appointment. Under Article 9, an equity receiver is a lien creditor; Section 9-102(a)(52)(D) defines a "lien creditor" to include "a receiver in equity from the time of appointment." With the powers of a lien creditor, the receiver's interest in the copyrights would be superior to SC1 and SC2's unperfected interests in the copyrights under Section 9-317(a)(2)(A).

187. **Answer (D) is the correct answer.** Because a search today (September 1, 2019) against "Quantum Technologies" will not reveal Omega Bank's earlier filing against "ZeeTech," the name change has rendered the earlier filing seriously misleading. *See* §9-506(c). Therefore, the earlier filing will perfect Omega Bank's security interest in collateral acquired before the name change and within four months thereafter, but not its security interest in collateral acquired by ZeeTech/Quantum more than four months after the name change. *See* §9-507(c). Quantum acquired Item #1 on April 15, within four months of the name change in February. But Quantum acquired Item #2 on July 15, more than four months after the name change in February. Therefore, Omega Bank's original filing continues to perfect its security interest in Item #1, but it does not perfect a security interest in Item #2.

Meredith did not become a "lien creditor" with respect to Item #1 until August. Omega Bank had a perfected security interest in Item #1 on the purchase date of April 15, and its interest in Item #1 remained perfected, notwithstanding the name change. Therefore, Omega Bank's security interest is not subordinate to Meredith's lien under Section 9-317(a)(2). Instead, Omega Bank has priority in Item #1, **making Answer (B) an incorrect answer.**

Meredith did not become a "lien creditor" with respect to Item #2 until August. Omega Bank's earlier filing is not effective to perfect its security interest in Item #2 for reasons discussed above. Therefore, Omega Bank's unperfected security interest in Item #2 is subordinate to Meredith's lien, giving Meredith priority in Item #2. **Answer (A), then, is incorrect.**

Answer (C) is incorrect because the facts provide sufficient information to resolve the priority dispute in both pieces of equipment.

In summary, Omega Bank has priority in Item #1, and Meredith has priority in Item #2. Answer (D) says as much, **making Answer (D) the correct answer.**

188. Under Section 9-323(b), the sheriff should pay $110,000 to Bank and $10,000 to Hannah. That statute makes Bank's security interest subordinate to Hannah's property interest "to the extent that the security interest secures an advance made more than 45 days after [Hannah] becomes a lien creditor." Rephrased, Bank's security interest enjoys priority with respect to *all* advances funded on or before the forty-fifth day after Hannah became a lien creditor (this 45-day period is absolute and is not shortened if the secured creditor acquires knowledge of the competing lien during the period).

Hannah became a lien creditor on September 20, so advances funded by Bank on or before November 4 — $50,000 on September 1, $35,000 on October 1 and $25,000 on November 1 — are entitled to priority. The $20,000 advanced on November 15 is not protected because it was funded more than 45 days after Hannah became a lien creditor. So Bank is entitled to receive $110,000 (covering its first three advances), and Hannah is entitled to receive the remaining $10,000.

Observe that Bank cannot take advantage of the post-45-day-protection offered by Sections 9-323(b)(1) and (b)(2) because Bank had knowledge of Hannah's lien on September 20 (before the 45-day period ended) and did not fund the advances pursuant to a prior commitment entered into without knowledge of the lien.

189. Yes, this change would affect the distribution. It would require the sheriff to disburse to Bank the entire $120,000. Bank's agreement to loan $150,000 to Debtor in one or more advances means that all of the advances were funded "pursuant to commitment," a phrase defined in Section 9-102(a)(69). Even though Bank is not obligated to fund an advance if an Event of Default exists, all advances are funded "pursuant to commitment." This is so because Section 9-102(a)(69) explicitly states that an advance is made pursuant to

commitment even if "a subsequent event of default or other event not within the secured party's control has relieved or may relieve the secured party from its obligation." Because Bank funded the four advances pursuant to commitment as defined in Section 9-102(a)(69), all of the advances are protected against Hannah's competing $75,000 claim. That priority is supported by Section 9-323(b)(2) because the commitment was entered into on September 1, before Bank discovered Hannah's competing claim on September 20. As all of Bank's advances enjoy priority, the sheriff should pay the entire $120,000 to Bank.

190.   **Answer (D) is the correct answer.** Redbird Bank's filing on January 18, 2014, is effective for five years after the date of the filing. *See* § 9-515(a). Redbird Bank can continue the effectiveness of its original filing by timely filing a continuation statement during the last six months of the five-year period. *See* § 9-515(d). In this case, that six-month period is roughly July 19, 2018, through January 19, 2019. **Answer (A) is incorrect** because a continuation statement filed on July 10, 2018, is premature and, therefore, ineffective (even if recorded by the clerk). *See* § 9-510(c). **Answer (B) is incorrect** because a continuation statement filed on January 24, 2019, is too late and, therefore, ineffective (even if recorded by the clerk). *Id.*

The difference between Answer (C) and Answer (D) is that Redbird Bank wins under the former only if it timely files a continuation statement, whereas Redbird Bank wins under the latter even if it never files a continuation statement. Section 9-515(c) addresses the effect of a filing that lapses because the secured party fails to timely file a continuation statement. On the assumption that the secured party is perfected solely by its original filing, its security interest becomes unperfected *prospectively*.

This does not concern Redbird Bank, as its filing was effective when Bradford Industries became a lien creditor in December 2018. Section 9-515(c) also states that Redbird Bank's security interest becomes unperfected retroactively "against a purchaser of the collateral for value." Section 1-201 defines "purchaser" and "purchase" in a manner that requires a party to acquire a property interest in a "voluntary transaction." Lien creditors, by definition, acquire their property interests by judicial process, an involuntary transaction. Therefore, Bradford Industries fails to qualify as a "purchaser of the collateral for value." This means that Redbird Bank's security interest will become unperfected if it fails to file a continuation statement, but it will continue to enjoy priority against a lien creditor whose property interest (or "lien") arises while Redbird Bank's original filing was effective.

That is the case under the facts. Given that Bradford Industries is an involuntary creditor whose behavior is not dictated by the filing system, the result seems only fair. Redbird Bank need not file a continuation statement to preserve its priority against Bradford Industries. Redbird Bank has priority even if it never files a continuation statement. *See* § 9-515, cmt. 3 (Example 2). Therefore, **Answer (C) is an incorrect answer and Answer (D) is the correct answer.**

Priority (Secured Party v. IRS)

191.   **Answer (C) is the correct answer.** "Commercial financing security" refers to "(i) paper of a kind ordinarily arising in commercial transactions, (ii) accounts receivable, (iii) mortgages on real property, and (iv) inventory." 26 U.S.C. §6323(c)(2)(C). Accounts and inventory are expressly mentioned, **making Answers (A) and (D) incorrect answers.** Chattel paper ordinarily arises in commercial transactions, **making Answer (B) incorrect.** Equipment is not mentioned in the definition, **making Answer (C) the correct answer.**

192.   **Answer (C) is the correct answer.** Under the Federal Tax Lien Statutes (26 U.S.C. §§6321-6323), advances funded after the IRS files its tax lien notice may enjoy priority if the secured party funded the advances (i) within the 45-day period following the filing date of the tax lien notice *and* (ii) without knowledge of the tax lien notice. 26 U.S.C. §6323(c)(2)(A), (d). The IRS filed its tax lien notice on August 1, so the 45-day period ended on September 15. But Bank discovered the tax lien filing on August 21, within the 45-day period. So only advances funded prior to discovery are protected. Those advances aggregate $900,000, **making Answer (C) the correct answer** and **Answers (A), (B), and (D) incorrect answers.**

Appreciate that, unlike Section 9-323(b), the 45-day period under the Federal Tax Lien Statutes is not absolute. The period can be terminated by the secured party's knowledge of the competing tax lien, and the period cannot be extended if the debtor and the secured party have entered into a binding commitment without knowledge of the competing tax lien.

193.   **Answer (A) is the correct answer.** As used by ZinnMark Fashions (a clothing retailer), the dresses and shoes are inventory, a type of commercial financing security. 26 U.S.C. §6323(c)(2)(C)(iv). So **Answer (B) is incorrect.** Bank's discovery of the tax lien notice terminates the 45-day period of protection for advances funded after the tax lien notice is filed. 26 U.S.C. §6323(c)(2)(A). But Bank's discovery of the tax lien notice does not terminate the 45-day period of protection for collateral acquired by the debtor after the tax lien notice is filed. 26 U.S.C. §6323(c)(2)(B). So **Answer (C) is incorrect.** (The difference is justified because Bank's knowledge can affect its own funding decision but not necessarily the debtor's purchasing activity.) Because the collateral is commercial financing security and was timely acquired on September 7 (within 45 days following the filing of the tax lien notice on August 1), Bank's security interest enjoys priority, **making Answer (A) the correct answer. Answer (D) is incorrect,** as the relevant 45-day period of protection commences on the date of the tax lien filing, not the date of the assessment.

194.   **Answer (D) is the correct answer.** The computers, in the hands of a business that sells clothing, are equipment, which is a type of collateral not included within the definition of "commercial financing security." 26 U.S.C. § 6323(c)(2)(C). But the definition of "commercial financing security" becomes relevant only with respect to collateral acquired by the debtor after the IRS files its tax lien notice. ZinnMark Fashions acquired these machines on July 25, before the IRS filed its tax lien notice on August 1. So the fact that the collateral is not "commercial financing security" has no effect on priority, **making Answer (A) an incorrect answer. Answer (B) is incorrect** because the tax lien filing date, not the tax assessment date, dictates priority. And **Answer (C) also is incorrect.** If anything, Bank's lack of knowledge at the time of purchase should favor Bank, not the IRS.

Default

195.   **Answer (A) is the correct answer.** Section 9-601 states: "After default, a secured party has the rights provided in this part . . . ." Most, if not all, provisions in Part 6 (Section 9-601 through Section 9-628) mention "default." Therefore, understanding its meaning is rather important. As noted in Section 9-601, cmt. 3, "this Article leaves to the agreement of the parties the circumstances giving rise to a default." The term, then, is defined by the parties, and they should memorialize their understanding and agreement in the security agreement or one of the other loan papers, **making Answer (A) the correct answer.**

Answers (B), (C), and (D) are incorrect answers because Article 9 does not define the term.

196.   **Answer (B) is the correct answer.** Section 9-609 permits the secured party to take possession of collateral after default. "Collateral" is defined in Section 9-102(a)(12) as "the property subject to a security interest[.]" Property becomes subject to a security interest on attachment under Section 9-203.

Answer (A) is incorrect because the statute does not exclude consumer goods from the type of collateral that the secured party can seize.

Answers (C) and (D) are incorrect because the statute does not limit the remedy to security interests that are perfected or have priority. *See* § 9-609, cmt. 5 (discussing multiple security interests).

197.   **Answer (D) is the correct answer.** Article 9 does not permit a secured party to avoid or reduce liability for breaching the peace by taking any of the actions suggested in the other three answers.

Answer (A) is incorrect because Section 9-602(6) refers to Section 9-609 as a statute that imposes on a secured party a duty (to avoid breaching the peace) that cannot be waived or varied.

Answer (B) is incorrect. Section 9-603(a) does permit a secured party to draft standards measuring its duties if the drafted standards are not manifestly unreasonable. However, subsection (b) indicates that subsection (a) is inapplicable "to the duty under Section 9-609 to refrain from breaching the peace."

Answer (C) is incorrect. Comment 3 to Section 9-609 states in relevant part: "courts should hold the secured party responsible for the actions of others . . . including independent contractors[.]"

If BigBank wants to avoid breaching the peace, it may wish to consider taking collateral "pursuant to judicial process" under Section 9-609(b)(1), which is not subject to a breach of the peace limitation because the actions are taken under color of law as authorized by the judicial process.

198.   **Answer (B) is the correct answer.** Section 9-609(a)(2) allows a secured party, after default, to "render equipment unusable." Therefore, Article 9 does indeed permit AutoCorp to use the starter interruption device to render Tim's car unusable if Tim is using the vehicle as equipment.

Answer (A) is incorrect because Section 9-609 does, contrary to the answer, address the secured party's ability to render collateral unusable (permitting it if the collateral is equipment).

Answer (C) is incorrect for two reasons. First, the answer suggests that Section 9-609 permits a secured party to render consumer goods unusable. But the statute only mentions equipment, not consumer goods or any other type of goods. Second, Section 9-609 does not require the debtor to be in default for a minimum period before the secured party can take action to render the collateral (if equipment) unusable.

Answer (D) is incorrect because Section 9-609 does not require the collateral to be located at any particular place before the secured party can render it unusable.

Please note that some states have enacted non-uniform amendments to Article 9, or other applicable laws, which address the secured party's ability to use starter interruption devices, and other technology, to disable collateral or render it unusable.

199.   **Answer (B) is the correct answer.** Section 9-611(c) requires Ruth to send notice to the debtor and any secondary obligor. (It also requires Ruth to send notice to other parties with a property interest in the jewelry, but the facts do not suggest any such parties.) Carmen is the debtor, as she is the party who granted the security interest in the jewelry. Therefore, Ruth must send notice to Carmen. A guarantor is an example of a secondary obligor (Kevin has a claim for reimbursement from Elliott if Kevin has to pay Ruth under the guaranty), so Kevin also is entitled to notice. Elliott is the borrower and the primary obligor, but he is neither the debtor nor a secondary obligor. So he is not entitled to notice. Therefore, under the statute, Ruth must send notice to Carmen (the debtor) and Kevin (the secondary obligor), but she is not required to send notice to Elliott (the borrower and primary obligor). Carmen and Kevin are the only two parties mentioned in Answer (B), **making Answer (B) the correct answer.**

Answer (A) is incorrect because Elliott is not entitled to notice.

Answer (C) is incorrect because Elliott is not entitled to notice, and the answer fails to mention Kevin, who is entitled to notice as a secondary obligor.

Answer (D) is incorrect because the answer fails to mention Kevin, who is entitled to notice as a secondary obligor.

200. **Answer (C) is the correct answer.** When drafting the notice, Ruth needs to determine whether she should follow Section 9-613 or Section 9-614. Section 9-614 applies to a consumer-goods transaction. This transaction is not a consumer-goods transaction because Elliott borrowed the $3,000 for a business purpose, rather than for a personal, family, or household purpose. *See* § 9-102(a)(24) (defining "consumer-goods transaction"). Therefore, Ruth should follow Section 9-613 when she drafts the notice. Section 9-613(1)(D) mentions that the notice should inform the debtor of the right to an accounting (and any fee for it), **making Answer (C) the correct answer.**

Answer **(A) is incorrect** because Section 9-611 merely requires Ruth to "send" the notice. Statutory compliance does not require proof that the notice was "received."

Answer **(B) is incorrect** because it erroneously suggests that Ruth must give at least 20 days' notice. Section 9-611(b) requires Ruth to send a "reasonable" disposition notice. Section 9-612(b) offers a statutory safe harbor of 10 days (which the parties could agree to reduce, under Section 9-603(a), if the agreed-upon number of days is not "manifestly unreasonable"). Article 9 does not require a specific minimum period of notice, **making Answer (B) incorrect.**

Answer **(D) is incorrect.** Section 9-614(1)(C) requires Ruth to include in her notice a telephone number the recipient can call to discover the redemption price. But Section 9-614 does not apply because, as already mentioned, this is not a consumer-goods transaction. Therefore, Section 9-613 applies, and it does not require Ruth to include in the notice the telephone number. For this reason, **Answer (D) is incorrect.**

201. **Answer (D) is the correct answer.** Subject to Carmen's consent, Ruth can offer to keep the jewelry (now in her possession and no longer in Carmen's possession) and forgive the unpaid debt. *See* § 9-620(a).

Answer **(A) is incorrect.** Absent an effective waiver, Ruth is obligated to forego this desired exchange and instead must dispose of the collateral under Section 9-610 if Elliott has paid down a certain percentage of the unpaid $3,000 loan. But the statutory threshold is 60%, and under these facts Elliott has paid $1,600, or approximately 53%.

Answer **(B) is incorrect.** Even if the pieces of jewelry are treated as consumer goods by Carmen (perhaps a safe assumption), Ruth can move forward with the transaction. Section 9-620(a)(3) poses no hurdle because Ruth, rather than Carmen, has possession of the pieces of jewelry. And Section 9-620(a)(4) does not block the transaction because Elliott has not yet paid 60% ($1,800) of the original $3,000 loan.

Answer **(C) is incorrect.** Section 9-620, cmt. 11, reminds the reader that Ruth must make a good-faith offer and further gives an example of a transaction made in bad faith (the ratio of collateral value to unpaid debt is 10:1). In this question, the ratio of collateral value ($3,500) to unpaid debt ($1,400) is only 2.5:1, and the excess value of $2,100 is not sufficiently high to trigger good-faith concerns (at least in the opinion of the author who drafted this question). Remember that Carmen must consent to the transaction, and presumably she has some idea of the fair value of the items that will factor into her decision.

202.   **Answer (D) is the correct answer,** which may come as a surprise. Ruth is obligated to send her proposal to Kevin, the guarantor (and, therefore, a secondary obligor), only if she is proposing to forgive some (rather than all) of the unpaid debt. *See* § 9-621(b). Kevin will not object to Ruth's proposal, and therefore sending notice to him serves no purpose, because Ruth is forgiving all of the debt (leaving Kevin with no secondary liability). Because Ruth is not required to send her proposal to Kevin, **Answer (A) and Answer (B) are both incorrect.** Elliott is the borrower and the primary obligor, but he has no property interest in the jewelry, and he has no claim to the jewelry even if he honors his obligation to Ruth. Therefore, **Answer (A) is incorrect for this additional reason.** This leaves Answer (C) and Answer (D) as the possibly correct answer. Carmen, the debtor, is not mentioned in the list of parties to whom Ruth must send her proposal under Section 9-621(a). Section 9-620, cmt. 4, further clarifies the issue, noting that Ruth is required to send a proposal to Carmen only if Ruth intends to rely on Carmen's silence, rather than Carmen's authenticated record, as consent to the transaction. The call of the question is "must send," and, for the foregoing reasons, Ruth is not required to send a proposal to Carmen (but Ruth will need Carmen's consent in the form of an authenticated record). Therefore, **Answer (C) is incorrect and Answer (D) is correct.**

203.   **Answer (B) is the correct answer.** Section 9-615(a) addresses how BankTwo should distribute the proceeds. After deducting the disposition costs of $10,000 under (a)(1), Bank-Two may next apply the proceeds to its own remaining secured debt of $150,000 under (a)(2). After doing so, proceeds of $150,000 still remain. Should BankTwo pay any of that amount to BankOne or BankThree? Is Debtor entitled to any or all of the amount? Section 9-615(a)(3) states that any remaining proceeds should be paid to any creditor who is subordinate (junior) to BankTwo if BankTwo received a timely authenticated demand from that subordinate (junior) creditor to participate in the proceeds distribution. None of the bank creditors is asserting a PMSI, so the relative priority among the three banks is as suggested by their respective names: BankOne has first priority and therefore is senior, not subordinate, to BankTwo's position. BankOne, as the senior creditor, does not participate in the proceeds distribution. BankThree has third priority and is therefore subordinate, or junior, to BankTwo's position. But the facts indicate that BankTwo never received any replies from any party, including BankThree, so BankThree also does not participate in this distribution of proceeds. Therefore, the remaining proceeds balance of $150,000 is payable to Debtor as surplus under Section 9-615(d). In summary, then, BankTwo keeps $150,000 (the amount of its unpaid secured debt) and remits the $150,000 balance to Debtor. This distribution is reflected in Answer (B), **making Answer (B) the correct answer.**

Answer (A) is incorrect for two reasons. First, BankOne does not share in the proceeds distribution, and BankTwo will receive $150,000 (rather than $50,000).

Answer (C) is incorrect because BankOne does not share in the proceeds distribution.

Answer (D) is incorrect because BankThree does not share in the proceeds distribution. As a party holding a security interest subordinate, or junior, to BankTwo's security interest, BankThree can participate in the proceeds distribution. To be eligible, however, BankTwo must receive a timely notice from BankThree. BankTwo never received such a notice from BankThree, so BankThree cannot participate in the distribution.

204. **Answer (C) is the correct answer.** The respective remaining loan balances are calculated by taking the amount owed immediately prior to the foreclosure sale, and then subtracting from that amount any proceeds paid to that particular secured party under the distribution scheme of Section 9-615. Debtor owed $250,000 to BankOne, and BankOne received no proceeds. Therefore, Debtor continues to owe $250,000 to BankOne. Debtor owed $150,000 to BankTwo, and BankTwo received proceeds of $150,000. Therefore, Debtor owes zero dollars to BankTwo. Debtor owed $50,000 to BankThree, and BankThree received no proceeds. Therefore, Debtor continues to owe $50,000 to BankThree. Answer (C) reflects these results, **making Answer (C) the correct answer.**

Answer (A) is incorrect because Debtor continues to owe $250,000 to BankOne, and Debtor now owes zero dollars to BankTwo.

Answer (B) is incorrect because Debtor continues to owe $50,000 to BankThree.

Answer (D) is incorrect because Debtor continues to owe $250,000 to BankOne and $50,000 to BankThree.

205. **Answer (A) is the correct answer.** Section 9-617(a) is the applicable statute. Under that statute, the foreclosing creditor's security interest, and any subordinate (junior) security interests, are terminated by the foreclosure sale. Security interests that are not subordinate (junior) to the foreclosing creditor's security interest are not terminated. Instead, they instead survive the disposition and can be enforced against the winning bidder. Under the facts, then, the security interests of BankTwo (the foreclosing creditor) and BankThree (a subordinate creditor) are terminated, but the security interest of BankOne (the senior creditor) survives. This conclusion is captured by Answer (A), **making Answer (A) the correct answer.**

Answer (B) is incorrect because it fails to mention that BankThree's subordinate security interest also is terminated by the foreclosure sale.

Answer (C) is incorrect because BankOne's senior security interest survives the disposition.

Answer (D) is incorrect because BankOne's senior security interest survives the disposition, and BankThree's subordinate security interest does not.

206. The term "public disposition" is not defined in Section 9-102 or Section 1-201 (probably the first two statutes the reader will consult). Nor is it defined in Section 9-610,

Section 9-613, or any other Article 9 statute in which the term appears. The lack of any statutory definition may cause the reader some concern, given the term's importance. Guidance is found in Official Comment 7 to Section 9-610. "[A] 'public disposition' is one at which the price is determined after the public has had a meaningful opportunity for competitive bidding. 'Meaningful opportunity' is meant to imply that some form of advertisement or public notice must precede the sale (or other disposition) and that the public must have access to the sale (disposition)." *Cf.* § 2-706, cmt. 4 (permitting a seller, upon a buyer's breach, to dispose of goods by "public sale," which is described as "a sale by auction"). In summary, then, the key elements of a "public disposition" appear to be: (i) the public may participate (no segment is excluded, for example, as in a "dealers only" auction); (ii) the bidding is competitive (sealed bids may not be viewed as such); (iii) advertising precedes the disposition; and (iv) the public has access to the disposition.

207.   A secured party should be aware that it can purchase collateral at a public disposition but (as a general rule) cannot purchase collateral at a private disposition. *See* § 9-610(c). Also, when drafting its disposition notice, the secured party should remember that the notice needs to state the location, date, and time of a public disposition, but only the date after which any private disposition will be scheduled. *See* §§ 9-613(1)(E); 9-614(1)(A).

208.   Article 9 excuses notice to the debtor in four situations. First, notice is not required if the debtor authenticated, after default, a waiver of its right to receive notice. *See* § 9-624(a). Second, notice is excused if the collateral is "perishable" (e.g., fruits and vegetables). *See* § 9-611(d). Third, notice also is excused if the collateral "threatens to decline speedily in value" (e.g., seasonal products tied to a holiday that is about to come and go; tickets to an event that is about to happen). *Id.* Finally, the secured party is not required to send notice if the collateral "is of a type customarily sold on a recognized market" (e.g., shares of capital stock traded on the NYSE). *Id.; see also* § 9-610, cmt. 9 (discussing "recognized market").

209.   **Answer (B) is the correct answer.** Subject to the requirement that such a disposition must be commercially reasonable, Dean can dispose of the car by utilizing an Internet auction site. *See* § 9-613, cmt. 2 (last paragraph).

   Answer (A) is incorrect. Section 9-610(a) authorizes Dealer to sell the car "in its present condition or following any commercially reasonable preparation or processing." The language preceding the "or" seems to authorize Dealer to forego any minimal cleaning, and the "or" itself, as generally understood, seems to leave the choice to Dealer. But Official Comment 4 indicates that Dealer's decision to forego minimal cleaning is subject to the requirement that it (the decision) must be "commercially reasonable." Given the time and costs likely associated with minimal cleaning (dusting, vacuuming, washing), and the possible upside (in terms of higher bidding for a more attractive vehicle) to be gained, Dealer may have an obligation (under the statutory duty to engage in commercially reasonable behavior) to clean the inside and outside of the car before disposing of it.

   Answer (C) is incorrect. Section 9-610(d) informs Dealer that it makes certain warranties when it sells the car. Possible disclaimer is addressed in subsections (e) and (f).

Answer (D) is incorrect. Other than the statutory requirement of commercial reasonableness, Dealer is not otherwise constrained (by Bruce's use of the collateral, or otherwise) in deciding whether to sell the car at a public, or a private, disposition.

210.   **Answer (B) is the correct answer.** Section 9-607(a)(1) permits the secured party, after default, to "notify an account debtor . . . to make payment . . . to or for the benefit of the secured party[.]" Section 9-607(c)(1) requires the secured party to "proceed in a commercially reasonable manner" if it "undertakes to collect from . . . an account debtor[.]" **Therefore, Answer (B) is the correct answer.**

Answer (A) is incorrect because Lender's right to contact account debtors after Debtor defaults is statutory, not contractual. The preface language to Section 9-607(a) requires agreement, but only if Lender seeks to collect payments *before* Debtor has defaulted (not the case under the facts).

Answer (C) is incorrect because Section 9-607 does not require Debtor to be in default for any specific period of time before Lender can exercise its post-default collection rights.

Answer (D) is incorrect because Section 9-607 does not require Lender to notify the account debtors in writing, nor does it require Lender to give any notice to Debtor of its post-default collection efforts directed at the account debtors. (For a discussion of "notify," see Section 1-202(d).)

211.   **Answer (C) is the correct answer.** A secured party that attempts to recover a deficiency after breaching one of its statutory duties is subject to the "rebuttable presumption" rule. The rule presumes that if the secured party had complied with its statutory duties, then the disposition would have generated proceeds equal to the debt (leaving no deficiency). The presumption is rebuttable, so the secured party can offer evidence that compliance would have generated proceeds less than the unpaid debt, still leaving a deficiency (in some amount) that the secured party can recover. *See generally* § 9-626(a) and cmt. 3. Under this test, the court should enter a deficiency judgment of $3,700, calculated by subtracting the proceeds generated at a commercially reasonable disposition ($11,300) from the unpaid debt ($15,000), and **making Answer (C) the correct answer.**

Answer (A) is incorrect because Dealer offered proof that rebutted the presumption of no deficiency.

Answer (B) is incorrect. The rebuttable presumption rule requires evidence of the amount of proceeds generated by a commercially reasonable disposition, which for most forms of equipment (such as these four photocopiers) will be less than the fair market value (remember, nonjudicial foreclosures are distress sales that attract bargain hunters). Therefore, it is improper to calculate a deficiency under the rule by subtracting the fair market value ($12,500) from the unpaid debt ($15,000).

Answer (D) is incorrect because Dealer's own evidence revealed that a commercially reasonable disposition might have generated proceeds in excess of $11,000 (leaving a deficiency of less than $4,000).

212. The answer depends on whether the court adopts the rebuttable presumption rule, or the harsher "absolute bar" rule. Section 9-626(a) codifies the rebuttable presumption rule, but subsection (b) allows a court to apply a different rule in a consumer transaction. This transaction is a "consumer transaction" as defined in Section 9-102(a)(26) because Emily is using the harp as a consumer good. Under the "absolute bar" rule, MusiCorp is barred from recovering any deficiency if the disposition does not comply with Article 9, allowing the court to enter a deficiency judgment of zero dollars. The court also might decide to apply the rebuttable presumption rule and award a deficiency judgment of some amount. Under that rule, the presumption is a deficiency of zero dollars, but MusiCorp is given the opportunity to rebut that presumption by introducing evidence of what amount of proceeds would have resulted if MusiCorp had not breached its notice duty. Under the facts, it appears that the actual sales price would have remained the same even if Musi-Corp had sent notice to Emily. Under the rebuttable presumption rule, then, a court could enter a deficiency judgment against Emily in the amount as high as $4,000.

Bankruptcy (Excluding Voidable Preferences)

213.   **Answer (D) is the correct answer.** The filing of a bankruptcy case, under any chapter, automatically puts into effect the automatic stay of 11 U.S.C. § 362(a). This stay applies to any action to collect a debt, including foreclosure. It is effective without notice to any affected person.

The debtor's advance consent to collection action is irrelevant. A debtor generally cannot waive the protection of the automatic stay for a bankruptcy estate that is not yet in existence, although some courts uphold such waivers if they are specifically stated and appear to not result in a greater recovery for the creditor obtaining the waiver. **As a result, Answer (A) is incorrect.**

It also is irrelevant what buyers at any foreclosure know; the act of foreclosing the debtor's interest is the act that violates the stay. **That makes Answer (B) incorrect.**

Finally, although a creditor can request definitive documentation, the lack of such documentation does not affect the existence or scope of the stay. The stay goes into effect automatically, without a separate court order, and without notice. The prudent course of action, then, is to postpone the foreclosure and to check on the debtor's statement (through checking the court docket on PACER, the electronic access point for bankruptcy court dockets, for example). As a result, **Answer (C) is incorrect** as it is clearly not the best course of action for the bank to take.

214.   **Answer (C) is the correct answer.** If a secured creditor has possession of collateral that is the debtor's property, it is in a delicate position. It cannot foreclose or sell the property due to the automatic stay of 11 U.S.C. § 362(a). But it is entitled to adequate protection of its interest, and if that adequate protection is not forthcoming, the secured party is entitled to have the automatic stay lifted so that it may foreclose.

The exact amount and form of adequate protection is a subject left to a bankruptcy class. But the secured party is entitled to be put in the position it was in when the bankruptcy case was commenced. That means that one standard method of adequate protection is to pay the secured creditor an amount equal to the decline in value of the collateral due to depreciation (this is especially the case with personal property; land may not be so reliably declining in value). Because the secured creditor is entitled to some adequate protection, simply giving back the collateral is not the best option, **so Answer (D) is incorrect.**

What if the secured party does nothing? There is a split of authority here. The majority rule is that the act of passively holding onto an asset constitutes 'exercising control' over it, and such action violates Section 362(a)(3) of the Bankruptcy Code. *Thompson v. Gen. Motors Acceptance Corp.*, 566 F.3d 699, 703 (7th Cir. 2009); *Weber v. SEFCU (In re Weber)*, 719 F.3d 72, 81 (2d Cir. 2013); *California Emp't Dev. Dep't v. Taxel (In re Del Mission Ltd.)*, 98 F.3d 1147, 1151 (9th Cir. 1996); *Knaus v. Concordia Lumber Co. (In re Knaus)*, 889 F.2d 773, 775 (8th Cir. 1989).

The Tenth Circuit disagrees. *WD Equipment, LLC v. Cowan (In re Cowen)*, 849 F.3d 943, 948 (10th Cir. 2017). Going with the majority for now, it would appear that holding on to the equipment collateral would be a violation of the stay, making **Answer (A) and Answer (B) both incorrect** (and Answer (B) is particularly bad, because that course of action would both violate the stay and expose the bank to a claim of tortious interference with contract).

215.   **Answer (A) is the correct answer.** Under 11 U.S.C. § 362(d), a court shall grant relief from the stay if (i) BigBank's security interest is not adequately protected (11 U.S.C. § 362(d)(1)) or (ii) Karen has no equity in the vehicle and the vehicle is not necessary to an effective reorganization (11 U.S.C. § 362(d)(2)) — and because this is a Chapter 7 liquidation, it is a given that the vehicle is not necessary for an effective reorganization. Under 11 U.S.C. § 362(g)(1), BigBank (as the party requesting relief) will have the burden of proof on Karen's equity in the vehicle, and under 11 U.S.C. § 362(g)(2), Karen (the party opposing the relief) has the burden of proof on all other issues, including the issue of adequate protection. This allocation of proof is correctly stated in **Answer (A), making it the correct answer and Answers (B), and (C), and (D) incorrect answers.**

216.   **Answer (D) is the correct answer.** The automatic stay is "automatic" and does go into effect regardless of whether any alleged violator of the stay knows or should know about it. But Answer (C) indicates that not only will the court find a violation — which did occur — but will award damages for that violation. While the operation of the stay is automatic — here resulting in rendering Lost's actions null or giving Henry the absolute right to nullify them — damages require more. Section 362(k) requires a "willful violation of the stay." If one exists, then "an individual injured by any willful violation of a stay provided by this Section shall recover actual damages, including costs and attorneys' fees," even for prosecuting the relief from stay motion and any appeals therefrom. *America's Serv'g Co. v. Schwartz-Tallard (In re Schwartz-Tallard)*, 803 F.3d 1095, 1101 (9th Cir. 2015). In addition, in appropriate circumstances, the individual debtor may recover punitive damages. 11 U.S.C. § 362(k)(1). Here, when Lost applied the account's balance to the loan, it did not have notice of Henry's individual filing. Any violation of the stay, then, would not be "willful," and no damages would flow. **Answer (C) is thus incorrect.** But once Henry calls Lost and tells it that he had commenced a bankruptcy case, Lost then had actual notice of the filing, and its actions thereafter in refusing to release the funds constituted a separate and independent violation of the stay — at a minimum, it was exercising control over estate property in violation of Section 362(a)(3). For that violation, Lost may be liable in damages for actual loss, including, in some circuits, emotional distress damages. *See*

Sternberg v. Johnson, 595 F.3d 937 (9th Cir. 2009). Because the statute limits damages to the period after it learned of Henry's filing, it limits recovery to the period of Lost Bank's "willful" violation—its inaction in the face of a void or voidable act—**making Answer (D) the correct answer.**

Answer (B) is not correct because Section 9-109(d)(13) only excludes "deposit account[s] in consumer transaction[s]." Under Section 9-102(a)(26)(i), however, a "consumer transaction" is one in which "an individual incurs an obligation primarily for personal, family, or household purposes. . . ." Here, the facts state that the loan was incurred for business purposes, and thus the security interest is within Article 9, thus negating the premise of the answer.

Answer (A) is not correct because Lost Bank acted after it received actual notice of the existence of the stay; bankruptcy law does not require formal notice to be given for consequences to attach. Once it received Henry's telephone call, it acted at its peril by proceeding as if nothing had occurred. In short, Lost could not rely on the fact that it did not receive proper notice; the fact that it received actual notice was sufficient for its later actions to be deemed "willful."

217.   **Answer (B) is the correct answer.** Because the trustee cannot set aside the security interests of either creditor, this question is merely an Article 9 priority dispute. MedCo, a seller-financer, is claiming a purchase-money security interest in the kidney dialysis machine under Sections 9-103(a) and (b)(1). Because MedCo filed its financing statement on August 25, within 20 days after delivering the machine to Clinic on August 9, MedCo's security interest in the machine enjoys priority under Section 9-324(a). Bank's security interest in Clinic's remaining equipment enjoys priority under Section 9-322(a)(1) because Bank filed its financing statement on July 7, before MedCo filed its financing statement on August 25. Clinic owes $80,000 to MedCo, and the kidney dialysis machine has a value of $90,000. Under Section 506(a) of the Bankruptcy Code, a creditor has a secured claim to the extent of the value of its security, so MedCo has an $80,000 secured claim. Clinic owes $120,000 to Bank, and Bank's claim is secured in an amount equal to the remaining collateral: $60,000. Under Section 506(a), if a secured creditor's debt is more than the value of the collateral, the creditor has an unsecured claim for the deficiency. The balance of Bank's claim, $60,000, is thus an unsecured claim. So Bank has a $60,000 secured claim and a $60,000 unsecured claim, and MedCo has an $80,000 secured claim. This result is found in **Answer (B), making it the correct answer and Answers (A), (C), and (D) the incorrect answers.**

218.   **Answer (C) is the correct answer.** Normally the act of filing a post-petition financing statement violates the automatic stay. 11 U.S.C. § 362(a)(4), (5). But post-petition perfection is permitted by 11 U.S.C. § 362(b)(3) if "the trustee's rights and powers are subject to such perfection under Section 546(b) of this title. . . ." Under 11 U.S.C. § 546(b)(1), a trustee's rights and powers are subject to any state law provision—which includes Article 9—that permits perfection to be effective against a lien creditor who had acquired its lien prior to the secured party's perfection. The applicable Article 9 provision here is Section 9-317(e),

which permits a purchase-money creditor to enjoy priority over the competing (and prior) claim of a lien creditor if the purchase-money creditor's interest is perfected no later than the twentieth day after the debtor receives possession of the collateral. As Dealer (a seller-financer) can claim a purchase-money security interest in the refrigerator under Sections 9-103(a) and (b)(1), and because Dealer timely filed its financing statement within the 20-day period, Dealer can invoke the protection afforded by Section 9-317(e). Therefore, Dealer did not violate the automatic stay by filing its financing statement after Restaurant filed its bankruptcy petition.

Answer (A) is incorrect because the refrigerator is equipment, and a purchase-money security interest is automatically perfected only in consumer goods. § 9-309(1). **Answer (B) is incorrect** because only individuals can exempt property from the estate. 11 U.S.C. § 522(b) (indicating that "an individual debtor" may exempt property). And **Answer (D) is incorrect** because Section 544 simply gives the trustee in bankruptcy the status of a lien creditor, and because a lien creditor's property interest (its lien) could be "primed" under Section 9-317(e), so could the trustee's interest under Section 544(a).

219.   **Answer (C) is the correct answer.** In bankruptcy, Section 552(a) of the Bankruptcy Code nullifies after-acquired property clauses (all X, now owned *or hereafter acquired*). 11 U.S.C. § 552(a). Although this nullification is the clear result with respect to after-acquired property clauses, the Bankruptcy Code makes an exception if the lender's security interest is acquired through the proceeds provision of Section 9-315. 11 U.S.C. § 552(b)(1). The purpose of Section 552(a) is to free up assets needed by the bankrupt debtor to secure post-petition financing in favor of a creditor that will insist on a first-position security interest in unencumbered collateral. It is also a recognition that no new value is extended by virtue of a security interest obtained solely due to an after-acquired property clause.

Under Section 552(b), Bank has a security interest in inventory worth $400,000 to $450,000 calculated as follows: $300,000 (collateral that existed on the petition date) + $100,000 (admitted proceeds of pre-petition collateral) + perhaps $50,000 (depends on whether the post-petition accounts were generated by the sale of pre-petition inventory). The $50,000 allocable to the sale of Google stock does not represent pre-petition collateral or its proceeds, and thus is not included. As to accounts, Bank has a security interest in accounts worth $350,000 to $400,000 calculated as follows: $250,000 (collateral existed on the petition date) + $100,000 (proceeds of pre-petition collateral) + perhaps $50,000 (the post-petition inventory may have been acquired with cash proceeds of pre-petition accounts, and thus would be proceeds of proceeds, which Section 552(b) also recognizes). The $50,000 allocable to the donated equipment does not represent pre-petition collateral or its proceeds. So Bank has a security interest in accounts and inventory that aggregate $750,000 to $850,000, **making Answer (C) the correct answer** and **Answers (A), (B), and (D) incorrect answers.**

220.   **Answer (A) is the correct answer.** The strong-arm clause, a moniker given to 11 U.S.C. § 544(a)(1), gives the trustee the status of a hypothetical lien creditor as of the petition date, together with the rights and powers associated with that status, including the right

to "avoid any transfer of property of the debtor" that could be avoided by such a lien creditor as of the petition date. This gives the trustee no independent rights; it only gives the trustee the powers that state law gives lien creditors generally. Working in tandem with Section 9-317(a)(2), the strong-arm clause permits the trustee to avoid any security interest that is unperfected on the petition date, **making Answer (A) the correct answer. Answer (B) is incorrect** — it quotes language from the actual and constructive fraud tests of the fraudulent transfer provision, 11 U.S.C. § 548(a). **Answer (C) is incorrect** because it does not matter when the security interest was perfected, as long as it was perfected before the bankruptcy filing (this will matter, however, for preference purposes, but not under Section 544(a)). And **Answer (D), also incorrect,** is a reference to 11 U.S.C. § 522(f), which permits a consumer debtor to avoid certain judicial liens on, and nonpossessory, nonpurchase-money security interests in, property that otherwise would be exempt in the absence of the encumbrance.

221. **Answer (C) is the correct answer.** This question focuses on fraudulent transfers and their effect on the transfer of property (so if you are not covering fraudulent transfers in your course, ignore this question). Under the law of fraudulent transfers, a transfer may be set aside notwithstanding compliance with various formalities. It can be set aside in two situations: the first is if the debtor made the transfer with the actual intent to hinder, delay, or defraud his or her creditors; the second is if the transfer is for less than a reasonably equivalent value and the transferor, after the transfer, is left in a poor financial state, such as insolvency.

Given the power of fraudulent transfer law to override formalities, **Answer (A) is incorrect.** Put another way, fraudulent transfer law will ignore formal title, or title registration systems. Similarly, because fraudulent transfers look at the intent or the financial state of the debtor/transferor, the financial state of the recipient is irrelevant. That **excludes Answer (B) as a correct answer.**

Because this was a gift transaction, with no expectation that Henry would recover or reclaim the car, it does not appear to be a transaction that creates a security interest, and thus filing a financing statement would do no good. This **eliminates Answer (D) as an answer.**

This leaves Answer (C). Under Section 2(b) of the Uniform Fraudulent Transfer Act, if a creditor can show that the transferor/debtor was not paying his or her debts as they become due, then a presumption of insolvency is created. Insolvency, in turn, is otherwise defined as having more liabilities than assets. But if the creditor shows that the transferor/debtor is not paying its debts as they become due (as set forth in the facts of the question), it is up to the debtor/transferor to show that he or she was *not* insolvent. If the debtor does not make that showing, then he or she will be assumed to be insolvent.

But in addition to a bad financial state such as insolvency, the creditor must show that there was a lack of reasonably equivalent value for the transaction. Here, in a gift transaction, not only is the value not reasonably equivalent, there is no value given whatsoever (gifts are always for no value; in the corporate setting, the analog would be guaranties, or dividends or distributions of profits). With both insolvency and a lack of reasonably equivalent value, the transaction may be set aside for the benefit of Henry's creditors. Thus, **Answer (C) is correct.**

222. **Answer (C) is the correct answer.** This fact pattern presents the classic leveraged buyout, which can be held to be a fraudulent transfer. *See Boyer v. Crown Stock Dist., Inc.*, 587 F.3d 787 (7th Cir. 2009); *Official Comm. of Unsecured Creditors of Tousa, Inc. v. Citicorp North Am., Inc. (In re TOUSA, Inc.)*, 422 B.R. 783, 866 (Bankr. S.D. Fla. 2009), *quashed in part and rev'd in part*, 444 B.R. 613 (S.D. Fla. 2011), *aff'd in part and rev'd in part*, 680 F.3d 1298 (11th Cir. 2012). But before we can get to that conclusion, the question is structured so that we have to assess the transaction under both preference and fraudulent transfer law.

Note first that, from the perspective of Article 9, Fred's security interest is valid and properly perfected. The security agreement describes a broad range of collateral, using Article 9 terms as is permitted by Section 9-108. The financing statement uses an "all assets" description as is permitted by Section 9-504. And the financing statement is filed in Delaware, where GI is located for purposes of Article 9 under Section 9-307. But this question points out that more than Article 9 has to be consulted when the debtor has filed a bankruptcy petition.

Is there a preference or a fraudulent transfer? First, preference law requires a "transfer," and fraudulent transfer law will set aside certain transfers. Transfers are defined very broadly in the Bankruptcy Code. Under the Bankruptcy Code, the term "transfer" "means — (A) the creation of a lien; (B) the retention of title as a security interest; (C) the foreclosure of a debtor's equity of redemption; or (D) each mode, direct or indirect, absolute or conditional, voluntary or involuntary, of disposing of or parting with — (i) property; or (ii) an interest in property." 11 U.S.C. § 101(54). Here, the transfer is the transfer of a security interest from GI to Fred; this transaction gave property rights to Fred.

But preferences require that the transfer be "to or for the benefit of a creditor," 11 U.S.C. § 547(b)(1), and "for or on account of an antecedent debt owed by the debtor before such transfer was made," 11 U.S.C. § 547(b)(2). Here, there is no indication that the creation of the security interest was for anything but the debt created simultaneously with the sale of the GI stock (ignore for the time being any security interests created pursuant to the after-acquired property clause — they are likely to be minor in comparison to the main transfer). In addition, the reachback period for preferences is usually only 90 days (unless the transferee was an insider), and more than 90 days has passed under the facts since the March 1 closing. Thus, the transfer cannot be a preference, because there appears to be no antecedent debt, and any transfer was outside the reachback period, thereby **disqualifying Answers (B) and (D).**

Is it a fraudulent transfer? In addition to transactions made with the actual intent to hinder, delay, or defraud (which does not seem to be present here), fraudulent transfers include transfers that are made for less than a reasonably equivalent value, *and* that either rendered the debtor insolvent (or nearly so) or were made at a time at which the debtor was insolvent (or nearly so). 11 U.S.C. § 548(a)(1)(B).

Was the transfer for a "reasonably equivalent value"? Probably not. GI, as a separate entity with separate creditors, did not receive anything in return for the grant of a security interest in its assets. It is as if it guaranteed Alice's debt and received nothing in return. (Note: most gift transactions, or transactions without consideration such as the payment of dividends, will be made for less than a reasonably equivalent value.)

Was GI insolvent or nearly so when it granted the security interest? The test for constructively fraudulent transfers under 11 U.S.C. § 548(a)(1)(B) requires *both* a lack of reasonably equivalent value and a shaky or insolvent financial state. Specifically, 11 U.S.C. § 548(a)(1)(B) requires one of the three adverse financial states[2]; namely that the debtor: "(I) was insolvent on the date that such transfer was made or such obligation was incurred, or became insolvent as a result of such transfer or obligation; (II) was engaged in business or a transaction, or was about to engage in business or a transaction, for which any property remaining with the debtor was an unreasonably small capital; [or] (III) intended to incur, or believed that the debtor would incur, debts that would be beyond the debtor's ability to pay as such debts matured. . . ." Insolvency, under the Bankruptcy Code, is a balance sheet test. It requires a "financial condition such that the sum of such entity's debts is greater than all of such entity's property, at a fair valuation. . . ." 11 U.S.C. § 101(32).

While there is not enough information here to find without question that GI was insolvent (no financial information at all is given), the speedy decline of GI and its inability to attract any new capital given Fred's security interest probably means that GI was insolvent (no one would lend on its assets in a junior position) or that it had "unreasonable small capital" (because it could not raise any based on its other assets). Given the likelihood of a colorable fraudulent transfer action, **Answer (A) is incorrect, leaving Answer (C) as the correct answer.**

223.   **Answer (C) is the correct answer.** First Bank is perfected in all collateral. The facts give the value of that collateral as $6,000,000. What is the secured claim in bankruptcy? That is determined by 11 U.S.C. § 506(a)(1) and 11 U.S.C. § 506(b). Under 11 U.S.C. § 506(a)(1), "[a]n allowed claim of a creditor secured by a lien on property in which the estate has an interest, . . . is a secured claim to the extent of the value of such creditor's interest in the estate's interest in such property." This states that the secured claim has a maximum value of $6,000,000, the value of the collateral. Thus, **Answer (A) is incorrect.**

We also know that bankruptcy will not give First Bank more than its state law claim. That means that we figure out what the debt is under state law, and that also is a maximum value. Here, we know that there is at least $5,000,000 in principal outstanding. Thus, the claim is at least $5,000,000. Is it more? Under state law, that is, under Article 9, First Bank was careful to note that attorneys' fees were also debts that would be secured by the

---

2. The 2005 amendments added a fourth condition to Section 548(a)(1)(B). Item (IV) does not relate to the financial condition of the debtor; rather, it states, as a condition of equal relevance, that the debtor: "(IV) made such transfer to or for the benefit of an insider, or incurred such obligation to or for the benefit of an insider, under an employment contract and not in the ordinary course of business."

collateral. If First Bank had not indicated that its attorneys' fees were part of the obligation secured, they would just be unsecured claims (that is, not secured by the collateral).

Knowing that interest continues to accrue under state law, we now know that **Answer (B) is incorrect**, because the $5,000,000 answer does not account for any accrued interest and attorneys' fees. Whether these additional amounts—the accrued interest and attorneys' fees—will be added to the secured claim in bankruptcy is a function of 11 U.S.C. § 506(b). That Section states that "[t]o the extent that an allowed secured claim is secured by property the value of which . . . is greater than the amount of such claim, there shall be allowed to the holder of such claim, interest on such claim, and any reasonable fees, costs, or charges provided for under the agreement or State statute under which such claim arose."

So in cases such as First Bank's, in which the agreement provides for attorneys' fees and costs, post-petition interest and reasonable attorneys' fees and costs will accrue post-petition and be added to the secured claim. First Bank will not get more than its actual claim, **making Answer (D) an incorrect answer. That leaves Answer (C) as the correct answer.**

224.   **Answer (A) is the correct answer.** Here, the changed fact is the reduced value of the collateral. For all the reasons listed in the preceding answer, the secured claim in bankruptcy cannot exceed the value of the collateral. Thus, it is irrelevant, for purposes of calculating the secured claim, what the amount secured by the debt would be under state law. Under 11 U.S.C. § 506(a)(1), then, the secured claim is limited to the value of the collateral, or $4,000,000. **The only answer consistent with this answer is Answer (A), making Answers (B), (C), and (D) incorrect.**

225.   **Answer (D) is the correct answer.** This question again involves fraudulent transfer law. Here, there were transfers to Beelzebub (the foreclosure) and to Lucy's, Inc. (the foreclosure sale). Under 11 U.S.C. § 548(a)(1)(A), a trustee may avoid any transfer made or obligation incurred within two years of the petition date if the transaction was made with the intent to hinder, delay, or defraud creditors. (Before 2005, the lookback period was only one year.) Because the lookback period is now two years, **Answer (A) is incorrect.**

It is also irrelevant that Lucy's, Inc. may have been solvent. The actual intent standard of Section 548(a)(1)(A) applies notwithstanding the financial condition of the debtor at the time of the transaction. The law only looks at the intent with which the transaction was made. **As a result, Answer (C) is incorrect.**

That leaves Answer (B), which focuses on Beelzebub's intent, and Answer (D), which focuses on Lucy's intent. Under Section 548(a)(1)(A), the intent of the recipient of the transfer is irrelevant. Their intent may affect their defenses, but it does not factor into the basic elements of the cause of action. As a consequence, **Answer (B) is incorrect.** As to Answer (D), a corporation's or LLC's intent is the intent of its owners or officers engaged in the transaction, and the intent specified in Section 548 is in the alternative: the trustee need only establish an intent to hinder, or an intent to delay, or an intent to defraud to prevail. Indeed, Section 4(b)(11) of the Uniform Fraudulent Transfer Act states that a badge of fraud — that is, a set of facts from which one can infer proscribed intent — exists if "the debtor transferred the essential assets of the business to a lienor who transferred the assets to an insider of the debtor." *See also Voest-Alpine Trading USA Corp. v. Vantage Steel Corp.,* 919 F.2d 206, 212 (3d Cir. 1990). **As a result, Answer (D) is correct.**

It also may be the case that the transaction left Lucy's, LLC, with unreasonably small capital. Because it received dollar-for-dollar reduction in debt — which is value under Section 548(d) — it likely received reasonably equivalent value, although some courts might collapse the transaction.

This answer can be answered affirmatively under state law as well — the Uniform Fraudulent Transfer Act and its 2014 successor, the Uniform Voidable Transactions Act, (enacted in 46 states) provides for a four-year statute of repose and all of the essential elements of avoidance as Section 548 of the Bankruptcy Code (both statutes were essentially drafted by the same person). The bankruptcy trustee has access to such law under Section 544(b) of the Bankruptcy Code.

Bankruptcy (Voidable Preferences)

226.   **The correct answer is Answer (C).** A preference is a transfer, usually of money (but not necessarily). What makes it "preferential" is that the retention of the transfer will allow the recipient to fare better than other similar creditors. If someone who is paid $500 on the day before a bankruptcy that pays 10 cents on the dollar gets to keep the whole $500, then in this sense, that creditor is "preferred."

Preferences are provided for in Section 547 of the Bankruptcy Code. Section 547(b) contains the elements (or definition) of a preference; Section 547(c) the defenses, and the other sections have presumptions and definitions of various terms.

Section 547(b) sets forth six elements of a preference. For a transaction to be a preference, there has to be

1. A transfer (defined in Section 101(54) of the Bankruptcy Code) of an interest of the debtor in property

2. The transfer must be to or for the benefit of [a person who is already] a creditor

3. The transfer must be for or on account of an antecedent debt . . .

4. The transfer must be made while the debtor is insolvent, (defined in Section 101(32) as having liabilities in excess of assets)

5. The transfer must be made within 90 days before the date of the filing (or within one year if the recipient is an "insider" (defined in Section 101(31))—the "reachback" period

6. The transfer must "enable such creditor to receive more than such creditor would receive if the case were . . . under chapter 7 . . . [and] the transfer had not been made . . . ."—the "improvement" test.

In the question, Lima Bank receives a transfer of cash on December 1. Lima is a creditor and the payment is on account of a debt already in existence (a so-called "antecedent" debt"). We don't know if SpotCo is insolvent, but the Bankruptcy Code helps the trustee: it sets up a rebuttable presumption of insolvency during the 90 days preceding the bankruptcy filing. 11 U.S.C. § 547(f). Because the transfer was made the day before bankruptcy, the presumption applies, and the transfer was made during the reachback period.

So all the elements thus far have been met. The one lacking is the improvement test. But that is easily met. Unless the bankruptcy will pay unsecured creditors 100 cents on the dollar, then any payment on an unsecured debt during the reachback period will be preferential. Why? If the recipient of a transfer gets to keep it, they keep 100% of its value. In the question, they will get to keep $1,100,000. But if the bankruptcy will pay less on the dollar than that (and the national average for chapter 7 bankruptcies is about 10-15%, with a little more than 90% of all bankruptcies paying nothing), then keeping 100% is better than something less than 100%. *So one rule to keep in mind is that any payments on* ***unsecured*** *debt during the applicable reachback period are almost always a preference.* As a consequence, **Answer (C) is correct**, because it captures the entire transfer, and **Answer (D) is incorrect**, because it does not.

Preference law also makes no distinction between principal and interest. It simply looks at what was paid before bankruptcy during the reachback period, and compares it with what would have been paid as a bankruptcy dividend on the same claim. As a result, **Answers (A) and (B), which make such distinctions, are incorrect.**

227.   **The correct answer is Answer (D).** Here, the only difference is that the creditor perfected its interest outside of the reachback period. But that difference makes, so to speak, all the difference. The change does not affect the first five elements of a preference. There still is a transfer to a creditor during the reachback period.

But what differs is the improvement test. In bankruptcy, secured creditors will receive dollar-for-dollar distributions on their claims. So a creditor who is oversecured will be paid in full.

That makes a difference here. Lima Bank is not being preferred. It would have been paid 100 cents on the dollar after bankruptcy, so to receive that much before bankruptcy is not preferential. This leads to a second rule: *Payments to fully secured creditors who were perfected outside of the reachback period are almost never preferential.*

For this reason, the trustee will not be able to establish all of the elements of a preference, and the trustee will recover nothing, making **Answer (D) correct**, and making **Answers (A), (B), and (C) incorrect**, because they each assume some recovery.

228.   **The correct answer is Answer (B).** The change here is that the secured creditor is no longer fully secured. They are partially secured. Under the Bankruptcy Code, this means that Lima will have two claims: a secured claim for the value of the collateral, or $500,000, and an unsecured claim for any deficiency after application of collateral proceeds—here, $600,000.

The presumption when payments on partially secured claims are made is that the first proceeds are applied to the unsecured debt. Here, that would be the first $600,000 of the $1,100,000 payment. From the first rule above—payments on unsecured debts are preferential—this portion of the payment will be preferential. The last dollars in are then applied to the secured claim—here, $500,000. This leads to the third rule: *Payments on undersecured claims are preferential to the extent of any deficiency.* That means in this case that $600,000 of the $1,100,000 payment will be preferential, **making Answer (B) correct. Answers (A), (C), and (D) are thus incorrect**, as they do not reach the same amount.

Qualification: The third rule has an exception. If the collateral no longer exists after payment to the creditor, the payment is not preferential. To see this, conceptualize what occurs in the case where a payment is made to an undersecured creditor who is secured by equipment. The payment is made, but the collateral remains. In short, the secured creditor keeps the collateral, and reduces its deficiency. But if the payment comes, say, from the payment on an account, then the account is satisfied and no longer exists. In this case, it is as if the collateral's value was directly paid to the secured creditor. Contrary to the first example in which the equipment collateral was unaffected by the transfer, with accounts or other self-liquidating collateral the collateral is diminished, but not the deficiency claim.

229. **The correct answer is Answer (D).** The key to this question is to see that there are two transfers. One is the transfer the prior questions dealt with: the $1,100,000 payment. The other is the transfer of the security interest in November, which is within the reachback period. Whether the transfer of the money results in any improvement is determined by the validity of the November transfer of a security interest. If unavoidable, then the payment is also unavoidable.

But the November transfer did improve Lima Bank's position, because secured creditors are always paid in full. As a result, the trustee would sue to avoid the creation and perfection of the security interest on November 15 as a preference, rendering Lima Bank unsecured as of the time of the December 1 payment, and then sue to set aside the payment as well (in practice, this is all done in one complaint). That makes **Answer (D) correct**, and **Answers (A), (B), and (C) incorrect**.

This gives rise to a fourth rule: *any action to secure a previously unsecured debt during the reachback period is likely to be preferential.*

230. **The correct answer is Answer (D).** Here, the issue is really just a spin on Question 229. Although the security interest was granted in July outside of the reachback period (and that's when it was enforceable against the debtor under Section 9-203(b)), it was not perfected until November, inside the reachback period. Without the perfection, we know that the trustee could have set aside the interest under the strong-arm power of § 544(a). So the perfection must mean something—and it does. Section 547(e)(2)(B) says a transfer occurs on the perfection date rather than the date of attachment if the perfection occurs more than 30 days after the transfer is effective (attachment, right?) between the parties. Here, it was effective when Section 9-203(b) says there is attachment; that is, when there was an authenticated security agreement, value given and the debtor having rights in the collateral. In the question, that is July 1.

Perfection, however, did not occur until November 15, more than 30 days after attachment, and with the reachback period. As a consequence, the transfer of the security interest, although effective on July 1, did not occur for preference purposes until November 15. 11 U.S.C. § 547(e)(2)(B). Because this occurred during the reachback period, it is the equivalent of securing a previously unsecured debt, and is thus preferential and can be avoided. This makes **Answer (D) correct.**

Answers (A), (B), and (C) are incorrect because they do not take into account the avoidability of the perfection on November 15.

231. **Answer (C) is the correct answer.** Under 11 U.S.C. § 547(e)(3), a transfer cannot occur until the debtor acquires rights in the collateral. Debtor acquired rights in the Item on the sale date, June 8, under UCC § 2-501(1)(b) ("identification occurs . . . when goods are shipped, marked, or otherwise designated by the seller as goods to which the contract refers"). As Bank had previously filed a financing statement, its security interest in the Item became perfected on June 8. That is the date of transfer. **Answers (A) and (B) are incorrect** because Debtor did not, at either of those times, have any rights in the Item. And **Answer (D) is incorrect** because Debtor need not have possession in order to have sufficient rights in the Item to use it as collateral.

232. **Answer (A) is the correct answer.** Under 11 U.S.C. § 547(b), the trustee can attack as voidable preferences "any transfer of an interest of the debtor in property." Angela's payment of $500 is a transfer, as is Elliott's conveyance of a security interest in his investment portfolio. But neither Angela nor Elliott is the "debtor." Kirk, the party in bankruptcy, is the debtor. Therefore, because the transfers were made by non-debtor parties, the transfers cannot be attacked by the trustee as voidable preferences. There was no "transfer of an interest of the debtor in property." **Answers (B), (C), and (D) are all incorrect** because they suggest that Angela's payment of $500, Elliott's grant of a security interest, or both, can be attacked as voidable preferences.

As easy as this requirement seems to be, you should be very careful when dismissing a preference analysis solely because the transfer did not come from the debtor. For example, the requirement that the transfer be of property of the estate has not stopped courts from recharacterizing a transaction when the effect, but not the letter, of the transaction is to transfer property that would have been property of the estate. This can be seen when someone assumes the debt of another as part of the purchase price for assets (as when a buyer of a business's assets agrees to assume the existing business lease). Payments on that assumed debt from and after the transfer, while made directly from the non-bankrupt buyer, are held to be indirectly made by the bankrupt debtor, because the assumption is part of the consideration the debtor received (in the case of the lease, it is treated as if the buyer paid the lease payment to the debtor, who then turned around and paid it to the landlord). This was summarized by the Seventh Circuit as follows:

> In those cases in which courts have held that a preference was given in the context of an asset sale, there is a fairly direct, traceable link between the consideration given for the debtor's assets and the funds used to pay the creditor. For instance, a debtor may sell its assets to a third party, and, as part of the purchase agreement, the third party may agree to assume the debtor's liabilities. When the third party subsequently pays a creditor of the debtor, courts have allowed the bankruptcy trustee to recover the payment as a preference. *See* [Mordy v. Chemcarb, Inc. (*In re* Food Catering & Housing, Inc.), 971 F.2d 396, 397-98 (9th Cir. 1992)]; Sommers v. Burton (*In re* Conard Corp.), 806 F.2d 610, 611-12 (5th Cir. 1986). In such cases, the third party's assumption of the debtor's debt is consideration for the sale of the

debtor's assets. *See In re* Food Catering, 971 F.2d at 398. The debtor effectively transferred to the creditor its right to receive a portion of the sale price equal to the amount of the debt. *See In re* Conard Corp., 806 F.2d at 612. The result is the same when, instead of transferring the money directly to the creditor, the third party deposits the money into an escrow account over which the debtor has no control. *See In re* Interior Wood, 986 F.2d at 231. Nor does the result change when the third party, rather than the debtor, specifies which creditor will receive the funds paid into the escrow account. *See* Feltman v. Bd. of County Comm'rs of Metro. Dade County (*In re* S.E.L. Maduro (Florida), Inc.), 205 B.R. 987, 992-93 (Bankr. S.D. Fla.1997).

Warsco v. Preferred Technical Group, 258 F.3d 557, 565 (7th Cir. 2001).

233. **Answer (D) is the correct answer. Answer (A) is incorrect** because the presumption can be rebutted by the secured party. **Answer (B) is incorrect** because 11 U.S.C. § 547(g) places the burden of proving nonavoidability of the transfer on the secured party. **Answer (C) also is incorrect.** For example, debtor borrows money on July 1, and the security interest attaches on July 3 and is perfected on July 25. Because the security interest is perfected within 30 days of attachment, the attachment date is the date of the transfer under 11 U.S.C. § 547(e)(2). But the debt date of July 1 remains antecedent (or prior) to the transfer date of July 3. So **Answer (C) is incorrect.** And **Answer (D) is correct** under 11 U.S.C. § 550(c). This position was reaffirmed by the addition of Section 547(i) in 2005. The effect of Sections 547(i) and 550(c) is to permit lenders to extract guaranties from insiders (almost all guaranties tend to be executed by insiders) without worrying that its preference period exposure will be extended from 90 days to one year.

234. **Answer (B) is the correct answer.** The "substantially contemporaneous exchange" exception, codified at 11 U.S.C. § 547(c)(1), can preserve any type of transfer, so **Answer (A) is incorrect.** The "enabling loan" exception," found at 11 U.S.C. § 547(c)(3), preserves only security interest transfers, **making Answer (C) incorrect.** The "floating lien" exception of 11 U.S.C. § 547(c)(5) preserves only security interest transfers in specific types of collateral, so **Answer (D) is incorrect.** But the "ordinary course of business" exception, codified at 11 U.S.C. § 547(c)(2), preserves only transfers "in payment of a debt," **making Answer (B) the correct answer.**

235. **Answer (C) is the correct answer.** The "floating lien" exception of 11 U.S.C. § 547(c)(5) permits the secured party to preserve its perfected security interest in inventory and accounts as of the petition date if the deficiency as of the petition date is not less than the deficiency on the later of (i) the date on which the secured creditor first gave value and (ii) the first day of the preference period (generally the 90th day before the petition date). But the security interest on the petition date is voided to the extent that the deficiency on the petition date is less than the deficiency calculated on the earlier date. The statute requires knowledge of the debt amount and the collateral value on two, and only two, dates. One date is the petition date; the other date is the later of the two dates described above. Debt amounts and collateral values on other dates are irrelevant.

In this question, the deficiency on the petition date of October 1 is $200,000 (debt of $2 million and collateral worth $1.8 million). The ninetieth day preceding October 1 is approximately July 1. But Bank did not loan money until July 16, so this later date is the date on which the other comparative deficiency is calculated. That deficiency is $300,000 (debt of $2.0 million and collateral worth $1.7 million). Comparing the two deficiencies reveals that Bank has improved its position by $100,000 (the deficiency decreased from $300,000 to $200,000). This amount is subtracted from the collateral value on October 1 ($1.8 million), leaving Bank with a perfected security interest in collateral worth $1.7 million (**making Answer (C) the correct answer and Answers (A), (B), and (D) incorrect answers**).

236.   **Answer (C) is the correct answer.** Here, we have a non-purchase-money security interest in a consumer good — the security interest in the television was not given as part of its purchase. As such, Friendly had only an unperfected security interest in the television. Being unperfected, however, does not mean unenforceable; indeed, attachment alone is sufficient for the security interest to be enforced. So Friendly could repossess the goods. It had that right under Section 9-609, and it accomplished the repossession without a breach of the peace. Therefore, **Answer (D) is incorrect.**

Friendly's sale, however, is not in accordance with Article 9. It does not give proper notice under Section 9-611(c), and the process of sale is likely not commercially reasonable under Section 9-610(b), given its timing and the ultimate purchaser. But that may not matter, if the teller who purchased the set paid an amount equal to its fair market value. Moreover, such actions would affect Friendly's deficiency, not the sale itself.

Thus, the focus should be on Friendly's actions taken to recover the $2,500. **Answer (B) is not correct** because the repossession of the television set achieved perfection by possession. The strong-arm power of 11 U.S.C. § 544(a)(1) that gives the trustee the status of a lien creditor only avoids transfers made with respect to property if a lien creditor could have obtained a better lien upon the property — and that is typically restricted to unperfected security interests. That leaves Answer (A) — under which Friendly keeps the money — and Answer (C) — which requires a preference analysis.

Is the receipt of the $2,500 preferential? Here, our determination that Friendly's security interest was unperfected before repossession matters. Under Section 547(e)(2)(B), the transfer of the security interest occurred when perfection occurred; that is, when the collection agent, the secured party's agent, repossessed the television. That repossession occurred within the reachback period, and thus is avoidable, because it converted a previously unperfected claim into a perfected one.

After avoidance, the debt is unsecured and clearly preferential, **making Answer (C) the correct answer and Answer (A) the incorrect answer.**

237.   **Answer (C) is correct.** First, the payment is preferential under 11 U.S.C. § 547(b) — it is a transfer, of property of the debtor, made within 90 days of the filing, at a time when the debtor was (presumed) insolvent (see § 547(f)), and, because the creditor is undersecured,

it enables the creditor to receive more than it would had the payment not been made and the debtor's assets distributed under chapter 7 (see § 547(b)(5)). Because the creditor is unsecured, the payment is deemed applied to the undersecured portion of the claim, and because that portion is unsecured by definition, the payment/transfer is preferential. **As a result, Answer (A) is incorrect.**

The answer then turns on whether the bank can prove a defense, and the defense most applicable here is the ordinary course of business defense found in Section 547(c)(2). After 2005, this defense has only has three elements. They are: (1) the debt was incurred in the ordinary course of business of the debtor; (2) the debt was incurred in the ordinary course of business of the transferee; and (3) the transfer (i) was made in the ordinary course of business of the debtor and the transferee; *or* (ii) was made according to ordinary business terms.

Here, the facts state that there was nothing unusual about the creation of the debt. The only question is whether Ladle's collection practices, being different from the industry norm, matter. And it appears that they do not. The clerk pays the amount owed with a regular check, which would seem to be within "ordinary business terms." **That means that Answer (C) is correct.**

Answer (B) is incorrect because, notwithstanding the physical presence of the collector sent, the facts state that no breach of the peace occurred, and that the collector was civil and behaved at all times. Moreover, so long as the payment was made on ordinary business terms, the manner in which collection was made does not matter.

Answer (D) is incorrect for the same reason. So long as the transfer—here the payment—was made according to ordinary business terms, the defense protects the transferee. The result might be different if the payment was demanded and made in cash or by wire transfer, because those might not qualify as ordinary business terms. But then the practices of both the debtor and the bank would be at issue as to whether such form of demand and payment were in the ordinary course of business of the debtor and the bank.

Practice Final Exam: Answers

Answers

Practice Final Exam

238. The secured loan does not fall within the scope of Article 9. Section 9-109 is the scope provision of Article 9. Subsection (d) mentions several matters to which Article 9 does not apply, including "an assignment of a claim for wages, salary, or other compensation of any employee." *See* §9-109(d)(3). Dave's commission falls within the language as "compensation," so Article 9 will not cover the amended transaction.

239. **Answer (B) is the correct answer.** The promissory note can serve as collateral, even if itself is secured by a mortgage on real estate (which, as a general rule, cannot serve as Article 9 collateral). *See* §9-109(b) and cmt. 7 (Example 1).

   Answer (A) is incorrect. Section 9-109(d)(11) excludes from Article 9 coverage rental income from real estate.

   Answer (C) is incorrect. Section 9-109(d)(9) excludes from Article 9 coverage "an assignment of a right represented by a judgment[.]"

   Answer (D) is incorrect. Section 9-109(d)(8) excludes from Article 9 coverage this type of interest in an insurance policy.

   Note that we are excluding some forms of property from the scope of Article 9. We are not concluding, however, that the property excluded from the scope of Article 9 cannot serve as collateral in a generic sense. The property may indeed serve as collateral. But law other than Article 9 will apply.

240. **Answer (C) is the correct answer.** Only one person is offering any property as collateral for the loan, and that person is Diana (offering eight pieces of jewelry). This makes Diana the only "debtor" as that term is defined in Section 9-102(a)(28).

   Meredith, Tim, Lisa, and Grace are "obligors" under Section 9-102(a)(59) because they are personally liable to repay the $10,000 loan, as signatories on either the promissory note or the guaranty. (Diana may or may not be an obligor, depending on whether she has agreed to be personally liable for repayment, in addition to her agreement to offer collateral.) Article 9 does not define "primary obligor," but it does define "secondary obligor" in Section 9-102(a)(72). If Meredith pays the loan, she has no recourse against any other party to recover the payment. Therefore, Meredith does not fit within the definition of "secondary obligor" (presumably ascribing to her the undefined term of "primary obligor"). If Tim, Lisa, or Grace make any loan payments, they have a right of reimbursement from Meredith, as the primary obligor. This right of reimbursement makes each of

259

them a "secondary obligor." Also, if Diana's collateral is applied against the loan, then Diana has a right of reimbursement from Meredith as the primary obligor (giving Diana the status of "secondary obligor").

Answer (A) is incorrect. True, Meredith is a primary obligor. But her parents, who have rights of reimbursement against Meredith, are secondary obligors.

Answer (B) is incorrect. Secondary obligors include not only Grace, but also Tim, Lisa, and Diana.

Answer (D) is incorrect. Meredith is a primary obligor, but Diana (who has a right of recourse against Meredith if Diana's collateral is applied against the loan) is a secondary obligor.

241.   **Answer (D) is the correct answer.** The reader's initial reaction to the question is that Law Firm has no "inventory" because its primary business is to offer legal services, rather than sell or lease goods (the traditional connotation of the word). But Article 9 defines "inventory" in a manner that is not limited to goods sold or leased. The term also includes goods that are "used [up] or consumed in a business." *See* § 9-102(a)(48)(D). Law Firm's letterhead stationary is an example of goods that Law Firm uses up or consumes in its legal practice. **Therefore, Answer (D) is the correct answer.**

Answer (A) is incorrect because amounts payable to Law Firm by its clients are not goods. Instead, they are most likely accounts (or, less likely, instruments or chattel paper).

Answer (B) is incorrect. The photocopiers are goods, but they are not inventory. Law Firm is not in the business of selling or leasing (as lessor) photocopiers, and their extended expected life removes them from being "materials used or consumed in a business." *See also* § 9-102, cmt. 4.a. (fourth paragraph). As used by Law Firm, the photocopiers are equipment.

Answer (C) is incorrect. Coins and bills in a petty cash drawer are "money" as defined in Section 1-201. "Money" is expressly excluded from the definition of "goods." *See* § 9-102(a)(44) (last sentence). Because inventory must be a good, and money is not a good, the money cannot be inventory.

242.   **Answer (C) is the correct answer.** This question requires knowing the type of organization each possibility represents. "L.L.C." refers to a limited liability company. "Inc." refers to a corporation. "L.L.P." refers to a limited liability partnership. "L.P." refers to a limited partnership. Section 9-102(a)(71) defines "registered organization." Paraphrasing, an entity that is created (or birthed) by filing particular paperwork with a state official is a registered organization. Helpful guidance is found in Section 9-102, cmt. 11. The fourth paragraph mentions that "corporations, limited liability companies, and limited partnerships ordinarily are 'registered organizations.'" It also mentions that "a general partnership is not a 'registered organization.'" PEB Commentary No. 17 (possibly reprinted in your softback statutes book) indicates that a limited liability partnership can be viewed as a general partnership (and, therefore, not a registered organization).

In summary, then, **Answer (C) is the correct answer** because a limited liability partnership is *not* a registered organization. **Answers (A), (B), and (D) are incorrect answers** because limited liability companies, corporations, and limited partnerships, respectively, *are* examples of registered organizations.

Why is it important to know whether an organization is a registered organization? The reason is that a secured party should file its financing statement in the state where the debtor is located (*see* § 9-301(1)), and the debtor's location can turn on whether it is or is not a registered organization (*compare* § 9-307(b)(2) and (3) *with* § 9-307(e)).

243.   **Answer (C) is the correct answer.** Section 8-102 provides definitions of "security entitlement, "securities intermediary," and "entitlement holder." Article 1 defines "purchaser" (and the related term "purchase"). And Sections 9-102(b) and (c) incorporate both definitions (among others) into Article 9. Each piece or slice of a broker-managed investment portfolio account can be considered a "security entitlement." Therefore, the Amazon shares can be viewed as one or more security entitlements (the number might vary, depending on whether the 400 shares were purchased in a single block or multiple pieces), **making Answer (C) the correct answer.**

When a customer has a broker-managed investment portfolio account, the customer is viewed as the entitlement holder and the broker is considered the securities intermediary. Therefore, **Answers (A) and (B) are incorrect** because BAMCO (rather than The ZinnVestments Group) is the entitlement holder, and The ZinnVestments Group (rather than BAMCO) is the securities intermediary.

Perhaps surprisingly, Article 9 defines "purchaser" (and the related term "purchase") in a manner much more liberal than "buyer" and "buy." In fact, any "voluntary transaction creating an interest in property" creates a "purchase" and a "purchaser." *See* § 1-201(b) (29), (30). So a transfer by gift is a transfer by purchase under the UCC. Furthermore, an "interest in property" expressly includes a "security interest." *See* § 1-201(b) (29). Therefore, Lender— in its role as the secured party—is a purchaser of the collateral (at least within UCC terminology). Answer (D) suggests otherwise, **making Answer (D) an incorrect answer.**

244.   **Answer (A) is the correct answer.** Generally, a description of collateral by "type" (e.g., chattel paper, inventory, etc.) is acceptable. *See* § 9-108(b)(3). But the general rule is subject to some exceptions, one of which pertains to commercial tort claims. Section 9-108(e)(1) states that a description "only by type . . . is an insufficient description" of a commercial tort claim. *See also* § 9-108, cmt. 5 (offering an example of an acceptable description of a particular commercial tort claim). As written, then, the collateral will not include any of TZCorp's rights in commercial tort claims that exist when TZCorp authenticates the security agreement. (Also remember that the after-acquired property clause fails to reach any of TZCorp's post-authentication rights in commercial tort claims. *See* § 9-204(b)(2).)

Answer (B) is incorrect. This transaction is not a consumer transaction (the debtor is not a consumer), so Article 9 permits TZCorp's deposit accounts to serve as collateral. *See* § 9-109(a)(1), (d)(13).

Answer (C) is incorrect. The debtor is a corporation, not a consumer, so the omission of "consumer goods" is appropriate (and inclusion would make no sense). True, consumers are TZCorp's primary customers, but TZCorp—rather than those consumer purchasers—is the debtor. And it is TZCorp's usage—rather than the usage by TZCorp's customers—which dictates the appropriate collateral description.

Answer (D) is incorrect. Fixtures are "goods." *See* § 9-102(a)(41). Goods are either consumer goods, equipment, farm products, or inventory. *See* § 9-102, cmt. 4.a. The collateral description mentions equipment, farm products, and inventory, the only types of goods in which TZCorp (an organization, rather than a consumer) will have rights. Therefore, the description indirectly covers TZCorp's fixtures through its specific reference to the only types of its goods that could be or become fixtures.

245.   **Answer (D) is the correct answer.** Richard had an enforceable security interest in the car, so he can claim an interest in proceeds if allowed by Section 9-315. *See* § 9-203(f). The check represents proceeds of the car because Trent received the check in exchange for the car. *See* § 9-102(a)(64)(A) (defining "proceeds"). Section 9-315(a)(2) gives Richard an enforceable security interest in proceeds that are "identifiable," or traceable to the car. Presumably Trent has no other explanation for the large check, other than it represents the purchaser's payment for the car that Trent no longer owns. Identifiable proceeds are collateral. *See* § 9-102(a)(12)(A). Therefore, Richard has an enforceable security interest in the check. Because Richard never perfected his security interest in the car, his security interest in the check, as proceeds, also is unperfected. *See* § 9-315(c). Nevertheless, it has attached and is enforceable (and will become perfected if Richard ever obtains possession of the check). **Therefore, Answer (D) is correct.**

Answer (A) is incorrect. Sections 9-203(f) and 9-315(a)(2) provide Richard with an enforceable security interest in the check, whether or not the collateral description in the security agreement includes any reference to "proceeds" from the disposition of the car.

Answer (B) is incorrect. True, Richard's security interest in the car was unperfected. Lack of perfection in the original collateral does affect whether Richard's security interest in the proceeds is perfected, but lack of perfection in the original collateral does not dictate whether the security interest in the proceeds is enforceable.

Answer (C) is incorrect. There is a "20 days" rule in Section 9-315(c) and (d), but that rule addresses extended perfection, rather than the enforceability, of a security interest in proceeds. Enforceability is addressed in Sections 9-203(f) and 9-315(a)(2), neither of which refer to any 20-day period.

246.   Because the security agreement failed to include a future advance clause, Templeton Finance will have a secured claim no greater than the initial loan of $5 million. The security agreement did include an after-acquired property clause, so the value of the collateral is $7.2 million. Because the value of the available collateral meets or exceeds the unpaid initial $5 million loan, Templeton Finance has a fully secured claim for $5 million, but no more. Templeton Finance also has an unsecured claim of $2.5 million (the

sum of the April and August advances). The surplus collateral value of $2.2 million does *not* secure Templeton Finance's two unsecured loans because the parties failed to include a future advance clause in their contract.

247.   The security agreement included a future advance clause, so Templeton Finance might have a claim secured by the collateral equal to the sum of all advances: $7.5 million. But the security agreement failed to include an after-acquired property clause, so the collateral is limited to the equipment owned by Clinic on the date of the agreement: $4.6 million. Therefore, Templeton Finance has a secured claim of $4.6 million, and an unsecured claim of $2.9 million (total debt of $7.5 million, minus the secured claim of $4.6 million). Templeton Finance has no security interest in the medical equipment acquired by Clinic in May and June because the parties failed to include an after-acquired property clause in the contract.

248.   **Answer (D) is the best answer.** A search against the debtor's current legal name of "ZinnCo," using the filing office's standard search logic, is not likely to reveal the earlier filing against "BAM Corp." Therefore, under Section 9-506(c), the debtor's name change has caused Bank's financing statement to become seriously misleading. Nevertheless, the filing against "BAM Corp." remains effective to perfect a security interest in equipment acquired by the debtor (i) prior to the name change and (ii) within four months after the name change (section 9-507(c)) — even if the perfected or unperfected status is examined (as in this question) on a date long after the four-month period has concluded (e.g., November 1). ZinnCo acquired Item #1 in May, within four months after the name change on March 15, so the original filing remains effective to perfect Bank's security interest in Item #1. ZinnCo acquired Item #2 in July, but without a specific date, it cannot be determined whether the purchase falls inside, or outside, the four-month period. If ZinnCo acquired Item #2 on July 10, then the original filing continues to perfect Bank's security interest in Item #2. But if ZinnCo acquired Item #2 on July 20, then Bank's filing fails to perfect its security interest in Item #2. Without more information, then, the perfected or unperfected status of Bank's security interest in Item #2 cannot be determined with certainty. Finally, ZinnCo acquired Item #3 in September, more than four months after the name change in March, so the original filing does not perfect Bank's security interest in Item #3. **Answer (D) then, is true, and Answer (C) could be true.** But **Answer (D) is the better answer** because the perfected status of Item #1 is known with certainty, whereas the perfected status of Item #2 is not.

         Answer (A) is incorrect because the name change has no effect on attachment, merely perfection.

         Answer (B) is incorrect because Bank has a perfected security interest in at least Item #1, and perhaps Item #2.

249.   **Answer (C) is the correct answer.** As a general rule (and no applicable exceptions apply in this case), a "security interest . . . continues in collateral notwithstanding sale . . . thereof unless the secured party authorized the disposition free of the security interest. . . ." *See* §9-315(a)(1). Therefore, **Answer (A) is incorrect.** But this statute says only that the sale

has not destroyed attachment; it does not address whether Bank must refile against Purchaser to remain perfected. Section 9-507(a) addresses the continued effectiveness of Bank's financing statement. Under that statute, Bank need not refile against Purchaser; instead, its financing statement filed against "BAM Corp." remains effective to perfect the security interest in the Item — even after the sale to Purchaser. (Because a financing statement filed against a seller [BAM Corp.] can remain effective against a buyer [Purchaser] under Section 9-507(a), a creditor of a buyer [Purchaser] "must inquire as to the debtor's [Purchaser's] source of title and, if circumstances seem to require it, search in the name of the former owner [BAM Corp.]." § 9-507, cmt. 3. For additional discussion, including an examination of competing policy arguments on this matter, see PEB Commentary No. 3 in your statutes book, keeping in mind that the statutes discussed therein have been renumbered.)

But what if Purchaser is an entity organized under non-Delaware law and therefore is "located" in a state different from the state in which Bank filed its financing statement? Section 9-316(a)(3) addresses this situation and continues the effectiveness of Bank's filing for one year. The question asks for analysis as of November 1, a date that is within one year of the sale in March, so Bank's filing in Delaware continues to perfect its security interest in the Item, regardless of where Purchaser is "located." For this reason, **Answer (C) is correct and Answer (D) is incorrect**. Note, however, that Section 9-316(b) does require Bank to file a new financing statement against Purchaser in the jurisdiction of its location (if not Delaware) within the one-year period if Bank wants to enjoy continued and uninterrupted perfection in the Item.

Answer (B) is incorrect because the location of the Item has no bearing on whether Bank's security interest in the Item remains perfected after the sale by BAM Corp. to Purchaser.

250. BFS's customer contracts evidence payment obligations of each customer to pay the balance thereunder, as well as a security interest in the furniture sold. As such, they are chattel paper under Section 9-102(a)(11). A security interest in chattel paper may be perfected by filing, § 9-312(a), but also by possession of the chattel paper, § 9-313(a). At a minimum, Xbank should file a financing statement against BFS listing chattel paper as the collateral. (BFS will have a perfected security interest in the furniture covered by the chattel paper because the retention of title is equivalent to obtaining a grant of a security interest (see § 1-201(b)(35)), the security interest in the furniture is purchase-money (it enables the customer to acquire the furniture), and the furniture will be consumer goods in the hands of the buyer. Under such circumstances, perfection by BFS in the furniture sold is automatic without the filing of a financing statement. § 9-309(1). But that is for BFS only; Xbank wants to have a security interest in the contracts themselves, and their proceeds, and Xbank can obtain that interest without BFS having a perfected interest in the furniture sold. Of course, if Xbank ever has to foreclose or collect on the chattel paper, it would like to have a priority secured claim to the furniture.)

Although filing guarantees perfection, it does not guaranty priority. A secured party that has possession of chattel paper will have priority in both the paper and its proceeds (payment of the obligation evidenced by the paper) over a secured party who claims perfection by filing only. § 9-330(b), (b). The exception to this rule is if the chattel paper itself bears a legend that it has been assigned to another, as the priority of a purchaser with possession depends on taking without knowledge that the purchase violates the rights of another, and placing a legend on chattel paper conveys this type of notice. § 9-330(f). So Xbank should also request that BFS change its standard form to include a legend to the effect that the chattel paper has been assigned to Xbank.

As to proceeds, a purchaser with possession only has priority in payments to the extent they would have priority under Section 9-322. Section 9-322(c)(2)(B) extends a possessor's priority to any cash proceeds of the collateral. As a result, if another secured party has possession of the chattel paper, it has priority to checks or other cash proceeds paid by the customers to reduce their liability under the chattel paper. The obvious way to avoid this is to periodically take possession of the contracts.

One other way to avoid this might be to require BFS to change its standard form to require customers to remit payments to a lock-box under Xbank's control. That would give Xbank perfection in the checks remitted (both by possession of the instruments, § 9-313(a), and as cash proceeds of existing collateral, § 9-315(d)(2)). By possessing the contracts, Xbank would also have priority in the checks, § 9-330(d). If the checks were then endorsed and deposited into an Xbank account for BFS's benefit (pursuant to a power of attorney between BFS and Xbank), that control would be maintained as Xbank would be the customer of the account, and thus perfected under Section 9-104, and would also have priority under Section 9-327.

251.   **Answer (B) is the correct answer.** BAM Technologies can satisfy its tracing burden by linking the cash and note with the equipment sold, so the cash and note—proceeds under Section 9-102(a)(64)—are identifiable. Therefore, BAM Technologies has a security interest in the proceeds under Section 9-315(a)(2). As a result, **Answer (A) is incorrect.**

That security interest is perfected for at least 20 days under Section 9-315(c), *but only if* the security interest in the original collateral (the equipment) was perfected. MediCorp, the debtor, is a corporation and, therefore, a registered organization under Section 9-102(a)(71). Section 9-301(1) tells the secured party to file its financing statement where the debtor is located. Section 9-307(e) states that a registered organization such as MediCorp is located in the state of its creation. MediCorp is organized under Delaware law, so Section 9-307(e) deems it to be located in Delaware. That is where all financing statements filed against MediCorp should be filed.

But BAM Technologies filed its financing statement in California, the state in which MediCorp operates its hospitals and clinics. BAM Technologies thus filed in the wrong state, leaving its security interest unperfected in the equipment. Because its security interest in the equipment is unperfected, its security interest in the proceeds is also unperfected. Therefore, **Answer (B) is the correct answer** and **Answer (C) and Answer (D) are incorrect answers. Answer (C) also is incorrect** because the time of the filing (assuming the filing is recorded in the correct state) does not dictate whether the secured party can claim a perfected security interest in proceeds (although the timing may dictate priority).

252. First Bank has priority. The bank account is proceeds of proceeds of proceeds as to First Bank (inventory > account > check > deposit account). First Bank's security interest in the bank account is perfected because First Bank can identify that at least $50,000 can be traced to its original collateral (inventory), and the proceeds are cash proceeds. §§ 9-102(a)(9) (defining "cash proceeds"), 9-315(a)(2), 9-315(c), 9-315(d)(2). As to Second Bank, the bank account is proceeds of proceeds (account > check > deposit account). Second Bank's security interest in the bank account is perfected for the same reason as First Bank.

When two secured creditors claim a perfected security interest in the same collateral, the "first-to-file-or-perfect" rule of Section 9-322(a)(1) resolves the dispute. Because Section 9-322(b)(1) states that the perfection date for proceeds is the perfection date for the original collateral, First Bank has priority because its filing and perfection date of June 1 is earlier than Second Bank's filing and perfection date of August 1.

253. The contents of an effective fixture filing are summarized in Section 9-502(b). A fixture filing must include the same information as a regular financing statement. It also must (i) state that it covers fixtures, (ii) state that it is to be filed in the real estate records, (iii) provide a description of the real estate, and (iv) provide the name of the record owner of the real estate if the debtor does not have a recorded interest. Furthermore, Section 9-501(a) (1) dictates that a fixture filing be filed in the real estate records where the real estate is located (often referred to as a "local filing" or a "county filing"), whereas Section 9-501(a) (2) mandates that a standard financing statement be filed in a central filing office (and thus the term, "central filing") in the state where the debtor is located (see § 9-301(1)).

254. **Answer (D) is the correct answer.** Answers (C) and (D) both suggest that Quality Contractors should file a fixture filing, with the only difference being the location of the filing. Standard financing statements are filed where the debtor is located (see § 9-301(1)), and Meredith (a human) is deemed located at her primary residence (see § 9-307(b)(1)). Therefore, Massachusetts may appear to be the correct state in which to file a normal financing statement. However, a fixture filing is *not* recorded where the debtor is located, but where the relevant real estate is located. See § 9-501(a)(1). The fixtures will be affixed to real estate located near San Francisco, so Quality Contractors should file its fixture filing in the relevant California county. **For these reasons, Answer (D) is the correct answer and Answer (C) is an incorrect answer.**

A secured party whose collateral is, or may become, a fixture should always file a fixture filing. The primary reason for doing so is that the filing increases the likelihood under Section 9-334 that the secured party can win a priority dispute with a real estate encumbrancer (e.g., a mortgagee) that also claims the fixtures as its collateral. **Answer (A) and Answer (B) are incorrect** because they erroneously suggest that there is no reason to file a fixture filing. Quality Contractors does have a PMSI in the fixtures, which are consumer goods as used by Meredith, so its security interest in the fixtures is automatically perfected. *See* § 9-309(1). Even so, for the reason mentioned above, Quality Contractors should file a fixture filing. And **Answer (B) is incorrect for the additional reason** that Article 9 includes within, rather than excludes from, its scope of coverage the debtor's use of residential fixtures (including those that are consumer goods) as collateral. *See* § 9-109(d)(11).

255. **Answer (A) is the correct answer.** MegaHealth is a Delaware corporation and, therefore, a registered organization under Section 9-102(a)(71). Section 9-301(1) tells a secured party to file its financing statement where the debtor is located, and Section 9-307(e) tells the secured party that a registered organization is located in the state of its creation. Therefore, MegaHealth's creditors must file their financing statements in Delaware (state of incorporation), rather than Washington (state of chief executive office and operations). First Bank filed in the correct state, and Second Bank did not. MegaHealth acquired the Item in February, before it authenticated the security agreement in favor of First Bank, so the omission of an after-acquired property clause from the security agreement is not fatal in this question. First Bank has a perfected security interest in the Item, and Second Bank does not. This means that First Bank wins the dispute under Section 9-322(a)(2), which favors perfected creditors over unperfected creditors. Therefore, **Answer (A) is the correct answer.**

Answer **(B) is incorrect** because Second Bank does indeed have a security interest in the Item. Second Bank filed its financing statement in the wrong state, leaving it unperfected. But the security interest remains enforceable.

Answer **(C) is incorrect** because it erroneously states that First Bank's interest is unperfected and Second Bank's interest is perfected. The status of each respective security interest is just the opposite.

Answer **(D) is incorrect.** If both security interests are unperfected (which is not the case), then Article 9 favors the first security interest to attach, rather than declare a "tie" between the unperfected claims. Here, First Bank's security interest attached first (April, versus September).

256. **Answer (C) is the correct answer.** MegaHealth authenticated First Bank's security agreement in April. MegaHealth acquired the Item in July. First Bank's security agreement failed to include an after-acquired property clause, so its collateral does not include this Item (which is after-acquired property). First Bank has no security interest in it. As explained in the previous answer, Second Bank filed in the wrong state, leaving it with an enforceable, but unperfected, security interest in MegaHealth's equipment (including this Item). Therefore, what appears to be a two-creditor dispute is actually a one-creditor dispute. Second Bank is the only creditor that can claim an enforceable security interest in the Item, **making Answer (C) the correct answer.**

Answer **(A) is incorrect** because filing a financing statement first, and in the correct state, will not perfect a security interest that never attaches.

Answer (B) is incorrect because the omission of an after-acquired property clause from the collateral description prevented First Bank's security interest from attaching to this Item.

Answer (D) is incorrect because First Bank has no security interest in the Item, and Second Bank has an unperfected security interest in the Item.

257.   The court should award priority to Matthew if Esther filed her petition on March 1, 2018. It should award priority to Shelby if Esther filed her petition on April 1, 2018. The court must address whether Esther's relocation from Texas to Arizona may have had an adverse impact on Matthew's continued perfection. Section 9-316(a)(2) addresses Matthew's concern, stating that his security interest remains perfected for four months following Esther's relocation (Matthew gets four months of protection because his financing statement has more than four months of effectiveness remaining on its five-year life.) Esther moved to Phoenix on November 20, 2017. A dispute date of March 1, 2018, falls within the four-month period. Therefore, as of that particular dispute date, Matthew's security interest in the chess sets remains perfected. Because he filed in 2016, before Shelby filed in 2017, the court should award priority to Matthew under the general "first to file or perfect" rule of Section 9-322(a)(1). But a dispute date of April 1, 2018, falls outside the four-month period that began running when Esther moved from Texas to Arizona on November 20, 2017. As a result, the court should conclude (on April 1, 2018), under Section 9-316(b), that Matthew's security interest has become unperfected prospectively and, as against Shelby as "a purchaser of the collateral for value," retroactively. Shelby remains perfected. If the petition is filed on April 1, 2018, then the court should award priority to Shelby under the "perfected beats unperfected" rule of Section 9-322(a)(2), a result that is not affected by Shelby's knowledge of Matthew's prior loan and his Texas filing.

258.   **Answer (D) is the correct answer.** Lender's search against the debtor's current legal name of "Southwest Avionics, Inc." has failed to reveal Bank's previous filing against "Texas Avionics, Inc." Therefore, under Section 9-506(c), the debtor's name change has caused Bank's financing statement to become seriously misleading. Nevertheless, the filing against "Texas Avionics, Inc." remains effective to perfect a security interest in equipment acquired by the debtor (i) prior to the name change and (ii) within four months after the name change (*see* § 9-507(c))—even if the perfected or unperfected status is examined (as in this question) on a date long after the four-month period has concluded. The debtor acquired Item #1 on February 10, before the name change, so Bank's filing remains effective to perfect its security interest in Item #1. The debtor acquired Item #2 on June 10 and Item #3 on August 10, dates that fall within the four-month period that started on May 1 and concluded on or about September 1. Therefore, Bank's filing continues to perfect its security interest in those two items. The debtor acquired Item #4 on October 10, a date that falls after the four-month period concludes on or about September 1. Therefore, Bank's filing is not effective to perfect its security interest in Item #4. Bank remains perfected in Items #1, #2, and #3 by its filing, so it has priority in those three Items under the "first to file or perfect" rule of Section 9-322(a)(1) because it filed in January, and Lender filed in July. But Lender has priority in Item #4 under the "perfected beats unperfected" rule of

Section 9-322(a)(2), because Lender's filing perfected its security interest in all of the equipment, and Bank's security interest in Item #4 is unperfected. The debtor's name change has rendered Bank's filing seriously misleading, and Item #4 was acquired by the debtor more than four months after the name change. These priority results are correctly stated in Answer (D), **making Answer (D) the correct answer and Answers (A), (B), and (C) incorrect answers.**

259. **Answer (B) is the correct answer.** Under Section 9-324(a), a PMSI in non-inventory enjoys priority over a conflicting security interest if the PMSI is perfected "when the debtor receives possession of the collateral or within 20 days thereafter." Debtor obtained possession of the equipment on June 5, but Dealer did not file its financing statement until June 29 (a difference of more than 20 days). Dealer's failure to timely file its financing statement prevents it from invoking Section 9-324(b), leaving Lender with priority under Section 9-322(a) as the earlier filer. Therefore, **Answer (B) is the correct answer and Answer (A) is incorrect.**

Dealer provided seller financing for the equipment, which secures payment of its purchase price. Dealer, then, has a PMSI in the equipment under Section 9-103. Answers (C) and (D) suggest, though, that Dealer's failure to timely file its financing statement may have destroyed its PMSI, leaving Dealer with a generic security interest. That is not so. PMSI status is dictated by Section 9-103, not when (or if) the PMSI is timely (or ever) perfected. Dealer's security interest continues to remain a PMSI, notwithstanding its untimely filing and lack of superpriority. Therefore, **Answer (C) and Answer (D) are incorrect answers.**

Answer (D) also is incorrect because a filing, even a filing that is not timely under Section 9-324(a), is effective to perfect a security interest.

260. **Answer (B) is the correct answer.** Both Midtown Bank and Kirkland Corporation have perfected security interests in the 2,000 sets of golf clubs sold by Kirkland to HSI. Midtown Bank filed its financing statement on March 10, and Kirkland filed its financing statement on August 15. Therefore, under the general priority rule of Section 9-322(a)(1), Midtown Bank will enjoy priority because its filing date is earlier than Kirkland's filing and perfection dates. By its own language, however, the general priority rule is subject to other applicable priority rules found in Section 9-322 and elsewhere in Part 3 (e.g., the 9-300 series), one of which is Section 9-324, which affords superpriority to purchase-money creditors. Kirkland provided seller financing and retained a security interest in the golf clubs to secure the unpaid purchase price, so it has a PMSI. HSI will sell the sets through its retail stores, so the sets are part of its inventory. Section 9-324(b) and (c) address the superpriority available to secured parties with a PMSI in inventory. Parsing the statute reveals that Kirkland must satisfy four requirements in order to achieve superpriority. First, its security interest must be perfected when HSI receives the sets. *See* § 9-324(b)(1). Kirkland perfected its security interest by filing a financing statement on August 15. HSI received the three shipments on August 10, August 20, and August 30, respectively. Therefore, Kirkland cannot claim superpriority in the 300 sets from the first shipment (**making Answer (D) an incorrect answer**) but might be able to claim superpriority in the sets remaining

from the last two shipments. Second, Kirkland must send notice of its PMSI to Midtown Bank (a previous filer entitled to such notice under Section 9-324(c)) before HSI receives the last two sets. *See* § 9-324(b)(2). Kirkland sent notice on August 18, before HSI received the last two shipments on August 20 and August 30. Third, Midtown Bank must receive Kirkland's notice before HSI receives the last two shipments. *See* § 9-324(b)(3). Midtown Bank received the notice on August 22, after HSI received the second shipment on August 20, but before it received the third shipment on August 30. Therefore, Kirkland cannot claim superpriority in the 200 sets remaining from the second shipment (**making Answer (C) an incorrect answer**), but it may be able to claim superpriority in the 250 sets remaining from the third shipment if it meets the final statutory condition. Fourth, Kirkland's notice must state that it "has or expects to acquire a purchase-money security interest in inventory of [HSI] and describe the inventory." *See* § 9-324(b)(4). The facts state that the notice satisfied these requirements. Kirkland can satisfy all four of the statutory requirements with respect to the sets remaining from the third shipment, so it enjoys superpriority in 250 sets (**making Answer (B) the correct answer, and Answer (A) an incorrect answer**). It does not have superpriority in the 300 sets remaining from the first shipment or the 200 sets remaining from the second shipment, so Midtown Bank enjoys priority in them under the general "first to file or perfect" rule of Section 9-322(a).

261.   ZinnBank will win the priority dispute. ZinnBank can claim priority under Section 9-201(a) and Section 9-315(a) because a sale of camera equipment in exchange for a photocopier is not a customary transaction. Therefore, ZinnBank's security interest survived the disposition. For the same reason, the exchange of camera equipment for a photocopier prevents Gwen from acquiring the camera equipment free of ZinnBank's security interest under the protection afforded by Section 9-320(a) to a buyer in the ordinary course of business. Gwen finds no help in Section 9-320(b) because ZinnBank had filed a financing statement and Markers was holding the camera equipment as inventory (rather than consumer goods). And ZinnBank's security interest remained perfected following the sale to Gwen under Section 9-507(a), so Gwen finds no help in Section 9-317(b). Therefore, ZinnBank wins any priority dispute with Gwen and, accordingly, Ethan (her non-buyer transferee).

262.   **Answer (A) is the correct answer.** ZinnBank's collateral includes current and future equipment, so its security interest extends to the photocopier (equipment in the hands of a camera equipment store). Its interest in the photocopier is perfected by its Texas filing. The security interest survives the sale to BizSmart under Section 9-315(a) because Zinn-Bank has consented to dispositions in the ordinary course of business. Rephrased, Markers can sell its inventory, but not anything else (including equipment).

Ashley, paying cash for the photocopier and buying it from BizSmart, which had held it as a unit of inventory, appears to be a buyer in the ordinary course of business. Nevertheless, Ashley cannot claim the protection afforded by Section 9-320(a) because Markers, rather than BizSmart, created the security interest in favor of ZinnBank (observe the statutory language, "a security interest created by the buyer's seller"). **Therefore, Answer (C) is an incorrect answer.** Ashley cannot win under Section 9-320(b) even if she uses the photocopier primarily as a consumer good, because that provision applies only if the seller (BizSmart) also used the photocopier as a consumer good, which is not the case. Ashley also loses under Section 9-320(b) because ZinnBank had filed a financing statement. **Therefore, Answer (B) is an incorrect answer.** Absent additional facts involving a change in jurisdiction and application of Section 9-316(a), ZinnBank's security interest remains perfected in the photocopier under Section 9-507, so Section 9-317(b) offers no solace. No other Section affords buyer protection to Ashley, so she loses to ZinnBank under Section 9-201 and Section 9-315, **making Answer (A) the correct answer.**

Answer (D) is incorrect because ZinnBank's ability to claim a perfected security interest in identifiable cash proceeds does not automatically preclude ZinnBank from continuing to enjoy priority in the collateral that generated the proceeds.

263. **Answer (A) is the correct answer.** The Section that resolves priority disputes between secured parties (Fidelity Bank) and lien creditors (Heather) is Section 9-317(a)(2). That Section states that the rights of a holder of an Article 9 security interest are subordinate to the rights of "a person that becomes a lien creditor before the earlier of the time: (A) the security interest or agricultural lien is perfected; or (B) one of the conditions specified in Section 9-203(b)(3) is met and a financing statement covering the collateral is filed."

The magical date here is July 5, when Heather became a lien creditor. On that date, Fidelity Bank did not yet have an attached security interest in any assets of Mockingbird Industries, because it had not yet given any value (no funds had been advanced, and the loan agreement did not obligate Fidelity to make loans; it only agreed to an illusory "consideration" of making such loans).

Fidelity's security interest did not attach until July 7, when Fidelity Bank gave value in the form of a loan. Because Fidelity Bank had previously filed its financing statement, its security interest became perfected on the attachment date of July 7.

On these facts, Fidelity Bank did not have priority under Section 9-317(a)(2)(A) because its perfection date of July 7 is after July 5, the date on which Heather acquired her lien.

But it did have priority under Section 9-317(a)(2)(B). Under Section 9-317(a)(2)(B), a secured creditor can obtain priority over a preexisting lien creditor if, at the time the lien creditor acquired that status, (i) there was on file a financing statement covering the property subject to the lien creditor's lien; and (ii) any of the "agreement" conditions specified in Section 9-203(b)(3) had been met. In most cases, the authentication of a security agreement that adequately describes the collateral will satisfy this condition.

Here, on July 5, Mockingbird had signed, on July 1, a security agreement describing collateral that ultimately became subject to Heather's lien. Also by that date, Fidelity had on file a financing statement covering the same collateral (the "all assets" filing, even though it was only valid as to the description in the signed security agreement, see § 9-510, cmt. 2, ex. 1). As a result, **Answer (A) is correct.**

Answer (B) is incorrect because Section 9-317(a)(2)(B) permits a secured creditor to obtain priority over an existing lien creditor in exactly the circumstances provided, as shown above.

Answer (C) is incorrect, and a red herring, because an "all assets" filing is permitted. *See* § 9-504(2). Recall, however, that such a supergeneric collateral description is not acceptable in the security agreement. *See* § 9-108(c). Also remember that an "all assets" filing cannot expand the collateral beyond the description found in the security agreement. *See* § 9-504, cmt. 2 (last paragraph) and § 9-510, cmt. 2, ex. 1. Perhaps rephrased, a filing cannot perfect a security interest that never attaches.

Answer (D) is incorrect because claiming a PMSI will not help Fidelity Bank under these facts. Sometimes priority does turn on the PMSI status of the security interest under Section 9-317(e), but that statute requires the PMSI to attach *before* the lien arises (with perfection occurring thereafter). Here, Heather's lien arose before Fidelity Bank's security interest attached. Therefore, even if Fidelity Bank held a PMSI it would lose the dispute.

264. The answer would change. If Heather acquired her lien creditor interest before Fidelity Bank satisfied one of the requirements of Section 9-203(b)(3), then Section 9-317(a)(2)(B), relied on in Question 263, would not apply. Under the revised facts, that is what happened. All that existed on June 28 was a filed financing statement, and nothing more. A financing statement filed before the lien arises, without more, is insufficient to give priority to the filer.

As a result, Fidelity Bank's security interest does not enjoy priority. That result makes sense under the general principle of *nemo dat* (you can only give that which you have). Fidelity Bank acquired a security interest that was subject to Heather's lien because the lien arose before the security interest attached.

265. **Answer (D) is the correct answer.** The fact that the car is parked on Tim's driveway—private property—does not trigger a breach of the peace (assuming Repo Company has free access to the car and is not opening gates, fences, garage doors, etc.), **so Answer (A) is an incorrect answer.**

Owners of motor vehicles often leave personal items in a parked and locked vehicle, and rarely will those items fall with the collateral description found in the security agreement. If placing personal items in the vehicle will prevent the secured party from repossessing the car, then owners in default can easily frustrate the creditor's ability to exercise one of its most valuable remedies. Perhaps the creditor should be obligated to remove the personal items from the car and just leave them nearby, but such action will extend the time necessary to seize the vehicle (increasing the likelihood of a confrontation or altercation) while exposing the debtor to additional loss of personal property. The law should not, and does not, approve either result, **making Answer (B) an incorrect answer.**

The law does permit the secured party to take the car, even if it contains non-collateral contents. The debtor may bring an action for conversion, seeking damages for any damage to the non-collateral contents. Additionally, the secured party cannot use the non-collateral contents as leverage to extract payment from the debtor. Instead, under the case law, the secured party should make the non-collateral contents available to the debtor once the vehicle is secure. **Therefore, Answer (D) is the correct answer and Answer (C) is an incorrect answer.**

266. **Answer (B) is the correct answer.** Section 9-623 extends the right to redeem collateral not just to the debtor, but also to other parties, including a secondary obligor. Grace is a guarantor, a common example of a secondary obligor. Therefore, Grace can redeem the collateral, **making Answer (A) an incorrect answer.** Because future scheduled payments have been properly accelerated, the redemption price is $8,750, rather than the single missed payment of $550. *See* § 9-623(b) and cmt. 2. **Therefore, Answer (B) is the correct answer.**

Answer (C) is an incorrect answer. Section 9-623 does not condition the exercise of redemption rights on any specific dollar amount of secured debt, or the type of collateral sought to be redeemed.

Answer (D) is an incorrect answer, for two reasons. First, Section 9-624(c) does permit a debtor and a secondary obligor to waive their redemption rights, but that waiver must be authenticated by the waiving party after default. A waiver clause found in the guaranty, presumably authenticated by Grace before Meredith defaults, is not enforceable. Second, under Section 9-624(c), a redemption waiver is not enforceable in a "consumer-goods transaction" as defined in Section 9-102. The secured debt is the purchase price of the car, which Meredith uses primarily as a consumer good, so the transaction is a "consumer-goods transaction" as defined in Section 9-102(a)(24). This means that Grace cannot waive her redemption rights.

267. **Answer (A) is the correct answer.** Any time a statute imposes a notice duty, the reader should determine whether the duty focuses solely on the giving of notice or also on the receiving of notice. Section 9-611(b) addresses this issue, informing the reader that Dealer "shall send" a disposition notice. The notice may be effective, even if the Resort never receives it. **Therefore, Answer (A) is the correct answer.** Appreciate, though, that litigation may trigger an investigation into why the notice was not received, and Article 9 acknowledges that in some cases the secured party may be under a duty to "try again." *See* § 9-611, cmt. 6.

Answer (B) is an incorrect answer. Section 9-611(b) requires the notice to be "authenticated" by Dealer. The term, when read with the accompanying term "record" (both defined in Section 9-102), contemplates written and electronic forms, but not oral communications.

Answer (C) is an incorrect answer. A notice sent at least 10 days prior to the earliest time of disposition meets the safe harbor of Section 9-612, but the 10-day period is "not a minimum requirement." *See* § 9-612, cmt. 3. A notice sent less than 10 days prior to the earliest time of disposition may comport with the contractual agreement of the parties or otherwise be commercially reasonable.

Answer (D) is an incorrect answer. Neither of the notice templates in Sections 9-613 and 9-614 require Dealer to include in its disposition notice the date, time, or filing number of its UCC-1 financing statement.

268. Yes, Dealer should order a UCC search report against the Resort before it sells the piano. Section 9-611(b) requires Dealer to send its disposition notice to the recipients listed in Section 9-611(c). Those recipients include other secured parties who have timely filed financing statements against the piano. *See* § 9-611(c)(3)(B). Dealer must order a UCC search report to discover those filings and the names of other secured parties to whom Dealer must send its notice. Absent the search report, Dealer may fail to send a notice to a party otherwise entitled to it, triggering potential litigation.

269. **Answer (B) is the correct answer.** Because Simon and his family use the horse for recreational pleasure, the horse is a "consumer good" as defined in Section 9-102(a)(23). When collateral is a consumer good, First Bank must send its notice only to the debtor and any secondary obligor. *See* § 9-611(c). Simon, who owns the horse that is serving as collateral, is the debtor; Rachel, the guarantor on First Bank's loan, is a secondary obligor. So **Answer (B) is the correct answer.**

   Answer (A) is incorrect because it is underinclusive (it does not mention Rachel, the secondary obligor).

   Answers (C) and (D) are incorrect because Article 9 does not require First Bank to send the disposition notice to other secured parties when the collateral is a consumer good.

270. First Bank should distribute the remaining $75,000 according to the payout scheme found in Section 9-615(a). After deducting its reasonable expenses, it can keep for itself an amount sufficient to pay off its secured loan: $15,000. What should it do with the remaining $60,000? Under Section 9-615(a), First Bank must remit proceeds to *subordinate* creditors who have provided to First Bank an authenticated demand for proceeds. Remington Farms, who gave written demand, is not a subordinate creditor. True, it never filed a financing statement. But Remington Farms engaged in seller financing, so it can claim a PMSI in a consumer good. Therefore, its security interest was automatically perfected on attachment (*see* § 9-309(1)), giving it priority under Section 9-322(a) over the competing claims of other subsequent secured creditors like First Bank and Second Bank. For this reason, Remington Farms is not a subordinate creditor and cannot claim any of the proceeds. (Remington Farms remains protected, however, because its senior security interest survives the disposition and can be enforced against the successful buyer by foreclosing on the horse in the buyer's hands. *See* § 9-617(a) (discharging the security interests of the foreclosing creditor and *subordinate* creditors).) Second Bank is a subordinate creditor. However, Second Bank is not entitled to any proceeds because First Bank never received from Second Bank an authenticated demand for proceeds. Therefore, the remaining $60,000 proceeds revert to the debtor, Simon, as "surplus" under Section 9-615(d).

271. Purchaser paid $78,000 for a horse appraised at $120,000, giving Purchaser a profit (at least on paper) of more than $40,000. But the appraised value probably ignores any

existing liens or encumbrances on the horse. Under Section 9-617, Remington Farms continues to have a perfected security interest in the horse after the foreclosure sale to secure its unpaid debt of $45,000. Subtracting this amount from the appraised value of $120,000 results in a discounted valuation of $75,000. Purchaser paid $78,000. Unless the horse continues to appreciate in value, Purchaser's paper *profit* of $42,000 has become a paper *loss* of $3,000. Now the deal does not look so "great."

272. **Answer (B) is the correct answer.** Under 11 U.S.C. § 544(a)(1), also known as the "strong arm clause," the trustee can "avoid any transfer of property of the debtor" (which includes the creation of a security interest) that could be avoided by a lien creditor on the date of the petition, *regardless* of whether such a lien creditor actually exists (that's why it is sometimes referred to as a "hypothetical" lien creditor). And under Section 9-317(a)(2), a security interest is subordinate to the property rights of a lien creditor (e.g., the bankruptcy trustee) if, when the lien arises, the security interest is not perfected (or, in less frequent situations, when perfection has not occurred solely because the secured party has not given value when the lien arises). Taken together, these two statutes permit the trustee to destroy (that's a technical term for "avoid") any security interest that is unperfected on the petition date. Therefore, you must determine whether Secured Party's security interest was perfected on September 13.

Debtor is a Delaware corporation, making it a "registered organization" under Section 9-102(a)(71). Therefore, to the extent that Secured Party is relying on a financing statement for perfection, it must file the financing statement in Delaware, because registered organizations are deemed to be located where they are organized or incorporated. *See* §§ 9-301(1); 9-307(e). Secured Party is perfected in Answer (A) because it filed its financing statement in Delaware. That is the proper place to file, not because the collateral was in Delaware, but because Delaware is the law under which Debtor was created. The collateral location is irrelevant, so no subsequent filing in Illinois is required. Secured Party remained perfected on the petition date in the Illinois collateral by the Delaware filing, so the trustee cannot avoid the security interest under 11 U.S.C. § 544(a)(1), **making Answer (A) an incorrect answer.**

Under Section 9-305(c)(1), Secured Party should have filed its financing statement in Delaware to perfect a security interest in investment property. Instead, Secured Party filed in the state where the stock certificate was located (Georgia), a mistake that left Secured Party unperfected on the petition date. Therefore, the trustee can avoid Secured Party's unperfected security interest under 11 U.S.C. § 544(a)(1), **making Answer (B) the correct answer.**

For reasons already mentioned, Secured Party is perfected in Debtor's Texas-based inventory by the Delaware filing. Normally a post-petition filing is ineffective because it violates the automatic stay under 11 U.S.C. § 362(a)(4). But subsection (a) is expressly subject to subsection (b). And 11 U.S.C. § 362(b)(3) permits a post-petition filing "to the extent that the trustee's rights and powers are subject to such perfection under Section 546(b) of this title...." Under that Section, the trustee's avoiding powers "are subject to any generally applicable law that—(A) permits perfection of an interest in property to be effective against an entity that acquires rights in such property before the date of perfection. . . ." The "generally applicable law" here would be Section 9-317(e), which permits a secured party to perfect its purchase-money security interest after the lien creditor obtains a competing property interest and yet enjoy priority over that competing property interest, so long as the secured party files its financing statement within 20 days after the debtor takes delivery of the collateral. Secured Party timely perfected its purchase-money security interest and can invoke the protection afforded by Section 9-317(e). Therefore, the post-petition filing did not violate the automatic stay and is effective to prevent the trustee from avoiding the security interest under 11 U.S.C. § 544(a)(1). So **Answer (C) is an incorrect answer.**

And Secured Party's security interest in the bank account became perfected by "control" under Section 9-104(a)(1) at the moment of attachment and remained perfected on the petition date. No affirmative action to perfect is necessary if the account is maintained with the secured party. Thus, the trustee cannot avoid the security interest under 11 U.S.C. § 544(a)(1), and **Answer (D) is an incorrect answer.**

273. **Answer (D) is correct.** This question raises issues of equitable subordination, which is specifically provided for by Section 510(c) of the Bankruptcy Code. Under the terms of Section 510(c),

> the court may—
>
> (1) under principles of equitable subordination, subordinate for purposes of distribution all or part of an allowed claim to all or part of another allowed claim or all or part of an allowed interest to all or part of another allowed interest; or
>
> (2) order that any lien securing such a subordinated claim be transferred to the estate.

This Section thus gives the estate the power to subordinate both the claim of a creditor and, if that claim is secured, the lien that secures it. Because both may be affected, **Answer (B) is incorrect.**

This subordination is of allowed claims. It is thus irrelevant as to whether the creditor has complied with other laws, such as Article 9's provisions on perfection or foreclosure. Accordingly, **Answer (C) is incorrect.** Similarly, as the doctrine addresses harm to creditors, the consent or acquiescence of the debtor before the filing of the bankruptcy case is also irrelevant, and thus **Answer (A) is also incorrect.**

Still, to subordinate either the claim or the security interest, the court must find that it is appropriate to do so "under principles of equitable subordination." The basic outline of this doctrine is usually stated as follows: (i) the claimant must have engaged in some type of inequitable conduct; (ii) the misconduct must have resulted in injury to the creditors of the bankrupt or conferred an unfair advantage on the claimant; and (iii) equitable subordination of the claim must not be inconsistent with the provisions of the Bankruptcy

Act. *See, e.g., Benjamin v. Diamond (In re Mobile Steel Co.)*, 563 F.2d 692, 700 (5th Cir. 1977). The first prong, inequitable conduct, covers a wide range of dastardly acts, including actions constituting "a secret or open fraud, lack of faith or guardianship by a fiduciary; an unjust enrichment, not enrichment by *bon chance*, astuteness or business acumen, but enrichment through another's loss brought about by one's own unconscionable, unjust, unfair, close or double dealing or foul conduct." *In re LightSquared Inc.*, 511 B.R. 253, 348 (Bankr. S.D.N.Y. 2011) (quoting *80 Nassau Assocs. v. Crossland Fed. Sav. Bank (In re 80 Nassau Assocs.)*, 169 B.R. 832 , 837 (Bankr. S.D.N.Y. 1994) (in turn quoting *In re Tampa Chain Co.*, 53 B.R. 772, 779 (Bankr. S.D.N.Y. 1985)). In addition, although there is a substantial minority, the majority of cases require conduct by a non-insider (such as Sinister in the question) to be "gross and egregious." *In re LightSquared, Inc.*, 511 B.R. at 348.

Here, Sinister's actions likely qualify for equitable subordination. Inducing trade creditors to deliver goods to a debtor for which the secured creditor has an after-acquired property clause has long been viewed as fraudulent; indeed, it has its own name: "feeding the lien." Moreover, Sinister tried to be cute in disguising its intent to proceed. Combined with its micro-management of BBH, actions that are inconsistent with a debtor/creditor relationship, Sinister engaged in "inequitable conduct." The first prong is thus satisfied.

The second prong is satisfied through the injuries to the lumber suppliers. They would not have shipped the lumber had they known of Sinister's true intent. Finally, no other clause in the Bankruptcy Code addresses this type of conduct, and so the estate can likely seek to subordinate payment of Sinister's loan to the payment at least of the creditors who were duped into lumber delivery, and to strip Sinister of its security interest to the extent necessary to effectuate the subordination. Accordingly, **Answer (D) is the best answer,** as equitable subordination certainly provides cause to worry for Sinister under the facts of the question.

274.   **Answer (D) is the correct answer.** The only transfer in Answer (A) is the loan repayment. But the loan was repaid by Debtor's brother, not the bankrupt party (Debtor). Therefore, the loan repayment does not represent a "transfer of an interest of the debtor in property" under 11 U.S.C. § 547(b), making **Answer (A) an incorrect answer. Answer (B) also is incorrect.** Dealer is fully secured at all times (the collateral is always worth at least $80,000 — the amount of the original credit). Because Dealer is fully secured, Debtor's loan repayment of $35,000 does not permit Dealer to receive more than it would under a Chapter 7 liquidation if the payment had not been made. If Dealer keeps the $35,000 it will file a proof of claim for $45,000, a fully secured claim. If Debtor never made the $35,000 payment, then Dealer will file a proof of claim for $80,000, also a fully secured claim. In both instances Dealer is repaid in full. Therefore, the trustee cannot satisfy 11 U.S.C. § 547(b)(5), **making Answer (B) incorrect. Answer (C) is incorrect** because the transfer occurred on May 1, a date that falls outside the 90-day preference period preceding the petition date of August 15. 11 U.S.C. § 547(b)(4)(A). **Answer (D) is correct** because all elements of 11 U.S.C. § 547(b) are present. The transfer is Debtor's grant of a security interest to Finance Company (a pre-petition creditor) in early February, within the 90-day period preceding the petition date of April 25. And the transfer permits Finance Company

to receive more than it would in a Chapter 7 liquidation without the security interest. If Finance Company keeps the security interest, it will file a proof of claim for $10,000, a fully secured claim. But if Debtor never grants the security interest, Finance Company will file a proof of claim for $10,000—an unsecured claim. So the transfer does favor Finance Company by converting an unsecured claim to a secured claim (the type of behavior that the voidable preference statute seeks to avoid).

275. The trustee wins, at least to the extent of $999,000. A payment can be recovered as a preference under Section 547 of the Bankruptcy Code if it is made (i) to or for the benefit of a creditor, (ii) on account of an antecedent debt, (iii) within 90 days of a bankruptcy filed, (iv) while the debtor is insolvent, and (v) if the payment would allow the creditor to recover more than if the payment had not been made and the creditor had simply received a bankruptcy dividend. 11 U.S.C. § 547(b)(1)-(5).

Here, the payment was to a creditor on account of an existing (antecedent) debt. It is within 90 days (one month plus five weeks would be about 65 or 66 days). Under Section 547(f) of the Bankruptcy Code, Construction, Inc., would be presumed insolvent during the 90 days before its Chapter 7 filing.

That leaves the last element—the improvement test. Although BankOne was fully secured at the time it made the loan, the truck's destruction by the meteor reduced the value of its collateral to $1,000. Under the Bankruptcy Code, that $1,000 would be the extent of its secured claim; it would have an unsecured claim for the balance of its $1 million debt. If allowed to keep the $1,000,000 it will do much better than if it had not been paid; no unsecured creditor of an insolvent debtor is paid in full.

Index

Topic	Questions
absolute bar rule	
see default	
accessions	88, 108
account debtor	
defined	15
accounts	
see scope	
defined	8, 10, 13, 15, 20, 54, 86, 140, 183, 241
after-acquired property clause	
application	34, 36, 37, 38, 42, 87, 99, 124, 125, 142, 150, 151, 246, 247, 255, 256
commercial tort claims	42
consumer goods	36, 141
in bankruptcy	219
omitted from financing statement	48, 87, 133, 143, 161
agricultural lien	27
attachment	
see generally	28–43, 88
timing of	123, 125, 132, 145
authentication	
see financing statement	
see security agreement	
automatic stay	
see bankruptcy issues	
bankruptcy issues	

Topic	Questions
see generally	213–237, 272–275
after-acquired property clauses	219
automatic stay	213–216, 218, 272
exempt property	218, 220
fraudulent transfers	220, 221, 222, 225
secured and unsecured claims	217, 223, 224, 228, 274
strong-arm clause	115, 218, 220, 230, 272
voidable preferences	222, 226–237, 274, 275
breach of the peace	
see default	
buyer in ordinary course of business	134, 163, 166, 167, 168, 170, 172, 174–178, 261, 262
cash proceeds	
see proceeds	
certificate of deposit	9
certificate of title	53, 59, 80
chattel paper	
see scope	
defined	1, 10, 15, 20, 54, 69, 70, 101, 102, 140, 162, 183, 250
circular priority	118
commercial tort claims	
see after-acquired property clause	
see scope	
description	244
commingled goods	89
consignments	
see scope	
consumer goods	
see after-acquired property clause	
see purchase-money security interest	
defined	2, 5, 8, 14, 36, 68, 80, 116, 141, 173, 174, 176, 180, 269
consumer-goods transactions	14, 160, 200, 266
consumer transactions	4, 14, 40, 151, 212, 216, 244

Topic	Questions
continuation statements	55, 56, 127, 128, 190
control	
deposit account	16, 40, 53, 80, 99, 130, 132, 133, 149, 272
investment property	19, 80, 82, 126
letter-of-credit right	53
copyrights	10, 81, 184, 185, 186
credit card receivables	83
debtor	
defined	11, 31, 69, 74, 101, 131, 182, 183, 199, 240
jurisdiction, see financing statements (where to file)	
default	
see generally	195–212, 265–271
absolute bar rule	212
application of foreclosure proceeds	203, 270
breach of the peace	111, 197, 265
commercial reasonableness	209, 211, 236
debtor's liability for post-foreclosure deficiency	204, 211, 212
definition	195
disposition of collateral	200, 203, 206, 209, 211, 212, 213, 236
effect of foreclosure sale on property interests	205, 271
notice of foreclosure sale	26, 199, 200, 207, 208, 211, 236, 267, 268, 269
payments by account debtors to secured party	210
rebuttable presumption rule	211, 212
recognized market	26, 208
redemption	266
removal of fixtures	111, 112
rendering collateral unusable	198
repossession of collateral	196, 265
strict foreclosure	25, 201, 202
deposit accounts	
see control	
see scope	
defined	8, 10, 40, 92

Topic	Questions
dual status rule	157–160
see transformation rule	
entitlement holder	23, 24, 243
entrustment	172
equipment	
defined	8, 80, 83, 110, 142, 155, 163, 176, 177, 181, 241, 262
farm products	18, 27, 104, 105, 166
federal tax liens	191–194
financing statements	
authentication	48, 109
authorization	48
collateral description	49, 83, 86, 87, 88, 150, 180, 222, 263
contents	49, 253
debtor's name	60–65, 67, 141, 142, 144
definition	52
effect of collateral dispositions	74, 85, 101, 134, 135, 163, 175, 176, 249, 261, 262
effect of name changes	138, 139, 187, 248, 258
effect of relocation of chief executive office	78, 79
effect of relocation of debtor	75, 85, 97, 136, 137, 249, 257
lapse	56, 128
rejection by clerk	51, 56
search reports	45, 46
secured party's name	66
where to file	44, 49, 67, 73, 74, 76–79, 97, 110, 126, 135, 146, 152, 170, 222, 242, 251, 254, 255, 272
fixtures and fixture filings	17, 44, 48, 59, 104–118, 244, 253, 254
fraudulent transfers	
see bankruptcy issues	
future advance clause	
application	37, 38, 246, 247
omitted from financing statement	48
general intangibles	
defined	10, 20, 53, 83, 140

Topic	Questions
goods	
defined	2, 8, 17, 27, 41, 104, 108, 171
information statement	47
instrument	
defined	10, 20, 41, 54, 70, 83, 91, 140, 183
inventory	
defined	18, 41, 72, 104, 161, 163, 168, 174, 177, 241
investment property	
defined	9, 19, 53, 80, 126, 151, 243
lien creditor	
defined	179, 185, 218, 236, 263
lowest intermediate balance rule	
see proceeds	
money	13, 17, 53, 54, 83, 91, 241
noncash proceeds	
see proceeds	
obligor	
see secondary obligor	
defined	11, 240
patents	10, 81
payment intangibles	
defined	10, 20, 83, 140, 184
perfection	
see generally	44–83, 251
see financing statement	
attachment as a predicate	48, 71, 72
possession of collateral	39, 54, 69, 80, 82, 102, 103, 119, 121, 250
priority	
in fixtures	110, 113–118, 254
secured party v. buyer of collateral	164–178, 261, 262
secured party v. IRS	191–194
secured party v. lien creditor	56, 179–190, 218, 263, 264, 272
secured party v. secured party (no PMSI)	56, 98, 102, 103, 119–140, 217, 252, 255, 256, 270

Topic	Questions
secured party v. secured party (PMSI)	89, 141–163, 217, 259, 260, 270
proceeds	
cash proceeds (defined)	13, 85, 86, 87, 91, 94, 98, 148, 150, 154, 162, 169, 252
lowest intermediate balance rule	22, 43, 94, 95, 96, 98, 99
security interest in	43, 84–103, 129, 169, 245, 251
purchase-money security interest	
see priority	
defined	155, 156, 157, 161, 173, 180, 181, 218, 250, 259
in bankruptcy	217, 218
in consumer goods (automatic perfection)	68, 80, 97, 107, 110, 116, 117, 141, 173, 175, 180, 218, 236, 254
in fixtures	110
pursuant to commitment	189
real estate collateral	
see scope	
rebuttable presumption rule	
see default	
registered organization	12, 44, 76, 77, 78, 110, 126, 146, 152, 242, 251, 255, 272
reservation of title	
see title retention	
scope	
agricultural lien	27
consignments	5, 182
deposit accounts	4, 40, 216
insurance policies	3, 43, 54, 90, 239
judgments	239
real estate collateral	2, 3, 6, 7, 9, 239, 254
sales of accounts	1, 131, 183
sales of chattel paper	1, 69, 102, 131
sales of instruments	1
sales of payment intangibles	1
statutory liens	6
substance over form	6

Topic	Questions
tort claims	3
wages	2, 238
secondary obligor	
see obligor	
defined	199, 240, 266, 269
secured party	
defined	131, 182, 183
securities intermediary	23, 24, 243
security agreement	
authentication by debtor	29, 30, 31, 119, 120
contents of	29, 30, 87
description of collateral	30, 32, 33, 41, 83, 87, 151, 169, 244, 263
oral	28, 35, 39, 40, 119
strong-arm clause	
see bankruptcy issues	
supporting obligation	21
tax refunds	10
termination statements	57, 58
title retention clauses	6, 88, 152, 162, 182, 250
trademarks	10, 81
transformation rule	160
see dual status rule	
value	29, 71, 102
voidable preferences	
see bankruptcy issues